VARIETIES OF UNBELIEF

*Atheists and Agnostics
in English Society
1850-1960*

Susan Budd

HOLMES & MEIER PUBLISHERS, INC.
IMPORT DIVISION
101 Fifth Avenue, New York, N. Y. 10003

LONDON EDINBURGH MELBOURNE AUCKLAND TORONTO
HONG KONG SINGAPORE KUALA LUMPUR NEW DELHI
NAIROBI JOHANNESBURG LUSAKA IBADAN
KINGSTON

I SBN 0 435 82100 8

First published 1977

77-363322   *6·80*

Published by Heinemann Educational Books Ltd
48 Charles Street, London WIX 8AH

Text set in 11/12 pt Monotype Ehrhardt Roman, printed by
letterpress, and bound in Great Britain at The Pitman Press, Bath

CONTENTS

PREFACE

My interest in the history of atheists and anti-clericals in Britain began by accident when I was searching for a way of looking at the relationship between beliefs and their social context. I became increasingly interested in and impressed by the humanists themselves and by the mid- and late Victorian period, a world close to and yet very remote from ourselves. My doctoral thesis contains a more detailed and documented historical account of these movements than is presented here. I have tried since to understand the ideas which these movements represented in the context of the changing world-view of the last hundred years, in which the decline of religion has been so central a part. To the many historians who have helped me to begin on this impossible task, I can only offer my thanks for their generous help with a project that they must often have disapproved of. I am particularly grateful to Bob Young, Sydney Eisen, Gillian Sutherland, Brian Harrison and Hugh McLeod. Together with so many other of his post-graduate students, I owe much to the painstaking help of my supervisor, Bryan Wilson.

An important source of material for my study has been the minute-books and libraries of the humanist bodies themselves, and I am deeply indebted to the kindness and generosity of their officials who willingly allowed an outsider access to their records, and helped me in other ways; to Mr H. J. Blackham and Miss Spiller of the British Humanist Association, Miss Palmer of the South Place Ethical Society, Mr McIllroy and the Executive of the National Secular Society, and Mr Hawton of the Rationalist Press Association. Many secularists and ethicists generously helped me with books, manuscripts and reminiscences, and I am especially grateful to Mr Hutton-Hynd, Mr F. J. Corina, Mr Hammersley, Mr C. Kensit, Lady Fleming, and Mr Fincham of the London Positivist Committee. The journals and annual reports of these movements, together with several collections of papers are deposited in the British Library and the British Newspaper Library, and I am indebted to all the librarians of these institutions who over the years patiently provided me with books, as I am to the librarians of the Bodleian, Senate House, the Bishopsgate Institute and the Co-operative Union, and many other collections.

My warmest thanks go to those who made it possible for me

to write this book; to my sister Judith Stephenson who looked
after my baby, to my neighbour Ena Blyth who lent me a place to
work away from nappies and housework, and to my husband
Alan who has suffered and helped with this project for far too
long.

ACKNOWLEDGEMENTS

The author and publishers are very grateful for permission to quote from the following works: C. B. Campbell; *Humanism and the Culture of the Professions*, (Unpublished PhD. thesis, London 1968); Malcolm Quin, *Memoirs of a Positivist*, (George Allen and Unwin Ltd, 1924); and Harry Snell, *Men, Movements and Myself*, (J. M. Dent and Sons Ltd., 1936). Chapter 5 appeared in an earlier version in *Past and Present*, No. 36, and we are indebted to the Past and Present Society for permission to republish it here.

The cover illustration is taken from H. A. Bowler's 'The Doubt —Can These Dry Bones Live?', and the author and publishers are grateful to the Trustees of the Tate Gallery for permission to reproduce it.

INTRODUCTION

Formerly I was led by feelings . . . to the firm conviction of the existence of God, and of the immortality of the soul. In my Journal I wrote that whilst standing in the midst of the grandeur of a Brazilian forest, 'it is not possible to give an adequate idea of the higher feelings of wonder, admiration and devotion which fill and elevate the mind.' I well remember my conviction that there is more in man than the mere breath of his body. But now the grandest scenes would not cause any such convictions and feelings to rise in my mind. It may be truly said that I am like a man who has become colour-blind . . .

The Autobiography of Charles Darwin

Somewhere between the tilled and fertile plantations of the sociology of collective behaviour and the history of ideas there lies a wasteland. It is the study of how ideas are adopted, simplified, made usable and incorporated into social activity not by those great men who create them or make them their own, but by ordinary men and women whose lives are changed by what they may not fully understand, who form the membership of those movements and currents of opinion which themselves play a part in history. They are the link between ideas and social context, between figure and ground, the medium through which thought and material life must pass to meet. They are the reality behind those handy conceptual ragbags, the 'spirit of the times' and the 'general social context', in which ultimately all chains of causes are lost or abandoned.

The problems of this area of study are many, and it is only now that sociologists and historians are beginning to be fruitfully influenced by each other's work that we can see that what was taken to be the faulty methods of another discipline was in part the intractable nature of the material. The methodological and epistemological issues involved in defining the historical and sociological approaches are too many and too complex to be entered on here, but many of them are part of an important and enduring distinction which can be made inside all fields of enquiry. Radcliffe Brown termed the two approaches the nomothetic and the ideographic; the attempt to analyse underlying structures and the attempt to trace specific causal chains.

It is hard to look at the complex and densely woven fabric of social reality from either viewpoint. As historians rightly complain, the analyst of structures loses the uniqueness of time and place, the sense in which a river has indeed subtly changed the second time that we step into it. Sociologists flourish in thin fields; where we know very little, it is easier to generalize. They have on the whole been little concerned with the defects of historians, being content to plunder their findings for their own purposes. The impetus among historians to look for general structures seems to have come from within the profession itself. There are those sufficiently influenced by Marxian views on historiography and by the intellectual changes which led to the modern social sciences to look at the general recurring interactions below the surface of events, and those, often the same people, who study the social and economic history of the common man in the last century or so, where the data is so voluminous and overwhelming that statistical analysis and generalization is the only alternative to drowning.

What I have tried to do in this account of the movements which have attempted to destroy Christianity or to replace it by reason or by religions of socialism or ethics, is not to write their history nor to locate them in terms of the sociological fields of enquiry to which they are tangentially related. Rather, I have looked at their history in terms of several repeated patterns of events which have seemed to me to be significant in explaining the paradox that the ideas which these movements represent are for the most part very dominant in our society, yet the organizations themselves are small and lacking in social influence. In such an enquiry, the significance of an event lies in its typicality. This has been well put by Erikson:

> When a student is primarily concerned with learning how a different society developed or changed from one period to the next, he naturally looks at those pivotal events which seem to 'make' history—decisive battles, important shifts of national mood, the appearance of new ideologies and new technologies. But when the student is primarily concerned with the underlying structures of society, he must look for his data in the ordinary cycles of everyday life, in the habits and behaviour of everyday people, for these point to a dimension of history which can only be learned by observing how often commonplace events reoccur.[1]

I have been concerned with the attempts of ordinary people to think about general issues and abstract ideas, and less with the conclusions that they reached than with the premises from which they began. Such a kind of enquiry is beset with methodological difficulties. Ordinary people record their ideas even less than the more mundane facts about their lives, and what they take for granted they do not mention. It is easier to give an account of a movement in terms of the activities and ideas of its leaders than to

[1] K. T. Erikson, *Wayward Puritans; a study in the Sociology of Deviance*, Wiley, New York, 1966, p. 164.

try to assess the views and nature of its members, though ultimately the latter are just as important. A related but less obvious difficulty is that men view and recall events in 'historical' rather than 'sociological' terms; they notice and remember unusual events, the activities of prominent and committed men. They are uninterested in the data of the sociologist—exact and repeated estimates of membership, its characteristics and its views, the ways in which meetings are conducted and the assumptions under which activities are carried on. Their lack of interest means that these facts are neither noticed nor recorded, so that the scholar can only infer them from what is preserved. Just occasionally, the extent to which attention is naturally focused away from a sociological perspective is pointed up by the rare individual who happened to see events in a more general light, and to search for structural explanations; the accounts of these natural sociologists differ widely from those of their contemporaries. Goblet D'Alviella provided a valuable comparative account of English liberal religions in the 1870s which focused on exactly those issues of ritual and its psychological acceptability to different social groups which are now of interest to us; and George Standring gave an acute analysis of the organizational reasons for the success and failure of the National Secular Society in a period when few would have noticed this sort of factor. Such observation is rare.

Most of the material which I read in journals and minute-books could not be exactly analysed in ways which were very illuminating for the central issues of my enquiry. The laborious analysis of membership lists, for example, was less fruitful than attendance at humanist meetings, which enabled me to see the subtle difficulties over modes of procedure which were occasionally referred to in the sources for earlier periods. Ultimately, I chose to focus on questions where for the most part the material which I could gain was scanty and impressionistic, and I have made extensive use of quotation to show its limited nature.

There are subtler but equally important difficulties involved in writing about the history of ideas. If we divorce them from their social context we none the less view them in terms of our own time; we try to give them the coherence and importance to their time that we would like them to have had. But the social meaning of an idea lies in its context and its meaning to its users; and this is something which changes over time.[2] The most abstract thinker

[2] Q. Skinner, 'Meaning and Understanding in the History of Ideas', *History and Theory*, 8 (1), 1969, pp. 3-53.

does not live in a vacuum, and the ideas of ordinary men are far more dependent on conventional assumptions and connections. To the intellectual, such ideas may seem inconsistent and fragmentary, but this is because they still bear the impress of their social origins.

There are many examples of these processes in the history of the humanist movement. The general intellectual question, 'Do Science and Religion conflict?' rapidly became embedded in a mass of polemical literature, and those who approached it did so on the whole through the polemic. As a consequence, when we look at the process of the loss of religious belief among men and women during the last century, we find a wide variety of books referred to which their readers felt had been a revelation to them. But many of them were neither new nor usually considered powerful arguments for atheism—the Bible, for instance—whereas others did not so much present scientific accounts of the natural world from which the reader could deduce conclusions for agnosticism or religious belief, as arguments to show that 'science' supported one side or another of the controversy, so that science itself had become reified and mythologized. In other words, the context in which arguments and evidence were presented was all-important. Why did parts of the Bible come to seem immoral to the mid-nineteenth century? What was the 'shape' which science and religion had for each group, and how did they actually experience it? This is not to argue that men are not really influenced by abstract beliefs, nor that such beliefs are predetermined by their social and economic circumstances; it would be impossible to argue this in the context of a movement whose ideas were often either unpopular or unfashionable, and afforded little social reward or psychological gratification to its members. Rather, as Weber showed, men often adopt beliefs in a relatively 'pure' form, but change them so that they make sense within a given social context.

Facts and Inferences

Despite the rapid growth of historical and sociological research into the process of secularization in nineteenth- and twentieth-century Britain, some of the most important parameters of the situation still elude us. We now have an accurate enough picture of church-building and church attendance to know that after the rapid growth of Methodism and evangelical influence at the start of the nineteenth century, church attendance slowly declined to a point where by mid-century about a half of all those who could have attended church on a census Sunday actually did so. The decline continued slowly in nonconformity and Anglicanism to the present, church attendance being more frequent amongst women, the middle class, small towns and rural areas (though some of those have a long tradition of low attendance). London, the centre of most of the activity described in this book, was not strongly affected by the evangelical revival and always had lower levels of religious practice. Concern began to be widely expressed in the 1860s at the absence of the working classes from church, and by the 1880s at the signs that middle-class people too were beginning to cease regular attendance and in more subtle but important ways to reject the social and moral authority of the church. Until very recent years, when baldly asked by survey researchers if they considered themselves Christian or believed in God very few of the British population indeed have answered 'no'.

These facts are clear, but not easy to interpret. We do not know what relationship the variables that we can measure, such as church attendance, bear to the really significant dimensions of the situation: the loss of power of religious institutions to control and shape the framework in which moral, social and scientific ideas are presented to the general public. Dimensions of private religiosity— saying prayers, grace, reading devotional literature, referring to religious explanations of events in everyday life—escape us almost completely.[3] So does the way in which the same behaviour at different points in time or amongst different groups would have been assessed differently. Saying grace proceeded from being something so normal as to be unnoticeable to something done on special occasions or by the devout, to something some people do but which is a bit formal and outmoded these days.

Depending on the social judgement as to whether a particular religious act is only decent or absurdly and ostentatiously over-pious, those who perform it and the way in which they will defend it will differ. The meaning of the act of church attendance is not constant, either over time or between social groups. In mid-Victorian England, its overwhelming connotation was that of social

[3] For a sensitive exploration of such issues and a wealth of material about religion in London, see H. McLeod, *Class and Religion in the Late Victorian City*, Croom Helm, London, 1974, and for research into different dimensions of religious experience and how they are related see R. Stark and C. Y. Glock, *American Piety: the Nature of Religious Commitment*, University of California Press, Berkeley, California, 1968.

and moral respectability. Working-men, however much their moral respect-worthiness could be piously conceded, could never become socially respectable. If they rejected the world of the respectable for the radical culture of the secularist and a counter-notion of the intellectual independence and self-help which alone was worthy of respect, the respectable could retort by pointing to their ungodliness and associations with drink and radicals as themselves proof of their moral depravity. The middle class, who *were* respectable, were required to demonstrate this and their responsibility to their class by church attendance. In both cases, not to attend church was a personal failing. By the end of the century, the churches were much less confident and inclined to blame their inability to reach the masses not only on the distractions of new ideas, associations and patterns of leisure, but on the complacency of some of their members. Increasingly during the twentieth century, both churches and people have come to see low church attendance as due to the churches' 'failure' to 'be relevant', and 'bear witness' to their message. The *meaning* of church attendance as a significant moral and social boundary has been almost completely eroded. Class solidarity and consumption patterns are now more important than respectability, and morality is widely seen as the arbiter of religion and not *vice-versa*.

It is difficult to assess the changing shape and influence of 'public' religion in various aspects of people's lives during the last century; it is even more difficult to assess the changes which religion underwent in their private lives. This book is concerned with the views and experience of religion by a group who were outside it and largely opposed to it. In consequence, it treats of Christianity largely as if it were homogeneous and a public institution, ignoring the aspects which made it also a world of private meaning, a symbolic universe, a hope and consolation, or part of the pattern of life in a particular community. Humanists perceived Christianity largely as a system of knowledge and the churches as institutions of social control; they were inclined to underestimate its role both as a vehicle of revolt and of social reformism. This book must inevitably share many of their biases.

It would have been interesting to investigate more closely the external environment in which these movements operated—the changes in social, intellectual, religious and political life during the period—and to try to compare various humanist views of social reality with those of other social groups. Unfortunately, not only would this make the work impossibly lengthy, but I do not possess enough historical knowledge of the changes in the formal knowledge and institutions of theology, science, politics, et cetera. This is partly because what is needed as a basis for comparison is the sort of historical account which has only just begun to appear, which is concerned to assess and describe changes at each social level rather than to provide an account of an élite and their views of social reality. What we need, for example, is not an account of the growth of scientific knowledge but an assessment of changing social attitudes to scientific knowledge; how much have various social groups known about it, and what have they felt about it? Only then is it possible to see to what extent rationalist views of science are distinctive and to what extent conventional.

Without this knowledge, it is difficult not to present the humanist movement as much more of a contra-culture, set against society, than it actually was. And yet it is clear that the forces which brought about changes in the position of religion and in theology also had their effect on atheists and anti-clericals. The moralism and possessive individualism of the early Victorians was as true of the secularist as of the Methodist. The currents of community consciousness and neo-Hegelianism flowed into Anglo-Catholicism and the ethical movement alike. The humanist groups stand in a complex and varied relationship to the intellectual and social history of our times. They are neither antitheses to nor substitutes for religion, but are as religion is, the product of the search of men in particular times and places to link together the ideas available to them and the dilemmas which bear upon them.

Moral Lanterns

The description of humanists and their activities in this book is impossibly high-minded. By this, I do not mean that they are in reality depraved, but that like religious believers, much of the time they are uncertain and doubtful, inclined to mock or qualify in private what they treat with official solemnity, distracted by personalities and enjoyments from their highest purposes, and in general are like other human beings.

The history of contact between Christians and humanists and the records of belief that they left necessarily treats of their beliefs as if they were of great importance to them, as they would indeed have been at that particular moment. How much of their lives they actually devoted to thinking about such issues must have varied greatly, but just as sympathetic observers of the poor saw a host of men essentially indifferent to religion but with a vague sense that it was a comfort and that if they did their best God would not disapprove too much, humanists must often have felt that humanist ideals were just that, and it was the fellowship and the attempts at honesty and argument that mattered. The journals of the movement reflect patterns of cheerful sociability; the charabancs of secularists who drove out to picnic on the Pennines and bait the Methodists, the tea-parties and soirées, the group of ethicists who still walk together in Epping Forest every Sunday and read Shakespeare to one another. And those who can remember outspoken atheists and rationalists as members of their families give us a glimpse of an even richer fabric; a secularist who loved dogs and had all his Dalmatians brought to his funeral, a family with a set-piece row every Sunday lunch as to whether the father was home late from the pub to plague his hard-working wife and was too lazy to go to chapel or whether he had been striking a blow for reason and freedom, a prostitute whose favourite reading was Bradlaugh and Ingersoll. The meaning of humanism lies as much in private life as in public, but it is public life which leaves a trace.

The difficulty, which will be discussed at length, of defining what it is that these movements are united by, extends to a difficulty in finding a collective term for them. They are more than merely anti-religious or anti-clerical, and some of them have not been opposed to religion but seen themselves as substitutes for it or evolving beyond it. Their members are not all atheists, but most see themselves as united by something more positive than agnosticism or unbelief. 'Advanced thinker' would now be too vague, and 'infidelity' misleading. I have chosen to refer to them collectively as *humanist*, but humanists themselves usually reserve the term for the British Humanist Association and its members. The Association was formed in 1962, and is seen as uniting rationalism and ethicism as earlier and less comprehensive versions of humanism. Humanists themselves define their movement by referring to a host of distinguished antecedents from classical antiquity onward, and critics dispute their sole claim to this lofty heritage.

It may be helpful to the reader at this point to be reminded of the central thread which links together the secular, rationalist, ethical, positivist and other related movements in Britain. The negative assumption is that supernatural religion is erroneous, and that this error has important consequences. The positive assumption is the belief in free discussion, the devaluation of any claim to authority except that of the scholar or scientist, a belief in morality as a guide to behaviour, and in the *power* of men to shape their world and determine their futures. The common assertion that humanists view man as basically good is mistaken; it would be more accurate to say that they see him as powerful. They attribute his malice and aggression to his social and biological circumstances, and accordingly demand that he try to assume responsibility for himself and his society. It is in this weak sense that humanism is a progress ideology. Progress does not happen in the nature of things, but only in so far as scientific knowledge is applied to problems. The barriers which prevent this are identified as fatalism, superstition, and irrational thinking, which are seen as more or less conterminous with religion or its derivates. The attack on religion is that by diverting men's energies and attention to their fate in a future life, it hinders the realization of such happiness as they can achieve on earth.

1 DEISTS AND DEMOCRATS: THE ORIGINS OF THE SECULAR MOVEMENT

Lady Clarinda. Next to him is Mr. Toogood, the co-operationalist [Robert Owen], who will have neither fighting nor praying; but wants to parcel out the world into squares like a chess-board, with a community on each, raising everything for one another, with a great steam-engine to serve them in common for tailor and hosier, kitchen and cook.
Captain Fitzchrome. He is the strangest of the set, so far.

Thomas Love Peacock, *Crotchet Castle*

The first Secular Society was founded in 1851. But secularism can only be understood as part of the radical tradition of English urban working-class life; it developed from older radical movements, it shared its members with them, and to a very great extent it continued to advocate and discuss their traditional objectives. The old anti-clerical strain of the Enlightenment, the attitude which saw science, nature and reason as somehow leading to a more rational society, crystallized out of the old radical tradition into the secular movement. In this metamorphosis, the name of Thomas Paine appears time and again. His writings and the mythology which had gathered round his life and his opinions provided much of the bond between social and political radicals and the more purely intellectual and philosophical concerns of secularism. The apparent failure of political and trade union activity in the late 1840s lent plausibility to a movement aimed at moral regeneration and the destruction of superstition.

The two most important sources of secularist membership were moral-force chartism and Owenism, especially the latter. Both bodies were losing support during the late 1840s and many members transferred to the secular movement; in some cases local branches became transformed into secular societies. Secularism was thus one of the organizational links between the radical socialists of the early part of the nineteenth century, and the birth of the mass trade union and labour movement in the 1880s and 90s. It built up its membership from among the chartists and Owenites, and lost most of it again to the new socialist bodies. The process of its rise was mirrored in its decline. The specific reforms with which secularism came to be identified—a secular state, neo-Malthusianism, and republicanism—were often advocated as if they were *alternatives* to economic reforms and socialism, a complete programme of social reform in themselves.

The anti-clerical tradition in Britain did not begin with the secular movement; it had been strong in many of the nonconformist denominations, and in associations formed by radical artisans from the 1790s on. Nor was it the first to hold meetings to press anti-religious views; an eighteenth-century observer of working-class political activities in London described numerous open-air speakers advocating the reform of Christianity. This had forced the magistrates to prohibit field speaking in 1798.[1] Various attempts had been made to convert sporadic popular protest into regular indoor meetings.[2] The new radical and revolutionary political organizations were sympathetic to atheism; the London Corresponding Society was divided into a deist and an atheist section. Reid described how the infidels infiltrated the Benefit Societies:

> Here, after the business of the evening was over, the disciple of Paine was sure to introduce the subject of religion; and by these means, several copies of the *Age of Reason* were circulated, from the reading of which many of its victims dated their conversion.[3]

In fact, as Reid observed, advanced political opinions were assumed to entail advanced religious ones: '. . . the idea of a *Deist* and a good *Democrat* seemed to have been universally compounded . . .'

Radicalism and Infidelity[4]

The link between political radicalism and what were sometimes euphemistically known as 'advanced religious opinions' was a general one, made up of many subtly varying strands. The French Revolution had an immense influence on both radical and conservative thinking in Britain. Not only the ideas of the *philosophes* had travelled across the Channel, even more importantly they had

---

[1] W. H. Reid, *The Infidel Societies of the Metropolis*, Hatchard, London, 1800, pp. 17–18. And see E. Burke, *Reflections on the Revolution in France, and on the Proceedings in certain societies in London*, Dodsley, London, 1791.

[2] One example was the Friends of Morality Association of 1796 formed to preach the new gospel of morality. In practice, like many later secular meetings, its meetings concentrated on passionate denunciations of organized religion by any member of the audience who chose to take the rostrum. Its anarchic existence was short.

[3] W. H. Reid, op. cit., pp. 5–6, 20.

[4] In the nineteenth century, this meant an open absence of religious belief.

created a set of identities. On the one hand there was an immense sense of enthusiasm for science, for education, for materialism with a dash of home-brewed utilitarianism, for the remaking of men, societies and constitutions on a wholly rational and material basis which should be freed of all the oppression and superstition of the past. On the other hand there was the conviction that all the agents of unjust authority—kings, landowners, armies, priests—were bound up together, and that to attack 'priestly thinking' in the name of science and progress would be not only to liberate the minds of men, but to shake government to its very foundations. Radical thinkers drew an implicit distinction between government and society. The latter was both indestructible and naturally self-regu-lating, or at least easily re-ordered according to the latest scientific blueprint; the former was unjust and (the most radical argued) unnecessary. 'Society is produced by our wants and government by our wickedness', said Paine. 'Society is in every state a blessing; government even in its best state but a necessary evil.' Because this distinction could be taken for granted, radicals could devote most of their energies to the demolition of the established order without being too concerned as to what should replace it. Reason and science would provide.

One of the consequences of this situation was that the content of the 'new knowledge' was often very cloudy in the minds of its supporters. In fact, its content probably was far less important to many of them than the fact that it no longer came from a clergyman or representative of the established order, nor was it presented within a religious framework. The conservative mob who smashed Priestley's laboratory had recognized that the new science lay out-side the established order. The moral importance that the radical artisan attached to the idea of unfettered enquiry, to individual freedom of conscience, and consequently to universal education and being able to choose and argue about knowledge cannot be over-estimated, nor can the extent to which some conservatives feared it. The very strength of their determination to keep godless and materialist French philosophy from the labouring classes acted to reinforce the radical view that merely disseminating new knowledge would bring about fundamental social changes.

For the working-class radical, being able to read was increasingly important. Societies in different parts of the country kept in contact by issuing and distributing newspapers and pamphlets, and the new ideas were appearing in books and newspapers that were not too costly for the most prosperous workman, especially if he banded together with others to form a Mutual Improvement Society. For the first time, some polemicists were writing *for* the uneducated in simple and direct terms; the *Age of Reason* and the *Rights of Man* were early and immensely successful examples of the genre. There were other reasons as well which made it desirable for the working-man to be literate. As industrialization proceeded, more skilled jobs came to depend on it. The self-help ideology of the early part of the century laid great stress on education; radical leaders repeatedly counselled their followers to educate themselves, both as a means to worldly advancement and to acquire an independent mind. 'Self-thought', advised Holyoake, '. . . is the first means of self-help.'[5] The new evangelical sects not only pressed each man to read his Bible, but the Old Dissenting and Methodist Sunday schools were much more likely to teach him how to do it and much other knowledge as well than those of the established church.

The self-educated artisan was of great social importance as the main interpreter of ideas to others of his class. The more enlightened middle classes approved of his attempts at self-education; they hoped that education would 'gentle the masses' and that they could be educated away from revolution, idleness and even sexual excess.[6] But the process of education itself, whether through Mechanics' Institute, Methodist Class or Mutual Improvement Society, was often conducive to radicalism and deism or unbelief. This was partly due to the hostility of the 'respectable'; where Mechanics' Institutes were run by artisans, outsiders tended to assume they were atheistic, and the prejudice against them made them more radical. Harrison talks of 'the ambivalent role of adult learning as alternatively a movement of protest and a means to promote social acceptance and harmony.'[7]

By means of education a man could become a radical and yet respectable artisan who might hope to rise to the middle class, to become perhaps a radical journalist, a clerk or small manufacturer or Methodist minister. The secular movement and previous radical movements such as Owenism derived much of their power and

[5] G. J. Holyoake, *The Logic of Life, Deduced from the Principle of Forethought*, Farrah, London, 1868, p. 4.
[6] J. F. C. Harrison, *Learning and Living, 1790–1960*, Routledge, London, 1961, p. 78; R. K. Webb, *The English Working Class Reader, 1790–1848*, Allen & Unwin, London, 1955, pp. 16, 34, 38.
[7] J. F. C. Harrison, op. cit., p. 13.

popularity from being educative; their journals and their meetings were concerned with a wide variety of new ideas and information.

The defenders of the *status quo* were disturbed by many aspects of these intellectual ferments. Irreligion might be tolerated amongst the nobility and established classes, whose loyalty to Church and Constitution was guaranteed by their social position and who could be relied upon to maintain some degree of religious practice; amongst the poor the rejection of religion could only lead to political subversion. Wilberforce wrote to Lord Milton after Peterloo to confiide his fears that

> the enemies of our political constitution were also enemies to our religion . . .
> Heretofore they inveighed against the inequality of property, and used every
> artifice to alienate the people from the constitution of their country. But now
> they are sapping the foundations of the social edifice more effectually by
> attacking Christianity. The high and noble may be restrained by honour;
> but religion only is the law of the multitude.[8]

The Law regarded the Church and State as a single entity; Christianity was not only part of the law of the land, but one of its major supports. Not until 1842 was even the 'reverential examination' of religious truths admissible. To question the church meant an automatic attack on the social order; blasphemy was an offence first against the State, the 'peace of our Lord the King', before being 'to the high displeasure of Almighty God, to the great scandal of the Christian Religion.' It was inevitable that radicals would be led to attack the Anglican Church.[9]

For those outside the established church, some way had to be found to accommodate a wide variation of religious beliefs and to preserve and justify freedom of speech and opinion. So it came to be accepted by the 1830s that Truth could ultimately be expected to prevail, that all of the new ideas were probably part of science and progress and in the meantime should be tolerated and investigated. The programmes of many working-men's institutions had a curiously giddy and eclectic air. Phrenology, mesmerism, astrology, jostled with more orthodox political and scientific topics to produce a crop of eccentrics in the best English tradition, such as a Pestalozzian instructor and agile gymnast in one of the Halls of Science,

---

[8] R. I. and S. Wilberforce, *Life of William Wilberforce*, 1838, p. 40, quoted in Ursula Henriques, *Religious Toleration in England 1787–1833*, Routledge, London, 1961 ,p. 206.
[9] Henriques, op. cit., pp. 207–9; W. S. Holdsworth, 'The State and Religious Nonconformity: an Historical Retrospect', *Law Quarterly Review*, Vol. 36, 1920, pp. 339–58.

who had found his own way of evading the Corn Laws by avoiding all cooked foods.[10]

Until the religious census of 1851, it was not clear to what extent working-class men in industrial cities had ceased to attend church, but as early as the 1800s concern was being expressed at their absence, which was attributed by both radicals and conservatives to the effects of reading and hearing about the new ideas. Richard Carlile wrote triumphantly in 1828 that 'one thing is certain, however the cause of the Bible may prosper among the red, brown and black savage animals abroad, it decays among the dirty white-brown ones at home.'[11]

But as the more acute pointed out and were to continue to do so throughout the century, those who had abandoned the churches were not on the whole hostile to religion, but to the churches themselves and especially to the established church:

> There is a sort of subconscious and unrecognized feeling of antagonism to the Church as an institution or corporate body, and to the parson as a paid teacher of religion.[12]

Indeed, the most outspoken radicals and infidels were deeply moral men; they asserted, and it was the main grounds of their attack, that religion as it was currently understood was immoral.

Meetings and Martyrs

The secular movement took form under the leadership of Holyoake in the 1840s. The vitality of radical culture in the earlier period and its connections with anti-clericalism and contemporary political life can perhaps best be conveyed by describing in detail some of the centres and personalities of 'Infidel London' in the early part of the century.

The most socially exalted and intellectually influential was the South Place Society (as it was later known), whose history stretches unbroken from 1795 to the present. It evolved through all the

---

[10] Letter from H. G. Wright, August 1841, to G. J. Holyoake (Bishopsgate Institute).
[11] Richard Carlile, in *Lion*, 9 May 1928, quoted in G. A. Williams, *Rowland Detrosier*, St Anthony's Press, York, 1965, p. 2.
[12] R. Mudie-Smith, *The Religious Life of London*, Hodder and Stoughton, London, 1904, p. 26.

phases of 'advanced' religion, being first Universalist, then Unitarian, then Liberal Unitarian, then becoming an Ethical society and finally part of the Humanist movement.[13] At its period of greatest influence it became the focus and forum for 'advanced' thought of all kinds in London: the intellectual standards of its pulpit and congregation were pitched at an exceptional level. Its ministers and congregations were courageous in their support for unpopular causes, and radicals who came under attack often found that an important contact with the established classes was to be gained from the South Place pulpit.

The Society's first minister, Elhanan Winchester, had been a Baptist minister in New England who had been converted by a young woman in a stage coach, whom he had been haranguing on the torments of Hell. A true apostle of natural religion, she converted him to Universalism, a millenial belief in an almost universal salvation, which was regarded at the time as literally revolutionary in Calvinist New England. Winchester came to London, established contact with advanced Unitarians and gradually gathered a congregation of 'the middling classes' who had seceded from other congregations.

He was succeeded by one of his converts, William Vidler, like himself an ex-Baptist preacher from a poor rural family, who had left his Sussex congregation over the issue of a final redemption of all of mankind. Division once begun becomes a habit; the issue of immortality led to part of the Parliament Court congregation seceding in 1799 to join the Freethinking Christians, a more working-class and radical variant of Unitarianism, which denied the immortality of the soul. Vidler finally proclaimed himself a Universalist and lost his wealthier members as a result, and a further schism took place over his wish that communion should be open to all who wished it. The congregation was considerably depleted and impoverished by the time that W. J. Fox took over in 1816.[14]

Around W. J. Fox, first a leading Unitarian minister and later an outstanding orator for the Anti-Corn Law League and a radical M.P., gathered a society of wealthy and intellectual religious radicals.

[13] It was named successively the Philadelphians, the Universalists, the Society of Religious Dissenters, South Place Unitarian Society, South Place Society, the Free Religious Society, and the South Place Ethical Society.

[14] S. K. Ratcliffe, *The Story of South Place*, Watts, London, 1955, pp. 2–5; W. Kent, *London for Heretics*, Watts, London, 1932, pp. 77–8; D. G. Rowell, *Death and the Future Life in the Religious Thought of Nineteenth Century England*, Cambridge Ph.D. Thesis, 1968, pp. 97–100; Minutes and Annual General Meeting of Parliament Court Chapel for 1808.

Fox's congregation after its removal to South Place Chapel in Finsbury was composed of the local wealthy Unitarian manufacturers and city families, with a sprinkling of intellectuals such as Harriet Martineau and Robert Browning who were protégés or friends of Fox, and a few radical artisans such as William Lovett and James Watson. Fox came from Norwich and, like his father, had been a hand-loom weaver. He attended an Independent chapel, educated himself and rose to be a clerk, and organized the local weavers into a branch of the London Corresponding Society. Having gone to an Independent College to train as a minister he was converted to Unitarianism. His oratorical powers were soon evident, and earned him a congregation at Chichester and a growing place in the Unitarian community.

By this period, the Unitarians had begun to emerge as the wealthiest group of dissenters, with an interest in the progress of scientific knowledge and social reform. Theologically, they spanned a great distance from fairly orthodox old dissent to the liberal wing, who were so far from attaching any importance to either revealed Christianity or to the Scriptures that they were usually considered to be no better than deists or even atheists, especially since they followed a courageous policy of giving protection and pulpits to notorious radicals such as Joseph Priestley. Because of this, and their exclusion from the ruling élite, Unitarian congregations were tightly knit by intermarriage and concentrated in certain areas, where they often came to play a leading part in civic affairs. Theologically, many of them saw the source of religion in the aspirations and desires of men, and relied on intuition rather than revelation or scriptural authority both for the basis of belief and for knowledge of the material world. Many of them were materialists and necessitarians, and one aspect of Unitarians which struck their contemporaries most forcibly was their absence of proper religious emotion; they were 'cold and critical', highly educated and interested in furthering science and education.

Fox had shared the general view that they had little true religion; they read their sermons and even their prayers, 'which I regarded as perfectly unnatural.' At first he found them impervious to his oratorical powers, and bemoaned the time when 'the candle of orthodoxy shone upon me'. 'Shall I call up the times when listening crowds heard with visible emotion, when trickling tears proclaimed the vividness of the feelings, the pathos of my eloquence, the power of grace?'. But he soon became a convert to the virtues of natural religion as the basis for virtue, and orthodox religion came to seem mainly a state of 'mind and feeling' which

> does not build up intelligence, does not develop the faculties, does not humanize and raise the entire character, nor shape it for public usefulness, it does not tend toward the expansion of our nature in the individual. It takes little account of man upon the earth in the aggregate. Its bearing on conduct is feeble, irregular and incidental . . .

The criticisms contain his programme for the uses of religion.[15]

One of the fascinating aspects of 'advanced' religious groups which will be demonstrated many times in this book, is that they support by contrast the truth of the Durkheimian view of religion as a seamless web. Theology, eschatology, metaphysics, ritual practices, the exact comportment of priest and congregation, the setting and symbols associated with the act of worship, all are bound together into a coherent whole by the cake of custom. Any element may come to seem natural and appropriate by use; but to take conscious thought about making the behaviour of worshippers or the form of service exactly appropriate to theology usually involves both leader and congregation in a mass of uncomfortable inconsistencies. Fox accepted the pulpit of the Parliament Court congregation, but he was already uneasy with the role of nonconformist minister and wanted his introduction to his new flock to 'be kept perfectly clear of anything which may look like *Ordination*, to which ceremony under every form I have a strong dislike, from its tendency to transform a preaching brother into a priest . . .'[16]

The startled Committee acquiesced. But as was conventional among old dissenting congregations, they saw themselves rather than the minister as in charge of services and the chapel, and resisted Fox's innovations and tried to exclude him from their meetings. He in turn could appeal to the congregation over their heads, since it was his highly successsful preaching which crammed the pews and boosted their rents. Fox and the chapel began on a steady movement away from the religious service and into radical intellectual life, supported on the whole by the Committee. In 1819 he preached a famous and influential sermon on the duties of Christians toward

---

[15] H. McLachlan, *The Unitarian Movement in the Religious Life of England*, Allen and Unwin, London, 1934; F. E. Mineka, *The Dissidence of Dissent : the Monthly Repository, 1806–1838*, University of North Carolina Press, Chapel Hill, 1944; S. K. Ratcliffe, op. cit., pp. 5–7; M. S. Packe, *John Stuart Mill*, Secker and Warburg, London 1954, p. 119; Richard Garnett, *The Life of W. J. Fox, Public Teacher and Social Reformer, 1786–1864*, Bodley Head, London, 1909, pp. 23, 31, 27.
[16] Minutes of Parliament Court Chapel, 14 February 1817.

deists, in which he accused orthodox religion of suppressing free speech and the use of reason, for example by Richard Carlile's recent imprisonment for selling the *Age of Reason*. The conservative members of the congregation protested; the Committee approved, and started weekly classes in biblical criticism.

Fox's position as a leading Unitarian minister was jeopardized when he left his wife and set up house with Eliza Flower, one of his wards. At about the same time, he had been responsible for introducing Harriet Taylor, a member of the congregation, to John Stuart Mill. Radical connections were thick on the ground. The Flower sisters were the daughters of a Unitarian printer who had been imprisoned over the *Age of Reason*, and Eliza's sister married another member of the congregation, whose previous father-in-law had been Francis Place. At the time, he was contributing a series of articles advocating freer divorce to Fox's influential *Monthly Repository*, which only added to the consternation of the congregation and of middle-class radicals generally. Fox resigned from South Place and was asked to return several times, vigorously protesting that since he had rejected the sacerdotal role the congregation should not be concerned with his private life. This ended with an excited meeting in which he justified his views on divorce to the congregation. Finally Fox was asked by a large majority to stay, fifty families withdrew to the Carter Lane Unitarian congregation and South Place was largely disowned by the Unitarian church. The episode profoundly affected the relationship between Fox and his congregation. He abandoned the pastoral role; he was no longer to be called 'reverend', to go on pastoral visits or administer the sacraments, and his sermons increasingly became speeches on social and political issues.[17]

Once he had ceased to be a minister Fox found that his obvious métier was as a politician and radical journalist. His relationships with Harriet Martineau, J. S. Mill and many of his congregation cooled; they may have supported his liberal opinions, but like other English campaigners for greater personal liberty they thought it both tactically prudent and ethically essential to act themselves with the greatest moral rectitude. The Committee protested at his withdrawal from South Place, but his reputation as a radical leader had grown too great for them to hold him. As a temporary expedient,

[17] M. S. Packe, op. cit., pp. 123–38, 14–89; R. Garnett, op. cit., pp. 155–71; F. Fox, ed., *Memoir of Mrs Eliza Fox*, Trübner and Co., London, 1869, pp. 191–2.

a series of deputies were appointed to carry on the bulk of the work—
one was 'too theological', but introduced the congregation to the
new German biblical scholarship before he left to become a lecturer
at an Owenite institution; another was 'a young clergyman who has
doubts on his faith', and frightened the congregation with his
atheism. The Committee never despaired of getting Fox back; he
wrote in 1846 that 'I do not know how the Finsbury folk will get
on—from all I hear, they seem to have only two ideas in their
heads, those of paying their seat-rents, and having me, and find
their brains exceedingly dislocated and obfuscated by any other
consideration.'[18] But finally they were forced to admit defeat;
Fox had become M.P. for Oldham in 1847 and was no longer
prepared to act as minister. When it was clear that he would not
return, the most radical part of the congregation abandoned
South Place.[19]

Important though South Place was for recommending radical
views to the wealthy and intellectually distinguished, it was *sui
generis*. Only in London were there sufficient numbers of wealthy
and educated religious radicals to support such an institution.
It stood at one end of the line between those whose interest in
radical ideas and theologies was primarily intellectual, and the
poor workman who was radical by instinct, who taught himself to
read with the *Age of Reason*. The latter, if he had been in London
in 1830, would have been likely to find himself at the Rotunda cheer-
ing Robert Taylor, the 'Devil's Chaplain'. Taylor was an ex-clergy-
man and surgeon, who had founded the Christian Evidence Society
to prove the fallibility of the Scriptures. He held tumultous crowded
meetings where, dressed in his ecclesiastical gown, he would lecture
on the Bible and challenge clergymen to come and refute him. At
his trial for blasphemy in 1827 he conducted his own defence, which
mainly consisted of reading out portions of the Bible to demonstrate
their immorality. During his subsequent imprisonment he wrote the
Syntagma, an elaborate and learned argument against the Scriptures
which was extensively used by several generations of secularists to
confound the clergy.[20] Richard Carlile had just finished his prison
sentence for selling the *Age of Reason*, and, anxious to show his
defiance, joined with Taylor in attacking the Bible not only in

[18] D. Garnett, op. cit., p. 286, letter from W. J. Fox to Eliza Flower.
[19] Minutes of South Place Chapel, 1852–56. The number of seat-holders (the main
source of income) fell from 231 to 196 between 1853 and 1855.
[20] *Freethinker*, 22 May 1938, pp. 324–5.

London but around the country. They established the Rotunda which became the centre for radical and free-thought activities in London from 1829–31, until they were both imprisoned and radicals turned their attention to other aspects of Owenism.[21]

The radical agitations of this period tended to grow out of and form facets of one another. As each agitation succeeded the last, or another leader arose, many radical working-men would transfer their main interest to the new body, and sometimes a whole local society would change course. Leeds secularism, for example, was part of an evolution between republican, chartist, Owenite, co-operative, teetotal and political reformist issues and groups. Many radicals, especially if they were more middle-class or nonconformist, disliked secularist or deist ideas and often a secular and usually more radical wing would be distinguishable from the main body of advanced thinkers. Thus, Leicester Secular Society began with a group of men who had moved from an Owenite Social Institution to the Mechanics' Institute, but finding that the discussion there was too confining they moved on, while political and trade union groups also split off from the original Social Institution. The Secularist Glasgow Eclectic Institution had been the successor to the Zetetical Society and the Owenite Universal Community of Rational Religionists. Secularist bodies were formed as a reaction to the zeal of clergymen who attacked groups of working-men who seemed to be discussing religion too freely. When the Coventry Mutual Improvement Society, which met in the schoolroom of an independent chapel, began to hold discussions on religion, the elders expelled all forty men and reformed the society with a constitution to exclude freethinkers, who in turn formed a secular society.[22] Perhaps the most remarkable case was that of the Failsworth Secular Society in Lancashire, which had been formed as a Jacobin club. It had absorbed all the scholarly artisans of the district and had formed a small community with its own library, burial club, band, dramatic society, and free school for both adults and children. Out of this came both a Mechanics' Institute and a Mutual Improvement Society. Politically, the society was also very active; it had sent a deputation

[21] G. D. H. Cole, *Richard Carlile*, Gollancz, London, 1943, pp. 22–6; J. M. Wheeler, *Biographical Dictionary of Freethinkers*, Progressive Publishing Co., London, 1889, p. 312; G. J. Holyoake, *Life of Richard Carlile*, Austin, London, 1849, p. 14; S. Maccoby, *English Radicalism 1786–1832*, Allen & Unwin, London, 1955, p. 458.

[22] J. F. C. Harrison, *Learning and Living 1790–1960: a Study in the History of the English Adult Education Movement*, Routledge London, 1961; F. J. Gould, *History of the Leicester Secular Society*, published by the Society, 1900, pp. 6–8; *Reformer*, 15 March 1897, p. 21.

to Peterloo, and made many chartists and Owenites. The school later split into physical- and moral-force chartists, and as so often, the latter turned to Owenism and took over the school. The institution then established a shop and a farm on co-operative lines, and because they had turned to co-operation under the influence of Holyoake, they adopted his views on religion as well, and secularism became part of the programme of the Institute. The society's school was still in existence in 1958.[23]

Most radical workmen of the 1830s or 40s would have had some kind of interest in chartism or Owenism. Many members of both were opposed to established religion, though chartists were often Methodists and likely to be only anti-clerical, whereas Owenites had philosophical objections to all revealed truths.[24]

Some of the leaders of the ritualist party, notably Thomas Cooper, did move straight from chartism into leading positions in the secular movement, and a large number of secularists of the period had initially been 'moral-force' chartists. But ill-defined and protean though the ideas of both movements were, there was a considerable difference between the secularist tradition as exemplified by Holyoake which preached self-help, self-improvement and the social reformation which would be wrought by a rational morality, and the tradition of the proletarian revolutionary, rooted in political and economic union with his fellows in the struggle against Old Corruption. Holyoake strove to resist tendencies toward class conflict and violent action, and mocked at the 'unwashed and illkempt' chartists delegates who met in 1848 to consider allying themselves with the middle class. He was himself attacked by some provincial secularists for not being chartist enough, the substance of their complaint being that he did not support O'Connor, advocated neo-Malthusianism rather than Socialism, and had quoted with approval 'that cold-blooded political economist, John Mill'.[25]

The connections between secularism and Owenism were much closer. George Jacob Holyoake had been a social missionary, and when the movement was in decay and he proposed that an association should be formed to promote secularism, most

[23] P. Percival, *Failsworth Folk and Failsworth Memories*, Hargreaves, Manchester, 1901; *Freethought News*, Sept. 1947, pp. 13–14 and Oct. 1947, pp. 6–7.

[24] H. U. Faulkner, *Chartism and the Churches*, Columbia University Press, New York, 1961, pp. 15, 42–4; Thomas Cooper, *Life*, Hodder & Stoughton, London, 1872, p. 166; R. F. Wearmouth, *Some Working-Class Movements of the Nineteenth Century*, Epworth Press, London, 1948.

[25] *Reasoner* for 1848, esp. No. 116, p. 177; and No. 612, 17 February 1958, p. 49.

George Jacob Holyoake and the Formation of Secularism

Holyoake was born in 1817 into a Birmingham family of skilled craftsmen. His father was a foundry foreman of no visible religious beliefs, and his mother a devout Wesleyan. At nine he began work in his father's foundry, continuing his education at a Wesleyan Sunday School. In 1829, partly as a result of the family's temporary poverty after being forced to pay a church-rate, his younger sister died. This event made Holyoake not anti-religious but anti-clerical: 'I remember that, in our blind, helpless way, the Church became to us a thing of ill-omen. It was not disbelief, it was dislike, that was taking possession of our minds.' He was very interested in religion and attended various nonconformist chapels and Sunday schools, but at seventeen he began to thirst for secular knowledge and started to learn science at the Mechanics' Institute and a Unitarian Sunday School.[33] He remained an assiduous student all his life. His zeal and enthusiasm for the pursuit of knowledge led him, as it did so many autodidacts, both to exaggerate the social and moral benefits which it could bring to others as it had to him, and to idealize the educated and cultured classes.

Holyoake avoided Owenism for some time because of its irreligious reputation, but was converted to it after having attended a lecture of Robert Owen's by mistake. He left the ironworks and took a series of teaching and clerical jobs where he found the constraints on his freedom of speech irksome. 'Why the devil,' a fellow Owenite suggested, 'don't you turn *Social Missionary*, eh?'[34] He became an Owenite social missionary at Worcester and then at Sheffield, where he held services of rational religion, and classes in science on weekday evenings. His friend Hollick had written with further good advice: 'A knowledge of *Facts*, of *things*, not *words*. And the more common your facts are the better. Avoid being *learned*, above all things . . . Gather up all the everyday facts as to the condition of society, and trace them to their *causes*; then by contrast, show what *be* the case . . .'[35] But more general issues were to prove to be to avoid.

[Holy]oake's thinking was based in Owenism. Morality was in-[depen]dent of religion. At first he thought religion prevented the

Holyoake, *Bygones Worth Remembering*, Fisher Unwin, London, 1905, Vol. -45; Proof of an article by Holyoake on 'My Religious Days' in Bishopsgate

to G. J. Holyoake, from F. Hollick, 19 January 1840 (Bishopsgate Institute). February 1840.

Owenites saw this as a natural progression. In 1856, Robert Cooper could propose a toast to 'Robert Owen. He was the true founder of Secularism'.[26]

In describing Owen, most writers have found it easier to discuss those of his ideas which were concretely enough defined to have some practical outcome: New Lanark, education, co-operation and labour exchanges, and the Grand Consolidated Trades Union. To the judgement of hindsight and even to many of his contemporaries, Owen's ideas on philosophy and society and its reform seemed to be often no more than naïve and cloudy generalizations. To many contemporary radicals they were illuminating and exciting in a way that is now difficult to understand. But they formed the basis of secularism.

Owen's general views were derived from Scottish moral philosophy *via* the Manchester Literary and Philosophical Society. They were marked by constant references to reason, to the consistency and uniformity of the laws of nature, and to utilitarian philosophy. If existing society was not benevolent and rational, that was because it was artificial. The task of socialism was to extend natural laws to human life, so enabling the reformer to reconstruct society on a scientific basis. It was an inherent property of all desirable social change that it would be peaceful.

Owen had originally established a position of considerable fame and influence by the creation of a benevolent but practical industrial community at New Lanark, which became a place of pilgrimage for all the social reformers of the day. But the uneasiness that was felt in polite circles at his references to the abolition of property, including the human property that men acquired on marriage, was considerably increased by his statement in 1817—almost in passing —that no rational man could be expected to have any religion. Owen believed that men's beliefs and characters were solely due to the fact that they lived in a particular time and place. They were the creatures of nature and of their social circumstances, and so could not be responsible for their actions to a god. Religion was created by 'the false imaginations of our early ancestors', and in the form of priestcraft did much to prevent man's self-realization and happiness. It was therefore enormously important to educate children to understand the consequences of their actions, because this would

[26] Robert Cooper at a Halifax secularist gathering, *London Investigator*, Vol. II, 24 March 1856, p. 183.

enable them to dispense with religion and form correct ideas of morality and conduct. By education a new social character could be created which would enable widespread social changes to take place without upheaval.[27]

The reform of man himself was at the centre of Owen's concern. The ways which he chose to do it in were less important. Much of the meaning for co-operation as an idea to him was that it would prevent competitiveness. Many of his contemporaries found this approach to reform maddeningly vague; his views on education were a case in point. Like all teachers before and since, his instructors sometimes found the Old Adam strong enough in their charges to make them doubt that man could ever become wholly good and happy, however well he were treated. As one Owenite who wrote to rebuke Holyoake 'for your profanity in designating by the low name of "urchins" the temples of the Divinity', said, 'the child may—I grant often does—*seem* rather a pigstie than a gorgeous temple, yet is there even in the least beautiful a somewhat "within that passeth show".'[28]

Phrenology, an immensely popular subject in the middle of the nineteenth century, presented much the same message. George Combe had argued for phrenology as 'a moral science' which showed that the brain was the material instrument of the mind, of which nothing could be known directly, and that human faculties corresponded to the organs of the brain. Consequently concepts such as will and responsibility were merely descriptions of human behaviour not causes of it, and to talk of evil or moral responsibility for one's actions was absurd.[29] Holyoake, who was studying phrenology in 1836, found it a natural corollary of Owenism.[30]

After about 1829, working-class radicalism became permeated by Owen's ideas on economics, trade-unions, co-operation, rational religion and communist communities, and as Owenism became attached to a mass movement it began to seem more alarming. It began to be associated with infidelity, and socialism, a word which Owen had used conterminously with the 'science of society',

[27] Robert Owen, *The Life of Robert Owen; written by Himself*, facsimile of first edition of 1857, reissued by Knight, London, 1971, p. 16; J. F. C. Harrison, *Robert Owen and the Owenites in Britain and America*, Routledge, London, 1969.

[28] Letter from H. G. Wright, August 1841, to G. J. Holyoake (Bishopsgate Institute).

[29] A. Cameron Grant, 'Combe on Phrenology and Free Will: a Note on Nineteenth Century Secularism', *Journal of the History of Ideas*, Vol. 26(10), January 1965, pp. 141-7.

[30] Holyoake's Logbook of self-education, Bishopsgate Institute.

acquired a more sinister meaning. In 1834 the Grand Consolidated Trades Union foundered, and many Owenites turned to moral-force chartism. The Owenite movement began to separate into groups of men united by more specific intersts, many of whom followed Owen himself as he turned his attention to moral and religious questions. The local Owenite societies became groups of rational religionists, and from 1838 they began, when they could afford it, to appoint social missionaries. Their function was to educate the members of the local hall of science, who should together both find a retreat from the economic, social and religious pressures of society and provide their members with a glimpse of the New Moral World. The respectable radical working-men who used them were, sensibly and traditionally enough, prone to turn them into clubs.

Alfred Wallace described the evenings he used to spend with his brother, a surveyor's apprentice, at the London Hall of Science i 1837. This had already become a club for 'advanced thinke mainly Owenites, in which they could listen to lectures on Owe or secularism, read, play games and drink coffee. There library, and all the members seemed well versed in the w Owen and Paine.[31] But sometimes the disposition of t Owenites was rather more strenuous. Holyoake became missionary to the hall of science at Worcester, whe services on Sundays and gave classes in mathematics Most of the societies had lost any direct connection w After the failure of the Owenite community at Ha 1845 (the misdirection of which Holyoake had *Oracle of Reason*, much to the annoyance of the Ow of Owen's supporters turned to chartism or lo The northern societies ousted Owen from le increasing extent it was taken over by Holyoak *Reasoner* (1846-61) was mainly concerned of Owenism which interested him most, the begun in 1844 and of less interest to Owen communitarianism, and the attack on re

[31] Alfred R. Wallace, *My Life*, Chapman & Hal *Sixty Years of an Agitator's Life*, T. Fisher Un

[32] G. D. H. Cole, *Life of Robert Owen*, Macm *Utopian and Scientific*, Sonnenschein, Lond *Radical Leicester*, University College, Leice *Holyoake and the Secularist Movement in B* 1968, p. 12.

full development of morality, but later he came to think it irrelevant to it. Morality could be discovered and analysed by reason; should moral issues be discussed sufficiently rationally, the truth would emerge. Science (which he used interchangeably with reason) was revealing to men the operation of the natural world, and the contemporary systems of scientific morals of the utilitarians, Spencer and the positivists and the science of personality of phrenology would ultimately reveal the science of social life. Holyoake never made a stronger charge against religion than that it worked against social improvement. In his first editorial of the *Reasoner*, he argued that Britain was 'afflicted by no fewer than 23,000 clergymen', who

> cripple the moral energies of men, which humiliate their active spirit, and divert them from independence and social amelioration. From this immense *foci*, innumerable tracts, bibles and agents radiate over the world, chaining the Spirit of Progress to musty records and drivelling dogmas—and not one association rears its head against this vast organized error!

Because of the influence of Owen, Holyoake saw individual weaknesses and failures as the product of society and not of faulty beliefs and immorality, and remained throughout his life a democrat, co-operator and believer in universal education. His attitude to social reform was tolerant and humane; for example, he supported the general aims of the Temperance movement but found it often bigoted and unrealistic in failing to see that drink was not in itself an evil but the social pressures which drive men to drunkeness were, and that the real attraction of the public house was the warmth, attractiveness and sociability it gave to working-men who could find leisure and acceptance in few places else.[36]

The disentanglement of morality from religion was only the first step for secularism; Holyoake saw as its next task the development of a scientific morality, and it was for this reason that he urged the movement to discuss all the contemporary systems of morals, and 'to examine all things hopeful, respect all things probable, but *rely* on nothing which does not come within the range of phenomena, or common consciousness, or assume the form of a law'. The only test of the truth was 'the universal, fair and open discussion of opinion', and thus such discussion became immensely important to Holyoake.[37] He spent much time urging the importance of courteous debate and fair rules when debating with Christians, and the

---

[36] *London Investigator*, Vol. III No. 27, June 1856, pp. 224 *et seq.*
[37] Holyoake's view of the aims of freethought organizations, stated in the Free Discussion Festival of 1852, *Reasoner*, No. 294, 14 January 1852, pp. 129–30.

necessity of discussion after lectures. He had disagreed with Owen over this. Owen had wanted speakers to convert and exhort, and disliked discussion because 'it enabled factious individuals to destroy the effect of what had been said', but Holyoake rejected the hortatory approach, as he refused to become a leader and disliked being a teacher. But he also wanted Owenites and secularists to turn their attention to a positive philosophy, to self-help and self-culture. The objects of the London Secular Society, for instance, were to be 'The instruction of the members in matters appertaining to this life, the promotion of secular education, of rational amusements, and general culture.' From the first, he believed that whilst it was important for working-class radicals not to compromise over their objectives, it was vital for them to cultivate a restrained and courteous manner. Writing to his father in 1842, he explained that whilst his radical activity was very 'advanced' in its aims, 'I should wish to do it respectably—without forfeiture of that position which confers additional power on one's advocacy.'[38]

At first, Holyoake took part in many of the public debates between atheists and clergymen so popular with secularist audiences. Many secularists especially relished the triumph of the puny, small-voiced David over the Christian Goliath—often in the shape of a renowned Christian controversialist, the Reverend Brewin Grant. Holyoake's account of an early encounter at Rochdale showed the extent to which debate between Christian and secularist had already become standardized.

> It is all over with Christians when they come to declamation, delinquencies and Deathbeds. The French Revolution, the Earl of Rochester, Infidel Death-Beds, and the Marriage Question [neo-Malthusianism] were not introduced. If I had my choice of topics, I would prefer debating these to any others. On no points is victory so easy or so sure.[39]

Holyoake was always under pressure to show his militant opposition to religion by taking part in these debates, but he grew to dislike them and finally to refuse to take part. The intellectual positions of both sides had become so established that open discussion was impossible, and they aided the tendency of some secularists to attack anything to do with Christianity.[40] Whilst he realized that

---

[38] Letter to his father, 11 March 1842, Co-operative Union, Manchester.
[39] *Reasoner*, No. 118, 1848, p. 215.
[40] *Reasoner*, No. 89, 1848, pp. 151–2. An 'Old Areopagite' had rebuked the *Reasoner* for conniving with Christianity by going on using Christian dates, and suggested a secularist calendar; Holyoake considered that 'there is no objection to be taken to anything useful because it is Christian.'

attacks on religion drew large readerships and audiences, he thought them fatal to the long-term health of secularism. Without some positive principles, 'Secularism will fall back into the aimlessness and chaos of old Infidelity, which never had cohesion except when persecution was present, and could never keep a party which commanded respect when persecution was still.'[41]

There were many paradoxes to Holyoake. He was genuinely liberal, tolerant and humane in his dealings, sincerely committed to the open mind. At the same time he was acerbic and testy with those of his supporters whom he considered to have overstepped his elaborate and idiosyncratic notions of the boundaries of courtesy. His Owenism made him a radical thinker, and in many ways he remained one. He had an acute sense of the limitations and lack of satisfactions in the lives of working-class people. Yet as he aged, his realistic perception that secularism needed to make its peace with Christian liberals so they could work together for reforms and that atheists could be seen to be respectable citizens mainly by their personal example, led him to befriend ostentatiously the liberal clergyman or well-connected radical. But his overtures were mingled with an obstinate punctiliousness which insisted that he *was* none the less an atheist, materialist, democrat, et cetera.

'The Last Trial for Atheism . . .'

By 1839, the general social prejudice against infidelity was very great and Owen, alarmed at the extent to which Owenism was being reduced to infidelity in the minds of the public, ordered the social missionaries not to foment religious dissent. The rational religionists, as they became called, now had sixty-two branches but could muster audiences which totalled over fifty thousand. The attacks on and prosecutions of the chartists in 1840 led to a split among the Owenites on their policy toward established religion. As they agreed, priestcraft was opposed to the education and improvement of the poor, but Owen and a majority of the Central Board wanted to abandon existing society and create a new community, a New Moral World. There seemed little point in raising opposition by attacking Christianity directly. In an attempt to check the rapid growth of the halls of science, the authorities revived an old statute

[41] *Counsellor*, No. 2, September 1861, p. 7.

forbidding all except ministers to take collections or teach on Sundays, and the Central Board advised its missionaries to sign a declaration which would permit them to teach on the grounds that they were Protestants and believed in the Gospels. Holyoake and several others refused to do so, apparently as much through indignation at the Central Board's cowardice and dishonesty as through strong irreligion. 'Did you mark that L. Jones, on behalf of the Social Body, undertook to prove, at Liverpool, that they believed in a personal Intelligent God. I congratulate you upon your conversion; when did *you* have your call?'[42]

One of those who refused to sign, Charles Southwell, founded the *Oracle of Reason* in a deliberately provocative attempt to force the socialists to decide how to treat his inevitable arrest. After his imprisonment Holyoake took over the editorship, and wrote to other Owenite lecturers advocating that they should separate theology from socialism. Many of the branches divided into two groups. One group regarded the destruction of religion as essential—'Socialism seeks the improvement of society, but that cannot be accomplished without the destruction of superstition. Socialism teaches certain views of human nature, and there again it must come into collision with popular faiths. If as a society we shrink from encountering the religious world we shall be treated as hypocrites or cowards . . .'[43] The other group considered themselves to be religious, or thought the issue not important enough to be the cause of division and persecution.

Holyoake and other missionaries of the anti-religious wing tried to introduce the discussion of rational religion into the societies under their care without antagonizing too many members or alerting the Central Board. One of them thought his Fabian tactics had been successful; 'Twelve months since, when I arrived here, the branch was a hybrid, unitarian kind of concern. The members were fond of hearing the nonsense sometimes spoken about "Socialism being genuine, primitive, practical or some other sort of Christianity". A word against Religion nearly frightened them from their seats. A few withdrew their names; but we had a much larger accession, and now they take strong meat like men. From our rostrum things are

---

[42] Letter from Chilton to Holyoake, 26 December, 1841 (Co-operative Union, Manchester).
[43] Letter from H. Jeffery to Holyoake, 23 March 1842 (Co-operative Union, Manchester).

now said which were never spoken publicly in Edinburgh before.'[44] In 1842 Southwell was imprisoned for blasphemy, and from this time onward, Holyoake began to attack religion more forcibly and to attribute more malevolent effects to it than he had done. It was also at this time that he began to describe himself as an atheist, the militant's phrase.

The significance of the terms 'atheist' and 'agnostic' will be touched on later, but they were only part of the debate which all the sections of the humanist and anti-clerical movement in Britain have intermittently held over what they should call themselves and their philosophy. The amount of effort devoted to this has been striking, but in context not surprising. There were and are unavoidable ambiguities in the purposes of these movements, since members have on the whole been united by what they do not believe but anxious to do more than go on attacking it. The search for the right word to describe themselves was partly a search for the bond which united them. The Owenites were divided in their views; some thought that socialism *was* a religion, others (who later became Christian socialists) thought some kind of religious basis was essential to create a community life which would withstand the *laissez-faire* pressures of capitalism, and some, as Holyoake was at first, were outspokenly anti-clerical. Richard Carlile argued to Holyoake the practical costs of this—'I quarrel not so much with your taste as with your judgement in the matter'—that if Christians saw his name advertised outside halls of science they 'will not enter the Den of Infamy'.[45]

In 1842, Holyoake gave a lecture to a group of chartists and socialists in Cheltenham on the Owenite scheme for Home Colonization. A preacher in the audience asked him why there was no provision for chapels in the communist communities, and Holyoake replied that poor men could not afford the worship of God. 'If poor men cost the State so much, they would be put like officers on half-pay. I think that while our (economic) distress lasts it would be wise to do the same thing with the Deity.' The local press accused him of blasphemy and he was arrested and charged. When released on bail he walked to London, the 'Infidel Metropolis', where his impending trial gave him access to leading deists and advanced thinkers, and he was adopted by Carlile. He spoke at the Rotunda, was introduced round radical London, and collections on his behalf were

[44] Letter to Holyoake from H. Jeffrey, 7 April 1842 (Co-operative Union, Manchester).
[45] Letter to Holyoake from Richard Carlile, 16 October 1842 (Co-operative Union, Manchester).

made at various Owenite and chartist meetings. He defended himself at the blasphemy trial with a virtuoso speech of inordinate length in explanation and defence of his opinions. He was imprisoned for six months in conditions of great privation and hardship, and during this time his daughter died of hunger.[46]

His trial and imprisonment were of permanent consequence for the strength of Holyoake's position in English free-thought. Radicals of all kinds rallied to his side. There was tremendous admiration for those who had been imprisoned for defending their beliefs, and imprisonment had become to some degree a touchstone of merit, a guarantee of genuine devotion to a cause. In the conflict between militant and respectable groups, Holyoake's genuine sufferings were a trump-card to be produced whenever his devotion to secularism was called in doubt. The continued loyalty of many freethinkers to Holyoake no matter how conciliatory he became was due partly to his extreme courage and militancy in the face of attack on his principles. To a later generation, his imprisonment 'had left him with a sort of martyr's halo which strengthened his appeal to us young "Freethinkers".'[47]

After Holyoake's release, he moved to London. He found its active radical and intellectual life so pleasant that he never left it again for a long period until the end of his life. Few provincial freethought centres thrived for any length of time, since the 'Infidel Metropolis' acted as a powerful magnet. The attractions of London were many. A belief so unusual as secularism could usually only attract a large and vigorous body of adherents in a very large town. London freethought was protected and stimulated by the society of powerful and intellectual middle-class religious and political radicals who were centred mainly on South Place Chapel. Holyoake's trial, for example, was made into an issue for freedom of expression; his case was raised by Roebuck in the House. In London the breakdown of the traditional local working-class community was already

---

[46] Account of the trial in G. J. Holyoake, *The Last Trial for Atheism in England*, Trübner and Co., London, 1871. In the preface to this, the fourth edition, Holyoake explained that even if he had known there was any word to describe a state between Theism and 'flagrant Atheism, . . . I should not have used it. When the *right* of freethought was in question, critical niceness of defense would have seemed like higgling with the enemy' (p. 15).

[47] Bradlaugh was never imprisoned, except for a night in the clock-tower of the Houses of Parliament. When Bradlaugh attacked Holyoake for his cowardice over the Knowlton trial, Holyoake replied that his sufferings for free speech had been greater; he did not use legal quibbles to get off, and was not supported by £2,000 of donations. *Secular Review and Secularist*, 7 July 1877, p. 64. Quotation from M. Quin, *Memoirs of a Positivist*, Allen & Unwin, London, 1924, p. 46.

far advanced and nonconformity had taken little hold. Those who openly declared their atheism in small tight-knit communities were often forced to leave them; and London was an obvious place where greater freedom would be tolerated. And those who came to London for other reasons, cut off from local community life and wandering around London in their spare time, were often attracted into work-ingmen's clubs or the crowds round open-air speakers which introduced them to radical and secularist ideas. Thus the radical society of London had a larger and more stimulating group of 'advanced religionists' and atheists than elsewhere.

Holyoake became part of various radical agitations, for example the Anti-Persecution Union which he founded to help those charged with blasphemy. But as he went round lecturing at various halls of science and travelled out on the growing railway network to lecture in the provinces, it was obvious that the Owenite movement was breaking up.[48] As late as 1848 Holyoake still saw his task as rebuilding the movement through his journalism and by travelling round lecturing, and although the Owenites of Lancashire and Yorkshire were anxious for him to do this, both he and many other Owenites were becoming disillusioned with socialism and turned to work for more limited and realizable ends. Holyoake founded a number of societies to promulgate utilitarian and naturalist ideas,[49] formed the Central Secular Society in 1851, and in the following year opened the Fleet Street House, a bookshop and publishing house for the *Reasoner*, which became an informal meeting-place for all those interested in secularist ideas.

Holyoake was not the sort of man to lead a mass movement and he does not seem to have wanted to do so, although equally he found it painful to see Bradlaugh rapidly amassing supporters and influence. He had none of the attributes of the popular leader; he was small, slight, with a thin high voice which could not carry very far and with an intense dislike of any kind of rhetoric or incivility; he was a genuinely open-minded man. Such a temperament gained him respect but also a great many detractors, who suspected him of loving a lord in the shape of any well-connected figure or liberal clergyman. But Holyoake did not conceive of himself as the leader of an organization but as an editor and public figure involved with a

---

[48] J. F. C. Harrison, op. cit., p. 250.
[49] He expected utilitarianism to extend the principles of naturalism to morality. 'Utility is the natural resting place of morals. Upon this basis politics have been put, and it only remains to bring religion to this standard.' *Reasoner*, No. 27, 1847, pp. 1–3.

wide variety of radical agitations. Rather than as a mass movement in its own right, he saw the secular movement as a body which could act against persecution, could educate and inform working-men about scientific discoveries, could provide some sort of focus for radical efforts, and which would demonstrate that free-thought was intellectually and socially respectable. Despite several attempts, he failed to establish a central body because he was too disposed to freedom to do more in the way of organization than hold annual Free Discussion Festivals of free-thinking sympathizers on the lines of those held by the ageing Robert Owen, to discuss 'What is to be done, and upon what principle to act to ensure a wide and effectual prevalence of their views'.[50]

London secularism was amorphous, composed of a series of radical bodies with overlapping memberships, some of whom might be interested in secularism, and of informal groups of men meeting in coffee-shops. The provincial societies were better organized, but the periodicals for the movement were mainly printed in London and the future of the movement was decided there. The reluctance of Holyoake to organize was made worse by the perennial difficulty of all radical movements: the very stiff-necked individualism which has driven their members out of conventional wisdom and associations makes them suspicious and resentful of any organizational curtailment of perfect liberty. Anti-clericals had an additional impetus for protest; for example, when Holyoake proposed that the officers of secular societies should be of good moral character and should subscribe to the principles of secularism, one member protested at even these constraints:

> We have in this outline a regular sectarian church of the most objectionable kind; a *secular order* with *clerical* and *lay* brothers; a secular *creed*; a secular *clergy*—a secular *episcopacy* of directors—a secular convocation of delegates—a central college of secular cardinals—with the editor of the Reasoner as Secular *Pope*.

To which, Holyoake returned tartly that 'according to Mr. Savage's easy use of words, any form of human polity might be called a church.'[51]

[50] *The Utilitarian Record*, April 1847, p. 39; *Reasoner*, 8 July 1846, p. 95.
[51] *Reasoner*, 15 December 1852, pp. 430–1.

2 MILITANCY AND RESPECTABILITY

The religion of the Dodsons consisted in revering whatever was customary and respectable: it was necessary to be baptized, else one could not
be buried in the churchyard; and to take the sacrament before death as a
security against more dimly understood perils; but it was of equal necessity
to have the proper pall-bearers and well-cured hams at one's funeral, and
to leave an unimpeachable will. A Dodson would not be taxed with the
omission of anything that was becoming, or that belonged to that eternal
fitness of things which was plainly indicated in the practice of the most
substantial parishioners . . .

George Eliot, *The Mill on the Floss*

Before examining the progress of the secular movement under the
presidency of Charles Bradlaugh the conflict between him and
Holyoake can be set in a wider context, because it was part of a major
debate which was constantly to recur inside the secular movement
and all other anti-clerical movements, and can conveniently be
examined here. The intellectual differences of opinion between
Holyoake and Bradlaugh were slight, but they disagreed over how
their beliefs should be furthered. These differences were discussed
and argued over as the difference between militancy and respectability, or a positive and negative secularism. All conflicts of opinion
within the secular movement and other humanist bodies have,
overtly or less overtly, engaged in some part of this central debate.
Thus apparently trivial discussions, for example of the use of the
terms 'agnostic' and 'atheist', or whether there should be songs at
meetings, involve more important and insoluble issues.

The secular movement faced, as all political and social movements
do, the problem of whether it should at all times stand by the
purest expression of its principles, regardless of how socially acceptable they were or how much desirable support they attracted, or
whether such principles should be expressed more moderately or
flexibly to encourage a larger membership and more effective role.
The militant secularist believed that to abate the anti-religious nature
of the movement destroyed its only legitimate purpose and that
only the fully committed, atheist member was worth recruiting.
His disregard for building up a mass membership was due partly
to a total rejection of the values of the outer, 'Christian' world.
If the militant chose to proselytize, he did so on his own terms. The

secularist who was prepared to be more moderate was willing to sacrifice purity for effectiveness. He would often justify this by claiming to make the movement more *respectable*—to make it accepted and valued within the existing legitimated forms of social protest. (The crucial importance of respectability is discussed again in Chapter 4.)

Conflict between factions inside political and social movements on this issue is often very bitter, partly because it is given a psychological interpretation. The militant assumes the moderate to be betraying the true purpose of the movement, attributing this to ambition, cowardice, or an unwarranted optimism that change can be brought about without a fight; the moderate feels the militant to be impossibly bigoted and idealistic, sacrificing for the sake of purity any chance the movement has to put its aims into effect. Such conflicts can be contained or controlled in several ways. They will be stilled by the success of the movement; they will also be solved by violent outside opposition. A more permanent solution is to form sub-groups containing the militants within them, but the humanist movement has formed separate societies with overlapping memberships.

The secular movement was not a successful mass movement (its greatest membership was about four thousand) nor has it been influential in improving the social position of atheists. It did achieve several crucial legal reforms concerned mainly with freedom of speech and publication, and on specific issues it acted as an effective pressure-group. But perhaps most importantly, it was there, acting as a *milieu* from which working-class radicals and campaigns could draw strength. Secularists were, much more than any of the other humanist groups ever were, perpetual outsiders.

One of the most interesting aspects of the secular movement is that it is undoubtedly a part of that elusive chameleon, working-class culture. It represents a later stage in the growth of part of the Liberty Tree so magnificently outlined in *The Making of the English Working-Class*. It is an unusual part, because it lies outside the traditions of socialism and nonconformity, and because of the stress on self-help and improvement, individualism and abstract arguments over morality. Because of this, commentators have sometimes dismissed secularists as if they were merely aping the manners of the middle class, suffering from false class-consciousness.[1] But in fact, as I hope to show in succeeding chapters, their ideas and the

---

[1] See for example Rosamund Billington, *Leicester Secular Society, 1852–1920; a Study in Radicalism and Respectability*, Dissertation, University of Leicester, 1968.

way that they tried to implement them sprang directly from their social experience.

The disagreements between Bradlaugh and Holyoake as to how secularism should best be realized were not only arguments about the right beliefs, how secularist meetings should be organized and what other aims secularism entailed, they were also implicitly arguments about how radical members of the working class should behave toward the ruling culture. Both men saw that something more than beliefs was at issue. The real question was, how could they win *legitimacy* for secularism? Religious beliefs could be combated and defeated and both men, true to the tradition of the *philosophes*, saw belief as the essence of religion. But in a society like nineteenth-century Britain religion was much more than that, as George Eliot with her unmatched understanding of provincial English life illuminated in the beliefs of the Dodsons. The strength of religion lay in its unexamined connections with every aspect of life, with its meaning as a *label* which marked off the church-goer who carried out religious practice scrupulously as part of his social duty from those simply outside the understood pattern of life, excluded from the routine of Sunday school with buns and band, and funerals with ham. It was this aspect of religion which was so baffling to the secularist. Religious beliefs could be combated; but the relations between religious practice and life in the community were so intimate that religion could not be made into a separate target.

'We are not bishops of a party . . .'

The debate which took place within the movement over the nature of religion and its connections with everyday life, and how those without religious beliefs should therefore treat a tradition of life in which religion was embedded, was not a debate between permanent factions. Each issue called forth different coalitions of supporters and attackers, and since members of the movement read the proliferation of magazines and pamphlets in which rival arguments continued to be presented rather than allowing the organization to define a central policy and commit itself to it, the debate itself came to be an important part of the culture of secularism. The distrust of the freethinker for centralized authority and the loose and largely unspecified relationship of the local branches to the central body meant that despite the loyal allegiance that Bradlaugh commanded throughout his presidency, Holyoake continued to be regarded as a leader of free-thought, to lecture to local societies, and to represent secularism to polite society.

In 1849, Holyoake summed up the result of eight years' effort in advocating atheism. In that time, his papers had not increased their readership. He considered that the failure of the movement was due to the legal disabilities of atheists (they could not take an oath, and so were unprotected by law, for example from unscrupulous shopmen), and the fact that atheists were feared and despised. 'The world regards the constant identification with unpopular opinions as dogmatism and intolerance.' Men dared not be seen with a copy of the *Reasoner;* even the notorious feminist Frances Wright 'was continually talking about her mortification and vexation and the utter impotency of her "mission" if it appeared in the Reasoner.'[2]

During the 1840s a gulf had grown between the middle-class and working-class radical. The removal of legal disabilities on dissenters had allowed the prosperous nonconformist to become more absorbed into established society. The evangelical revival had been slowly bringing about that combination of sentiment, propriety and domestic piety which we think of as characteristic of the Victorian middle class. As the upper layers of society grew in size, the informal code of conduct possible in a small-scale community was increasingly replaced by a formalized etiquette, by an increasing concentration on the forms of social life. The vivid, concrete and pungent prose of the earlier freethinkers gradually became more prolix, abstract and long-winded. Holyoake in particular laid increasing anxious stress on 'politeness', and wrote a book on public speaking for working-men. It is fascinating to speculate as to how far the speech forms and vocabulary of the wealthy and the poor were really diverging at this time as their social worlds became increasingly divided, and how far the anxious concern with form and etiquette had merely made people more conscious of existing differences. Holyoake tried to justify the reluctance of eminent radicals to become associated with the secularist movement; the 'unknown and insignificant', 'whose daily lives are near privation and whose position excludes them from society in its pleasant sense', would lose very little if they declared their atheism 'but it is a very different sacrifice

---

[2] *Reasoner*, 13 June 1849, pp. 369–72; letter to Holyoake from Isaac Ironside, 18 June 1947 (Co-operative Union, Manchester).

when a man of genius and means . . . exposes his name to the common defamation of every ignoble and ignorant partisan.'[3]

Holyoake and his associates became increasingly unhappy at the crudity of some articles in the *Reasoner*, which would 'delight the rabble of mutineers and the herd of coarse-minded Atheists, but which are calculated to repel men worth more than all these put together . . . a tone of perpetual sneer and snarl . . .'[4] His middle-class friends found the endless repetition of diatribes against religion increasingly distasteful; what should have been a '*means* of rescuing morality from the domination of future-world speculation, became an end—noisy, wordy, vexed, capricious, angry, imputative, recriminative and interminable.'[5] Like other leaders of movements drawn from the poor and excluded, Holyoake found that he had a ready audience as their representative among middle-class sympathizers once he had accommodated himself to their politer *mores*, and that they could offer him many more concrete benefits and social and political opportunities than his members could command. His growing allegiance to their judgements led to a bitter estrangement from his old allies, amongst them Robert Cooper and Charles Southwell. 'I am neither rich nor respectable, and so can be of no further interest to you', wrote an old friend reproachfully. 'You are now fairly admitted into the respectable circle. I desire to keep out of it. I cannot worship your new gods; but I do not wish to control your conscience. I only feel that our sympathy is broken . . .'[6]

Holyoake was more true to the radical tradition of independent outspokenness than they gave him credit for. He never concealed his change of opinions, even when the appearance of another potential leader who was prepared to vigorously attack the churches began to draw support away from him. His motives must have been partly personal; 'the two past years have been eleemosynary, propagandic and precarious', he wrote in his diary for 1856. Yet there can be no doubt that he had good grounds for thinking that a purely

---

[3] G. J. Holyoake, *John Stuart Mill as some of the Working-classes knew Him*, Trübner, London, 1873, p. 10.

[4] Letter to Holyoake from 'Lionel Holdreth' (Percy Greg), 18 July 1857 (Co-operative Union, Manchester). Greg was a middle-class supporter of Holyoake who took over the *Reasoner* during his illness in 1859, and did much to alienate secularists by his conservative politics and slighting references to their lack of education.

[5] S. D. Collet, *George Jacob Holyoake and Modern Atheism*, Trübner, London, 1885, p. 14.

[6] Letter to Holyoake from Thomas Cooper, 11 November 1853, (Co-operative Union, Manchester). And see Kurt Lewin's analysis of the ambivalent position of the leader of a minority group, 'The Problem of Leadership', in A. W. Gouldner, ed., *Studies in Leadership*, Harper, New York, 1950, pp. 192–4.

anti-clerical movement could have only limited vitality, although he does not seem to have realized that it could be strengthened not only by persecution but by a powerful charismatic leader who could use the rowdy emotional gatherings of workmen that middle-class reformers so disliked to bind men to him so that his campaigns would become their own.

'President of a British Republic'

Charles Bradlaugh, the son of a solicitor's clerk, whilst preparing himself for confirmation at an Anglican church in Hackney found some apparent discrepancies between the Gospels and the Thirty-nine Articles. The vicar reacted to his queries by complaints to his father about his atheistical tendencies, and Bradlaugh shrank from returning to church and began to go instead to the open-air debates in Bonner's Fields. He joined one group of regular arguers who were the followers of Richard Carlile, and having become further estranged from both his clergyman and his father left home in 1848 to lodge with Carlile's widow. He encountered the secular movement and the Holyoake brothers at the old Owenite St John Street institution, but was finally forced by poverty to enlist. He won some notoriety in the army as an ardent temperance advocate, but succeeded in buying his release in 1853 and finding employment in a law firm, where he acquired the basis for the legal knowledge which was so useful in his later career. He married into the old radical free-thought tradition; his father-in-law, Abraham Hooper, was a chartist, radical, teetotaller and anti-smoker. Neither the marriage nor Bradlaugh's career as a solicitor's clerk was a success.

He began to make a living as a propagandist, speaking first to outdoor groups and then travelling all over Britain to speak to any group who would have him. At first his audiences were small and he was shunned by many respectable freethinkers from amongst the labour aristocracy, and collected his small income from the donations of pitmen, factory workers and the notoriously infidel railway navvies. Occasional attacks and stonings from rowdy defenders of the faith added excitement to his meetings.

These experiences made Bradlaugh—'Iconoclast'—a very different sort of speaker from the more established, self-confident and almost painfully learned leaders of the secular community of London. An anonymous account by 'an old Chartist and Owenite' of his first

appearance as speaker at the St John Street Institution illustrated
vividly the snobberies of established radicalism.

When our host [Robert Cooper] entered into conversational criticism on
the new phases of philosophical thought, then the topic of society, I observed
that 'Iconoclast' listened without appearing to comprehend . . . Mrs. Robert
Cooper . . . drew him out, by enquiries as to his outdoor propaganda against
the biblical controversialists. This at once aroused his interest. His eyes
sparkled as he recited his triumphs over itinerating evangelists. He related
his adventures in Coffee-house discussions . . .
   I was anxious to fathom the extent of his educational and literary quali-
fications. The subject of the 'Immortality of the Soul' came up, in reference to
a new edition of Lectures which Mr. Robert Cooper was preparing for the
press, and I was greatly surprised at the paucity of knowledge possessed by
'Iconoclast' upon this subject . . . [They discussed the materialist/meta-
physical controversy as to the nature of the soul]. I soon found that 'Iconoclast'
had not studied those subjects. He was unable to enter into argument,
either in defence or opposition, upon theories which had reference to either
Kant, Reid or Macintosh. His mind was only saturated with textual contradictions of the Pentateuch, and he seemed never to have considered the
tendency of Hebrew Sadduceeism towards the comity of thought, which was
in antagonism to the Platonic Metaphysics of the age of the Apostles. In
opposition to those, he commenced to portray the horrors of Hell, as if engaged in one of his favourite lectures.
   I heard for the first time that evening the peculiar eloquence of 'Iconoclast'.
It was an old story. It was an hour of hyper-critical analysis of Mosaic texts.
It pleased the audience, who took their quantum of anti-biblical criticism as
other people in the same neighbourhood take their quantum of gin. It was a
fair sample of the orations of 'Iconoclast'. He supplied, then as now, a kind
of excitement which is dispensed elsewhere by Salvation Armies and sensa-
tional preachers. An *educated* audience could not listen to such harangues, if
frequently repeated.[7]

The process by which Bradlaugh took over the leadership of the
secular movement can be briefly summarized. A group of Yorkshire
secularists gave Bradlaugh enough funds to start the *National
Reformer* in 1860, which differed from previous freethought journals
in that it carried discussions of current news. At first his main support was to be found in the North of England, reported to be more
militant than the South, but in the previous year Holyoake had had
a nervous collapse and his absence from secularism for a year proved
decisive. The *Reasoner* died in 1861, and the leadership began to
revolve round the editor of the new journal. In the same year
Holyoake became part-editor with Bradlaugh, a reconciliation for

---

[7] Charles Mackay's libellous *Life of Charles Bradlaugh, M.P.*, Gunn, London, 1880,
pp. 104-6, probably produced by W. S. Ross, an eccentric figure who was a rival
secularist leader.

which many secularists had been pressing, but the difference between their ideas and personalities was too great for him to stay more than a few months. Some parts of the movement rallied to Holyoake; Bolton Secular Society resolved that he 'had led Freethought into a sphere which, for respectability and usefulness, it never before occupied', and several secular societies in the Midlands and that at Manchester supported him, as did the communities of secularists at Leicester and Failsworth, who continued to remain outside Bradlaugh's National Secular Society. But despite the confusion and recriminations over this process and the election of Bradlaugh in place of Holyoake as President of the movement, it is clear that the majority of the movement were with Bradlaugh in wanting secularism restricted to anti-theology.

Between 1851 and 1861, about sixty secularist groups were formed, mainly in London or the industrial communities of the North. Most of them had an interrupted existence—at the movement's greatest expansion, it still had not many more than sixty secure branches. At least fourteen of the societies started secular schools. Bradlaugh continued an active career as a travelling lecturer, and the *National Reformer* was edited by John Watts with his brother Charles until 1866, when Bradlaugh once again took over as editor and founded the National Secular Society, with himself as President. Its constitution supported universal education, employment, civil, religious and intellectual liberty. It declared 'the promotion of Human improvement and Happiness is the highest duty', and that these were powerfully obstructed by religion, 'when the intellect is impeded by childish and absurd superstition'.[8]

These principles were more militant and radical than those of Holyoake's society but a decade later the rules and principles had become much more conciliatory. Members then merely had to assent 'to promote the improvement and happiness of myself and fellows', and free-thought was now less *against* religion than *independent* of religion. 'By the principle of Freethought is meant the exercise of the understanding upon relevant facts, independent of penal or priestly intimidation.'

Bradlaugh remained as president of the secular movement from the 1860s to his resignation in 1890, the year before his death. He was well equipped to become a charismatic leader and a lasting legend inside the movement. He was very tall, massively built, with

---

[8] *National Reformer*, 13 October 1867, p. 234.

an imposing voice and manner; a great orator, with a powerful harsh voice. George Bernard Shaw remembered that

> He really did radiate terrific personal magnetism. You were conscious of it when you sat near him. He was the most magnetic person I have ever known, and the greatest orator. Henry George and Mrs. Besant were splendid and most convincing orators; but Bradlaugh was the heavy-weight champion of the platform.

Similar metaphors occurred to his contemporaries—'military', 'a granite character', 'trenchant', 'a fighter', 'strenuous' and 'resolute', 'a hero, a giant who dwarfed everything about him, a terrific personality', 'he was built on a bigger plan than any other man that I had ever met . . . I have seen strong men, under the storm of his passion, rise from their seats, and sometimes weep with emotion'. Even his detractors judged him on the same grandiose scale; he once asked Madame Blavatsky who he had been in a previous reincarnation, 'and even as he spoke, I saw a black cloud form itself behind his head, and on it was written in letters of a horrid grey, the name "Torquemada"!'[9]

Bradlaugh justified his extraordinary power in a movement devoted to freedom by stressing that the times were those of crisis. As he was annually re-acclaimed President, he remarked that he and the office itself only existed as a 'fighting President'. He dramatized the enormous and menacing power of organized religion—'no man ever saw a religion die'. Members of the movement and contemporaries were fascinated by his size, his energy and strength. The 'replies to letters' column in the *National Reformer* frequently carried reassurances that Bradlaugh's height was over six feet, and of his having resisted ten policemen when ejected from the House. Stuart Headlam, who used to speak against Bradlaugh at the London Hall of Science in the 1870s and 1880s with many expressions of mutual esteem being exchanged, saw that 'it was really the boldness of the secularist speakers that frequenters of their Halls of Science admired; to these sturdy workmen, Bradlaugh seemed to stand for courage, for honesty, for "freethought" . . .'[10] He became the embodiment of the legend that the secular movement created for itself; feared and hated by those who opposed it, whom he combated by force of personality and an agile use of the law; tender and helpful

---

[9] Appreciations in J. P. Gilmour, ed., *Champion of Liberty, Charles Bradlaugh*, Watts, London, 1933; H. Snell, *Men, Movements and Myself*, Dent, London, 1936, p. 31; P. C. Kegan, *Memories*, Kegan Paul, London, 1899, pp. 355–6.
[10] F. G. Bettany, *Stuart Headlam*, John Murray, London, 1926, p. 47.

toward the helpless. He devoted every morning and endless correspondence to acting as a legal adviser to secularists and any other members of the working class who asked him for help. His frequent law suits provided the movement with both a recurrent source of excitement and some vividly dramatized heroes and villains, and also with an important source of moral legitimacy; by this means Bradlaugh was defending the just laws of the nation against corruption.[11]

It was inevitable that this style of leadership allowed for neither delegation nor division. Despite the democratic apparatus of an annual conference with voted members where policy was to be voted on and the president elected, Bradlaugh's dominance was certain. Within the secular movement all disagreements rapidly turned into issues of principle; no one took much interest in creating a stable organization. George Standring, an acute and perceptive observer, regretted that Bradlaugh never made 'any provision for what I may call automatic working. The society was a potent machine for utilizing and distributing the impulses which its president never failed to impart to it, but the development of individual initiative was a matter that never received due attention.'[12] After 1870 or so, power in the movement, even after Bradlaugh's death, could only be held by claiming his mandate.

'Mr. Bradlaugh the Model Protestant'

The core of Bradlaugh's objection to Christianity was that it required submission to authority. As such, it was intolerable. There were only two possible religious positions: 'One, the completest submission of the intellect to authority: to some book, or church, or man. The other, the most thorough assertion of the right and duty of individual thought and judgement.' The Old Owenite

---

[11] This theme appeared in a secularist's sonnet to Bradlaugh:

> They hate because they fear him. Not for flaws
> Of Speculation, not so much for even the Hell
> They love—because they send its foes to swell
> Its lost (us not forgotten)—but because
> In him they see the interpreter of laws
> Working against their wrong, the axe to fell
> The forest of corruption . . .

'Omicras', *National Reformer*, 14 September 1883, p. 215.

[12] George Standring, 'Reminiscences of the Secular Movement', *Reformer*, 15 March 1897, p. 12.

quoted earlier who complained that Bradlaugh did not know about any recent theological or philosophical developments had missed the point; Bradlaugh's attack on religion began and ended at first with its origin, the Bible. His own doubts had been raised by its inconsistencies; his listeners heard the books of the Old and New Testament 'assailed as incompatible with history, with science and with each other; but above all they are denounced as incompatible with justice and right'. That was how he impressed a man who had been a 'vague radical freethinking theist', whose 'opinions chiefly consisted of aversion to parsons and landlords', and who found Bradlaugh's 'fiery scorn, his lofty indignation, his absolute conviction' even more impressive than anything that he actually said.

Bradlaugh was much nearer to the radical nonconformist tradition than either he or they were aware of. The insistence on an intimate knowledge of the Bible and of little else, on the supremacy of the individual judgement, and the absolute certainty that there was only one right, one truth, and one morality did not strike many of his listeners as strange; the nonconformist chapels in which religion had taken its *shape* for them had stressed the same things. That religion was a set of beliefs about the supernatural and the after-life which underpinned moral conduct was a part of taken-for-granted reality for both sides. The dislike for any worldly form of religious authority was as characteristic of many radical nonconformists as it was of secularists. Stuart Headlam was once interrupted in a Christian Socialist lecture where he was putting forward his liberal but high-church views on the mediating role of the priest by a working-man who cried out 'Atheist as I am, sir, atheist as I am, no man shall stand between my soul and my God'.[13]

In 1870, Bradlaugh and Holyoake restated their views on the prospects for free-thought in a public debate on 'Is Secularism Atheism?'[14] There was a careful avoidance of any direct hostility or implication of leadership between the two men—'Mr. Holyoake has the right to his opinions, and the right to express them, for we are not bishops of a party, we are not leaders of a party, we are only men of a party.'

Holyoake argued that the principles of secularism did not necessarily include atheism; the purpose of the movement was the construction of a scientific morality, not the denial of the existence of

---

[13] Bettany, op. cit., p. 87.
[14] The debate from which subsequent quotations are taken was printed in the *National Reformer*, 20 March 1870, pp. 177 *et seq*.

God, and to call it atheist would merely alienate support, especially respectable support. The secular movement, he pointed out, despite Bradlaugh's activities and 'arguing with the clergy', was 'unadvanced in position'; still meeting above public houses—'The most ordinary sects build or hire temples and other places where their people decently meet. Mr. Bradlaugh, with all his zeal and appeals, finds today that all London can do is to put up this kind of place in which we now meet opposite a lunatic asylum . . .' Why was the party so small, poor and disreputable? Because it insisted that its members be atheists and infidels.

> The truth is that there are liberal theists, liberal believers in another life, liberal believers in God, perfectly willing to unite together with the extremist thinkers, for secular purposes, giving effect to every form of human liberty— but they refuse to be saddled with the oppobrium of opinions they do not hold, or do dislike.

To this Bradlaugh replied that it was in fact only the poor and the militant who were prepared to fight for the extension of liberty and the truth, and in the classic retort of the militant sectarian, he rejected the judgements of outsiders about secularists. 'I know the leading men among them who have made themselves prominent, and I do not care what kind of a character religious men may put round the word Atheist. I would fight until men respect it . . .'[15] Fighting in his opinion had achieved far more for freethinkers than compromise ever did. 'I say we need a bold front to the enemy. Is it not true that the bold front which we have taken here during the last decade, has won a wider recognition than ever before accorded?' Christianity could not be bypassed or ignored for the sake of collaborating with Christians in political matters, because organized religion interfered with all men's lives.

> Christianity will not allow you to exist side by side with it. It claims a right to dominate you. You talk of 'ignoring the priest'. You cannot. He takes your children in the cradle, he modifies the teaching in the class book, in every phase and walk of life . . . his claim is to dominate and control all thought. You must go boldly to them in your Freethought propaganda and break their teeth, or else they bite those members of your party who are weakest. (Loud Applause).

To attack Christianity was not merely destructive; Christianity was a total falsehood and its removal would mean the replacement

---

[15] Bradlaugh in fact *was* an agnostic by T. H. Huxley's definition. He did not deny the existence of a God, but was prepared to deny that there was any evidence for the existence of any God which had so far been claimed. He was a monist, but it never seems to have occurred to him that moral statements were not material ones.

of error by truth, in itself a positive change. Therefore, his conclusion was, 'We do oppose theology. We do make war on the Church. We do say that the Bible has had a position taken for it which no book has a right to have', and whilst 'all men who are Secularists are not yet Atheists, I put it to you as also perfectly true, that in my opinion the logical consequence of the acceptance of Secularism must be that the man gets to Atheism if he has brains enough to comprehend. (Loud Cheers).'

But to the secularist of long standing, after the first flush of liberation and militancy had passed anti-theological arguments began to prove wearisome and fruitless. The debate between Christian and Atheist became increasingly routinized; 'the discussion consisted, more than anything else, in accusations and counter-accusations of not coming to the point, and the accusations and counter-accusations were equally true . . . And so this vain show of battle went on for three hours, until for one, I got thoroughly tired of it . . .'[16], and so did many secularists. Those who stayed in the movement did so, on the whole, because they believed that the destruction of religious beliefs was in itself a positive act. This meant that secularists had to ensure that some of their audiences *were* still believers, and one way of doing this were the debates with Christian controversialists who brought with them an audience of potential converts. But to an audience largely ignorant of theology, only a swingeing attack on scriptural religion or the evils of priest-craft would create much response, and by the 1870s many secularists were uneasily aware that in an age of growing theological liberalism, their targets were more and more irrelevant.

> . . . and so it is somewhat painful, and savours of a *fiasco*, when, after a vigorous pounding of the doctrines of literal inspiration, eternal punishment, election and reprobation, forensic views of the atonement, etc., etc., the thought arises that, perhaps for forty miles around, there is not a single man—not even a clergyman—who would think of controverting a single word . . .[17]

Many secularists were honest and psychologically sensitive enough to recognize that the public debates between Christian and secularist

---

[16] Report of a debate between Bradlaugh and Thomas Cooper, an ex-secularist turned Christian, at the London Hall of Science, *London Christian Times*, 3 February 1864, p. 201. Collyns Simon, a Christian Controversialist, complained to the *National Reformer* that having read 'your most useful' journal for many years, 'there appears to be, from time to time—almost every three or four months—a fresh crop of controversialists upon this subject—who seem to enter, in each case, without apparently having overheard what had been said upon a previous occasion'. 26 August 1866, p. 138.

[17] J. Whiteley, *Secular Review*, 8 June 1878, p. 354.

had unpleasant undertones. They attracted large audiences but many of them came for the show, and the discussions after the lectures became repetitious with contentious and meaningless arguments. The search for reason and truth was abandoned for the enjoyment of the fight; lecturers replied roughly and aggressively to those who questioned them, and provoked 'unhealthy' laughter at their discomfiture. Long-established 'militant' secular meetings often acquired a resident Christian Evidence questioner, who became 'a well-known and almost affectionately regarded figure.'[18] But despite these doubts the absolute right of free speech was so important both to the ideology of secularism and in its traditions that the leaders refused to stop it; 'we must fight to live, and debate is our war'.

Yet another characteristic that marked Bradlaugh as true heir to the protestant evangelical tradition was his marked attention to his own set of the proprieties. He created his own traditions and routines, which gave his meetings an agreeably ritualized shape. He was always exactly punctual, and always dressed entirely in formal black—like a nonconformist minister, observed his detractors. He was adamant in insisting on certain aspects of 'respectability'—he would not allow any card-playing or drinking at the Hall of Science, and reminded open-air speakers 'to be careful of their language as well as earnest in their advocacy'.[19] But the happy mean of militant expression without offensiveness to anyone was impossible to achieve.

'Positive' and 'Negative' Secularism; the Form of the Meeting

One important reason for the perpetual uncertainty as to the purposes and activities which were proper for the secularist meeting was that freethinkers themselves usually changed considerably after they had joined a local society. They often joined a society in a state of fury at the injustice that had been meted out to other freethinkers by the churches. The maltreatment of Charles Southwell had been for his friend Holyoake 'the cradle of my doubts and the grave of my religion', and in much the same way Bradlaugh's attacks on the churches turned bitter after the persecution of himself and

---

[18] Discussion on the role of discussion in meetings, *National Reformer* 21 November 1886, *et seq.*
[19] Bradlaugh's editorial, *National Reformer*, 19 June 1887.

Carlile's family. The loss of religious faith itself (described in a later chapter) had often happened several years previously; the decision to join the secular movement was prompted by an incident which suddenly dramatized the antipathy of respectable society for atheism. Bradlaugh's violent expulsion from the House of Commons when he attempted to take his seat was an incident of this kind; the freethinker suddenly seemed to realize that ultimately, as an atheist, he was not a full citizen, that his opinions were so feared and hated that a policy of conciliation and moderation was useless. Thus he found himself in a position of self-sustaining rebellion, an attitude to society which could find no channel except violent hostility to the symbols of the respectable *mores* which excluded him.

After several years in the movement, the secularist was likely to have become satiated with attacks on religion and to have noticed that many members, especially the wealthier and more respectable, disliked them and that by leading outsiders to see atheists as aggressive, violent and anti-social figures they were hindering the social acceptance of atheism. Many men who had held extremely 'advanced' and militant opinions in their youth found that as they aged, the same opinions had become far more generally accepted. They had also usually been involved with agitations for other reforms, and had found that their acceptance among more orthodox and influential reformers depended on their playing down their atheism. At this point many gave up active involvement with the movement, although they still called themselves secularists and their interest would revive if a national leader spoke at their local branch, or was involved in a spectacular political campaign. Secular societies were like Turkish baths, a leader remarked resignedly; good to pass through, but not to live in.

Holyoake and some of the movement, principally the older and more 'respectable' secularists, thought that the answer to this situation was to create more 'inner life' in the branches themselves, or 'positive' secularism. In order to foster a sense of communion and friendship among their members they turned naturally to the religious forms which seemed to fulfil this purpose for others. The desire for something equivalent to the fellowship of a united congregation fixed on various parts of the nonconformist prototype that most members had been familiar with. The commonest wish was for a secular hymn-book; many members had missed 'music to rational poetry, in our too prosaic and cheerless assemblies.' Indeed, one member confessed, 'many a time since having become a freethinker, have I attended some church or chapel, that I might again the more vividly recall those departed muscial pleasures of the past.' In order that God might not have all the best tunes, several hymn-books were compiled.

Many secularists advocated more 'positive' meetings because they hoped that in this way they would be able to attract women and their children. (The vast majority of freethinkers were men; reports of meetings which mention the proportion of women put them at between none and less than a quarter of all attenders.) Unless the movement succeeded in attracting women, particularly the wives of members, it could never be based on family membership, and children would grow up outside the movement. Each secularist would have to be a convert and the movement would have to recruit vigorously to maintain even a constant membership. The National Secular Society often urged local societies to try to recruit more women, and in order to attract them it was believed that secular meetings had to be accommodated to the greater emotional and ritual needs which held them to the churches; '. . . their ritual wants are satisfied by the ceremonies observed on such occasions.'[20] Women were thought to find the rites of passage of family life more important than men did, and so to wean them from the churches ceremonials for burials, marriages and christenings were devised.[21] It was a nineteenth-century convention that women, children, churches and the home were somehow bound up with what were called the 'softer' emotions, and when Stalybridge Secular Society debated as to whether they should found a secular church to attract women and children, those in favour of it argued that 'a Secular Church should largely avail itself of the emotional faculties from which arose the good and beautiful in human character.'[22] (The feeling that women and religion had an intrinsic connection with unselfishness was an important theme in the movement's later contacts with socialism.)

Some large secular societies, not necessarily those who had conceded the need for ceremony in other respects, established Sunday schools. These were not only to ensure a supply of future members,

---

[20] Austin Holyoake advocating secular ceremonies, *National Reformer*, 12 January 1868, p. 27.

[21] The main service-books were devised either by Annie Besant, the wife of a clergyman, or by Charles Watts, the son of a Wesleyan minister.

[22] *National Reformer*, 18 June 1871, p. 398, and 2 July 1871, p. 15. So many members objected to the term 'church' that finally they compromised with 'United Secular Institution'.

but also to give working-class children a better education and to remedy the defective moral education which was provided by religious instruction in schools. Some of these secular Sunday schools were drawn into the social pattern of the local church schools, going on outings and teas together with the Sunday schools of liberal denominations. The Failsworth Secular Sunday School joined in the local Whit Walks with their own brass band. Few of these schools lasted long enough to rear a generation of freethinkers. but those that did, for example at Leicester and Failsworth, provided a solid basis of membership for exceptionally long-lasting societies.

Bradlaugh, whilst adamant on promoting respectability in the sense of the prevailing code of proper social behaviour, was opposed to all use of religious equivalents. 'Is the cult to be a rearranging of what is called "divine service" on non-supernatural lines; a singing of "human hymns" and a style of platform address which deals generally with the moral emotions but does not discuss, or at least at times avoids, questions of concrete action?' His conception of the purpose of the secular movement was a very specific one. In part it existed simply to break down the legal handicaps which atheists suffered, and he sometimes implied that when this was done the movement would disband, thus lending it an air of transience in which there was no room for an 'inner life'. It would achieve its end by attacking the churches. 'Without such wars with other creeds constantly and persistently maintained, Secularism has neither force, nor character, nor purpose as a party. To call it "a new religion" is misleading. It is not a religion.' And indeed a few years earlier, Halifax Secular Society had been expelled for registering itself as a religious institution.

To the militant freethinker, a concern with the 'inner life' of a branch usually meant a neglect of militant proselytizing. The societies which had schools 'were not generally those which were most active in direct propaganda'. The militant also professed himself puzzled at those who hankered after reminders of religion. Bradlaugh believed that 'the desire for these things [hymn-books, congregational singing and devotional readings] is mainly an emotional survival of old ecclesiastical habit, and I cannot see what good they do apart from gratifying these surviving emotions.' Paradoxically, the intense admiration and affection that many secularists felt for him made them thrust priestly duties upon him; he found himself, slightly unwillingly, officiating at namings, marriages and funerals.

How far Bradlaugh really did adhere to the narrowly rational and pragmatic theory of human conduct and emotion that he propounded is in doubt; when Mrs Besant promoted a more social and ritual aspect of London secularism, he seemed to concur willingly. His blindness to the possible functions of ritual was and is common enough amongst radicals; not only might the use of a quasi-religious form for expressing a 'positive secularism' have stilled the doubts of those who wondered whether there was any, but ritual and ceremony generally have the useful function of meaning many things to many men.

In a movement in which so much depended on words—for argument, debate, definition and allegiance—secularists were forced to make their meanings absolutely clear and consistent. But as a group they were not formally educated, and disdained the exact and hair-splitting mode of expression of the educated but ineffectual agnostic. Words could only show them their differences more clearly and divide them, except in the passionate oratory of those whose lives had shown that they were dedicated to the ends of the movement. In the end, leaders appealed to their members on the basis of their lives, and as the external circumstances of the movement changed during the 1880s, it was Bradlaugh himself who held the militant and the moderate together.

3 SEX AND SOCIALISM: THE ZENITH AND DECLINE OF THE SECULAR MOVEMENT

Two principles, according to the Settembrinian cosmogony, were in perpetual conflict for possession of the world: force and justice, tyranny and freedom, superstitition and knowledge; the law of permanence and the law of change, of ceaseless fermentation issuing in progress . . . There was no doubt as to which of the two would finally triumph: it would be the power of enlightenment, the power that made for rational advance and development . . . Much still remained to be done, sublime exertions were still demanded from those spirits who had received the light. Then only the day would come when thrones would crash and outworn religions crumble . . .

Thomas Mann, *The Magic Mountain*

Charles Bradlaugh became president of the secular movement in 1861, and resigned in 1890 shortly before his death. During his presidency, the movement attained its largest membership and widest influence. Those who were attracted to the movement were very often those who supported Bradlaugh and the various reforms that he championed—neo-Malthusianism, freedom of speech and publication, republicanism and the right to affirm—and who saw secularism as simply an adjunct or basis to these reforms. After Bradlaugh's eventual entry into Parliament in 1886 support for him from the secular movement began to diminish, partly because he was inevitably less active in the movement, and partly because it became more and more evident that he was opposed to the growing socialist doctrines of the 1880s. By the forcible extension of his atheist opinions into political life, Bradlaugh caused a new outcry against atheism which did much to unify the secular movement and give it purpose. By creating a central body—the National Secular Society—to which local societies were affiliated, Bradlaugh was able to use the movement as an effective vehicle to support his campaigns. But by using it in this way, he and his supporters moved away from the mainstream of working-class political and intellectual activity. The story of Bradlaugh's various campaigns and the success that they had is well known; the focus of attention here is on the effect that they had on the freethought movement.

Perhaps the most interesting of these campaigns, both in terms of the repercussion that it created within the movement and also for what it reveals about the attitude of various radical groups to sexual morality, was that for neo-Malthusianism. This neologism came to mean the knowledge and advocacy of mechanical means of birth control, but in its wider sense it meant the right of men and women to intervene in the natural process of bearing the number of children that God had intended for them. The subject was so hedged with taboos that in retrospect it is often difficult to determine exactly what any individual was arguing for, but perhaps even contemporaries were not always sure.

The early socialists, from whom the secular movement had taken its general mental map of worldly improvement, had often argued for birth control. Their arguments had two general themes. Politically, active working-class men were kept in poverty and subjection by their large families, forced to depend on charity, unable to free their talents and energies to enable them either to succeed within society or to attack its arrangements. The role of the churches in perpetuating large families was symptomatic of the general alliance between priest, state and employer to ensure an over-supply of docile and inexpensive workers. In addition, the political and social equality of women was unattainable whilst they were at the mercy of their own fertility. A free and open communion between the sexes would never be possible until its biological consequences could be controlled. It was at this point that reformers diverged and conservatives pounced.

Some reformers—for example, Owen in some of his more philosophical-radical moments—argued that marriage made women chattels and they should enter free unions instead. But whilst the secular movement was widely accused of this, particularly since it was clear that Bradlaugh and Annie Besant, both separated from their spouses, were attracted to each other, the freethought movement was opposed to such bohemianism. Bradlaugh's arguments for population control were less concerned with personal happiness than with the political importance to the poor of being able to limit their families. Poverty was not only a source of misery in itself but 'is in fact the impassable barrier between man and civil and religious liberty . . . There is a miseducation in poverty, which distorts the human mind, destroys self-reliant energy, and is a most effectual barrier in the way of religious liberty.'

During the mid-Victorian period, the solution to the problem of family limitation that was most generally advocated was that men should marry late. (There could be no greater proof of the inability of the Victorians to think clearly about sexuality than the wide-spread advocacy of this policy, which was both conducive to great unhappiness and prostitution and ineffectual, since it was not usually proposed that such men should marry women of the same age as themselves.) To the neo-Malthusians within the freethought movement, this solution demonstrated yet again the contribution of the churches to human misery and especially to the miseries of the poor, who would have to wait far longer than the rich until they could afford to marry. Bradlaugh quoted a letter from

A forced Bachelor—hindered from marriage by poverty; not daring to marry because his wretched wages are insufficient to feed, clothe and shelter himself, and give him no hope if he marry, other than of a careworn wife and shoeless, ragged, hungry children—asks us, in terrible earnestness, how he can be thankful to a Deity who places the barrier of misery between the writer and love.[1]

Bradlaugh had advocated neo-Malthusianism in very guarded terms in the earliest issues of the *Reasoner* in 1860, and this had led to a breach with his co-editor Joseph Barker, who was dismissed by a majority of the shareholders, turned a complete *volte face* and set up an *Unbounded Virtue* party based on High Toryism and the union of church and state. Bradlaugh had founded a Malthusian League but little interest was expressed in it, and it did not survive for long. But the connection with George Drysdale, a Scottish doctor who advocated in *The Elements of Social Science* that population control should be compulsory and marriage should be abolished, may have been the reason for the ban in 1862 on all freethought publications by W. H. Smith, who even then controlled most railway station bookstalls and have continued to ban freethought literature.[2]

Pamphlets advocating birth control had always had a steady sale from freethought booksellers, including the Holyoake brothers. But by the mid-century, the growth of the evangelical reaction against licence and lack of propriety led to the extension of the laws against obscenity. In 1857 the police were empowered to search for and destroy stocks of obscene publications, and in 1868 obscenity was redefined so as to include literary and scientific works. Inevitably, the issue acquired a new meaning in the contemporary debate on respectability and its relationship to the social system. A division was assumed between reason and the emotions or passions; the

---

[1] *National Reformer*, 22 December 1872, p. 393.
[2] W. A. Smith, who built up the book-selling empire, was largely concerned to better the reputation of the notorious railway bookstalls by 'scrupulous care devoted to excluding all pernicious literature', as the D.N.B. has it.

latter were the province of women but also of the sexually incontinent lower classes.[3] The respectable man turned from the expression of passion to pursue wealth or other public ends, and contemporary descriptions of the heroes of the self-made man myth laid some stress on the extent to which they repressed emotional freedom and the most harmless appetites. Bradlaugh, obsessively overworked, teetotal, puritanical and punctual, was a figure cast in this mould. Since the respectable norm especially for women was a profound ignorance about sexuality and reproduction, the mere provision of information became an increasingly explosive act.

The Knowlton Trial

In 1876, a Bristol bookseller was arrested for selling Charles Watts' edition of Knowlton's *Fruits of Philosophy*. He was found guilty, not because of the work itself but because of some illustrations with which he had interleaved the book. The London freethinkers began to debate whether to contest the right to publish the book. Bradlaugh at first decided that since Knowlton advocated free love and the book was 'coarsely' written it was indefensible, but Annie Besant, who of all the freethought leaders was probably the most totally ostracized by respectable society at the time, persuaded him that the freethought party ought to contest the case. Watts then refused to be martyred, and Bradlaugh, furious, dismissed him from the sub-editorship of the *National Reformer* and he and Mrs Besant withdrew from his publishing house and started their own. Watts retaliated by founding the *Secular Review and Secularist* together with G. W. Foote, to protest about the high-handedness and autocracy of Bradlaugh within the movement and the bad effects which attempting to defend Knowlton would have on its reputaton. Bradlaugh repeatedly stated that whilst he approved of the birth control information in both *The Elements of Social Science* and *The Fruits of Philosophy*, he emphatically disagreed with their arguments for free love and general licentiousness, but most freethought leaders knew well enough that his opinions would be deliberately distorted.

> Yet, because he had expressed a qualified approbation of the *Elements*, . . . these gutter friends of Christian Evidences took to saying that he 'recommended it', without any sort of reservation. Some of them went to the length

[3] Peter T. Cominos, 'Late Victorian Sexual Respectability and the Social System', *International Review of Social History*, Vol. 8., Parts 1 and 2, 1963.

of calling it the Secularist's Bible. They would pick out a few strong sentences from hundreds of pages; one about the evils of legal marriage, another about the evils of celibacy, and perhaps another . . . about the social uses of prostitutes. Having read these passages to an ignorant, inconsiderate audience, as samples of the whole volume, they would exclaim 'Such are the tenets of Secularism! Such are the teachings of Bradlaugh!'.[4]

Holyoake fully approved of birth control, and was the only leading secularist to do so not as part of a political programme but because he could see that it would give rich and poor alike more chance of happiness and personal dignity. But he felt that the manner of advocating it was all-important. 'On a question such as family limitation, delicacy of phrase and purity of taste are everything.' He was only prepared to tolerate *The Fruits of Philosophy* because it superseded Richard Carlile's even coarser *Every Woman's Book* in the publication lists of the movement. He was especially concerned that Mrs Besant should realize the impact of such publicity on her social position—it would mean ruin to her 'as a lady'. She and Bradlaugh brought out an edition of *The Fruits of Philosophy* in 1877, and were arrested and prosecuted. 'The impetus which it gave to the Society was enormous. In all parts of the country members flocked into our ranks; for, though the advocacy of Malthusianism was not part of our duty as Secularists, yet the right of free publication was one for which many Freethinkers had suffered . . .'[5] When Bradlaugh and Mrs Besant tried to involve Holyoake in the trial he reminded them of his earlier and greater martyrdom, protested about being subpoenaed as a witness, and resigned from the National Secular Society because of the *National Reformer*'s refusal to print the letter. The discord spread within the movement, and branches and minor leaders began to join one faction or another. Those branches which tended toward a religious form of meeting, were antagonized by the 'arrogant and overbearing' London leaders or had a high proportion of pro-respectability members, opposed Bradlaugh, but the majority of branches supported him.

Bradlaugh and Mrs Besant found that the publicity for *The Fruits of Philosophy* made its sales rise dramatically; they sold five thousand copies in a few days, and one hundred thousand in three months. Mrs Besant's later *The Law of Population*, a more refined

---

[4] G. W. Foote, *The Hall of Science Libel Case*, Forder, London, n.d., pp. 4–5.
[5] S. Standring, 'Twenty Years of Retrospect', *Reformer*, 15 July 1898, p. 129.

description of methods of population control, was to sell hundreds of thousands of copies and she received many letters of thanks from the wives of poor men and of clergymen. The importance of the Knowlton case was not that information about birth control had previously been unavailable but that many had been ignorant of it, and that the norm of sexual propriety meant that the issue could not be publicly discussed. The enormous publicity surrounding the case altered this, and thus eventually it altered public attitudes to sexuality itself.[6]

The actual trial of Bradlaugh and Mrs Besant was prolonged and involved, with an adverse verdict being reversed on a technicality. During its course much hostility against them developed in the secular movement, particularly to Mrs Besant, for having involved it in such a damaging issue. They offered to resign from the National Secular Society, but Holyoake retorted that the executive was not empowered to accept their resignations and that most of the provincial societies would support them. At the annual conference, an attempt was made to abolish the presidency on the grounds that it was too powerful. No one dared to attack Bradlaugh directly, although accusations of his autocracy had been growing. Sydney Gimson, a Unitarian manufacturer and leader of the large and influential Leciester society, asked him to resign, as he had become too controversial a figure to head the secular movement. The majority of secularist delegates supported Bradlaugh, but local members from Nottingham were opposed, and they and most of the other leaders voted against him. Amidst uproar and confusion, the presidency was retained by a short margin, and Bradlaugh appointed vice-presidents from amongst his loyal supporters. The dissentients set up the British Secular Union, which 'provides for those who are dissatisfied with the constitution of the National Secular Society'.[7]

Much of the hostility of the other secularist leaders to Bradlaugh's decision to fight the Knowlton case was because they seem to have thought that he could not possibly win. His victory came as a complete surprise, and strongly reinforced his control over the movement. But their fear about the effect on public opinion was largely justified. Attacks on the movement were in the near future much more likely

---

[6] See J. Banks, *Prosperity and Parenthood*, Routledge, London, 1954, for an assessment of the importance of the trial.

[7] N.S.S. Executive Committee Minutes, 19 April 1877; *Secular Chronicle*, 18 August 1878, p. 82.

to be on the grounds that atheism entailed immorality and loose living. Mrs Besant suffered especially. Her daughter was removed from her supposedly immoral influence by a law suit; she was refused entry to various scientific institutions at the University of London; and the executive of the National Sunday League asked her to retire from its vice-presidency, since they wanted Lord Thurlow as president, who could not be expected to consort with a person so polluted.

This reaction was exactly what the 'respectable' secularist party had feared. Since atheists were prone to be accused of immorality anyway, they feared that any action which damaged their claim that the movement was respectable in its advocacy and aims would result in their being shunned by respectable and powerful radical groups such as the National Sunday League. The number of self-declared agnostics among public figures was growing; but none of them would support the secular movement over issues such as neo-Malthusianism, and most were reluctant as a result of such associations to acknowledge it at all. But the 'respectable' did not see that it would be difficult to defend freedom of thought and publication, the basic tenet of secularism, without defending Knowlton; and Bradlaugh and Mrs Besant, if they had made no social gains for freethought, had made legal ones. (Even Mrs Besant's failure to retain custody of her daughter had aroused public opinion and thus established *de facto* the principle observed thereafter, that a father should not be able to remove his children from his wife without her consent.) But Holyoake, Foote, Charles Watts and the other founders in 1877 of the British Secular Union were very conscious of the damage the loss of respectability could do, and the events of its short life may be seen as a conscious attempt to acquire all the connotations of 'respectability'.

The British Secular Union had a similar constitution to the National Secular Society, advocating 'the promotion of political, social or religious reform in any wise tending to increase the secular happiness of the people'. Its structure was ostentatiously democratic —no presidency, but a council elected by the annual conference, all of whose meetings were to be reported in print. They emphasized that they were not in rivalry with the secular movement, but were an auxiliary group. They opposed 'Bible-bashing' or arguments about the existence of God, in favour of more integrative methods— Sunday schools instead of outdoor propagandists.

Their members came from the same areas as those of the National

Secular Society and must have in the main been the same people, with a rather larger number from the wealthy Midland manufacturing towns and London. The London meetings were held at the South Place Institute, under the aegis of middle-class advanced thought. The form of their meetings reflected the assumption that religious-like meetings were more respectable. The final mark of success came with the election of the Marquess of Queensberry as President in 1881, and the appointment of Pasteur, Renan and Hugo as honorary members. This especially delighted Holyoake. By 1882, the Union claimed to be 'the most respectable and influential organization of Freethinkers in Great Britain.' The surface amity of the national leaders towards each other's organizations concealed the fact that often a fierce struggle for the control of local secular groups was taking place. In Glasgow, it was reported, a group of young pro-Knowltonism secularists had joined the local branch of the National Secular Society, and then joined the Glasgow Eclectic and Secular Institute, a rival body, in an attempt to vote it over to the Society. They did not succeed, but so many other members left in disgust that they formed a third society, which affiliated itself to the Union.

There were layers and layers within respectability, however, and Queensberry resigned because 'I cannot say that I feel quite satisfied with the associations I find Secularism has drawn me into'.[8] As the agitation over Knowlton died down and was replaced by the much more generally defensible attempt to have the religious oaths which members of Parliament had to take supplemented by the Right to Affirm, the British Secular Union lost its *raison d'être* and began to decline.

Yet another theme in the debate on birth control now appeared. The newly emerging socialist consciousness of the 1880s was on the whole opposed to birth control since it represented an individualist means of curing a social problem; the cause of human misery and overcrowding was the unequal distribution of wealth and misallocation of resources, which would be cured by economic and political action. Many of the supporters of the Union were not only more respectable but also more socialist than the militant secularists, and joined the Fabian Society after its formation. Foote, who was not a socialist, made his peace with Bradlaugh and rejoined the National Secular Society.

[8] Letter to Holyoake, n.d. (Co-operative Union, Manchester).

The Oath: Bradlaugh becomes a Public Figure

During the early 1880s Bradlaugh became a national figure and support for him grew both within the secular movement and nationally as he struggled to take his seat in the House of Commons. He was elected as a Liberal M.P. for Northampton in 1880, but was unable to take his seat in the Commons until six years, eight law-suits and four re-elections later.[9] At first he had refused to take the oath; later he had been willing to take it, but the House had refused to let him do so. Support for him was universal within the secular movement and the issue revitalized it. Branches were reactivated, Bradlaugh's meetings crowded to the doors, new recruits attracted and enthusiasm whipped up to great heights. The outcry against Bradlaugh in the press, which was added to by the Anglican and Catholic clergy, did much to bind the society together and make it more militant. Holyoake and other secularists who counselled moderation and co-operation with Christians had based their appeals on the fact that attacks on atheism had been decreasing in violence since the 1840s, and the churches were becoming more liberal. Now a new outcry had begun against atheists, in which, significantly, the main charge was not that they mocked at God and religion but that they were revolutionary and sexually licentious. The growing number of distinguished figures who were openly agnostic refused to lend Bradlaugh public support—J. S. Mill had been the conspicuous exception, and had lost his own seat as a result. Considerable class hostility against them grew within the movement, which felt with some justice that they neither knew nor cared how the churches, whilst debating theology on equal terms with the scholarly sceptic, still oppressed the poor.

The six years of Bradlaugh's struggle passed in constant agitation and law-suits. The National Secular Society was actively involved both as a subscription agency and by providing active workers for Bradlaugh in Northampton and elsewhere. Many of the members joining at this time did so out of political sympathy with Bradlaugh rather than identification with his religious opinions. He became the symbol of a solitary, wronged but obdurate man fighting the massed forces of reaction; his supporters compared him to Horatius. In

[9] W. L. Arnstein, *The Bradlaugh Case*, Oxford University Press, London, 1965, gives a full account.

the early 1880s everyone seemed to be talking about him, and little
boys sung ballads about him in the market-place:

'He'll stick to it, he'll stick to it,
If they throw him from the window, the door he will
come through it'.[10]

During this period of struggle many nonconformists supported
and voted for Bradlaugh and as a result he stressed increasingly
that his political and anti-theological activities were separate. He
now lectured twice every Sunday at the London Hall of Science,
once on religion and once on politics. He tried to emphasize to the
secular movement the non-theological nature of his political agitation. It would be 'unjust in the extreme', he said, knowing what he
owed to the radical nonconformist boot- and shoe-workers at
Northampton who voted for him, and the nonconformist members
of the Commons who supported him, to pretend that their fight
for him was for anything but equal political rights for the atheist.
His attacks on religion were changing; he attacked the Bible less
and less, which must have been offending nonconformity, and
increasingly focused on the unjust position of the established
church and the arbitrary authority of Catholicism.

(Anti-Catholicism had always been a popular chauvinist and
working-class prejudice. It had increased from the later 1840s with
the influx of Irish immigrants who were thought to depress the
wage market. The introduction of the doctrines of Papal Infallibility
in 1870 outraged middle-class liberal opinion also. Such notions
seemed essentially unenlightened—to violate ideas of scientific
proof, individual freedom and the role of debate within a liberal
state.[11] The civil allegiance of Catholics seemed questionable, and
the Irish question did little to endear their faith to the English
political élite. The secularists were torn between an instinctive
sympathy for the under-dog and triumph at finding that in this
case their opinions about the reactionary nature of religious authority
were being adopted.)

Like his intensely respectable moral code, Bradlaugh's very
unrevolutionary politics had passed largely unnoticed until his years
of struggle to enter Parliament had made him both more widely

[10] *Freethinker*, 3 June 1943, p. 7; Ben Turner, *About Myself*, Humphrey Toulmin,
London, 1930, p. 48.
[11] Little research has been done on the role of anti-Catholic feeling; but see E. R.
Norman, *Anti-Catholicism in Victorian England*, Allen and Unwin, London, 1968.

known and separated him from his old associates. He alienated some of his old radical friends by rigidly upholding the etiquette of the House—he felt his position too insecure to risk a snub,[12] and like other radicals who move into the English social élite, he found their manners mesmerizing. Belfort Bax thought that the principal bourgeois objection to infidelity was that its old radical associations had led to it being seen as part of the attempt to overthrow private property. Once it became obvious that Bradlaugh was opposed to socialism, 'on his coming down firmly on the side of the sanctity of existing economic and social order and of private property in the means of production, they willingly forgave, or at least condoned, his Atheism.'[13] Bradlaugh became accepted by the middle class for just those reasons that were leading many of his younger secularist supporters to part company with him.

During the 1870s and 80s socialist ideas began to gain in popularity amongst working-men, and Thomas Okey noted obvious indications 'both on the platform and in the audience of the Hall of Science that the Marxian Bible, or rather the earlier Communist Manifesto, had begun to leaven English Democratic Thought.'[14] The freethought and socialist movements began to move apart, and those men who were members of both felt that relations between them grew increasingly strained.

During the 1880s British society generally came to seem less settled and secure than it had been since the hungry 1840s. The economy faltered under growing international competition and a severe recession. The 'rediscovery of poverty' demonstrated the hopeless plight of unimaginably large sections of the English people caught helplessly in ill-health, appalling living conditions, the vicissitudes of the trade cycle and sweated labour; these evils were summed up together in the phrase of the day, 'the social problem'. It was widely agreed that this was very grave, insoluble without huge efforts on the part of all of society; disagreement came over how it could be solved and whether a revolution would be necessary. In particular, for a whole generation of political and social thinkers, the key question became whether *laissez-faire* could be abandoned, and how it could be replaced without destroying individual liberty.

[12] For example, he forbade 'M.P.' to be put after his name in advertisements for his secularist lectures.
[13] E. B. Bax, *Reminiscences and Reflections*, Allen & Unwin, London, 1918, p. 36.
[14] T. Okey, *A Basketful of Memories*, Dent, London, 1930, pp. 61–2.

The Challenge of Socialism

A socialist tradition defined the ruling class in terms of employers and capitalists, and oppression as stemming from the economic structure of society. One of the difficulties for the independent artisan faced with this new philosophy was that coming as he did from a social and political tradition which had emphasized independence, self-education and self-help, socialism appeared to deny, or at least to devalue, individual liberty and the freedom for working-men to rise by their own initiative to attain the real benefits and self-respect that the middle class already had. The debate among historians as to the role of Methodism and of nonconformity generally in preventing class antagonism and consequently revolution in nineteenth-century Britain has focused on the organizational and other ties between chapels and working-class politics, and also on the influence that religious ideas had on radical ideologies. But in addition, nonconformity represented a way of life—sober, respectable, morally earnest, interested in education and science but often anti-intellectual in its setting up of conscience as the arbiter of knowledge, seeing men as defined and redeemed by their own efforts. As Halévy pointed out, this *weltanschauung* was essentially lower middle class, but it penetrated the culture of the craftsman and the skilled workman. It was as strong among the radicals who left the churches as among those who remained, and so their natural animosity was directed not at the socialist's version of the enemy, the middle class of small manufacturers and professional men whom in so many ways they resembled and emulated, but against the aristocracy and the established church.

Bradlaugh and the secular movement had been very active in the short-lived republican movement of the 1870s, and many secular branches had become republican clubs. In Bradlaugh's inaugural address as president of the London Republican Club in 1871, he sketched out an essentially pre-industrial analysis of Britain's social ills. The monarchy and aristocracy were above all expensive and useless. They used their political power in their own interests to produce cripplingly high taxation and rents, they misused land and held landless labourers in subjection, they prevented the parliamentary process initiated by the Commons, and by their alliance with the bishops of the Anglican Church they enslaved men's minds by religion and their children's by control of the schools.

These growing evils would be remedied by a social revolution, but Bradlaugh wanted the nation 'to strive to make that revolution gradual, peaceful, and enduring, rather than sudden, bloody, and uncertain'. Far from being a revolutionary, Bradlaugh had an exaggerated respect for British institutions. The equality that the republicans wanted, he pointed out in a distinction which was to become wearily familiar, '. . . is no dead-level equality of either property or person, but that equality which, ensured by a fair educational start in life to all, shall secure also to the lowest in the State the right—if he have courage, honesty, virtue, intelligence enough—to climb to be the highest.'

Perhaps the most fundamental aspect of Bradlaugh's dislike of socialism was his belief in the moral virtue of self-help, which he was unable to disengage from *laissez-faire*. 'He was always in favour of self-help and individual responsibility, and was naturally hostile to everything that might weaken those precious elements of English life.' His own life, after all, had been a conspicuous example of the success which could be gained through hard work, intellectual independence and self-education. He opposed the socialist ideas of the 1880s because they were Germanic and consequently 'not suited to English conditions'. English radicals were often intensely chauvinist; Britain, unlike other countries, had the free institutions that made revolution unnecessary: the press, the right to vote and demonstrate, trade unions and co-operative societies. These were the more important to Bradlaugh since he had fought for so many of them.

Both Bradlaugh and Holyoake actively supported foreign revolutionaries and revolts but not the home-grown kind. Many of the reforms that secularists proposed (and others such as Social Credit that were being discussed by contemporaries), were seen as alternatives to socialism. Bradlaugh believed that small, planned families, land reforms and the control of extravagant state spending on the civil list would ensure social justice and a high enough standard of living for all. In their turn, many early socialists saw these reforms as irrelevant, for they too had a uni-causal theory of change.[15]

Bradlaugh had never attempted to conceal his beliefs in free

[15] In 1896, for example, a member of the N.S.S. was debating with a socialist from the East End on 'will Socialism or neo-Malthusianism more benefit the English People?' *Freethinker*, 19 January 1896, p. 42. And see J. F. C. Harrison, *Learning and Living*, Routledge, London, 1961, p. 250, and C. Bradlaugh, *England's Balance Sheet*, Freethought Publishing Co., London, 1884, and *Some Objections to Socialism*, Freethought Publishing Co., London, 1884.

enterprise, but perhaps they only became a reality to most of the secular movement when he entered Parliament. Much hostility was created when he refused to support the Employer's Liability Bill; John Burns accused him at a meeting of the Leicester Secular Society that by this he 'shall betray the people to serve the Capitalist and the Landlord.' He was such an influential figure among the radical working class that socialist leaders were forced to attack him. Hyndman accused him in the first issue of *Justice* of using his prestige among the workers to induce them to neglect their own interests.

To the socialist, the secularist's interest in abstract ideas and neglect of the realities of economic life was preposterous. 'These men . . . occupy themselves about creation and revelation, and miracles, and the authorship of the ten commandments, when they are losing half the results of their labour by reason of the existence of a non-working class which lives upon profits and dividends.'[16] Beneath the relatively superficial arguments between secularists and socialists as to which reforms should be supported lay enormous disagreements as to the nature of social change, though true to the pragmatic tradition of English political argument, they were rarely acknowledged openly.

Both sides, for example, agreed that 'selfishness' was responsible for 'all our social evils'. But how was this to be altered? 'How are selfish men to be induced to regulate their social proceedings to the dictates of benevolence?' To the secularist it was obvious that morality was based on ideas; it had been supported by religious beliefs, or so virtually everybody in English society believed, and so to change morality one needed a more scientific system of beliefs—utilitarianism, for example. Because secularists devoted so much time to attacking religion, they implicitly believed that it was extremely important, both in determining men's attitudes and in supporting the injustice and privilege with which the established church seemed so bound up. And of course, most people in England would have agreed with them that religion was indeed the basis of social order. Consequently, an incredulous Hyndman found that many working-men 'supposed that a general social emancipation would ensue if once the Gods departed'.

For many working-men, the core of the issue as to whether they should abandon the old radical tradition and cast in their lot with

---

[16] J. M. Robertson, analysing the appeal of the Guild of St Matthew to reformers and the failure of the N.S.S., *National Reformer*, 7 October 1888, pp. 226–7.

the socialists did indeed seem to be whether the theory—so easily understood, so often proved in their worldly experience—that any able man could better his lot, if given the chance, by individual struggle and effort was to be abandoned for the less easily comprehended claim that it was the social *system* itself which was at fault. As many secularist speakers shrewdly pointed out, did the socialists, eager as they were to destroy the old system, propose to eradicate the greed and injustice of the human condition merely by legislating for the structure of the new system? That sounded all too like Owen.

Socialists believed that ideas were a product of the economic structure—'Therefore, in his worship of the "idea", the *bourgeois* Freethinker is like the Christian, attributing miraculous powers to the figments of men's brains'—but to the secularist, man was 'always under the dominion of his ideas, and it is these that are the chief determinants of social conditions.'[17] Societies were created by shared values, not by economic life. It was not an issue which was to be resolved rapidly.

Tom Mann's intellectual pilgrimage must have been like that of many radicals in the 1870s and 80s. In Birmingham in the 70s, he recalled, there had been no socialist group, but radical life was dominated by the large and influential freethought movement. Like many freethinkers, he worked in the temperance movement because he thought of social improvement in terms of individual salvation. But he was convinced by a period of fluctuations in employment in which the virtuous and the slack alike were laid off that something in the environment must be at fault. He became interested in vegetarianism, Malthusianism and Henry George's land reform proposals, but finally in 1880 his life was revolutionized by his sudden discovery that social evils could not be cured by urging men to lead 'godly, righteous and sober lives', and he became a socialist and member of the Social Democratic Federation.[18]

Gradually, and especially during the depression years of 1884–7, support for socialism began to gain ground amongst the radical working class; and amidst great emotion many of Bradlaugh's old allies became estranged. The Northumberland and Durham miners, for example, had always been staunch supporters of Bradlaugh and the secular movement—the National Secular Society

[17] F. J. Gould, *Hyndman*, Allen & Unwin, London, 1928, pp. 86, 90–3; letter from M. Streimer and reply from C. Cohen, *Freethinker*, 15 July 1917, p. 446.
[18] T. Mann, *Tom Mann's Memoirs*, Labour Publishing Co., London, 1923.

had a large number of branches among them. Until the 1880s, many of the miners were strong radicals who would not support the Eight Hours movement or state intervention in any form, and Bradlaugh was always a welcome and popular speaker at the Miners' Gala. But in 1884–8, a prolonged strike and period of low wages had led the miners to adopt socialist principles and form many branches of the Social Democratic Federation. In 1889, Bradlaugh refused to attend the Gala, for the miners had attacked him over his policy on the Employer's Liability Bill. Many of his speeches to secularists showed his sorrow at what he perceived as their desertion.

The growing unrest among members of the secular movement had led Bradlaugh to a public debate with Hyndman on socialism in 1884. Hyndman conceded that socialists should be atheists, but claimed that secularists did not realize the necessity for economic change. The debate was widely read and discussed in radical clubs and secular societies, and although at the end of the debate Bradlaugh seemed to have triumphed through force of personality and his oratorical powers, the final result was to convert many secularists to socialism. Many of the more active and able secularists became socialists, John Burns, Harry Snell, Tom Mann, George Lansbury, Hunter-Watts and Annie Besant among them. Mrs Besant continued to lecture to secularists but her main interest was now in converting them to Fabianism. Edward Aveling, a secularist and intimate friend of both Bradlaugh and Mrs Besant, had been won over to socialism by other methods. Annie Besant observed waspishly that 'In 1882 he took to reading at the British Museum, and unfortunately there fell into the company of some of the Bohemian Socialists, male and female, who flourish there.' She meant Eleanor Marx.

The secular movement was placed in an insoluble dilemma. The secretary reported to the N.S.S. conference in 1888 that:

> . . . many political clubs had been founded in London in the last seven years, and many members had gone to these, remaining Freethinkers but giving their activity to politics. They had further lost a number by Socialism, some leaving because Socialism was advocated on the Freethought platform, some because the President refused to become a Socialist.[19]

Bradlaugh's Death

In 1889, Bradlaugh announced that he must relinquish the presidency through overwork and ill-health. He did so unwillingly, for

[19] *National Reformer*, 4 May 1884, p. 310; 27 May 1888, p. 345.

he had always vowed to remain President until the Blasphemy Laws had been abolished, which he had been unable to achieve.

> Mr Bradlaugh . . . could for some moments scarcely speak from emotion, and appeared as though he would actually break down. Old men, many of whom had come from various parts of the kingdom, were also observed to be overcome by their feelings during the proceedings, and furtively wipe away the welling tears.[20]

Mrs Besant, Edward Aveling and George Bernard Shaw, all possible future secularist leaders, had become socialists and Mrs Besant refused to stand for president, since socialists were a minority among the older members of the society. In addition she had forfeited Bradlaugh's support by becoming a theosophist, which to almost all secularists but herself seemed to be incompatible with secularism. She correctly foresaw that only Bradlaugh would be able to hold together the militant and respectable wings, refused to work under Foote, and resigned. G. W. Foote was elected as President in 1890, and in the following year Bradlaugh died, worn out by constant public speaking, financial worry and overwork.

By the time of Bradlaugh's death, he had become almost universally respected, if not esteemed. He united the secular movement simply because the majority of members admired and trusted him so much that their usual individualism was subdued. He had been able to convert the London Secular Society into a flourishing centre with a thousand members, with science classes, concerts and glee clubs, discussion groups and expeditions, a library and classes and examinations for open-air propagandists. The respectable world had accepted him to such an extent that they were apparently unable to believe that he was not really a Christian—thirty hours after his death, his daughter had begun to receive enquiries asking if it were true that he had had a change of heart on his death-bed. After she had left the National Secular Society because Foote had attacked her father she and her husband ran a journal for the old Bradlaughites in which she refuted once a year the latest series of fabrications about Bradlaugh. Most of them asserted that he had told the writer in confidence that he really believed in God, or wished that he could. Even in India, when the Congress Party of Lahore named their new Hall after him because he had fought for their constitutional liberty he had somehow strayed into a religious pantheon; the speaker 'prayed that God's protective hand might rest over the building,

---

[20] *Freethinker*, 23 February 1890, p. 93.

and that under its benign auspices the soldiers of constitutional liberty in India might carry high the sacred torch which Bradlaugh had lighted to guard their way.'[21] His daughter organized excursions every year of the 'Old Guard' to his grave in Brookwood cemetery, or to the river Lea where he had fished, and reminisced with other freethinkers about the battles that he and they had fought in a more rugged age.

Bradlaugh's very success in gaining some degree of legitimacy for atheists had weakened the *raison d'être* of the secular movement. The experiences of persecution and prejudice which had created recruits were now less frequent, and in a political climate in which its ideas seemed increasingly irrelevant many freethinkers either turned to new campaigns or urged the movement to commit itself to socialism. One secularist thought at least three-fifths or three-quarters of members in the 1890s were socialists, and consequently it seemed even more incredible that a movement whose proudest tradition had been its fight for freedom and the poor was now 'too busy discussing the first chapter of Genesis to hear the cry of the outcast, too absorbed in the edifying pastime of proving the impossibility of the Flood story, to heed the bitter wail of the starving workers'.[22] Foote was placed in an impossible dilemma; he was not a socialist, and even if he were to commit the movement to socialism he would lose both the Liberal 'Old Guard' and also any grounds for the movement's distinctiveness. He inherited problems that Bradlaugh had been unable to solve, but his own high-handedness, financial mismanagement and attacks on the Bradlaugh legend made matters worse. He was forced to sell the London Hall of Science, and the large and active secularist community which had grown up there was disbanded.

Most of the leading secularists left the National Secular Society declaring that Foote was impossible to work with. With the exception of Mrs Besant they joined the newly formed Rationalist Press Association, which had been formed by G. J. Holyoake and Charles Watts to provide a more respectable, scholarly and financially viable organization which would proselytize by means of circulating literature on rationalism and science, rather than open-air speaking. Those members of the secular societies who wanted a more 'positive' and ritualist expression of their beliefs were attracted into the Labour

[21] 'An Indian Bradlaugh Hall', *Reformer*, 15 December 1900, p. 748.
[22] S. Standring, *Truthseeker*, August 1894, p. 11; *Secular Work*, July 1896, p. 6.

Churches, and as a result the debate over the form of the secular meeting ceased.

Holyoake had effectively moved out of the National Secular Society, which had become far more militant than he thought necessary or reasonable, and his final breach with Foote came over the 'Atheist Shoemaker' affair. In 1889, the Reverend Hugh Price-Hughes in connection with his mission work in the East End published a pamphlet *The Atheist Shoemaker*, about a leading secularist who was a shoemaker, who had fallen ill and was converted to Christianity on his death-bed. Such a figure was part of the Christian mythology of the period. The indignant secularists asked for the name of the man, and to prove the case Price-Hughes sent Holyoake, who was a friend of his (they had met at 'Lady Aberdeen's soirée', and identified one another as gentlemen beneath the creed) two lay sisters to vouch for the story, and Holyoake believed them and confirmed its truth. Death-bed conversions never impressed him; with his usual good sense, he considered that what men did when they were sick and desperate was worth less than the record of their rational moments. Foote was furious at this, and at Holyoake's decision to continue to conceal the dead man's name. He was contacted by the shoemaker's relatives, whom he triumphantly produced to announce that the widow had lied; the shoemaker had always been a Methodist, though the approach of death made him a more conscientious one. Foote was triumphant and clearly unwilling to let the matter drop; Holyoake expressed concern that secularists had become so obsessed by trivialities, and he and his supporters also became chiefly involved with the Rationalist Press.[23]

'God in the Labour Movement . . .'

Before going on to describe the later history of the secular movement, which is largely that of its decline to a very much smaller anti-religious pressure group, some account must be given of the other movements which drew support away from it in the 1890s. In the early 1890s, the two other humanist groups—the Rationalist Press and the Ethical Union—were founded. Despite the obvious antagonisms and differences of opinion between these three groups, their history

[23] Dorothea H. Price-Hughes, *Life of Hugh Price-Hughes*, Hodder & Stoughton, London, 1904, pp. 295–8; Hugh Price-Hughes, *The Atheist Shoemaker*, Hodder & Stoughton, London, 1889; and *Freethinker*, issues of 31 January to 11 March 1894.

on the whole has been that of co-operation and some friendliness. All three have considered that they are fighting for the same general ends, and that the fact that their members often belong to one or both of the other groups is not surprising. None the less, the two later groups did rob the secular movement of members, particularly the more middle-class, educated and less hostile to religion. The secularists were inclined to resent their 'polite atheism', to feel that it was prompted by class condescension—'an agnostic is an atheist with a tall hat on'— and to feel that the heroic fighting past of the secular movement which now enabled others to be openly agnostic and still members of established society was being neglected. Foote, a literary journalist by profession, felt especially slighted by the neglect of the movement by agnostic scholars—for example neither Bury nor Stephen mentioned it in their histories of nine-teenth-century rationalism. And yet such 'kid-gloved agnostics' seemed willing to work for the other two movements.

In the 1890s, the socialist movement also began to take on a mass organizational form. The I.L.P. was founded in 1893, the Labour Church movement and the first Socialist Sunday School in the previous year. These developments drew much of the labour movement away from the Marxist atheism of the S.D.F. towards a position of religious neutrality or even of friendliness to religion. Those secularists who were also socialists tried to combat the in-creasing leniency toward religion which an influx of socialists who were also nonconformists was bringing in. They regarded the growth of all forms of Christian Socialism as merely proof that the churches had succeeded in taking over and perverting the ends of the socialist movement. 'Maddening to see socialists glad to pretend that "Jesus was a Socialist" . . .' Some secularists were even prepared to argue against communism on the grounds that it had been practised by the early Christians.

In London, where nonconformity had little hold on the working class, both secularism and the S.D.F. were strong. But in provincial towns many socialists were unwilling to sever their ties with religion completely, and in any case uncertain as to whether socialism could or should be reduced to purely economic issues. The founder of the Labour Churches, John Trevor, saw them as 'an organized effort to develop the religious life inherent in the Labour movement, and to give to that movement a higher inspiration and a sturdier indepen-dence in the great work of personal and social regeneration that lies before it.'

Trevor had been driven from fundamentalism by his horror of hell. He became a Unitarian minister, but had been influenced by the more organicist and communitarian conception of religion which had taken over American Unitarianism via the New England Transcendentalists. (This particular intellectual current flowed directly into the university settlement movement and then the ethical movement on both sides of the Atlantic.) Trevor became an assistant to Phillip Wicksteed, warden of a settlement founded by the Unitarians in the attempt to liberalize religion and make it the basis for working-class community life. But the working classes would only attend the settlement's club, and could not be persuaded to either an interest in the uplifting religious lectures or the expositions of socialism by Beatrice Potter and Graham Wallas.[24] Trevor then abandoned the Unitarian church because all religions, however theologically liberal, seemed too socially conservative and too divorced from the day-to-day struggle of most working-men. He knew that many workmen were unwilling to attend the established churches because they felt out of their class and feared that they might be suspected of attending to seek charity, since this was the motive for churchgoing of so many of the poor.

Previously, it seemed to him, God had worked through the churches to do good in the world, but in the 1890s the only body which was trying to relieve misery and bring about the peaceable kingdom was the labour movement. Therefore, God must be working through the labour movement, and working for political and economic change was working for God. Trevor called together in Manchester a group of workers from liberal religions and the labour movement and explained, to hearty applause, that he proposed to found a Labour Church which would enable the labour movement to achieve its ends without resort to violence or revolution. The new movement was to be a religion without theory, based on current ideas and morality and committed to social reform. Whether members believed in convential Christian dogma or not was their affair. One of the bases on which the Churches were founded was that reform needed both changes in social arrangements *and* a change of heart—'the development of Personal Character and the improvement of Social Conditions are both essential to man's emancipation from moral and social bondage.'

In 1891, Trevor and Robert Blatchford had also founded the first I.L.P. branch in Manchester, and the two organizations began

[24] J. P. Trevelyan, *Life of Mrs. Humphry Ward*, Constable, London, 1923, pp. 86–7.

to grow rapidly; the labour churches were mainly founded by local I.L.P. branches, and many of them were merely used to mollify the respectable so that the I.L.P. could hold a meeting on a Sunday. The Plymouth Labour Church was an offshoot of the local Gas-workers' Union. The vast majority of the churches that sprang up so rapidly from 1892 to 1896 were in the manufacturing towns of Lancashire and the West Riding. There were some in London and the Midlands, but the labour movement in London was too influenced by both secularism and the S.D.F. to allow a strong Labour Church.

The members of the churches were mainly the skilled and respec-table working class—Trevor was distressed at how few unskilled workers attended. These members were younger than the secularists, and after a time socialists began to comment favourably on how many women were attracted to the meetings, a sign of the extent to which they had become part of respectable working-class community life. The meetings displayed an enormous variety of ritual forms. Some were barely distinguishable from an I.L.P. meeting, some were very closely based on the routines of the Methodist chapel but with a socialist tinge; readings from *Looking Backward* for example or ending the service with the singing of the Red Flag and then a Benediction. Most of the leading socialists spoke in the churches, but some were opposed to them; John Burns thought them 'a waste of time and tissue, and calculated to lead to the disintegration of powerful forces'. At their best, the churches' speakers did achieve great emotional rapport with their audiences.

Although the political speakers at the churches brought many men to them, they also brought problems which were familiar to every group that tried to create a blend of a religious and a secular meeting. Exactly how religious were the Labour Churches to be? Trevor was vague on the point but insisted that if they were to be-come merely a political organization, they would be 'no more than a Fabian Ethical Society', and would die. He dismayed his more Christian members by announcing that Christ had by no means been a socialist. As the labour movement grew and shed its earlier millenial and redemptionist ideals, disagreement and confusion as to the role of the churches meant that their membership declined—they decreased from fifty-four in 1895 to twenty-two in 1900. As they declined, they became on the whole more political, and the theo-logical ritual—the hymns, the prayers (always a difficulty), and the confessions of fomenting discord between groups, of capitalism, of sweating children for merchant's profits, of sins against agricultural workers—were abandoned. Some of the churches were taken over by the Ethical Union and a few by secularists, and after 1900 they rapidly declined.[25]

The cause of their decline lay partly in the general decline of church attendance among all social classes at the beginning of the century, which made religion seem a less and less likely candidate for the source and focus of a new society. But in addition, the process of structural differentiation by which religion and politics were increasingly defined as occupying separate and noncompeting spheres, each with a metaphysic and a moral code peculiar to itself, meant that those who wished to attend chapel and be socialists found less conflict in doing so, and those who abandoned chapel altogether found their general philosophy in a more securely based socialist movement.

One remaining use which religious routines still seemed to have, however, was to recruit and educate men into socialist ways of thought, and it was felt that children in particular before they could become politically active needed to be taught about the ethical values of socialism. The Socialist Sunday School movement, which was closely associated with local I.L.P. branches, became widespread during the decade following the decline of the Labour Churches. It was founded in Glasgow and by 1900 had only spread as far as Yorkshire, but it grew rapidly in the first two decades of the twentieth century—mainly in Scotland, Yorkshire and Lancashire—to a peak of 149 schools in 1920. Compared to the Labour Churches, the Socialist Sunday Schools were more explicitly concerned with politics as a *separate activity* from Christianity. The socialists who worked in the movement did so either because they were interested in trying out educational innovations or because they saw the movement as a means of making converts to socialism by educating a new generation. These relatively limited and concrete aims carried their own difficulties, however. For example, should children be taught to *understand* society, or should the schools create the emotional responses which were needed if they were to *transform* it? The 'scientific' socialists rejected any idea that children could be educated in ethics, since ideas were socially determined. But the majority, who thought that they were not merely passing on knowledge but

[25] My main source of information on the labour churches is D. F. Summers, *The Labour Church and Allied Movements*, Ph.D. thesis, Edinburgh, 1958; but see also Chap. 6. of K. S. Inglis, *Churches and the Working Class in Victorian England*, Routledge, London, 1963, and Chap. 8. of E. Hobsbawm, *Primitive Rebels*, Manchester University Press, Manchester, 1959.

trying directly to inculcate socialist ideals, turned to the familiar ritual means of hymn-books and creeds. (The hymn-books were divided into 'ethical' and 'socialist' sections.) The younger teachers in the Sunday Schools were inclined to criticize this 'ethical' approach as over-respectable and preaching merely a general moral altruism rather than specifically socialist economic and political aims. To what extent, too, should children be told about the conflicts and disagreements among their elders?

Just before the First World War, the ethical wing of the Socialist Sunday Schools had gained the support of the positivists and the Moral Instruction League. F. J. Gould, a leading humanist whose main interest was in moral education, helped them to systematize both their ideas and their teaching material. In the early stages of British socialism many socialists were pacifists, and so all left-wing organizations experienced internal upheavals and splits during both the Boer War and the First World War. The Socialist Sunday Schools were pacifist and consequently acquired many members who belonged to either the C.P.G.B. or the left wing of the I.L.P. The schools drifted away from the central growth of the labour movement and were increasingly beset by the sectarian quarrels of revolutionary socialism. In the 1930s, they rapidly dwindled to a remnant in London and West Scotland.[26]

'Secular Societies are like Turkish Baths . . .'

During the 1890s and 1900s, the secular movement declined in size and even more in influence. The more ritualist members and even whole secular branches joined the Labour Churches; those who wanted a more educated and up-to-date anti-theological propaganda found it produced by the Rationalist Press. Several further attempts were made by secularists who were socialists to commit the National Secular Society to socialism (the unsuccessful campaign to elect George Bernard Shaw to the presidency is one of the more fascinating might-have-beens of history) and there were several rival bodies set up—in 1896, 1898, 1903 and 1947—to try to win members away to socialist free-thought. All of them were unsuccessful.

Although there were frequent accusations of the leaders' mishandling of things—in 1913 Foote complained members were still

[26] F. Reid, 'Socialist Sunday Schools in Britain, 1892–1939', *International Review of Social History*, Vol. XI (1), 1966, pp. 18–47.

'going round saying "what would Bradlaugh have done?"'—even Bradlaugh could have done very little. Church-going in Britain was declining now not only among the working class but among the middle class as well, and the interest in theology, which had been the most popular category of reading matter until the 1880s, had almost entirely disappeared. The detailed attack on the Bible was thus no longer something which had much meaning, and secularist propagandists increasingly found Christians indifferent and uninformed about their theological beliefs. As the funds of both the central body and the branches dwindled secularist meetings were forced into the open air, and the penumbra of ungovernable and eccentric figures who had always been found in the open-air crowds round atheist orators grew more prominent.

Several of these outdoor militants displayed alarming leanings towards free love, spiritualism and anarchism, and the pamphleteers and outdoor speakers who were now prosecuted for blasphemy struck many secularists as obscene and offensive rather than courageously outspoken. One, for example, was fined £5 in 1913 for saying at an open-air meeting at Blackburn 'that when the Lamb of God descended into Hell, the Devil swore because there was no mint sauce with the roast lamb.'[27]

Foote and the next president of the N.S.S., Chapman Cohen, tried to shift the activities of the movement away from open-air speaking. In the nineteenth century working-class movements preached and proselytized mainly by public speaking, for not all the population were literate, books were expensive, and attending public meetings was an established pattern of behaviour. The secular movement, denied the use of halls and forced to publish and distribute its literature itself, had often held open-air meetings in parks where its pamphlets were sold. With the spread of alternative channels of communication—the popular press, radio, and the cheap editions of the Rationalist Press—public speaking became less important as a means of conveying ideas or opinions. The leaders of the movement began to withdraw from it; 'Hyde Park is becoming too much a Babel to be of much utility to an intellectual propaganda', said Cohen in 1907, and an open-air speaker summed up thirty years of effort in 1936, but doubted if he had converted six people.

Whilst the tradition of open-air speaking is hard to reconcile with the sophisticated pressure group which the leaders increasingly wanted, it had and has an enduring vitality. Cohen himself became

[27] *Truthseeker*, 1913, No. 1, p. 5.

a secularist via open-air debates in Victoria Park where he built up a large following, and religious revival meetings, which harked back to an older oral tradition, also sparked off secular activity. About ten secular branches were formed in South Wales immediately after the revivals of 1903–4, and two secularist speakers who are still active founded open-air branches in Halifax and in Kingston-on-Thames when they stood up to protest against clergymen. Local branches became increasingly detached from the central body; the kind of man who was a successful open-air speaker and could keep a branch going was not likely to accept the guidance of a central organization which could offer little in the way of speakers or money. The branches dwindled in number, and so did the interest in them of the central society. Several were drawn away by the upsurge of communism in the 1930s, but the majority of freethinkers found the control of intellectual life in Russia too alien to the traditions of secularism.

The central society in turn began to rely more on recruiting individual members directly, who were linked with it via the journal, the *Freethinker*, and supported the Society's activities as an anti-religious pressure group over issues such as the abolition of religious instruction in schools, or the banning of family planning advertising. Freethinkers were cheered by the decline in church attendance, which they assumed both to indicate a rejection of religious belief and to be 'almost entirely due to the work of Freethinkers'.

From the First World War onward, the religious background of the majority of the movement's members appeared to change: having been mainly drawn from nonconformity, increasingly they became converts from Catholicism. Perhaps as a result of this, or perhaps because Catholics were more conspicuous in an era when working-class members of other denominations had mainly ceased regular church attendance, the attacks of the secular movement on religion were increasingly directed at Catholicism, and interest in political or social issues diminished. Whilst the concentration on attacking religion served to prevent much potential conflict it also probably resulted in a more rapid turnover of membership. The fear of Catholicism was often linked with politics; examples of informal pressures and influence by the Catholic lobby were cited, and the freethought movement was seen as an agent of resistance to Catholicism on behalf of both the working class and socialism.

The executive of the Society, under the presidency of David Tribe who took office in 1963, became increasingly unhappy with this policy. It ignored developments in Catholic theology—'He [Tribe] referred to the Modernist trends in Christian apologetics, the emphasis on symbolism rather than literalism, and the pseudo-science of Père Teilhard de Chardin, which secularists must be aware of and refute. Mr. Ebery [a leading open-air speaker] suggested that fundamentalism was still far from dead; witness the Roman Catholic Church, Jehovah's Witnesses, etc. . . .'[28] Tribe also wanted the movement to move away from mere anti-clericalism and to take a more active interest in social and political affairs, to co-operate with other humanist bodies and progressive pressure-groups and exploit 'the most imaginative use of modern promotion and public relations techniques (in the elevation, not the glossing over, of our solid Secularist edifice); unremitting militancy, but careful avoidance of anything that suggests the cranky, the parochial, or the vituperative.'[29] It was an inherent part of this policy that he did not want the secular movement identified as part of the working class; he considered that the other humanist bodies were wrong to regard it as such.

The secularists who disagreed with him were those who were active in branch life and who feared that any lapse from militant anti-theology would compromise the purposes of the organization. 'The present seeming obsession with sex, abortion, and so-called "free art" . . . will not get us much further along our proper road.'[30] They were proud of the movement's distinctively working-class and militant traditions, and inclined to view the other humanist bodies as middle-class agnostics who were too soft on religion. To broaden the objectives of the movement seemed to be foolish since it was essentially a militantly anti-clerical organization, the only one in Britain.

The National Secular Society had gradually changed its structure. The executive was no longer primarily interested in secular branches, whether outdoor or indoor. Their number had dwindled from about fifty-two at the start of Foote's presidency to about eleven active ones. They were concerned rather that supporters of the secular movement's policies should subscribe to the *Freethinker* and support their activities as a pressure group, hoping to operate in this way rather than as a mass movement. Whilst still protesting their

---

[28] Debate on propaganda techniques at the 1962 Annual Conference, *Freethinker*, 29 June 1962, p. 206.
[29] The Executive's Annual Report for 1963/4, p. 5, and see that for the following year.
[30] Letter from J. C. Cartwright, *Freethinker*, 30 June 1967, p. 207.

militancy, the executive still seemed to be moving away from anti-theology in the late 1960s; the *Freethinker* had become less concerned with attack on religion and more with general social comment. The editor of the *Freethinker* claimed to be both militant and an agnostic, but the debates between the supporters of militancy and respectability, positive and negative secularism, agnostics and atheists were still being continued. It would appear that the secular movement had reached an *impasse*. Whilst the executive might have largely rejected anti-theological militancy the movement had no other distinctive rationale, for since the nineteenth century its role had shrunk largely to that of anti-religion, whilst the Rationalist Press had taken over its educative and propagandist functions and the ethical movement its role of creating an active network of branches for social and political activity. These organizations could fulfil these purposes more successfully for their members, for they were both larger and wealthier than the National Secular Society.

The open-air speakers and those who still attended secularist meetings had a rationale and a tradition for their actions. Their methods of argument may appear crude and repetitive, and in an age when the mass media dominate the formation and transmission of ideas and opinions, the network of open-air speakers who still debate in market-places and on street-corners is puny in comparison. But I collected much anecdotal evidence during the course of my research to suggest that many of these secularists are respected figures in the life of working-class communities, especially those of the industrial cities of the North. Their intransigence and their frequent contempt for the compromises and place-seeking of party politics keep them detached from any position of social power, but their passionate defence of truth and real interest in gaining a general philosophy of life has been an inspiration to many men. Their arguments may seem belligerent and oversimplified to the intelligentsia, but their *experience* of religion, and of the effects that it has on men's lives, is different from theirs. They are the heirs to a great tradition, to the continued vitality of a radical culture which exists outside established methods of thought.

4 THE MEMBERSHIP OF THE SECULAR MOVEMENT

The old blacksmith usually, in virtue of his standing among us, presided over our meetings. One night, while he was so presiding, somebody spoke of Tom Paine. Up jumped the chairman. 'I will not sit in that chair', he cried in great wrath, 'and hear that great man reviled. Bear in mind he was not a prize-fighter. There is no such person as Tom Paine. Mister Thomas Paine, if you please.'

W. G. Adams on Chartism in Cheltenham in the 1840s in
Memoirs of a Social Atom

The secular movement is part of the general philosophy of humanism, but its characteristic cluster of emphases can be distinguished from the cultural traditions of rationalism and ethicism. The grounds for these separate emphases are interrelated; secularism is more anti-clerical and anti-religious, and is a movement with a mainly working-class membership. It had and still has links and affinities with a more general working-class tradition of opposition to established authority.[1] In order to understand the ideology of a social movement, it must be set in the social context in which it operates. Our view of a society is largely that of the dominant group within it, so that the very different nature of working-class experience may be over-looked.

In the last twenty years, sociological research has increasingly revealed the unequal treatment meted out to different social classes in education, medicine, working conditions and the whole array of personal social services. Benefits which were designed to be univer-sally and equally available have often failed to reach the sections of the population who need them the most. There are many reasons for this, and some of them are also applicable to the working classes' experience of the churches. The antagonism and friction that characterize the contact of many officials and professionals with their working-class clients were equally true of the contact between

---

[1] The anti-clerical tone of some working-class nonconformists was remarkably similar: 'The establishment is the enemy of public freedom. It has always deserved this odious name; it has ever been the friend of tyranny, the foe of freedom, siding with the strong against the weak, with the oppressor against the oppressed, and doing its utmost to maintain class privilege, and prevent the enactment of equal laws, and the enjoyment of equal rights'. A Primitive Methodist minister on the Anglican church, *Primitive Metho-dist Magazine*, 1875, pp. 18–19, quoted in R. F. Wearmouth, *Methodism and the Struggle of the Working Classes, 1850–1900*, Edgar Backus, Leicester, 1954, p. 112.

clergymen (who before the development of the welfare state often controlled the access of the poor to medical care, housing, education, employment and even food) and the nineteenth-century working-class sceptic. Their mutual antagonism, so puzzling to the more successful, educated and liberal members of late Victorian society, is explicable if we see that infidelity was often reacted to in terms of a classical Goffmanesque stigma.

'They do furiously rage against all Christians . . .'

Any social movement acquires through the particular policies it advocates a characteristic view of the world. In the mind of the abstainer drunkenness looms large, and drink and its attendant dissipations are the main social facts on which he focuses. In the same way the secular movement overestimated the influence of religion. All behaviour that was justified in religious terms (as so much was in Victorian England) was assumed to be *due* to religion. The secularist consequently spent much time trying to destroy religion because he believed that the illiberalism, irrationality and hypocrisy that were justified in terms of it were largely due to it. Freethinkers often had a simplistic view of the link between belief and action; unless Christians completely conformed to the tenets of their faith stated in the baldest terms, they were judged to be hypocrites or to have signified their *de facto* dissent from religion. The beliefs of Christians about atheists and secularists were similarly largely incorrect or oversimplified, but they formed the basis for their behaviour towards freethinkers, and thus acquired a social reality.

Christian and free-thinking combatants often become so habituated to their antagonists that they established a system of controversy and insult which scarcely affected or was affected by changes in the outside world. In particular, the Christian propagandist who devoted his efforts to attacking atheism was not affected by the increasingly liberal attitude towards it in the higher ranks of the churches or in the wider society. As far as he was concerned, God was still likely to strike the sceptic dead or ruin him in business, for his opinions and his morals were equally appalling. For example in 1903 the Anti-Infidel League was distributing a pamphlet *Beware of Infidelity*, which could have been issued a hundred years previously. It was Christianity which had founded almshouses, orphanages and so on for the 'relief of the suffering, the forsaken and the sad'. As for infidels,

WHAT ARE THEY OFFERING US INSTEAD?
Sensuality, Free Love, and a foul system by which animated nature can be destroyed, and increase of population prevented, thus opening up the way for
UNIVERSAL PROSTITUTION
with its attendant evils of disease and death. All this is taught in books recommended by Secularists, beside a great deal more which is too vile to mention.[2]

The secularist speakers who encountered such defenders of the faith would be hard put to it not to respond in a similar vein. If they laboured to refute the horrors of hell long after theologians had largely dismissed it, it was because they were speaking opposite men who still preached hell-fire against them. Such controversies would become almost self-sustaining and created a world of their own, much as detectives and prison-warders come to share a culture with those among whom they spend their lives. Special societies were set up to combat atheists, and churches near the places where infidels regularly conducted their meetings often specialized in preachers who attacked them.[3] When George Lansbury and his brother disobeyed their mother's strict orders by going to listen to the Infidels in Bonner's Fields, she would—if she found them out—take them 'to the small Primitive Methodist Chapel in Bonner Lane, where we received the message of Hell Fire and Brimstone, and a general naming of what was in store for us if we listened to the wicked men in Bonner's Fields'.[4]

Charles Bradlaugh's brother was set up as an anti-infidel speaker by the Christian Evidence Society, and wrote pamphlets which parodied and inverted those of his brother. Secularists were trained at the London Hall of Science to heckle in meetings of the Christian Evidence Society, and their familiarity with the arguments of the Shoreditch Christian Evidence speakers for the truth of a literal Bible made them easily victorious.[5] Church history focuses on the more intellectual, influential or innovating clergy; the freethinker

---

[2] Quoted in *Truthseeker*, April 1903; this pamphlet was being circulated among crowds at open-air meetings in Bradford; the secularists counter-attacked by issuing a similar pamphlet which mimicked the phraseology of the League.

[3] For example, the Society of Reasoners and the Victoria Park Mission. And Bradlaugh reported that the Bible Defence Association and the Christian Evidence Society were started to prevent the 'rapid spread of Secularism'. Report, *N.S.S. Almanack* for 1871.

[4] G. Lansbury, *My Life*, Constable, London, 1928, p. 28.

[5] T. Okey, op. cit., p. 36.

was more likely to meet a professional anti-atheist, or a local minister who would react aggressively to any questioning of his authority by the poor among his flock.

In the second half of the nineteenth century, most influential men had been affected in various ways by the intellectual challenge to religious authority. Doubt was a *problem*, something which was a besetting source of anxiety, which had to be striven against. The anti-clericalism of secularists was the more resented because they were attacking beliefs which had come to seem frail and precious. The theme that religion was a consolation was an important part of evangelical Christianity. To destroy faith, especially the faith of women and children, was felt to be brutal because it removed the only support in suffering which was available to their weaker natures.[6] Holyoake was sensitive to this argument, but thought that consolation could be found in intelligent, merciful and joyous Nature. Most freethinkers thought that it was better to learn to live without opium.

The fear of infidelity was inseparable from the fact that it was most common among the industrial working classes. The religious census of 1851 had shown that only about half of the population who might have gone to church did so, and it was obvious that church-going was at its lowest in the working-class communities of the large industrial cities. The more realistic argued that working-class non-church-goers were not usually atheists, but merely ignorant of Christianity or mildly hostile to the churches. But the connections between the radical political opinions of the more intelligent and articulate working-men and their anti-clericalism were obvious, and it was feared that they might influence their fellows. On Sundays the middle-class agnostic could shelter behind an advanced religious or Unitarian congregation which *looked* like a church; the poor met outside in large, excited crowds. Bradlaugh focused and accentuated such fears; he and his followers 'do furiously rage against all Christians and all Christianity'.[7] The sight of atheists haranguing large crowds in parks gave rise to fears of mob violence, and the association of secularism with republicanism and neo-Malthusianism could only increase such fear. Secularists were democrats; and arguments for democracy were regarded as

---

[6] W. E. Houghton, 'Victorian Anti-Intellectualism', *Journal of History of Ideas*, Vol. 13 (3), 1952, p. 304.

[7] Anon, 'Popular Infidelity in the Metropolis', *Journal of Sacred Literature*, March 1865, p. 329.

arguments for working-class revolution. The often ragged and un-kempt appearance of many men who attended outdoor secular meetings created much prejudice in an era when open poverty was regarded as shameful and immoral.[8]

More sympathetic observers of the anti-clericalism of working-class communities thought that it was connected with the general sense of frustration created by their lack of rights as citizens or the inability of even the most respectable and skilled to protect them-selves against falling into hopeless penury by ill-luck, ill-health or just living too long. Radical workmen resented the compulsion to attend church to receive even a minimal amount of charitable help. They equally resented the extent to which atheist work-men had to conceal their opinions to remain employed, and even shopkeepers feared they would lose custom.

> Today thousands of artisans dare not openly declare their Freethought opinions. Even in the middle classes the same thing prevailed. If you went into a shop suddenly, you might perchance find the shopkeeper reading the *Age of Reason*, or the *Rights of Man*, or the *National Reformer*, but on anyone coming in, such works would be hastily thrust under the counter . . .[9]

Freethinkers also resented the constant self-righteous attacks on atheism by those defending 'civilized life', whilst even the most restrained criticism of Christianity was automatically branded as wicked and immoralist. Doubtless well-meaning Christians considered that they had every right to force their presence upon known infidels and their families when they were dying. The attemp-ted death-bed conversion loomed large in secularist indignation, and was frequently reported. All in all, as one observer realized, 'the heretics of the working classes are the victims of many petty persecutions which never affect wealthy enquirers.'[10]

Many of these petty persecutions made it difficult for secularists to hold meetings except in the open air or in public houses. Churches and chapels controlled most of the meeting-places in schools or church-halls and usually effectively ran Mechanics' Institutes, and the freethinkers could only occasionally find a liberal Unitarian or independent group of radical artisans who would be prepared to let

[8] W. E. Houghton, *The Victorian Frame of Mind, 1830–1870*, Gale University Press, New Haven, 1957, pp. 55, 184–5.
[9] Charles Watts, speech to the Dialectical Society, *National Reformer*, 7 January 1872, p. 3.
[10] Anon., 'The Religious Heresies of the Working Classes', *Westminster Review*, reported in *National Reformer*, 11 January 1862, pp. 2–3.

them a hall. Some secular societies became large and wealthy
enough to buy their own premises; this was made easier if one or
more of their members or supporters were wealthy, as were the
Unitarian manufacturers Gimsons of Leicester, or Joseph Cowen
at Blaydon and Stella colliery in Northumberland. Where a meeting-
place was secured a settled community of freethinkers could grow
up, whose leisure time like that of the members of a small sect
would be spent in association with the secular community.

Such societies developed secular Sunday schools for adults and
children, educational facilities which were sometimes also Mutual
Improvement Societies, clubrooms and a calendar of dances, picnics
and educational excursions. The London Hall of Science had political
or social meetings on every night of the week in the late 1870s.
Bradlaugh helped with oratory classes for would-be open-air
speakers, and they were required to take an examination testing the
amount of anti-theological knowledge they possessed, with questions
such as: 'How would you meet the argument that the long legs of
the stag, the spatulate diggers of the mole, the thickening of the
fur of animals in winter, etc., are marks of design?'[11]

It was natural for those secularists enclosed within a community
of like spirits to accept and encourage the other aspects of fellowship
that were usually provided by the churches, whereas secularists in
more ephemeral or open groups found that without a community
structure to support them outside pressure was too strong. Wives,
who were rarely freethinkers and bore the brunt of social pressure
on atheists, were likely to default and send their children to a
Sunday school.

Those within secularist communities became less militant as they
were more insulated from the irritations of contact with the Christian
world, but most freethinkers were in a more exposed position.
When forced to meet in public houses or outdoors they were not
only more vulnerable to intrusion but their surroundings automatically classified them as disreputable. Though freethinkers
were widely regarded as 'rough' the few unprejudiced middle-class
observers who broke through the emotional barrier against them

[11] Question from one of the examination papers in General Science, Grammar and
Atheism, and the History of Christianity and Biblical Criticism, set for the Lecturing
Diploma of the N.S.S., *N.S.S. Almanack*, 1885, pp. 53–6. W. J. Ramsey used to meet
with a band of open-air speakers for instruction at Bradlaugh's house, before he moved
to St John's Wood and the more refined company and secularism of Mrs Besant.
Freethinker, 2 January 1916, p. 3.; A. H. Nethercot, *The First Five Lives of Annie
Besant*, Hart–Davies, London, 1961, p. 112.

found them surprisingly often respectable, worthy and educated. Secularists for their part were receptive to those Christians prepared to meet them on equal terms. Stuart Headlam who from 1875 to 1883 went to answer Bradlaugh's arguments at the London Hall of Science was impressed by the moral earnestness of the secularists who met there; 'How much nearer to the Kingdom of Heaven are these men in the Hall of Science, than the followers of Moody and Sankey'.[12] But less liberal Christians, his bishop among them, disapproved of his action.

The result of the separation of secularists from more liberal and educated Christians was that apart from reading their work their only source of even moderately informed Christian apologetics were the clergymen who would debate with atheists. A formal debate often lasting for several nights between a Christian minister and a secular leader was also a popular entertainment and would draw large crowds. Holyoake and Bradlaugh debated extensively in this way at first, but the debates were attacked by some members of both sides as being rowdy and pointless—ministers and atheists were accused of going round 'like a travelling raree-show', touting for hire. A strong element of snobbery was evident in such criticisms, as well as the conventional wish to keep religion from being a subject of open discussion.

> Why the Reverent Brewin Grant, or any other self-respecting person, condescended to appear in public against a debater of such vulgar proclivities and mean attainments [Bradlaugh] is not easy to conjecture. The objections raised against Holy Writ are simply the objections of uneducated impertinence and irreverence all the world over.[13]

It would have been better, the orthodox thought, if parsons did not help atheists by bringing up the issue of the reasons for unbelief, which could only result in their congregations falling into doubt. When J. F. Rayner started a secular branch at Southampton, which caused a good deal of local agitation and provoked a counter-attack from the churches, 'the net result of the anti-infidel campaign was to bring us a good many new members, and in other ways to help us in our enterprise; and I suppose the orthodox foe recognised the fact, for they adopted a Fabian policy ever afterward and lay very low.'[14]

[12] F. G. Bettany, *Stuart Headlam*, John Murray, London, 1926, pp. 48–51.
[13] C. R. Mackay, *Life of Charles Bradlaugh*, op. cit., pp. 123–4.
[14] J. F. Rayner, 'Reminiscences of the Secular Movement', *Reformer*, 15 March 1898, p. 9. But the local churches forced them out of their meeting-place and they had to meet in a public house.

In consequence many secularists had little conception of the development of liberal theology, and regarded works such as *Essays and Reviews* or Colenso on the Pentateuch as proof that such writers would shortly become atheists, or would be already, if they were honest.[15] Conversely, liberal Christians believed that 'a large majority of that audience are Secularists because they don't know what true Christian teaching is'.

> They have read Paine's *Age of Reason* and the works of Carlile and Robert Taylor, 'The Devil's Chaplain', and have thus picked up, at second hand, a few of those objections against divine revelation which have been answered a thousand times over . . . Of the real merits of the religion of the Bible, they are just as ignorant as are the inhabitants of Timbuctoo.

But though secularists may have known little of liberal theology, they certainly knew a great deal about biblical religion.

Charles Booth and other investigators found the most disturbing aspect of the religious beliefs of the poor was their ignorance of the doctrines of both Christianity and secularism. Formal disagreement with religious doctrines, Booth found, would 'mainly be among the very intelligent educated members of the more highly paid working-classes.'[16] The antipathy of many secularists to religion was based on unhappy experience with ministers rather than on intellectual objections, but the movement contained large numbers of men such as Booth described; self-educated artisans or superior workmen who had often used the classes and libraries of the secular societies to inform themselves on a wide variety of subjects. Beatrice Webb noticed in the 1880s that London dockers would dress up respectably on Sundays and go to listen to the secularist speakers in Victoria park where they would debate religious and philosophical issues earnestly from their readings of Spencer and Huxley.[17]

Much secularist discussion showed (and still shows) a keen interest in problems of philosophy and ethics; poor men spent all that they could to amass libraries. 'Many persons have remarked to

[15] The *National Reformer* greeted Colenso's book thus: 'The new year brings us into contact with a great and wonderful fact; and more important than wonderful. A Bishop of the established Church writes a book against the "Holy Bible", using all his great learning to destroy the very foundation of the Christian religion—to wit, the first five books of Moses. As Secularists, we ought to consider the best method of taking full advantage of this—we do not get bishops on our side every day. . . . The book ought to be a sledgehammer in the hands of every intelligent Secularist.' 17 January 1863, p. 7.

[16] Charles Booth, *Life and Labour in London*, Third Series, Macmillan, London, 1902, 'Summary of Religious Influences in London', p. 422.

[17] Beatrice Webb, *My Apprenticeship*, Longmans, London, 1926, pp. 257-9.

me that when they first came into contact with the propaganda of Secularism the new ideas not only made them think, but made them study . . .'[18]

These men were a puzzle for the unprejudiced Christian outsider, for the worthy infidel was until the 1890s or so a contradiction in terms. In 1847 Holyoake had reported an Anglican adult class which had discussed the problem of the worthy infidel and

> considered the moral character of infidels to be a more powerful weapon against the Christian religion than all the books which had ever been written against it.
> They were utterly at a loss how to account for infidels having such characteristics, seeing that they had not the Grace of God. The minister accounted for it thus: 'Infidels', says he, 'are persons whom the devil will be sure of having, consequently he leaves them to pursue their own ways; but Christians, whom he is not sure of, he is constantly tempting, and drawing them from the way in which grace would direct them.'

Until the 1870s secularist speakers and their supporters were regularly stoned.

> There are still [in 1897] Secularists alive in Glasgow who remember how, on Sundays, the street in which the 'Hall of Science' stood used to be lined with a gaping crowd who had assembled partly to spy upon those who passed in and out, to mark them for subsequent molestation, and partly to judge by ocular demonstration whether these children of Belial so far resembled their father as to have horns, short horns even, club-feet, and a posterior bulging answering to a coiled-up tail.

Even if beliefs about infidels were not usually so dramatic, many men remembered that they had doubted various aspects of Christianity for some time, but sharing in the general assumption that freethinkers were immoralists had hesitated to make contact with the secular movement until they had been astonished to meet secularists who were also respectable artisans of impeccable moral and social standing.

> The 'infidel' of my imagination was a willing and vicious son of Satan, whose diabolical work upon the earth he joyfully engaged himself to do, and dramatic stories of the deathbed agonies and repentances of unbelievers were, at that time [i.e. the 1870s] told to children from their earliest years. My astonishment when I first saw and heard an 'unbeliever' was therefore intense. There was nothing abnormal about him. He wore a black frock-coat, and he looked

---

[18] 'Chilperic', *Reformer*, 15 January 1898, p. 315. Bradlaugh amassed a very large library; a poor bill-poster in a London slum had a roomful of free-thought publications, B. Webb, ibid.; a secularist in 1861 was induced by secular writings to leave off bad companions and sign the pledge, and with the money saved he bought books to educate himself and became respectable.

as much like a highly virtuous elder of a nonconformist chapel as any man I had ever seen. Upon inquiry I learnt that he was a most respectable and respected citizen of the town, a confectioner by trade, a leader in the Co-operative Movement, a Liberal in politics, and, in religious opinion, an advanced Unitarian.[19]

Far from being disreputable, many freethinkers were cut off from the rest of the working class by their intense and rather solemn autodidacticism. Their avid reading and attendance at evening classes in science and theology were scarcely usual. As Thomas Okey's basketmaking family reproached him when they found him reading, 'Ah, Tom, *that'll* never bring you bread and cheese!'[20] Such a pattern of earnest self-improvement, often involving rejecting drink and with it a whole pattern of working-class sociability in order to study, was typical enough of some nonconformists; but secularists were isolated by their open atheism. The Reverend Tuckwell was warned by a clergyman that when he spoke at a co-operative meeting in a Lancashire manufacturing town, his chairman would be a notorious local atheist. Tuckwell with ostentatious liberalism befriended this 'strong, thoughtful man', and the impression he gained of him was similar to the impression that many other freethinkers made on curious outsiders.

> He was a quiet, meditative, rather melancholy man, scientifically half-trained, well read in history and literature, in his room two well-filled bookcases and a microscope. . . . We sat in my host's room for hours, talking over the mental anxieties which he had kept broodingly to himself for want of some counsellor whom he could trust. Chiefly theological, they bore also on the labour problem . . . I found he had won ill-will from his mates by opposing hopeless strikes.[21]

'I look with suspicion upon all respectability . . .'

Despite all the evidence to the contrary, it was so generally assumed that religion was the only possible agent which could impress moral notions on poor men's minds that it necessarily followed that atheists must be morally lax. Even the poor who did not attend church felt themselves superior to infidels, and the ungodly argued against

[19] H. Snell, *Men, Movements and Myself*, Dent, London, 1936, p. 29; this was in Nottingham in the 1870s.

[20] At work as a basket-maker, the foreman was one, it was whispered, 'What didn't believe in no God', and Okey remembered him buying an *Age of Reason*. But he was an educated man of integrity who read *The Times* nightly. T. Okey, op. cit., pp. 18, 32–3.

[21] W. Tuckwell, *Reminiscences of a Radical Parson*, Cassell, London, 1906, pp. 176–7.

them, the secularists complained, when they denied Divine Retribution. The attachment of many of the poor to a profit-and-loss conception of religion in which a few restraints in this world paid for happiness in the next meant that many liberal clergymen working among the poor found themselves unable to enlighten their parishioners. Headlam had abandoned his belief in hell for all sinners as morally revolting but when he preached his new views in the slums of Drury Lane, his congregation protested and a 'small and decent milliner' said, 'Oh, but Mr Headlam, if that is true, where is the reward of the righteous?'

In addition to the presupposition that freethinkers must be immoral, popular convictions were strengthened by the fact that some self-confessed atheists *were* immoral; or at least unrespectable. This fact was vigorously asserted by Christians and as vigorously denied by secularists, but even some leading freethinkers had offended against propriety. A group which asserted liberal opinions on personal matters and complete liberty of speech was bound to attract some who practised what most freethinkers merely preached. Anyone could attend a secular meeting, and contemporary accounts indicate that some of those who did, especially outdoor meetings, were very disreputable in opinion and manner. It was feared that because of their presence many respectable sceptics did not join the movement, and that the absence of women and children from meetings was because they were controversial and rowdy. Many older secularists were upset by this—'I have held Secularist views now for twenty years, and have found one uniform failing in Secular societies, and that is the disregard paid to the moral character of their members.' They were distressed partly because eccentric and quarrelsome behaviour prevented any sense of community emerging to replace the constant attacks on religion, but also because they were conscious that secularists were continually being watched by Christian outsiders who were quick to pounce on any evidence of immorality.

The ethic of secularism itself enjoined liberty to all men. If the

No person should be allowed to become a member [wrote a secularist in 1892] much less an officer, of a society, who is not of good moral character. Secular societies are not regarded in the same light as political clubs and similar institutions. They are looked at by the enemy outside from a moral and religious standpoint. In a community where religion and morality are widely regarded as inseparable, absence of religion is looked on as being synonymous with absence of morality. That this is so, every Freethinker is only too well aware.

Christian denominations shrank from pickpockets and prostitutes, this was all the more reason why the secular movement should not cold-shoulder them. The Owenites within the movement argued that it was man's environment and not himself which was responsible for his depravity, and the secularist (like the nonconformist) placed great emphasis on the moral significance of the act of individual choice. Those who chose freethought were thereby made socially redeemable. Respectability too, the key social concept of Victorian *petit-bourgeois* life, was an ambiguous goal. It had close links with the *mores* of the chapel, and the more radical secularists pointed out that it often had less to do with gentlemanly behaviour than with social standing. And since the working-class unbeliever could never become respectable, they argued, he ought not to stray into the paths of the righteous. Indeed, even Holyoake received many rebuffs from 'respectable' advanced thinkers to whom he had made overtures.[22]

The temperance movement was a major agency in defining a respectable, industrious and self-respecting life-style in mid-Victorian England. Many secularists were temperance advocates, and frequent proposals were made that the movement should either commit itself to teetotalism or at least form a temperance group within it; 'it is nothing less than moral and social suicide for Secularism to be directly or indirectly associated with the liquor traffic.' The leaders of the movement were sympathetic, but advocated moderation rather than abstinence. Holyoake, intelligent and humanitarian social observer that he was, saw the warm sociability of the public house, the only institution where working-men could freely meet and express what opinions they wanted and read what they liked, needed to be supplemented and not destroyed. Some secular societies opened clubs 'to provide members with

---

[22] His correspondence contains many letters which either criticize him for not being militant enough, or regret that he is not respectable enough for the writer to associate with. For example, Herbert Spencer, admittedly hypersensitive about his reputation, wrote in 1882 that 'you will understand . . . why I hesitated to respond to your request to arrange so that our voyage to the United States should be in the same vessel. Inevitably if we were fellow-passengers and had the daily intercourse that would naturally occur, the fact would be remarked and commented upon by American fellow-passengers, and reporters and interviewers would inevitably be informed of our intimacy and some such statement as that we had come over together, possibly with some purpose, would become current. The religious world is especially unscrupulous in its endeavours to injure antagonists . . . and as it would be their policy to damage me as much as possible—and as there either survives over there, or will be easily revived, the idea formed of you in early days so that you would be called by them "the notorious atheist Holyoake" or some such name, I think it very probable that the fact of our association would be used as a weapon against me.' Letter to Holyoake of 4 April 1882 (Co-operative Union, Manchester).

such means of recreation, amusement, instruction and social intercourse, as have a tendency to elevate the tastes and to contribute to
their intellectual improvement, without being dependent for these
purposes on the public house.' The secular movement was closely
associated with the growth of the educational and social aspects of
working-men's clubs. If they served alcohol, such clubs became all
too socially successful, and encroached on specifically secularist
activities.[23]

Secularists claimed, probably correctly, that a higher proportion
of their members were non-smokers and abstainers than of Christians.
But the temperance movement did not want such hampering allies,
and went to considerable lengths to deny and conceal the connections
between secularists and temperance.[24] They pointed to a confusion
in the secularists' beliefs which was indeed never resolved. If Owen
had held that men were bound by social laws and that poverty and
misery came from the workings of the environment, how could
secularists exalt that act of free choice which was at the heart of
temperance?

The influence of socialist ideas in the 1890s combined with the
great decline in public drunkenness weakened both the influence
of temperance ideas and, on a wider level, the concept of 'respectability' itself. It suddenly disappeared from secularist writings at
the turn of the century, and social divisions were afterwards conceived of in a less moral and more class-conscious way. Such an
enormous change must have been connected with the declining role
of the churches as a major agency in denoting social boundaries.
In contemporary discussion, the churches were increasingly criticized
for want of sympathy with the workers and maintaining class-
distinctions in their congregations.

A decade earlier, the secularist's denial of religious teachings had
been enough to make him immoral and unrespectable; now many
people, both working- and middle-class, condemned the churches
for abandoning the 'natural' morality that all worthy men adhered
to, and that Christ must therefore have represented.[25]

---

[23] Leicester Secular Society had a flourishing club, but there were frequent complaints
about the 'tone' of the entertainments and the visitors. Two members were expelled for
extra-marital relations, and finally liquor was stopped in 1902. Sydney Gimson, *Random
Recollections*, Vol. 11, (6), and N.S.S. Executive Committee meeting, 22 February 1876.

[24] B. Harrison, *Drink and the Victorians, the Temperance Question in England,
1815–1872*, Faber, London, 1971, pp, 173, 184.

[25] This theme appeared mostly in contemporary literature. See especially the results
of an inquiry carried out by officers among their men during the First World War,
D. S. Cairns, op. cit.

Who were the Secularists?

The information that is available about the membership of the secularist movement is both limited and non-representative. As in all movements the available official material refers mainly to the leaders of the movement, and those most active within voluntary associations invariably come from the uppermost social group of their membership. Thus whereas the magazines give an impression for the nineteenth century of a body largely composed of independent artisans and craftsmen, small shopkeepers and manufacturers, Christian contemporaries asserted that open-air secularist meetings were mainly composed of the very poor. Given that the Christians were likely to exaggerate their poverty, the journals reflect a too-wealthy sample. Yet such material as is available does make more explicable the process by which men became secularists and their attitude to religion.

Family Connections

Of the 382 members of the movement for whom biographical data is available only twenty-one were women, and of these fifteen were the wives and widows of freethinkers.[26] This confirms the frequent reports from secular societies that almost all of their members were men, and that few children of freethinkers grew up in the movement. From 344 biographies of secularists where information was detailed enough to make it reasonable to assume that another freethinker in the secularist's family would have been mentioned, only twenty instances occurred. The first generation of secularists often came

---

[26] The information about members has been compiled from biographies and pamphlets, but mainly from the accounts and (especially) obituaries of secularists printed in the journals of the movement, *The Reasoner*, 1852–61; *The National Reformer*, 1860–93; *The Counsellor*, 1861; *The Secular Chronicle* (Birmingham), 1872–79; *The Secularist and Secular Review*, 1876–84; *The Freethinker*, 1881–1965; *Truthseeker* (Bradford), 1898–1915.

Because the same information about members was not always given, the total number of cases in each category—such as age, or previous religion—varies in each case. In addition because most information was printed as obituaries and information about members of the movement was most abundant when it was at its largest and had an active branch life under Bradlaugh and Holyoake, the bulk of information about secularists is about those who joined the movement in the nineteenth century. No differences, other than those which are mentioned, were found between the secularists of an earlier and a later period, and so all the biographies have been analysed together.

from radical and socialist backgrounds but it was frequently stated that the radical father was not of 'advanced religious opinions'. A recent survey of membership found the percentage of women to be still very low—14 per cent—but this may partly have been due to the fact that in the case of married couples, husbands were the formal subscribers to the central society.[27]

Most secularists seem not to have entered the movement until middle age. Observers made constant reference to the lack of young men in meetings; they were attracted by Bradlaugh, but left again to join the socialist movement. Secularists sometimes commented on those who had joined the movement as young as twenty-four or thirty years old. C. B. Campbell's survey found that over a third of secularists were over sixty, and the main age-group were in their forties. A recent study of the Leicester secular society found that more than half of the members were over sixty.[28] The sex and age imbalance created a constant problem of recruitment, for by its nature the membership must be made up of converts.

Occupations

Most secularists who recorded their occupations came from the working class. This judgement sometimes must be tentative, since individual occupations change their relative positions—for example, the nineteenth-century secularists who were teachers, doctors and engineers were of lower social standing than their contemporary counterparts—and the subjective divisions between classes move over time.[29]

Local branches varied in their social composition; some were based on a place of work, usually a colliery—for example the group

[27] C. B. Campbell, *Humanism and the Culture of the Professions: a Study of the rise of the British Humanist Movement, 1954–63,* London Ph.D. Thesis, 1968, p. 285.
[28] C. B. Campbell, op. cit., pp. 249–51; R. Billington, op. cit.
[29] E. Royle, op. cit., Appendix IV. The data seem to refer to secularist leaders. Royle's data on secularists for the period up to 1861 showed a small majority of secularists to be middle-class, but his sources and classifications seem open to doubt. My data, which mainly refer to the mid-Victorian period, show an overwhelming preponderance of manual workers, 104 of 236 being semi-skilled or unskilled workers. The proportion of manual workers and 'poor' is an underestimate, since the information mainly relates to leaders and more prominent local freethinkers.
    C. B. Campbell's evidence on present-day members of the National Secular Society classified a third as manual workers and less than a third as professional and technical workers. Only half of his sample replied, and it is therefore probable that his figures are biased toward the educated and middle-class freethinker.

at Stella and Blaydon fostered by Sir Joseph Cowen which met in the Mechanics' Institute. Sometimes occupations formed a basis for a secular group, for instance the makers of railway engines at Swindon who asked Holyoake to talk to them, or a group of soldiers who set up a branch at their barracks in 1890. Some local groups were drawn from wealthier occupations, notably the society at Leicester; when its members purchased shares in the Secular Hall in 1873 there were seven manufacturers or owners of companies, six clerical and lower supervisory workers, four craftsmen, and twenty-two manual workers, mainly self-employed members of the hosiery and clothing trades. In the nineteenth century many independent craftsmen mentioned that they could be open secularists because they could not be pressured by employers, and some of these were the atheist cobblers and shoemakers of the popular stereotype. As working groups grew larger and more impersonal employers ceased for the most part to concern themselves with the opinions of their employees, though in firms where close contacts persisted, so might the attempts at control. Harry Snell remembered that in the poverty-stricken Nottinghamshire village where he was brought up in the 1870s, the few craftsmen and basket-makers lived in a separate row of cottages; only they were freed from the constraints of local employment, and only they were radicals and nonconformists.[30]

The large number of secularists who worked in the printing industry and kept bookshops in my sample is due not only to the tradition of radical independence of these occupations but to the over-representation of secularist leaders who earned a living by the production and distribution of radical literature. In general, nineteenth- and early twentieth-century secularists appear to have been drawn from the communities of the industrial or commercial working-clam—there are few from rural occupations and a large number fross occupations such as mining and weaving.

The picture that is suggested is that free-thought flourished in those communities where the links between the individual and older social allegiances had been broken down. When working-class men were migrants, gathered together in working groups and exposed to the authoritarian control of their employers rather than the softer bonds of an established community, then freethought seems to have been a likely response; among the railway navvies, for example, or

[30] H. Snell, op. cit., pp. 22–3.

the members of the armed forces during the two world wars, or in mining villages. It was not the only response, of course; such men have also been predisposed to Primitive Methodism, or communism, or criminality and drunkenness or high and persistent strike rates. And isolated freethinkers might equally be found in more settled communities.

Secularists for the most part appear to have been previously either Catholics or members of various nonconformist churches. Of ninety-one freethinkers who defined their previous beliefs, thirty-five had been Catholics, twenty-one Methodists, eight Presbyterians, six 'nonconformists' or 'fundamentalists', four Baptists, two Church of Christ and two from the Salvation Army, and one each from the Particular Baptists, the Bible Christians, the 'White' Quakers and the Plymouth Brethren. Nine had been Anglicans. The membership of those denominations has been mainly from the same social groups as the secularists themselves. But in the nineteenth century more working-class people were still, nominally at least, Anglican than any other religion. Why were they under-represented among the converts to secularism? Perhaps those whose attachment to religion was more nominal were even at that date describing themselves as 'Anglican', whereas the biographies of secularists suggested that they had usually been deeply religious. And many work-class Anglicans were rural, and well integrated into more traditional communities.

On a wider level, the Anglican working-man who was not an evangelical was bound to his church by custom and ritual. The nonconformist emphasis on a personal conviction of the *truth* of religion and of the Bible left religion separated from the routine of life, the symbolism which united men to the cycle of their own lives and the complex order of society. The secularists who had been nonconformists brought with them many aspects of this tradition into the movement: the attack on the established church as mingling worldly and spiritual power when religion was a matter of individual choice and belief and should be separated from the state; the campaign for freedom of belief and for equal civil rights for all; the familiarity with the Bible and the identification of religion as scriptural religion.

The shift from nonconformity to Catholicism as the main source of recruits may have been partly due to the influx of working-class Irish immigrants, who by migration weakened the network of familial and community ties which had bound them to the church and the authority of the priest.[31] Anti-Catholicism seems to have become a more dominant part of the general antipathy to the churches from the late nineteenth century on. As church-going declined and the Anglican church and nonconformist denominations began to modify the moral and theological doctrines that their members must follow, Catholicism became more conspicuous because it did not follow such a trend; church attendance remained high and the Church's attitude to knowledge and authority remained absolutist. The moral and especially sexual doctrines that it enjoined were both distinct and illiberal; in particular, it continued to condemn birth control.

The Context of Recruitment

In attempting to explain why a social group, a religion or a political party attracts the members that it does, perhaps the most crucial factor is the image or reputation of the group which is current in the outside world. (Different parts of the society may, of course, hold different views.) What initially attracts or repels individuals is not what the group is really like or stands for but what they believe it to be like. A group may be composed of men of extreme respectability and good standing but if it is identified as notorious it will be unable to attract suitable new members, and a self-fulfilling prophecy will result—a group identified as eccentric will attract members who share, or are at least indifferent to this characteristic. Some groups deliberately purvey an outré image of themselves; jazz musicians, bohemians, and movements of dissatisfied youth repel the adult and respectable by emphasizing characteristics which offend them. Some bodies which are generally disliked use 'front organizations' to attract the unsuspecting who having joined the group find after some time that its members and purposes are not what they had been led to believe. Similarly, some groups advertise themselves as open to all comers but are in fact more restricted—and newcomers not of the particular ethnic, religious or occupational slant as those who compose its membership will be likely to leave. Many social movements are more 'closed' than their formal tenets claim.

Such a situation is made the more complex because not only movements but their opponents try to build up such exterior images. Political groups try to define their opponents as either a

---

[31] Irish Catholics were more likely to leave the church, or at least be less obedient to clerical authority, on arriving in England. J. A. Jackson, *The Irish in Britain*, Routledge, London, 1963, pp. 137-51.

weaker version of themselves or at the extreme end of the political spectrum, and churches may similarly use such handy pigeon-holing, 'dangerous liberalism' on the one hand and 'die-hard orthodoxy' on the other. Some beliefs attract a largely automatic ridicule or dislike, and groups will also try to brand their opponents with such beliefs. In the case of secularism, the secularist movement and the nine-teenth-century churches were locked in a mutually sustaining system of antagonisms. The existence of each was of service to the other.

In the nineteenth century the infidel was of great symbolic importance to churchmen, especially to the orthodox. He could be used to rally men into the churches and religious enthusiasm, and to attack the encroachment of science, liberal ideas and/or the moral anarchy of which he was the foremost representative. The orthodox churchman used infidels as a stick to beat liberal or advanced think-ers; the threat of atheism always became more prominent when such groups resisted change. 'Advanced' clergymen and liberal dissenters found the atheist an embarrassing figure since on many issues his opinions coincided with their own. As general social support for religious institutions was withdrawn, attacks on atheists became less and less generally effective. Christians and atheists came to be seen as conducting a private war over an increasingly peripheral set of issues, and the atheist's position as a bogey was taken over by various other minorities.[32] The widespread prejudice against secularist meetings set up a filter through which only a few cate-gories of potential members were likely to pass; those who as a part of the radical tradition were relatively immune to social pressures, friends or relatives of freethinkers, and those who were unrespec-table already. To these were added those who came into contact with the movement by accident—by stopping to listen to open-air speakers, by reading literature idly—and found that their pre-conceptions were challenged.

Numbers

The number of men who were secularists at any time was always very much greater than the number of those who were actually

[32] M. E. Marty, *The Infidel-Freethought and American Religion*, World Publishing Co., Ohio, 1961, p. 140 *et seq.*, argued that in late nineteenth-century America the churches were perturbed by the intellectual rise of science and employed the infidel image to condemn it more widely. In turn, Ingersoll attacked scriptural authority because liberal Christians were embarrassed by it, and the orthodox found its literal interpreta-tion increasingly hard to support.

members of the society. Many men supported the movement only by reading its journal and debating the issues with friends. The very high turnover of members, who would often allow their contact with the movement to lapse until a fresh instance of persecution brought them back in again, made the movement's size uncertain. In 1851, Holyoake estimated that there were rather more than three thousand subscribers to the *Reasoner*, and in fact sales of the *National Reformer* never rose much above this level. Under Bradlaugh's presidency more emphasis was put on joining branches, and by the end of the 1860s, successful secular societies had memberships of over fifty and very occasionally of over one hundred. The Secular Almanack listed the number of branches affiliated to the National Secular Society from then on until the 1900s.[33]

The average size of branches continued to increase during the 1870s, partly as a result of the republican agitations. The London Hall of Science had over a thousand members in 1879, and a full programme of events nightly. The number of *new* members of the movement each year shows high turnover of up to a third of all members a year, and rapid influx during Bradlaugh's attempts to enter the House of Commons.

The membership of the Society reached a peak of about four thousand in the mid-1880s, and started to fall rapidly after Bradlaugh's resignation as a result of schism and disaffection. Not surprisingly, the situation became even less clear; the opponents

---

[33] *Number of Secular Societies affiliated to the N.S.S.*, compiled from the *National Secular Society's Almanack* and the *Secular Almanack*

Year	London	Provinces & Scotland
1870	7	30 (and 21 places with members)
71	7	46 („ 25 „ „ „)
72	8	49
73	6	37*
77	6	44
78	8	46 (and 4 societies outside N.S.S.)
79	7	49
1880	8	61
81	9	62
82	10	68
83	12	65
84	21	60 (and 33 omitted to send returns)
85	17	54 („ 24 „ „ „ „)
86	22	67 („ 4 „ „ „ „)
1890	15 ⎤ (now includes	37
91	18 ⎬ open-air	33
92	20 ⎦ societies)	51 (many 'meet when required')
94	18	46

of the officials of the National Secular Society claimed that the branches had few members and 'bogus branches' were kept on the books. An increasing number of societies were forced by lack of money to meet in public houses, or outdoors. Support has clearly been at a lower level during the twentieth century. A steady drain of secularists to left-wing groups has continued, and despite gains of membership during both wars the number of branches does not seem to have risen much above ten. A freethinker hostile to the executive estimated total membership in 1948 to be about seven hundred, and C. B. Campbell's survey in 1963 would suggest less than six hundred. No more precise figure is available.

Petty Persecutions

Those who have come into contact with secularists have commonly remarked on both the violence of their antipathy to religion and the fact that their attacks on it were often launched on theological bastions which had long since been abandoned. Because of this, influential Christians and agnostics alike have throughout its history dismissed the movement as if it were a problem of individual path-ology, or the vestige of an intellectual attack which was too out of date to be interesting. But social life is not homogeneous. Secularists attacked a theology which might be absurdly over-simplified and old-fashioned to the sophisticated, but it had plenty of supporters in the world that they inhabited. The harshness that secularists complained of when they encountered Christian ministers was in part a function of their social position. The poor were not thought sufficiently educated or intelligent to appreciate the combination of doubt yet commitment of liberal theologians; and among them, doubts about religion were more morally and politically dangerous.

95	18 (largely open-air)	42
96	15	28
97	15	48
98	12	49
99	9	48
1900	11	49 (but 17 were only individual members)
01	11	46
02	11	42
03	8	24
04	8	24

*Effect of republican agitation—many secular societies became Republican Clubs.

Some writers consider that the suspicion and dislike of religious scepticism declined steadily or reached its peak in the 1860s, and that the following decade was one of an increasingly powerful scientific counter-attack.[34] But social reality seems to have been different for the secularist; whilst physical attacks on atheists were not common after the 1860s or so, animosity to them was very high during the 1870s, and many secularists reported having been evicted by landladies or parents once their unbelief was discovered. After the mid-80s and Bradlaugh's entry to parliament hostility to them did largely die down, perhaps because the growing socialist movement made it possible to distinguish between religious and political dissent.

The doubts of the educated as to sacred authorities had no such tinge of the questioning and rejection of secular authority. The religion which was taught to the poor was often conservative, simplified, and used to point heavy morals about submission to just authority. The secularist attack on Christianity as fostering slavish submission and mindless obedience was the inevitable corollary of the use of religion as a means of social control.

This argument should not be over-simplified. Many religious currents ran strongly among the nineteenth-century poor which were intensely conservative and fundamentalist, and recent survey evidence from both Britain and the United States suggests that not only are the most conservative religious groups strongly working-class in composition and the most liberal upper middle-class, but that in given congregations, greater theological conservatism and fundamentalism is associated with lower class status and lack of education. The Unitarians and the Quakers, the most liberal in theology and the most prepared to protect secularists at a local level, were composed almost entirely of wealthy middle-class congregations. The liberal clergy who laboured among the nineteenth-century English poor amply reported the theological conservatism of their flocks, and often expressed admiration for the secularists' concern—unusual for their class—with moral issues and new knowledge. Why, then, did some men respond to the same general situation by a religious protest against or denial of worldly authority, some by a radical protest which might include secularism, but the majority by a greater or lesser indifference to both politics and religion, combined with a relative acceptance of the *status quo*?

[34] E. C. Mack, *Public Schools and British Opinion 1780–1860*, New York 1939, p. 289, saw suspicion of freethought as peaking with *Essays and Reviews*.

The answer is partly a question of individual personality, and partly a question of the kinds of explanation and allegiance which were available to each man, living where he did, when he did, and receiving the ideas that he did. This chapter and the next suggest some of the factors conducive to choosing the secularist alternative but can do no more, any more than with far better contemporary data we have succeeded in doing more than loosely predict men's voting patterns, the move to non-traditionalism, the retention of religious allegiance, or the resort to radical political activity.

5 THE LOSS OF FAITH

I well remember, when about seven or eight years of age, hearing a sermon read by a relation of mine, who was a great devotee of the Church, upon the subject of what is called *Redemption by the Death of the Son of God*. After the sermon was ended, I went into the garden, and as I was going down the steps, (for I perfectly recollect the spot) I revolted at the recollection of what I had heard, and thought to myself that it was making God Almighty act like a passionate man that killed his son when he could not revenge himself in any other way; and as I was sure a man would be hanged that did such a thing, I could not see for what purpose they preached such sermons. This was not one of those kinds of thoughts that had anything in it of childish levity; it was to me a serious reflection arising from the idea that God was too good to do such an action, and also too almightly to be under any necessity of doing it. I believe in the same manner to this moment; and I moreover believe that any system of religion that has anything in it that shocks the mind of a child, cannot be a true system.

Thomas Paine, *The Age of Reason*

Most of the discussion of the reasons for the decline of belief in religion in nineteenth- and twentieth-century Britain has been based on the experience of members of a small intelligentsia whose spiritual pilgrimages were recorded in some detail. These examples have led to an overwhelming emphasis on the intellectual rather than the moral or social causes of unbelief. The effects of developing scientific knowledge, especially Darwinism, and of the higher criticism have been seen as mainly responsible for weakening belief in the literal truth of scriptural religion for some, and for forcing others to abandon belief in God altogether. But the evidence which is available for secularists whose conversions were recorded between about 1850 and 1950 but occurred mainly in the sixty years from 1840 on, suggests a rather different picture of their reasons for rejecting Christianity.[1]

The evidence has been taken from the conversion experiences of

[1] The assumption is implicit in many writings about religion and science. See as examples, K. S. Inglis, op. cit., p. 2; A. O. J. Cockshut, *The Unbelievers*, Collins, London, 1964; A.W.Benn, *The History of English Rationalism in the Nineteenth Century*, Longmans & Co., London, 1906; W. Irvine, *Apes, Angels and Victorians*, Weidenfeld and Nicolson, London, 1920. Howard P. Murphy, 'The Ethical Revolt against Christian Orthodoxy in early Victorian England', *The American History Review*, Vol. 60, 1955, showed that the causes of the loss of faith of a few literary figures were in fact moral. Perhaps the most famous spiritual crisis induced by science was that of *Father and Son*, but Gosse's father was both a naturalist and the leader of a group of Plymouth Brethern—an exceptionally sharp confrontation of beliefs.

one hundred and fifty secularists which were recorded in some detail, with supporting evidence from nearly two hundred briefer biographies.[2] Accounts describing why freethinkers had rejected religion were often printed in their obituaries in the magazines of the movement, and the obituaries themselves were printed to refute one of the main popular arguments in favour of Christianity, the *Argument from Death-bed Repentance*. The atheist might find his infidelity sufficient for life, Christian apologists warned, but on his death-bed faced with the prospect of the unknown, he would be bound either to repent or to die in fear and horror.

Secularists tried to combat this by attempting to expose as lies the death-bed repentance stories most widely reported—a difficult task since the stories were usually reported anonymously and were sometimes true—and by writing obituaries of their prominent members emphasizing their high standard of morality in life and their composed and atheist deaths. The drama of the spiritual pilgrimage, into or out of faith or sobriety, to be relived again by being retold in meetings so that the manner of each man's conversion became general knowledge, was a product of the general cultural belief in individual responsibility and choice. Whether each individual was able to weigh up his own motives correctly is perhaps more doubtful.

The conversion to atheism usually followed two distinct phases: the conversion from Christianity to unbelief or uncertainty, which is the focus of this discussion, and the move from unbelief to positive commitment to secularism. Studies of patterns of conversion to Christianity during this period suggest that the typical conversion to Christianity or moment of personal conviction of salvation differed markedly from the loss of faith in it.[3] Conversions *to* Christianity occur earlier—the peak age being at about fourteen to seventeen, whereas the age of loss of faith given for this group of secularists is

[2] The journals used were the *Reasoner*, 1852–61; *National Reformer*, 1860–93; *Counsellor*, 1861; *Secular Chronicle* (Birmingham), 1872–79; *Secularist and Secular Review*, 1876–84; *Freethinker*, 1881–1968; *Truthseeker* (Bradford), 1898–1915, with the addition of the biographies of notable secularists and some others. Most conversion experiences were printed as obituaries and date from the nineteenth century. Because no differences are apparent (except those mentioned) between nineteenth- and twentieth-century conversion experiences, they are discussed together.

[3] For conversion to Christianity, see G. W. Allport, *The Individual and his Religion*, Constable, London, 1951; Elmer T. Clark, *The Psychology of Religious Awakening*, Macmillan, New York, 1929; Wilfred Lawson Jones, *A Psychological Study of Religious Awakening*, Epworth Press, London, 1937; E. D. Starbuck, *The Psychology of Religion*, Walter Scott, London, 1899; Alfred C. Underwood, *Conversion, Christian and Non-Christian*, Allen and Unwin, London, 1925.

usually between thirty and forty. Religious conversion, especially in its swift and emotional forms, is common among women and girls, conversion to secularism is not. Religious conversion often occurs in the group setting of a religious or revival meeting, but the loss of faith was a more individual process produced by solitary reading and thought, or the persuasion of a close friend or family member who was a freethinker.[4] Only eight of the one hundred and fifty secularists mentioned having been converted at a secularist meeting, three of these having been Christians who had gone to oppose Bradlaugh but were won over by his oratory.

Conversions to unbelief were often associated with a change from conservative to more radical politics, or a stronger interest in politics. No secularist is mentioned as having moved towards conservatism or become less politically interested, and two-thirds show some kind of socialist or radical interest. The intertwining of shifts in political beliefs with changing religious allegiances has not been mentioned in studies of conversion to Christianity, and their frequent appearance in secularist biographies, together with the large number of secularists who left the freethought movement to devote their time to politics, suggests that the conversion to unbelief was part of a shift from a religion which was seen as part of established society. For many individuals, secularism was a detour in their movement from religion to left-wing politics. Some secularists thought half the movement had been converted by hearing Bradlaugh speak on politics. But the association with radicalism is not sufficient to explain secularism, since many radicals and socialists remained Christians.

Beyond such a general delineation of the kinds of men who joined secular societies, some more individual causes can be found which had commonly led to their unbelief. These are the reading of the Bible and the classics of radical literature; the realization that Christian doctrines and ministers were wicked or politically reactionary; and the importance of beliefs about death. These causes could all have been intellectual discoveries; for example, Bible-reading could have led to the discovery of factual errors or impossibilities that demolished belief. In many cases it did; but the biographies suggest that what was crucial was the realization that the Bible, minister etc., was *wrong*—i.e. morally wrong.

The many men who saw intellectual errors in religious dogma probably became liberal Christians or syncretists rather than atheists.

---

[4] Twelve of the biographies mention conversion by a friend, workmate or spouse.

To become a secularist, it seems to have been necessary to dislike or fear the religious establishment as well as believing it to be mistaken.

The Causes of Unbelief:

Books

In forty-eight of the fifty-eight cases where influential books were specifically mentioned, one of them was the Bible, or *The Age of Reason*, or both. In the twentieth century Robert Blatchford's *God and My Neighbour* was also influential but Paine still remained a dominant influence, and the last conversion that can be dated that resulted from reading *The Age of Reason* was in 1939.[5] Paine, Blatchford and the Bible can be considered together as having exerted the same kind of influence, since the reasonings mentioned by those secularists who lost their faith by reading the Bible are very like the arguments used by Paine and Blatchford.

One reason for the dominance of the effect of the Bible and *The Age of Reason* must have been their enormous circulation. *The Age of Reason* was a bestseller from publication onwards—Carlile had sold two thousand copies in six months, and a further ten thousand were sold as part of the report of his trial, which was itself printed in most radical newspapers.[6] Both Blatchford and Paine partly owed the wide distribution of their books on religion to their political reputations. *The Age of Reason* was passed round by radical workmen —some freethinkers mentioned having been lent it by a workmate. The National Secular Society, which rightly always regarded *The Age of Reason* as a main agent of conversion, printed an edition of sixty thousand copies in 1937 which was sold out in two years.

In the 1850s and 60s, one pattern of conversion to unbelief appears with remarkable frequency. It is that of the nonconformist, often a Wesleyan, who becomes a class teacher or even a lay preacher, and in studying the Bible closely to prepare lessons from it discovers

---

[5] *God and My Neighbour* was mentioned five times as having been influential in the loss of faith; other authors read were also radical—Carlile, Voltaire, Robert Taylor— whereas only two secularists mentioned having read Darwin or Huxley *before* their loss of faith, and one Strauss' *Leben Jesu*. Many of them, however, found their views confirmed by reading such scientific and philosophical works after they had lost their faith.

[6] W. H. Wickwar, *The Struggle for the Freedom of the Press, 1819-1832*, Allen & Unwin, London, 1928, esp. p. 95.

inconsistencies and absurdities, and finds that he can no longer
regard the Bible as divinely inspired or literally true. The seeds of
doubt once sown, he goes on to consider not only the truth of
Biblical statements but their morality. Paine and many others found
the Bible too shocking to be believed. Theologians had attempted,
he said, to impose the Bible

> as a mass of truth, and as the word of God. They have disputed and wrangled,
> and have anathematized each other about the supposable meaning of particular
> parts and passages therein . . . Now instead of wasting their time, and heating
> themselves in fractious disputations, about doctrinal points drawn from the
> Bible, these men ought to know, and if they do not it is civility to inform them,
> that the first thing to be understood is, whether there is sufficient authority
> for believing the Bible to be the word of God, or whether there is not?
>
> There are matters in that book, said to be done by *the express command* of
> God, that are as shocking to humanity, and to every idea we have of moral
> justice, as anything done by Robespierre, by Carrier, by Joseph le Bon,
> in France; by the English Government in the East Indies; or by any other
> assassin in modern times. When we read in the books ascribed to Moses,
> Joshua etc., that the Israelites came by stealth up to whole nations of people,
> who, as the history itself shows, had given them no offence; *that they put all
> those nations to the sword; that they spared neither age nor infancy; that they
> utterly destroyed men, women and children; that they left not a soul to breathe;*
> expressions that are repeated over and over in those books, and that too with
> exulting ferocity, are we sure these things are facts? Are we sure that the
> Creator of man commissioned these things to be done?

To Paine, and to eighteenth-century religious liberals, it was obvious
that the Creator had not. They abandoned scriptural authority for a
natural religion in which the deity's benevolent intentions were to be
read by his gift of reason in the marvellous design of nature. Some
early secularists moved through a deist phase, but the effect of the
evangelical revival had been to set the scriptures and an emotional
conviction of the truth of Christian doctrine at the centre of religion.
But what if the moral emotions and the scriptures conflicted?

Freethinkers held that the Bible was of poor moral value, as well
as being an inaccurate record of events. In it the good were not
rewarded, in fact they were often gratuitously punished. It encouraged men to divert their attention from improving the lives of
themselves and mankind to a future life. Their attitude to the teachings of the New Testament varied from that of Leicester Secular
Society, who considered Jesus a great moral teacher and placed his
bust outside their secular hall with Paine and Socrates, to those who
considered most of his teaching immoral. Their criticisms, like

those of Paine and Blatchford, were simple and intuitively acceptable with a strong element of social criticism. One man thought that the Bible had too much blood in it. Joseph Symes, a local preacher at a Wesleyan College found that his faith was being sapped 'not as the result of "Infidel" reading, but arose from my study of the Bible itself'.

Later in the nineteenth century, the moral objections were supplemented by a more prudish one. When Mrs Annie Besant was sued by her husband for the return of their child in 1878, one reason given was that she corrupted her daughter's morals by not allowing her to read those parts of the Old Testament which she considered obscene and unfit for children. An otherwise unsympathetic judge agreed with her on this point.[7] The president of the National Secular Society pointed out in 1912 that

> The Bible is, at least in parts, an obscene book. The lowest animal functions are often called by their vulgar names; there are frequent, and sometimes very brutal, references to the generative organs; the stories of lust, adultery, incest aud unnatural vice are enough to raise blushes in a brothel. And occasionally, as in the Song of Solomon, the most passionate eroticism is decked out with the most voluptuous imagery . . .

'Bible-bashing' has been the main method of attack used by open-air secularist speakers to the present day. To induce doubt in the Bible was to remove the keystone from the arch of faith. Arthur B. Moss, an active propagandist, judged in 1887 that 'The usual road by which individuals in this country become Secularists, is, first, scepticism in regard to the alleged truth of some of the Bible statements; second, doubt in regard to all alleged revelations; third, doubt as to the existence of the Bible God; fourth, doubt as to the existence of a personal God at all; fifth, disbelief in all of the above; . . .'

Another simple observation, equally independent of any knowledge of science or of biblical criticism, was 'the opposition between the different sects of Christians, afterwards at the deadly hatred between the Jews, Christians, Mahomedans, Hindoos, Chinese, and c., and c., and between these and what they called Pagans and Infidels.' The very zeal with which each religion proclaimed its unique truth induced doubt in men as separated in time as Robert Owen and a freethinker writing in 1960.[8]

---

[7] Nethercot, *The First Five Lives*, op. cit., p. 136.
[8] *Freethinker*, 6 November 1887, p. 359; Robert Owen, op. cit., p. 3; and W. E. Huxley, who thought he had been converted by his experiences of Islam, *Freethinker*, February 1960, p. 43.

The Immorality of Christian Doctrines and Ministers

The loss of faith was often a painful experience. In the nineteenth century, and to a lesser extent in the twentieth, the self-confessed atheist was subject to social handicaps—he might be turned out of his home or his lodgings, be refused jobs, find his trade declining and be ostracized by parents and friends. One Balham landlady 'would rather have a confirmed drunkard, or have the place empty for seven years, than have an infidel'. In the nineteenth century, the poor could be intruded on while dying by Christian missionaries making a last attempt to save their souls.[9] The loss of faith was serious and unpleasant for metaphysical reasons as well—fears of a lonely and meaningless universe, or of obliteration at death. Thus those who for some reason began to doubt often consulted a priest or minister, and held that the treatment they received turned them against the church. Accounts of this kind may often have been exaggerated but those in relatively defenceless positions, as the poor and children were, seem to have been brusquely treated in comparison to the seriousness with which the doubts of the well-educated were handled.

Freethinkers sometimes came to see particular priests or ministers as immoral or hypocritical without having had previous doubts, and this became strong enough to carry them out of religion altogether. Often it was their realization of the shaky props on which revealed religion rested that made them turn against the priests who concealed the truth and pretended to special knowledge.

When Austin Holyoake began to discuss Robert Owen's doctrines with his brother and sisters, his faith began to falter. 'My belief in the infallibility of the Bible first gave way. Soon after commenced my disbelief in the possession of any special knowledge on the part of the preachers of the gospel of God and immortality of which they talked so glibly.' The priest's actions alone could lead to religious doubt. One child at a Catholic school was asked after a lecture on the nature of priesthood what he should do if a priest hit him. He was punished for answering that he would hit him back, and having lost faith in priests, at a later age lost his faith in Catholicism.[10] Another freethinker provides the only case of instantaneous conversion from Christianity to atheism, which took place at a famous

---

[9] *Freethinker*, 17 September 1882, p. 295. Attempts at death-bed conversion are commonly cited in the obituaries and elsewhere—one of the most recent was in 1957, *The Humanist*, August 1957, p. 27.

[10] Maurice Davies, *The Sun*, 25 April 1974, p. 20; Michael Blake in *Freethinker*, 23 September 1928, p. 620. His belief in God was destroyed by *God and My Neighbour*.

revivalist meeting at Aldershot. The preacher was grandiose and the peroration on salvation high-flown and emotional, and the young man suddenly saw himself as a sentimental fool. Alone, he refused to stand and be saved at the end, and immediately his friends drew away from him. To the preacher's questions, he replied that faith required reason as well as emotion; the revivalist denied that reason was necessary. He was rejected as an infidel, and the resultant social ostracism was so strong in his small local community that he was forced to leave Aldershot, and drifted into popular scepticism in London.[11]

Connected with the moral protest about the behaviour of priests was a moral protest about Christian doctrine as a whole. Freethinkers attacked it either as morally barbarous and a relic of primitive society, or thought that the teachings of Christ were acceptable initally but had been denied and distorted by the established churches. The weight of feeling behind the attack on Christianity was not that it was untrue but that it was wicked. One freethinker said, 'I lost my faith in Christianity because it conflicted with my own standards of right and wrong. In short, it wasn't good enough for my conscience.'

Christianity and Politics

Most secularists believed that religion contained nothing of value to humanity and that the churches' effect on political life was only to support corrupt ruling groups and reactionary policies. Priests were not only supporting a system of false beliefs, but were acting in the interests of the ruling classes by keeping the poor quiescent. The connection between secularism and radicalism seems to have brought men into the secular movement rather than caused their loss of faith, but often they both sprang from a common root in working-class thought and organization.

J. C. Farn, for instance, who related his life story in 1857, had been born to poor dissenting parents, but his father (who read the *Black Dwarf*) had been radical and anti-clerical. After an apprentice-ship to their harsh and tyrannical local preacher, Farn was introduced to radical literature by his workmates and joined the National Trade Union. He became convinced that poverty was a great social evil and that its cause lay in drink, which rendered the trades union move-ment ineffectual since its meetings were held in public houses. He

[11] *Freethinker*, 10 July 1921, p. 444.

joined a temperance movement, but his visits to the homes of the
poor convinced him that poverty was not solely due to drunkeness
but that both were a product of the factory system and lack of
education of the poor. He discovered arguments to be more effective
than religion in enabling drunkards to reform. He became very
opposed to the parsons and Christian workers in the temperance
movement, since they saw salvation as the remedy for poverty. He
came to London and educated himself at Birkbeck in order to
educate the poor, and to further this end became a social missionary
in the Owenite movement. His interests had become purely secular
and political, and the final link with methodism, his fear of hell-fire,
was broken when he read Charles Watts' book disproving the
existence of a future life; at the disintegration of Owenism he
moved on to free thought.

Later in the nineteenth century Charles Cattell, who had been
brought up Church and Tory, came from the Warwickshire
countryside to a Birmingham factory. He was preparing lessons for
his Sunday School class when he found biblical statements which
converted him *simultaneously* to liberalism, republicanism and freethought. Later still Joseph Bryce related in 1938 that when he had
doubted the doctrine of eternal punishment through reading more
liberal religious literature produced by the Anglicans, he revealed
this at his Presbyterian Bible class and was denounced by his
teachers and evicted by the minister. After joining and leaving
various other denominations he began to preach socialism to the
Church of Christ, for which he was ejected. His only remaining
religious belief was in the existence of God, but he became an atheist
after reading a secularist journal for its political views.[12]

For many freethinkers, unbelief was part of a general rejection
of conservative and established authority, but the movement had
little close contact with left-wing groups, whose leaders of whatever
religious persuasion were unwilling to forfeit the support of the
Christian majority. The number of militant and organized atheists
was always too small to make their support important. Even
Blatchford and the group who worked with him on the *Clarion*,
whilst they supported the Labour Churches and wanted to create a
religion of socialism could not do so because 'we had feared to
retard the advance of Socialism by mixing the acrimonies of religious

---

[12] J. C. Farn, *Reasoner*, 16 September 1857, p. 197 and subsequent issues; *Truthseeker*, December 1895, pp. 1–2; *National Reformer*, 23 March 1890, pp. 187–8; *Freethinker*, 1 May 1938, pp. 282–3.

controversy with our propaganda'. Those freethinkers who worked for other reform movements found that it was politic not to alienate support by mentioning atheism.[13]

Many freethinkers began by doubting religious authority and moved on to attack political and economic authority, but even though their loss of faith was permanent, they found a positive ethic in their political beliefs rather than in secularism and did not remain active in the movement.

Death

In nineteenth-century England, the emotional core of evangelical protestantism was the atonement, that act which had joined God and man in suffering and its consolation. The act of unbelief was in itself a rejection of the message of salvation and meant eternal punishment, whereas a sufficiently strong belief, it was somehow assumed, led one to die in a way which was itself a proof of salvation. The moral importance attached to the act of individual choice was echoed again in the doctrine of personal immortality. Arguments and assertions about death were consequently widely used by Christians to illustrate the failure of atheism as a philosophy at life's most searching moment, and by secularists to show how Christian lies about the after-life kept men in ignoble subjection. Death was an event of much greater social significance than it was to become after the First World War. It was more frequent—the crude death rate was halved between 1880 and 1935—and it was more emotionally and financially disruptive since, especially among the poor, relatively more children and young adults died. (The mortality rate of children under one fell from about 154 per thousand in 1900 to 57 per thousand in 1935.) The process of dying was openly discussed, and death-beds were an important theme in novels and moral homilies. In this context, the *Argument from Death-Bed Repentance* of anti-infidel lecturers was a powerful weapon.

The amount of discussion of death-bed literature in freethought

---

[13] Blatchford had reviewed Ernst Haeckel's *The Riddle of the Universe* very favourably in 1903, announcing that science had conquered religion. This had cost him so many *Clarion* readers and offended so many labour leaders that he was forced to drop all anti-theological material, A. Thompson, *Here I Lie*, Routledge, London, 1937, p. 105. 'Education, Temperance Societies, political and social reforms, Malthusianism, Science, art, morality, etc., are in the main manifestations of growing Secularism replacing religious follies, but Atheists who take prominent part in such work find it only wise and just and courteous to drop the Theological dispute when engaged in carrying out such movements.' W. P. Ball, *Freethinker*, 7 February 1886, p. 47.

journals is very striking until the end of the century, but such literature was important. Fr. Furniss, who produced lavishly illustrated and sadistic accounts of hell-fire as tracts for children, sold over four *million* copies.[14] It was assumed that the approach of death revealed truth; men's last words were peculiarly significant, and thus the frequent assertion that secularists jested at death had to be carefully disproved. Bradlaugh spent much time in denying that he had defied God to strike him dead in five minutes. Here is the argument in use at a secularist's lecture in 1860:

> On Sunday evening, Christopher Charles in the chair, a crowded audience attended the Odd-Fellows Hall, to hear Mr. Barker on the 'Sunday Question', and applauded him throughout, with few exceptions. Some little confusion was occasioned by men delivering tracts which told what an Infidel Captain (whom Mr. Barker said never had a daughter) told his daughter in his last hour. The Religious Tract Society have made infidels say many queer things, but I never before heard that they had spoken to young ladies who never existed![15]

The commonest form of the argument was to cite a supposedly real case of an atheist or indifferent Christian who refused to mend his ways until the approach of death brought him to realize the truth. Sometimes this was too late. In a popular book of tracts on his mission work in the East End, the Rev. C. J. Whitmore told the story of a blind secularist who, having fallen ill, at first had refused to see him but then repented. His death-bed was described in lurid detail.

> The strong form was struggling and writhing, and every feature was distorted and wrung with the intensity of his suffering. Heavy perspiration poured from his face; and his hands were clasped and working convulsively on the coverlet of the bed. 'O God! O God!' he groaned out between his pangs. 'I have deserved it, I know I have; but be merciful! be merciful! . . .'
>
> Trembling and horror-striken, the visitor drew near and knelt by the side of the bed, intending to pour out his heart in prayer; while the suffering man endeavoured to stifle his groaning and crying, that he might hear and join in the supplications. But as the visitor knelt, and his face sank upon his hands, there came upon him a cold and awful feeling that it was useless to pray; it seemed to him verily as if God had closed up heaven, and would not hear. . . .

[14] D. G. Rowell, *Death and the Future Life in the Religious Thought of Nineteenth Century England*, Cambridge Ph.D. Thesis, 1968, p. 301, on which much of this section is based. Geoffrey Gorer (*Death, Grief and Mourning*, Cresset Press, London, 1965) argues that death ceased to be a topic for social discussion in England during the 1920s.

[15] See that gadfly, G. B. Shaw, on the social reaction to 'Defying the Lightning—a Frustrated Experiment', in the Preface of *Back to Methuselah*; *Reasoner*, 29 July 1860, p. 122.

At length the cries and struggling ceased. But the end had come. 'I am in awful pain' groaned the blind man, 'but that is nothing to the agony of my mind. There all is darkness—no light! no hope! no God!' And thus he died.[16]

Alternatively, the infidel might have repented in time, in which case his death was made easier. The story of Richard D. illustrates the identification of infidelity, immorality, and politically subversive opinions.

Richard D. had been a careful hardworking man, and had laboured diligently to maintain respectability of condition. Unhappily he had adopted infidel principles, and these operated like a blight upon his welfare, and exercised their usual influence over his temper, for misery is the certain fruit of infidelity . . . His principles rendered him discontented and unhappy. He was perpetually railing against the Government, finding fault with the existing scheme of things, indulging bitter feelings toward all who were in circumstances superior to his own, and holding up everything religious to ridicule and scorn. Ministers of the Gospel were the objects of his peculiar dislike, to whom he invariably ascribed the most unworthy motives . . .

When Richard had been married about eight years, his health began to fail, and symptoms of consumption appeared . . . His principles were now put to the test. We know what Christianity has done in similar circumstances; it has sustained man in every species of sorrow. All in every age and condition who have confided in this Divine Consolation have found it a sustaining system, and a bright angel of mercy. But here infidelity utterly fails. If you visit the sceptic in sickness you will see in his careworn countenance and heavy look the sign of his distress . . . infidelity has no consolation to impart—it is a cold comfortless system, unsuited to man at all times, and especially unsuited to him in the time of his woe . . . the doctrines of the Gospel were, therefore, placed more forcibly before him, and faithful appeals made to his observation and experience for their confirmation . . . This was the turning-point in his experience . . .

Richard's bodily sufferings increased with the progress of the disease, but so soon as he began to exercise faith in the truths of revelation, and especially in the great doctrine of the Atonement, he became a partaker of Divine supports and consolations . . .

The closing scene presented satisfactory evidence of his entire confidence in the great truths of the Gospel, and especially of his firm trust in Christ, as well as of that change of heart with which true faith is always accompanied . . .

This case is one among many . . .[17]

Popular ideas about death influenced conversion to unbelief in two ways. Many freethinkers first began to doubt the morality of

[16] G. J. Whitemore, 'Blind, Body and Soul', from *Seeking the Lost, Incidents and Sketches of Christian Work in London*, Nisbet, London, 1876, pp. 239-40. For an infidel engine-driver who dies without repenting, see 'I cannot find the brake!', *British Workman*, June 1874, p. 215.
[17] T. H. W., 'The Conquered Infidel', *British Workman*, September 1872, p. 131. Another instance, 'The Smuggler's Death-Bed', in *British Workman*, No. 16, 1856, p. 62.

religion because of Christian doctrines concerned with death and the way in which such doctrines were used to check questions, and many who had lost any positive commitment to Christianity remained nominal believers through fear of death and hell. When for some reason this fear was removed they left the church and sometimes became secularists.

Percy Ward's account of his conversion was unusually detailed in that it gave the *order* in which he had relinquished dogma. Born into a Yorkshire family of methodist local preachers, he was saved at fourteen and became a speaker for the Christian Evidence Society. He lost his faith in eternal punishment because he was unable to believe in a God who had created earthly fathers more forgiving than himself. At eighteen, a methodist trial preacher, he received a shock to his faith when he read *The Age of Reason*, which convinced him that even atheists might be good men. While he was working as a local preacher his doubts increased, and in studying comparative religion he realized Christianity to be morally less advanced than many other religions. He rejected in turn doctrines of the Trinity, original sin, the atonement, salvation by faith, damnation for unbelief, heaven and hell, and unwillingly came to consider the Christian church to be the enemy of all human progress. He still wished to believe and prayed that he might be able to accept these doctrines to test the practical power of prayer. This failed and in 1895 he left the Methodist church. He lost his remaining faith in a personal God and individual immortality, and in the following year joined the National Secular Society.[18]

The Fear of Hell

When secularists named the Christian doctrines they found most objectionable, they were almost always those of eternal punishment, hell, the Atonement, and damnation for unbelievers. As Paine had felt as a child, these doctrines conjured up to them the picture of a God who was remorselessly punitive and morally more barbarous than mankind. The liberal and humanitarian temper of nineteenth-century England found such doctrines increasingly intolerable. Holyoake, for example, remembered how his own belief had been shaken when he saw how upset his mother had been, who had buried several of her children, when he had gone with her to the

---

[18] *Freethinker*, 1 January 1911, pp. 10-13; *Truthseeker*, March 1901, pp. 1-2.

Baptist chapel to hear the pastor preaching that there were unbaptized children in Hell 'not a span long'. The theological reaction to such moral revulsion was partly to widen the category of those who were saved, partly to emphasize that the grounds of salvation were in effect moral—that even heathens who were virtuous might at least escape hell—and partly to cast all such doctrines in a more personal and allegorical light. The close associations which were made in popular theology between a God who allocated men to hell and heaven and the ranking of the social and moral order (prostitutes et cetera were *ipso facto* excluded from the rewards of the righteous) came to seem increasingly abhorrent. Theologians realized that the use of the threat of hell as an agent of social control was alienating large numbers of working and even middle-class people, many of whom turned in the 1850s to an interest in spiritualism as a more acceptable and scientific eschatology.[19]

By 1880, infallibilist interpretations of Scripture had largely been abandoned, and the main drift of theological debate was over whether there was a future life at all. The post-Darwinian attack on the special status of man in creation and the erosion of the Cartesian dualism of body and soul led to increasing doubt about all doctrines of personal immortality. By the early twentieth century, samplings of popular opinion showed that religion had been ethicized. Most people had abandoned a scriptural hell for a vague belief in an unspecific afterlife, regulated not by religious beliefs but by behaviour. The pastors and officers who sampled the opinions of their men during the First World War were affronted to find that they were not prepared to accept that their suffering and sacrifice were ennobled and explained by the suffering of Christ. They no longer saw sacrifice as a moral act—surely 'the proof of some deep and strange misunderstanding?'[20] In view of the profound changes in theology during this period, it is odd to find that the proportion of freethinkers who mention being led to unbelief through dislike of teaching about death and hell does not decrease over time. Most of them were taught the doctrines at school; perhaps they were fading from the adult world but were still being retailed to children.

[19] See Rowell, op. cit., and D. P. Walker, *The Decline of Hell*, Routledge, London 1964, both of whom trace the modifications of belief in hell as occuring in the theology of the liberal denominations in the early years of the century and beginning in more conservative circles around the 1860s or so.
[20] A. C. Cairns, op. cit., p. 60; and see W. L. Courtney's *Do We Believe?*, an analysis of correspondence on this topic in the *Daily Mail* in 1904. The Broad Church philosophy that beliefs were less important than acts had become the dominant Anglican view.

Secularists held that most *de facto* atheists or agnostics were still nominal Christians not only because of the social consequences of open atheism but because of fear of the possibility of hell. Much secularist propaganda was aimed to remove the fear. Perhaps the most effective argument was used by Paine, who held the Judgement Day concept to be ridiculous; men could not be divided into sheep and goats because the moral world, like the physical one, contained gradations, most men being neither good nor bad.

> My own opinion is that those whose lives have been spent in doing good and endeavouring to make their fellow-mortals happy—for this is the only way in which we can serve God—*will be happy hereafter*; and after that the very wicked will meet with some punishment. But those who are neither good nor bad, or are not too insignificant for notice, will be dropped entirely. This is my opinion. It is consistent with my idea of God's justice, and with the reason that God has given me . . .

Many secularists wrote on the subject, perhaps the most widely read being G. J. Holyoake's *The Logic of Death* (1851) which sold fifty thousand copies. The arguments used were conditional enough to be nearly invincible.[21] Salvation, if there was such a thing, was not by faith but by works, i.e. helping one's follow-men. The best guide to securing an improbable future life was not that recommended by priests, who had no more knowledge than anyone else, but that shown us by reason and the natural world, both given as guides by a putative God. God either did not exist or was morally good, and in both events men should help their fellow creatures, the aim dictated by a purely utilitarian ethic. A good life in terms of a secular ethic was therefore the most effective insurance against hell. If God was evil or amoral, a rational man owed him no allegiance, since moral judgements were supreme. As John Watts expressed it,

> What if there be a heaven above,
> A God of truth, and light, and love?
> Will He condemn us? It was He
> Who gave the light that failed to see!
> If he be just who reigns on high,
> Why should the Atheist fear to die?

This kind of propaganda did detach some from religion, but it acted more to still the doubts of those already in the movement.

[21] G. T. Holyoake, *The Logic of Death, Or, Why Should the Atheist fear to Die?*, J. Watson, London, 1851; Chapman Cohen, *The Other Side of Death*, Pioneer Press, London, 1902; G. W. Foote and A. D. McClaren, *Infidel Death Beds*, Pioneer Press, London, 1933.

Freethinkers seem mainly to have lost their belief in hell through a sense of moral outrage, or by contact with a more liberal theology. One case showed clearly the importance that beliefs about hell could have in determining religious allegiance. Clark had been a deeply religious Anglican, who at sixteen was very upset by a hell-fire sermon he heard at a chapel meeting. He became more and more disturbed until his conversion to Primitive Methodism, and then went to Spurgeon's College and Glasgow University to train for the ministry. Whilst at Glasgow in the more liberal atmosphere of the upper ranks of the denomination, he heard ministers condemning eternal punishment as unethical. His initial enormous relief at this became alarm as he realized that his faith was slipping away. He tried hard by Bible reading to suppress his doubts, but could find no evidence for Christ's divinity. He was forced by his rapidly advancing opinions to leave first the Baptist and then the Unitarian ministry, and in 1883 left religion altogether and drifted to unbelief.[22]

Some of the freethinkers who described their loss of belief in hell felt an initial euphoria and freedom analogous to the Christian's joy at conversion, but in the case of the secularist it was usually succeeded by unhappiness at the social consequences of atheism.

Unrecognized Causes

From this unsystematic material, no firm conclusions can be drawn as to what the determining factors were which made these men lose their belief in God. The causes discussed above were those that the individuals concerned thought had influenced them. But as well as these conscious reasons for their loss of faith, there must have been many factors in their background and experience which predisposed them towards it of which they were unaware.[23] Some facts emerge from the biographies on which interpretations may be laid. These

[22] *National Reformer*, 1 June 1890, pp. 348–9, and subsequent issues.
[23] Some men, thinking back, could not remember why they had become secularists. Mr Wilson, speaking to Northampton Secular Society on 'How I became a Secularist', cites many of the influences other secularists encountered—the influence of workmates, the failure of the preacher—but his sunny disposition protected him from the usual solitary struggle. 'Mr Wilson said he could not tell how he became a Secularist. He was a Sunday School teacher, but this was because he liked people being brought together. He was a sceptic when at Sunday School. He did not attend Freethought lectures, but heard them discussed in the shop by working men. These discussions impressed him, he applied to his Pastor for advice, was accused of "Infidelity" and told not to worry about such things. He went to London and heard Owen lecture, which he enjoyed so much that he often went to the John Street Institution and gradually became a confirmed Secularist', *National Reformer*, 3 July 1870, p. 15.

cannot be very certain, since neither these circumstances nor contradictory instances would be thought to be important by the actors, and would not have been systematically included.

In the case of conversion *to* religious belief, social pressures can clearly be seen at work. The revival campaign is designed to bring many forces to bear upon its participants; approval and love for the saved, ostracism for the unrepentant. The birth of religious belief drew men into society and provided them with links which could lead to social esteem and success, as Christian proselytizers were quick to point out. For the man who lost his faith the process was reversed, and very few of these cases could be described as a response to social pressures. The causes of conversion to atheism seem rather to have lain in a relative isolation from social pressures—a strongly individual personality, a sense of being outside respectable society, or resenting it, or merely having become relatively detached from the opinions of family and friends. Such factors are suggested by the details from many biographies.

Secularists seem to have been relatively detached from close links with their families and local communities. Over half of this group of one hundred and fifty men had moved long distances during their lives, often from rural or small-town areas to large towns, notably London.[24] A few mentioned that they were forced to move because of the ostracism they suffered, or alternatively that it was as a result of moving that they came into contact with other beliefs, including radicalism and secularism. Migrants generally are likely to stop church-going, or experiment and join new and less orthodox religious groups. The declining social pressure to go to church is reflected in the fact that no twentieth-century freethinker mentioned it, except for two ex-Catholics from areas with strong Catholic communities.

It was mainly those who had been actively and sincerely religious who were converted to secularism. As a secularist proselytizer remarked, 'It is the hardest thing in the world to convert a "Nothingarian" to Freethought. A much easier task is to convert a sincere believer in Christianity, or for a matter of that, a sincere believer in anything.' As secularization or at least the non-practice of religion

---

[24] Secularists were probably more likely to have moved than the rest of the male working-class population, but in the nineteenth century migration, especially into towns, was very common but has not been precisely assessed. See A. Redford, *Labour Migration in England 1790–1850*, Manchester University Press, Manchester, 1964, pp. 62–7 and 183, and E. J. Hobsbawm, 'The Tramping Artisan', *Labouring Men*, Weidenfeld & Nicolson, London 1964, pp. 39–46. Migration and change of beliefs were sometimes regarded as linked by the secularists themselves.

proceeded in England, the available pool of active Christians to convert became smaller, although the secularists were always a fraction of their number. Whole communities seemed to react against a religious overdose, as in the rapid recruitment of secularists in the aftermath of the South Wales revivals. But these have been the last grass-roots revivals in Britain.

The reaction against overbearing ministers was another aspect of the process of recruitment only from those who had had close contact with religious institutions. As ministers lost much of their social prestige and education passed out of their control, fewer people found their lives so controlled by the demands of organized religion as to make them react against it. But a few occupations and situations remain where religious compliance is socially reinforced, and these seem to have been a major source of the secular movement's twentieth-century membership. Catholicism, the major twentieth-century source of recruits, demanded until very recently explicit conformity with church discipline on matters over which other major denominations had ceased to try to exert control. This is especially so in countries where the Catholic hierarchy has secular backing, resulting in migrant Irish secularists and even secularists from Italy and Malta. During the twentieth century and especially after the Second World War the ideal-typical picture of the methodist class teacher, studying his Bible and finding there gospel discrepancies and immoralities that make him lose his faith, is succeeded by another. This is of the child in the Catholic school who finds himself in revolt against the church and priesthood because they tell him things he knows scientists to have disproved, prevent his reading science or politics prejudicial to their views, or justify unfairness or hypocrisy by reference to religion.[25] During the two world wars, a number of secularists were recruited from the armed forces who were irked by enforced religious affiliation and compulsory church parades.

Another factor leading to unbelief suggested by some obituaries was conflict within the family. The view that religion is the product of a search for authority with God as a father-figure would presumably imply that atheism is partly due to the rejection of authority, especially of the father. Few secularist biographies are revealing enough to include this kind of information, but rebelling against a father was apparent in some of the more detailed biographies. Family

[25] See, for example, A. T. Brown, rebuked for saying men were descended from apes, *Freethinker*, 28 September 1962, p. 311, and many other letters and reports in that year.

conflict may also have accounted for the disproportionate number of secularist leaders who were the sons of ministers, or, in Mrs Besant's case, the wife of one. Several leaders and members had themselves been priests or ministers, and retrospectively some thought that they had been forced into the church by family pressure. Such transitions may seem dramatic, but when men accustomed to a ministerial role lost their faith and thereby their occupation, it involved a minimum shift for them to take up a similar position, but in an anti-clerical organization.[26]

In some cases, unbelief may have been part of the reaction to blocked upward social mobility. Many nineteenth-century secularists were obviously able and had attempted extensive self-improvement, but were still unskilled manual workers. This may partly account for the number of secularists who were miners, an occupation in which the chances of social betterment were very low indeed. The resultant sense of the injustice of society may have led them to attack its religion and social hypocrisy rather than its economic arrangements. Several secularists mentioned that it was the personal handicaps which barred them from social acceptance that made them become freethinkers. One was illegitimate and felt this put him outside respectable society; one was a secularist because his mother had left his crooked foot unoperated on, on the grounds it was God's will.

The Decline of Authority

The conclusions that can be drawn as to why this group of men lost faith in Christianity cannot be extended to cover the general decline of religion during the last hundred years, which has been partly a modification of belief but mainly the decline of support for religious institutions. But freethinkers, whilst they represented only a small proportion of all English atheists and agnostics were, even if atypical, at least more numerous than the intellectuals and scientists on whom discussion is often based. There were far more nineteenth-century working-class agnostics and atheists than middle-class, and a large number of these passed through or were casually associated with the secular movement. The loss of faith for these men rested on extreme individualism; an often anomic social

---

[26] Priests changing between organizations but unknowingly retaining the same role appear strikingly in D. R. Davies, *In Search of Myself*, Geoffrey Bles, London, 1962, and John T. Lloyd, *From Christian Pulpit to Secular Platform*, n.p., London, 1903.

situation; radical or socialist involvement and a strong moral sense. These causes were not sufficient nor even always necessary; but the revolution in scientific and theological thinking seems largely irrelevant. The loss of faith was not an intellectual but a moral matter.

One of the striking features of this picture of the experiences and impulses that led to the loss of faith is the extent to which they are timeless. Priests and parsons had long complained of the indifference of even rural working-men to religion, and the impulse to deny God must be as old as the belief in him. 'The Commissioner will have hard work with the Scotch atheists,' wrote Sydney Smith, in 1818; 'they are said to be numerous this season, and in great force, from the irregular supply of rain.' But the loss of faith did become a more common, lasting and self-confidently asserted experience. If the arguments for the existence of God did not change, why did an increasing number of men have the confidence to reject the authority of the church? At the heart of the process lies a changed attitude to authority, a rejection of tradition and a demand that all knowledge be made 'conformable to the moral sense'.

6 RATIONALISM AND THE RELIGION OF SCIENCE

> One of the most vigorous enterprises of the nineteenth and twentieth centuries has been the creation of a mythology of science—not in the invidious sense of a collection of lies, but of a compression of experience and dogma into symbols.
>
> Donald Fleming, *John William Draper and the Religion of Science*

The Rationalist Press Association was and is a limited company concerned with the promotion of rationalism through the distribution of cheap books and magazines, both to the subscribing members of the organization and to the general public. The complex dialogue within the other humanist movements as to what their goals are and how they may be reached, and the relationship between the dialogue and the social experience of the members has here largely been lacking or remained for the most part private and unrecorded. The Association has known little about its members, and has seen itself as providing them with a service in producing books at low cost, many of which initially were too controversial to be readily published elsewhere. Through its contacts with influential rationalists and humanists it developed into an informal pressure group, and through conferences, dinners, and journals it has tried to mould and promote a general philosophy. This philosophy, protean and uncertain in its outlines, has as one of its central elements a belief in science.

The major difficulty in trying to describe both the ideology of the Association and the philosophies of science with which it has been tangentially concerned lies in the very centrality of these beliefs—scientific humanism—to the beliefs which most influential members of British society hold. With few exceptions, such as the belief in the possibility of a synthetic philosophy and the importance of ceasing to rely on religious explanations, it is difficult to say where the views of the Association end and those of an educated twentieth-century Englishman of vaguely progressive inclinations begin. The very central and general quality of these ideas makes them complex and difficult to identify; their distinguishing mark, perhaps, is the greater articulateness, forcefulness and confidence with which the rationalist holds them.

It has frequently been observed that whilst we have many excellent studies of fringe movements, sects and parties, the majority bodies and traditions with their ambiguous, complex and familiar doctrines are because of their very closeness to us too camouflaged to be seen clearly. When members of a society can rely on holding certain assumptions in common, they need never mention them. The gaps between the ideas of a philosopher, said Russell, are the clue to his passions; this chapter attempts to describe not the ideas but the gaps.

The Rationalist Press has never had more than six thousand members, but the set of ideas which it tries to articulate and reinforce are in many of their aspects the most dominant ideology in British society. The Association has not acted as a social movement with a distinctive set of ideas and aims but as an organization which tries to increase the influence of a certain way of looking at the world by presenting a body of information from which, it is believed, certain conclusions will inescapably emerge. Many of the Association's members have probably seen it pre-eminently as a source of cheap books on science, ethics and the social sciences. The books which have been perennial bestsellers in the Thinker's Library series are an odd blend of radical classics—*The Age of Reason*, *The Rights of Man*, Ingersoll's *Liberty of Man*, works of science—*The Descent of Man*, *Psychology for Everyman*, and works which blend science and personal philosophy—H. G. Wells' *Short History of the World*, Mill's *On Liberty* and *Religion Without Revelation*. The ideas and philosophies which are contained in these and all the other works published by the Association add up to most of the science, philosophy and ethics of the last century. To assess this history far exceeds the scope of this book and of its author.

Despite such difficulties, there is no doubt that many members of the Association have seen it as a definite entity with distinct non-commercial aims, and as representing not only a particular variety of humanism but a particular sort of unbeliever, the middle-class materialist. As in the Left Book Club of the late 1930s, membership implies more than the formal connection. The beliefs and aims of members are made explicit and reinforced through occasional meetings and the letter-page of the journal. On very slender evidence, some of the members of the Association have seemed to resemble more closely than other humanists do the stereotype of the hard-headed, emotionless and positivist atheist. The Association has also been an agent in the dissemination of scientific knowledge on a popular level and of the associated ethic of *scientism* which has been so characteristic of our era.

Whilst there can be no doubt that science—or the image of science—has come to affect our view of the world as profoundly as it has affected our material experience in it, the process of isolating our views, intuitions and myths about science, and the ways in which we have learnt about them and made them part of our most instinctive assumptions, has hardly begun. Our lack of knowledge makes it impossible to assess how far the interest in science and the interpretations which were made of its nature and purpose inside the rationalist group have differed from the way in which all those who were broadly favourable to and interested in science have conceived of it. The Rationalist Press provides a reflection of the general process, but it is a distorted one. Unless we know how other groups outside the scientific establishment conceived of science, to define the characteristic views of the rationalist is to try to make bench-marks on a not yet visible surface. One way to begin is to describe the origins of the Association itself.

The Origins of the Rationalist Press

The history of the Association has been largely that of the Watts family. Charles Albert Watts founded the Association, and on retiring as managing director was succeeded by his son Frederick, who died in 1953 whilst vice-chairman of the Association. Charles Albert was the son of the secularist leader Charles Watts, who had been a friend of Holyoake. Charles had come to London as a young man to join his brother John, who edited Bradlaugh's journal the *National Reformer* and acted as printer to the freethought movement. Charles became a full-time lecturer for the National Secular Society in 1868, and after his brother's death took over the proprietorship of the *National Reformer* and his position as printer to the Society. After he had quarrelled with Bradlaugh over the Knowlton trial, he became the editor and printer of the journal produced by the rival Holyoake/Foote faction, but unlike them never rejoined the National Secular Society. He had apprenticed his son Charles Albert to Holyoake's brother Austin, who had also been a sub-editor on the *National Reformer* and was a printer and bookseller. There he became well versed in the business aspects of publishing freethought writings, and on Austin's death took over the business.

In 1885 Watts founded *The Agnostic*, a short-lived journal devoted to the thought of Herbert Spencer whom, in common with many contemporaries, Watts regarded with almost religious veneration. (His opinions were seen in such an *ex cathedra* light by religious liberals that when he began to talk about an Unknowable Creator of Space [and using capitals was a sign that these entities were being reified by mid-Victorians] John Morley was sufficiently worried by this 'weakening of Agnostic orthodoxy' to travel down to Brighton to remonstrate.) Watts was also engaged in a more literal attempt to deify Spencer in the services held at the Agnostic Temple in South London.[1] In the same year he founded the *Agnostic Annual* to explain and defend agnosticism, and *Watts' Literary Guide*, a guide and recommendation to the work of 'advanced' thinkers with summaries of their views. This was to prove a more successful venture because it met the need of a lower-middle class and working-class public unable to read most of this literature, since because of their controversial nature arguments were often couched in the most learned and qualified terms, and the books in which they appeared were often very expensive and excluded from public libraries.

The conditions for publishing were changing. The repeal of the paper duty in the 1860s and the spread of literacy had led to a rapid increase in the amount of popular literature. A large number of periodicals were established at every level of intellectual sophistication which actively discussed the latest developments in science, philosophy and ethics. Most of the leading scientists and thinkers of the day contributed to these discussions, and to the twentieth-century observer it is striking, despite the active controversies which men felt divided them so deeply, how unified a cosmos they present. In part this was because science was only on the verge of becoming intellectually differentiated from the rest of knowledge—the British Association could still present the significant developments of the last year to an educated audience. The 'Man of Letters' was a real entity, embodied at his most powerful and successful in the culture of the great editors and essayists described by John Gross,[2] and at his most desperate in the poverty-stricken scholars of *New Grub Street* and the strivings of some of Trollope's intelligent women, who like his mother had turned to writing in the search for financial independence.

[1] J. Morley, *Recollections*, Vol. 1, Macmillan, London, 1917, p. 114; *The Agnostic Annual* for 1885, p. 54.
[2] J. Gross, *The Rise and Fall of the Man of Letters—English Literary Life Since 1800* Weidenfeld & Nicolson, London, 1969.

Yet another source of the intellectual unity of Victorian middle-class culture was the extent to which all new ideas and knowledge were discussed within the context of natural theology. The increase in popular reading material had been at first mainly an increase in theology, the most popular reading matter of the 1860s.[3] However much or little individual scientists may have desired it, in the discussion of their ideas one can always hear the anxious voices behind the formal arguments. What will this do to religious belief? Is it reconcilable with nature as God's handiwork and man as his special creation? Will the theologians be able either to demolish or to reconcile this new knowledge with revealed truth? And what is there left that I can believe, and what do I have in common with men of goodwill who are agnostics/Christians?

It has frequently been said—and was at the time—that most of the essential points of Darwinism, particularly those parts which entailed a challenge to religious dogmas about the origins of the world and the special position of man in the natural creation are to be found in Lyell, Chambers and other works which antedated the *Origin of Species*. The significance of the Darwinian controversy lay in the social effects of the controversy itself, which made it impossible for even the most conservative or indifferent to scientific ideas to ignore it. Contemporary accounts are full of the surprised encounters of the intelligentsia with barbers, butlers, dockers, vapid young ladies and men on Clapham omnibuses who may know almost nothing of what Darwin, Spencer or Huxley are saying, but they know that evolution is important and part of enormous sweeping changes in the view of man and the universe. During the 1870s, John Morley thought, 'Evolution was passed on from the laboratory and the study to the parlour.'[4] It was the demand of the parlour, the counting-house and the discussion circle that the new ideas be made available to them that the Rationalist Press began to meet.

During the next forty years, the channels of communication within British society changed. The number of local scientific societies which were founded in each decade rose from two in 1811–20 to twenty in the 1870s, and fell again to four by 1911–20. In the 1860s, scientists were seeking to extend their relations with the public, and a lecture on science for the working class became part of

---

[3] L. E. Elliott-Binns, *The Development of English Theology in the later Nineteenth Century*, Longmans, London, 1952, pp. 3–6.
[4] J. Morley, op. cit., p. 88.

the programme of the British Association. The 1870s saw the setting up of the great debating societies among the men of science and letters in London, especially the Metaphysical Society of 1869 which met to discuss what those of every shade of faith and lack of it really did believe, and to what extent this left them with a common moral understanding and culture. The process reflected the growth in size of the intellectual élite which, like the social élite, now needed more formal institutions to define itself.

Lower down in the social scale came the growth not only of formal education but of a plethora of arrangements for lectures on science and general knowledge for working-men (who mainly turned out to be the lower middle classes), the setting up in 1872 of the University Extension Society, and the appearance of a host of literary and Browning societies, where polite suburbia met to talk about philosophical and moral ideas.[5] Contemporaries thought that late Victorians rarely read the scientific evidence themselves; it was its social and moral effects that were debated. To fuel these new interests, there was an increase in the production of inexpensive books which dealt with the new knowledge on a popular level, and behind them lay an increasingly self-confident assumption of the effect that this process of making knowledge widely available was going to have. Rationalism was the systematic and intellectual expression of this assumption.

The growing number of eminent scholars of 'advanced' opinions had, with a few exceptions from the earlier radical tradition such as J. S. Mill, avoided all contact with the secular movement. Not only did many of them (including Darwin) consider that their own intellectual scepticism might have pernicious results if it was adopted by the unsophisticated, but they differed from the working-class atheist in that their views on religion were not part of a general attack on corrupt authority. Above all, like many middle-class sympathizers with the radical working class, for example those who worked in the settlement movement, they found antipathetic the violent, unruly and emotional way in which issues were attacked and fine distinctions obliterated by working-men in debate. Contemporary accounts of debates such as those at Toynbee Hall were filled with an uneasy distaste; the smell, the tobacco fumes, above all, the lack of reverence for ideas and authorities which should be held

[5] Amy Cruse, *After the Victorians*, Allen & Unwin, London, 1938, pp. 13–14; F. A. Mumby, *Publishing and Bookselling*, Cape, London, 1930, p. 359; O. J. R. Howarth, *The British Association for the Advancement of Science—a Retrospect 1831–1931*, published by the Association, London, 1931, pp. 95, 104.

sacred. In Bernstein's terms, they disliked hearing such issues discussed by means of a restricted linguistic code.

C. A. Watts saw that none the less there was a growing demand for serious reading-matter on questions of science and ethics from a sceptic's viewpoint. In 1888 he and Holyoake had formed a Propagandist Press Fund to agitate for the reform of the blasphemy laws and for liberty of bequest. (Since anti-clerical activity was an attack on the state, all bequests for such a purpose could be overruled.) The Fund became an advisory body to assist Watts in spending the money which had been bequeathed to him for propagandist purposes, and it began to attract increasing donations from those who felt that open-air propaganda had had its day. In particular, some wealthy donors to the secular movement and many leading secularists who had been closely associated with Bradlaugh and had quarrelled with Foote joined the Association instead.

The publishing aspect of the Fund had proved such a success that in 1899 it was decided to form an Association 'similar to the S.P.C.K. and Religious Tract Society', and to appeal for members. The Rationalist Press Association announced its objects to be the publication of rationalist literature and its distribution to societies, members and the general public. There was the usual difficulty in humanist movements in finding a definition for the key-word—Rationalism, but finally it was agreed that 'Rationalism may be defined as the mental attitude which unreservedly accepts the supremacy of reason and aims at establishing a system of philosophy and ethics verifiable by experience and independent of all arbitrary assumptions of authority.'

The general principles which were to determine the choice of titles to be published were the need for books—especially inexpensive ones—to stimulate freedom of thought; to popularize science; to support a humanistic philosophy of life; to separate morality from all theological connections; to dissociate art and literature from theological influences, and to encourage secular education. The organization was registered as a limited company, which automatically created an undemocratic form whereby members could influence policy only by voting at annual general meetings, and initially a larger subscription gave a large number of votes. But it was apparent that the chairman and only full-time worker, C. A. Watts, took most major decisions. Leslie Stephen, Emile Zola, Ernst Haeckel, E. A. Westermarck and other leading scholars became honorary associates.

The new organization based its policy on the belief that in a period of universal literacy, the public could be most easily contacted and converted to rationalism by inexpensive books and pamphlets. This method of using propaganda required a move away from Bible-banging to more scholarly and milder arguments: 'persuasiveness rather than undue hostility toward the popular creeds'. C. A. Watts did not intend that the Association should try to attract a mass or working-class membership. 'While we have not forgotten the masses, our object has mainly been to influence and direct the middle and higher (i.e. educated) classes. When Rationalists have converted the intellect of the world and made heresy "fashionable", the great multitude will, as sheep, follow their leaders.'[6]

At the time when the Association was founded, the general mythology of science was exceptionally favourable to its position. From the 1860s on, there had been a wide public for ideas about the philosophical and social implications of evolution; rationalists and many others regarded Darwin's work as providing a scientific proof for the sociology of Herbert Spencer. The Darwinian controversy symbolized the conflict of religion and science. Its importance for social and political thought lay in the ease with which analogies could be drawn between biology and social life. Darwin seemed to have provided the key to many other questions, and natural selection became a kind of general revelation. Because of this, C. A. Watts felt that he could discard

the crude Bible-banging, the head-on onslaughts on Christianity, the long discussions on Bible discrepancies and atrocities, and our general secular aggressiveness. And as for labels, he did not like the word *atheism*—it alienated potential rationalist sympathizers . . . No! Mr. Watts wanted anthropology, evolution, and science in general to undermine the Christian religion—and he pointed out how he was commissioning Joseph McCabe to give lantern lectures on evolution and other subjects . . .[7]

During the 1900s, the Association did move toward making more direct contact with its membership, and prompted by Holyoake and John Watts, several ex-secularists were appointed as lecturers to the Association. There was a tentative move toward the formation of societies, but these were confined strictly to the discussion-group

---

[6] *Literary Guide*, 1 March 1895, p. 10; 15 December 1889, p. 3.
[7] H. Cutner, a secularist but also a member of the R.P.A., *Rationalist Review*, Vol. II(2), May, 1905, pp. 1–2.

pattern; all tendencies toward religious ritual were sternly discouraged. A few members felt that the emotional and aesthetic side of rationalism needed more acknowledgement, but the majority were strongly opposed to such 'artificial ritualism' and 'castrated church-mongering'. The London discussion group amalgamated with that of the South Place Ethical Society, who felt similarly estranged from the ritualism, socialism and philosophical idealism that Stanton Coit was fostering in the other ethical societies. The Association began to assume other responsibilities toward its members; advice on cremation, proposals for a rationalist school, rationalist post-cards, and the proposal to form provincial rationalist societies to bring members together. The Association took no active part in these activities except to supply literature until 1907, when it agreed to appoint honorary secretaries to recruit members, organize local lectures, sell books and organize societies. Those societies which were formed seem to have resembled closely the discussion groups of the W.E.A.(which had been formed three years previously), and the membership of local groups largely overlapped in many cases. For example, a rationalist group was formed in the Ogmore and Gawr valleys by a number of colliers who met to discuss *God and my Neighbour*, which had impressed them deeply. They met monthly to discuss a book, usually an R.P.A. reprint, and assailed the contemporary revivals by going to meetings to ask awkward questions, and writing to local newspapers.[8]

The Association also refused to be associated with any kind of political position or commitment. The majority of its directors and probably of its members were liberals, and had little quarrel with the established order. The ideas with which they were identified were widely accepted among the influential. Whilst members of the Association did at various times request it to be or accuse it of being aligned with various political groups, the Board was able to adhere successfully to a policy of complete political non-alignment and a Fabian permeation of the climate of educated opinion. Some members wondered whether they should declare their unorthodoxy at all, since it exposed them to 'unnecessary' persecution.

The directors were soon able to claim that the flood of cheap

---

[8] Report from John Cawker, *Literary Guide*, April 1908, p. 60. T. Brennan *et al.*, *Social Change in South West Wales*, Watts, London 1954, pp. 150-1, described a Methodist discussion group who also met at the same time and in the same area to read Blatchford, and became socialists although not (though nearly) atheists. For a description of the general ferment in working-class communities in South Wales in the 1900s as nonconformity merged into and fought with messianic socialism, see D. R. Davies, op. cit.

scientific and anthropological reprints was worrying the Christian denominations, and that many booksellers had been pressed not to sell such literature. The number of members and subscribers to the Association rose steadily from sixty-five members in 1899 to over a thousand in 1906, two thousand in 1910, three thousand by 1929 and four thousand by 1933. The success of the Association and its financial viability attracted donations which enabled further cheap reprints to be published and made possible the distribution of free literature which was sowed indiscriminately. One of the favourite techniques of supporters was to leave cheap reprints or copies of *Watts Literary Guide* in deserted railway-carriages, and occasionally new members reported that they had indeed been recruited by such random and anonymous methods.

The cheap reprints were mainly reissues of the writings of popularizers of science with a strong positivist flavour, and anthropological accounts of the superstitious origins of religion and of man's gradual emancipation through scientific and rational thought. For example, by 1902 about 155,500 cheap reprints had been disposed of, of which 45,000 were T. H. Huxley's *Lectures and Essays*, and 30,000 were Ernst Haeckel's *The Riddle of the Universe*, which had been singled out for special praise by Robert Blatchford in the *Clarion*. (In doing so, he had enormously increased both the popularity and the sales of Haeckel's works, but found that the anticlericalism of his article created much rancour within the labour movement.) In the following year, 1903, the highest sales were for a group of books highly characteristic of the Association's intellectual interests of the period; these were to remain bestsellers and to influence many rationalists. They were: T. H. Huxley's *Lectures and Essays* which sold 55,000; S. Laing's *Modern Science and Modern Thought* which sold 60,500; *The Riddle of the Universe* which sold 75,000; Herbert Spencer on *Education* which sold 60,000 and Grant Allen's *The Evolution of the Idea of God*, which sold 55,000.[9]

Why were these books so popular, and what did they mean to those who read them? They are all part of the impact of the evolutionary method of thought in the life sciences and social science, and most of them are mainly concerned with popularizing the Darwinian myth itself. The books published by the Association and the articles in the *Literary Guide* suggest that their members' interest in science seemed to pass through three broad phases, perhaps conterminous with a change in the general mythology itself. When

[9] R.P.A. Annual Reports for 1903 and 1904.

the Association was founded, biology was the most widely popularized science, and linked to it by social-evolutionary theory, anthropology simultaneously enjoyed a briefer vogue. After the First World War, popular interest shifted to physics and chemistry, and after the second, to medicine and the social sciences. It was only during the first period that the general 'myth' of science approached sufficiently closely to the Association's to make the popularization of scientific ideas an obvious way of advocating rationalism, and even then it depended on which science you chose. Had popular interest been focused on the changing views of matter which were being brought about by discoveries in chemistry, for example, rationalists would have found it less easy to be materialists.

The remainder of this chapter describes, first, the general programme of epistemology and the uses of knowledge which was characteristic of many rationalists at the turn of the century, and then tries to give some account of the contemporary ramifications of evolutionary theory, of the variety of inferences which were drawn from it for philosophy, morality and social life, and the way in which as these ideas were popularized they picked up the tinge and flavour of the ways of thought of different groups of people.

'The Laws of Nature are our Guide in Life . . .'

Thus wrote C. A. Watts in 1905.[10] His account of rationalism reiterates many of the themes of writings produced by the Association. Essentially, much of his argument depended on a curious faculty psychology. Reason is a mode of thought distinct from and opposed to faith, emotion, and the rigid adherence to dogma. It is 'man's highest intellectual power', the agency by which we gain our knowledge of the world. In the positivist fusion of facts and values so characteristic of previous decades, Watts considers that what our reason shows us as our highest duty is the promotion of individual happiness, justice and freedom. The ethical basis of social life lies in human nature—if we follow its promptings, social harmony will result. Virtue and vice are produced by the 'operation of natural laws'; were the causes of crime, like those of disease, to be discovered then vice could be prevented. Should we fail to obey the moral law, we will suffer for it; but by rational knowledge, we can

[10] C. A. Watts, *The Meaning of Rationalism*, Watts, London, 1905, on which this paragraph is based.

create the social conditions under which moral law will automatically be obeyed. Religion, by contrast, justifies its precepts by reference only to an unknowable future life and a rigid adherence to the traditions of the past.

The defence of freedom of thought in *On Liberty*, where the free interplay of ideas was simply the best method to ensure the emergence of truth, had been sharpened in Morley's *On Compromise* to the half-implicit belief that holding a minority opinion against the conventional wisdom was almost a guarantee that it would be the truth. In Watts it becomes the defence of complete liberty of thought and speech in all circumstances because progress depends on unbelief; indeed, on non-belief, for 'disbelief in an old system must ever precede the introduction of a new one'.

The benefactors of humanity (such as Spinoza, Goethe, Priestley, Newton, Voltaire, Paine and Harriet Martineau) have been unbelievers; and at this point 'sceptic' elides to 'atheist' and then to 'scientist', for 'unbelief in one thing must mean belief in the opposite', and whereas some things, such as mathematical axioms, are self-evident and must be believed, and other beliefs, such as in the invariant order of nature, can safely be based on experience, religious beliefs deal with entities for which we can have no evidence and which are therefore speculative and absurd. Watts draws a parallel antithesis between Christ and the scientist. Given that Christ was badly educated and lived in unintellectual circles, he did reasonably well but was by no means a model of virtue or wisdom. 'He revealed nothing of practical value, and taught no virtues that were before unknown . . . He taught false notions of existence; he had no knowledge of science . . . He lacked experimental force . . .' Our duty in the material world is to reveal the laws and the forces of nature 'which are our guide in life', its grandeur 'which is our inspiration'. Scientists, 'that noble and hardworking band of men', who teach us about nature are thereby exercising the highest duty of the most complex and sophisticated part of man, the last and final creature to evolve. Evolution through scientific discovery, which is the same thing as the advance of reason, will, however, continue; 'something new is constantly being brought to light to lessen the load of human woe and sorrow, and bring about harmony among mankind.'

Such a philosophy was and is easy to mock. It is crudely Panglossian and, even given the simplistic theories of motivation and personality of the nineteenth century, it represents an impossibly intellectualized and monochrome view of human nature and wishes.

The confusion between the socially beneficial uses of scientific
knowledge, its epistemological status and the men who pursued it
was common enough among rationalists, but had already been
trenchantly objected to by T. H. Huxley. Some of its subtler
confusions are more interesting, for example the firm commitment
to the Newtonian laws of nature combined with the exhortation
perpetually to doubt everything; or the insistence on the unitary
law which governed nature and human life and the consequent
attack on defences of religion in terms of miracles, first causes,
et cetera, because they breached this unity, combined with the
view that much can never be known and must therefore not even
be the subject of speculation. Like most evolutionists, Watts was
following not Darwin but Spencer when he identified evolution
with both a law-like process and social and moral progress.

Many of his themes were familiar axioms to the nineteenth century; the appeal to duty, the exhortation to doubt and yet to stand
by one's beliefs, and the conception of science as cumulative laws
with direct beneficial practical results. 'Has not science made the
world happy?' Edward Aveling had asked; 'Is not its very task and
joy to make the wheels of life move more smoothly? What happiness
has any creed yet wrought that can be for one moment compared
with the easement given to the hearts of men by the discovery of
the electric telegraph?'[11] It is noteworthy that although constant
reference was made in this literature to Darwin as a scientist and
his role in religious controversy, the picture of science that emerges
is Newtonian. 'Science' has become a myth.

At this period, i.e. the last decade of the nineteenth century,
science was rapidly being split into subspecialisms and developing
an internal culture.[12] (One of the reasons for the general impact of
Darwin was that he stood outside this world, and wrote in lucid
and attractive prose.) Natural theology, from being the context of
scientific debate, was becoming an increasingly excluded faction.
Consequently, to interpret scientific advance and its meaning to
the public, the popularizer, often a scientist himself, arose as both
interpreter and screen between the scientist and the general public.

In discussing scientific ideas it was almost impossible for the
popularizer (as it is for us) to avoid a Whig view of scientific history.

[11] E. B. Aveling, *A Godless Life the Happiest and Most Useful*, Freethought Publishing
Company, London, 1882, pp. 7–8.
[12] R. M. Young, 'The Impact of Darwin on Conventional Thought', in A. Symondson, ed., *The Victorian Crisis of Faith*, S.P.C.K., London, 1970.

Those scientific views which succeeded were mentioned by later workers as the basis of their own thought; the view that knowledge is cumulative is largely inescapable. So, too, is the internalist explanation of scientific discovery, the view that scientific theories grow from within science itself and not in response to the questions, theories and metaphysics which scientists bring to it as members of particular societies in particular times. Part of the special status of scientific knowledge, according to the 'myth' of science, is that it has a purely internal origin and validation.

The foundations of the 'myth' of science were laid down in the 1870s with the process of reinterpretation and absorption of Darwin's work and its generalization into a theory which was used not only to explain all processes of change but to justify them. Darwin had been anxious to create a picture of himself as a modest and practical naturalist, and was opposed to personifying causal processes as Forces or identifying them with moral progress. 'Never use the words higher and lower', he had written in his copy of *The Vestiges of Creation*.[13] But the parallels with social life were inescapable: his conception of evolution itself had formed as he read Malthus, just as Marx found in Darwin the germ of *Capital*. Around his ideas grew ever-thicker layers of interpretation, theory and generalization, as they were extended to aesthetic, political and metaphysical doctrines. The original statements became ever more general and moralized, and less clearly related to each other and the evidence.

If we are trying to study 'the manifestations of specific ideas in the collective thought of large groups of persons', it is misleading to look for established thought-systems in popular writings.[14] Their influence lies in the support that they have provided for very general assumptions or mental habits, of so vague a sort that they can be grafted onto thinking about any topic at all. From them, often no more is taken than a metaphor, an incantatory set of words and phrases, 'the survival of the fittest', 'the law of the jungle'.

There are few studies of the way in which ideas change as they percolate throughout a society beyond the reach of its intelligentsia, but in an excellent and pioneering analysis of the reviews of the theory of evolution in the popular press from 1859 to 1872, Ellegard showed how Darwin's ideas were dissolved in many different social

[13] Gertrude Himmelfarb, *Darwin and the Darwinian Revolution*, Chatto and Windus, London, 1959, p. 181.
[14] A. O. Lovejoy, *The Great Chain of Being*, Harvard University Press, Cambridge, Mass., 1961, p. 19.

solvents.[15] He found that in the periodicals intended for the less educated the theory was mainly used as a weapon in political and ideological warfare; in the popular press, 'the Darwinian theory was hardly referred to at all except in its relation to religion, [and] . . . little else was said about the Darwinian doctrine than that it represented man as descended from apes.' The secular movement had indeed largely seen science in this light; Bradlaugh had used Darwin as 'a stick to beat the Bible with'.[16]

Those periodicals aimed at the educated public presented the Darwinian controversy as largely that of the problems of inference and the interpretation of scientific evidence. It was commonly argued at the time that the glory of British science was that it was solely inductive, as opposed to the abstract and barren Continental deductive tradition. The *Origins* was accordingly accused of abandoning traditional empirical knowledge and making rash hypothetical assumptions rather than relying purely on facts.[17] The issue was at root connected to a boundary dispute between religion and science; with the abandonment of natural theology, religion had reserved for itself the realm of supernatural phenomena which obeyed their own laws, and science had now invaded that realm. Much contemporary antagonism to biology at the popular level was that it intruded in places where it had no right to be, in Genesis for example; men such as Darwin, Huxley, Tyndall and Lyell would 'peep and botanize upon their mothers' graves'. At first theologians had been inclined to dismiss Darwin's work as 'only a hypothesis', and consider that in challenging the traditional view of men's place in the universe 'science had overstepped its competence'.[18] Tyndall and other popularizers of science consequently claimed vigorously that science had the right, the duty to examine any hypothesis, any event, regardless of whether it offended common sense or traditional susceptibilities.

Those who were associated with the Rationalist Press endorsed this view enthusiastically. To the popularizers of science and those who rejoiced in its conflict with theology part of the attraction of Darwinism lay in the very ease with which analogies could be drawn

[15] A. Ellegard, *Darwin and the General Reader*, Göteborgs Universitets Arsskrift, Göteborg, 1958.
[16] A positivist's comment on Bradlaugh, S. H. Swinny in *Positivist Review*, No. 42, June 1896, p. 125.
[17] A. Ellegard, 'The Darwinian Theory and Nineteenth Century Philosophies of Science', *Journal of the History of Ideas*, Vol. 18(3), June 1957, pp. 362–93.
[18] T. Simonsson, *Face to Face with Darwinism*, C. W. K. Gleerup, Lund, 1958.

in political and social life; natural selection became a kind of general revelation. W. K. Clifford and his mathematical friends at Cambridge

> were carried away by a wave of Darwinian enthusiasm; we seemed to ride triumphant on an ocean of new life and boundless possibilities. Natural Selection was to be the master-key of the universe; we expected it to solve all riddles and reconcile all contradictions. Among other things it was to give us a new system of ethics, combining the exactness of the utilitarian with the poetical ideals of the transcendentalist.[19]

'System' and 'grand design' were among the key 'sacred words' of the late nineteenth-century religion of science. The insistence that science should be allowed to look at everything became the assumption that whatever it looked at would be brought into its sphere, made part of the same system of laws. J. W. Draper, an American popularizer whose view of science was convincing to many scientists, including Tyndall, believed that the 'world is not governed by many systems of laws, . . . but that there is a unity of plan obtaining throughout.'[20] This assumption was supported not only by the wide acceptance of Mill's *System of Logic* as a programme for the sciences of society, but also by the wish to eradicate the 'god of the gaps', i.e. the claim that there was a supernatural intelligence at work at those points where man's reason faltered and science had not yet provided an explanation.

A unitary system of laws which would explain the whole of reality was not merely intellectually desirable but emotionally seductive. In Jack London's autobiographical novel he described the effect of Spencer's doctrines on the half-educated *Martin Eden*:

> And here was the man Spencer, organizing all knowledge for him, reducing everything to unity, elaborating ultimate realities, and presenting to his startled gaze a universe so concrete of realization that it was like the model of a ship such as sailors make and put into glass bottles. There was no caprice, no chance. All was law. It was in obedience to law that the bird flew, and it was in obedience to the same law that fermenting slime had writhed and squirmed and put out legs and wings and become a bird.
>
> . . . All the hidden things were laying their secrets bare. He was drunken with comprehension.

And even Arnold Bennett, far more cautious and phlegmatic, found this aspect of Spencer wholly admirable.

---

[19] Introduction by F. Pollock to W. K. Clifford, *Lectures and Essays*, Macmillan, London, 1886, pp. 24–5.
[20] J. W. Draper, *The Influence of Physical Agents on Life*, New York, 1850, p. 6, quoted in D. Fleming, *John William Draper and the Religion of Science*, University of Pennsylvania Press, Philadelphia, 1950.

It is fascinating to see that at the heart of the emotional appeal of Darwinian biology to many men was the notion of a grand planned system. For example, Professor C. J. Patton recalled how he was 'carried away by Darwin's noble concept and by the grandeur of evolutionary processes acting according to fixed law and order in the universe', and that he was equally impressed by Darwin's moral meaning; 'his noble concept of man emerging hale and hearty from a long line of vigorous ancestry, and by the fact that he was surely destined to rise steadily and not to fall into sin immediately after he appeared.'[21] And yet the core of Darwin's work had been the demonstration that there was no system; that natural selection worked on variations thrown up by chance, was morally aimless and indifferent to the concerns of man. It was this that Tennyson and the liberal theologians had found so repugnant.

One of the reasons for this fact being so quickly lost sight of, especially among rationalists, was that Darwin's work was widely seen as complementary to Spencer's account of social evolution. Tyndall's famous 1874 address to the British Association, in which he had flung down the gauntlet on behalf of the scientific establishment to challenge theologians to try to exert any control over science at all or to check its inexorable progress, had linked the doctrine of natural selection to its extension by Spencer into psychology. His argument, as was common among evolutionists, had almost instantly begun to take a more optimistic and Lamarckian turn. Man had gradually developed actions and mental capacities which had become instinctual—'faculties which scarcely exist in some inferior races become congenital in superior ones'.

Darwin and Spencer were bracketed together as the basis for 'Modern Science'; Spencer's associationalist psychology, in which man's mind was largely a creation of the influence of the environment and education acquired a central importance in social evolution, gained great influence and in turn added to the general feeling that scientific ideas themselves could liberate men's minds. As Fleming says in his biography of John William Draper, one of the great popularizers of science, he '. . . consistently wrote of science as if it were synonymous with willingness to experiment in the face of authority, with hostility to any coercion of the mind', and Draper was only adding to a tradition of the history of science which was fully believed by most rationalists, in which the key figures are Copernicus, Kepler, Bruno, Galileo, Servetus and other martyrs

[21] *Books Which Made me a Rationalist*, Watts, London, 1942, p. 19.

to an oppressive religious establishment, bent on a suppression of the truth.[22] Haeckel and Huxley, the two greatest popularizers of Darwin and probably the two authors whose books were most widely sold by the Rationalist Press, both brought out strongly in their works the theme of the struggle of the scientific Prometheus against the chains of religion.

Darwin's Bulldogs

The way in which Darwin's work was interpreted varied not only between different social strata, but according to the different intellectual traditions and current conflicts of societies as a whole. In the United States, the debate took on a racial tinge almost at once, and social Darwinism, far stronger than it became in England, was widely used to justify the harshness and inequalities of rapid industrialism. In Germany where Darwin's views were very rapidly accepted, they were blended into the *Naturphilosophie* of the romantics and idealists, and he became merely an extension of the Hegelian picture of all of man's history as an evolving unfolding process. (It was in this Hegelianized and idealized form that many of the English churches were finally prepared to announce that they 'accepted Evolution'.[23])

The incorporation of Darwin's views into a general mythology was largely the work of Ernst Haeckel, whose work was immensely popular in both Germany and England. *The Riddle of the Universe* sold 100,000 copies in 1899, its year of publication, and by 1914 its English and German sales had reached over half a million and it had been translated into fourteen languages. Haeckel was strongly championed in England by Joseph McCabe, a lecturer for the Rationalist Press. He translated his work for the Association to publish, defended it against critics, and gave lantern-slide lectures to popularize his philosophy. He found that his audiences were more interested in Haeckel's thought than in any other scientific topic.[24]

[22] D. Fleming, op. cit., p. 126. The other great creator of the myth of science, Andrew Dickson White, author of the *Warfare of Science with Theology*, brackets Darwin and Spencer as the basis of contemporary science in much the same way.

[23] G. Himmelfarb, op. cit., p. 249; J. Kent, *From Darwin to Blatchford: the Role of Darwinism in Christian Apologetic, 1875–1910*, Dr Williams Trust, London, 1968, p. 28.

[24] J. McCabe, *The Riddle of the Universe Today*, Watts, London, 1934. His translations of Haeckel's works were published by Watts, *The Riddle of the Universe*, in 1901, and *The Wonders of Life, a Popular Study of Biological Philosophy*, to answer the questions most frequently asked of Haeckel, in 1904.

It is interesting to note the variations between the English Dar-
winians and *Darwinismus*. In Germany, Haeckel saw that Darwin's
work enabled a modern scientific outlook to be brought into harmony with the *Naturphilosophie* of the German idealists. Goethe
and the romantic movement had personified nature as the divine
source of all beauty and knowledge, and Haeckel treated evolution
as a cosmic force, a manifestation of the world soul, the creative
energy of nature. As the English mythology of science did, he
aggregated all processes of social change and physiological development to evolution. In the cooler atmosphere of mid-twentieth century science, Haeckel's philosophical flights found less sympathy
among biologists; he 'habitually perverted scientific truth', thought
Charles Singer, 'to make certain of his doctrines being more easily
assimilable.'[25]

Haeckel, like many English rationalists, conceived of nature in a
vitalist way. The whole universe was alive and conscious, a 'colossal
organism' which men could both study and worship. (It is a remarkable proof of the lability of ideas that this one had been the
basis of one of the main theological attacks on Darwin in England.
It had been argued against the picture of natural selection as a
chance and random process that in fact the 'laws of development'
were vital things, the outcome of an unconscious striving toward
progress.[26])

Haeckel began on an active career as a publicist for Darwin's
ideas, which he incorporated into a general philosophy of life called
monism. All knowledge was the same; scientific knowledge, the
true knowledge of nature, was overcoming the traditional erroneous
dualist and *a priori* ways of thinking that had been supported by
religions, which had served to separate man from awareness of his
origins in nature. The dominion of theologically based ways of
thought had been responsible for the discrepancies between the
immeasurable advances 'in a knowledge of nature and in its practical
application' and the 'state of barbarism' and even of regression in
moral and social life.

> In a great measure, its [political life's] evils are due to the fact that most of our
> officials are men without an acquaintance with those social relations of which
> we find the earlier types in comparative zoology and the theory of evolution,
> in the cellular theory and study of the protists. We can only arrive at a correct

[25] Charles Singer, *A Short History of Biology*, Oxford University Press, London,
1931, p. 481.
[26] A. Ellegard, 'The Darwinian Theory', op. cit., pp. 388–9.

knowledge of the structure and life of the social body, the State, through a scientific knowledge of the structure and life of the individuals who compose it, and the cells of which they are in turn composed.[27]

Man had weakened himself by ignoring his animal origins and imposing an erroneous intellectualism and humanitarianism on the running of human affairs. Catastrophe was imminent unless scientists arrived at a correct view of the world, and their methods of understanding were adopted as the basis of social life. The arrogant theological view of the uniqueness of man would have to be replaced by a consciousness of his place in the great scheme of things; and yet (a familiar ambiguity) 'the greatest and most commanding of all the works of life is unquestionably the mind of man.'

The cosmos was ruled by iron, invariable laws, which as we came to comprehend them would serve to displace religious faith; '. . . our clear modern insight into the regularity and causative character of natural processes, and especially our knowledge of the universal reign of the law of substance, are inconsistent with a belief in a personal God, the immortality of the soul, and the freedom of the will.' Just as the natural world had evolved, so had civilization; anthropology was a part of zoology, and Haeckel accordingly campaigned against the mixing of races or the genetically misguided policy of preserving the unfit to perpetuate themselves, and not allowing the struggle for survival to create a natural aristocracy of leaders. Morality was naturalistic; ethical conduct had arisen 'by adaptation of the social mammals to the conditions of existence, and thus may be traced eventually to physical laws.' Duty was a kind of moral instinct.

(It is indisputable that Haeckel believed in both the superiority of the Aryan race and the moral legitimacy of the struggle to survive, but Gasman's[28] argument that he was a proto-Nazi and provided a powerful impetus to the adulation of the nation state seems to proceed from false premises. Whilst Haeckel was an immensely influential figure in German intellectual life and National Socialism was a product of that life, by noting similarities we cannot infer causes. Haeckel also influenced Engels; but that did not make him a proto-Marxist. To argue in this way is the Whig view of history in reverse.)

[27] E. Haeckel, *The Riddle of the Universe*, p. 3.
[28] D. Gasman, *The Scientific Origins of National Socialism; Social Darwinism in Ernst Haeckel and the German Monist League*, MacDonald, London, 1971. For a contemporary view of Haeckel which saw him as a religious reformer, see E. E. Slosson, *Major Prophets of Today*, Little, Brown, Boston, 1914.

Haeckel believed that a crisis was being reached in the evolutionary process because of the increased resistance of Christian superstition (especially Catholicism) to the scientific knowledge which was starting to enable man to bring society into harmony with the laws of biology. Monism was not merely a science, but a philosophy which should satisfy man's religious yearnings. Haeckel proposed to the International Freethought Congress in 1904 that he found a *Monistenbund*, which would worship a new trinity of the Good (Christian ethics minus the asceticism), the True and the Beautiful (to be found in the study and worship of nature). The League acquired six thousand members in Germany and Austria, but Haeckel came to dislike the ritualized form that its meetings took, with their sermons and Christmas celebrations in the Lutheran style. Monistic missionaries held revival meetings where they called upon those who would leave the churches to stand up and be counted. But ultimately, as in England, left-wing anti-clericalism and the search for a new metaphysics which had led to an interest in Haeckel and meant that most monists were social democrats, was outgrown, and the *Monistenbund* subsided. Haeckel lost his influence in England and his favour with the Rationalist Press as well for a time because of his attacks on England during the First World War.

It is part of the unspoken assumptions of scientism that social and political life and thought are devalued where they are not run on scientific principles. The rejection of Christian doctrine because it was the basis for a resistance to the biological laws which governed nature and society alike was a theme which constantly recurred in rationalist writings, and contemporary religious apologists were equally anxious to reconcile God and biology. Science is presented in this way of thinking as a sort of knowledge which is created by a uniquely powerful method of reasoning; positivist, experimental, in short, rationalist, which is destroying emotive, intuitive, unsystematic, in short, mystical approaches to truth. The optimism about the progress of science is combined with a predominant note in many rationalist writings of steely resignation, of what can only be described as *grimness*. There is an adulation of hard-headedness which is a corollary of the Victorian view of science as essentially a practical and material form of knowledge, the feeling that the harsh demands which nature and reality make of mankind must be faced with stern endeavour and an indomitable will.

Far from being facile optimists, rationalists were likely to argue that the conditions of man's existence were not pleasant but challenging.

It was often implied that religious beliefs acted as false comforters to those weaker spirits who could not face reality without their aid; they covered the harsh reality of life with an illusory promise and glow. Indeed, some rationalists attacked Catholicism because of its emotionalism and sentimental Mariolatry rather than raising the much commoner objections to its claim to absolute authority. They betrayed a puritan uneasiness at the public display of emotion and the luxury and elaborate decoration of the churches.

> When one has seen Russian devotees flopping down by the dozen before a tinselled and jewelled ikon, and beating the pavement with their foreheads; when one has been introduced to the 'very miraculous' Virgins of Spain—little black fetishes who own extensive wardrobes of gorgeous doll's clothes which are solemnly changed from day to day . . . one begins to appreciate the decent dullness of an English Cathedral. Even Puritanism, detestable and obnoxious in many of its manifestations, was a step toward Rationalism. Let us not be ungrateful to our iconoclastic grandsires, or merely shrug our shoulders at an attempt to undo their work. It is a pity, no doubt, to destroy a beautiful image; but if the choice lies between smashing it and worshipping it—ho for the hammer![29]

At the turn of the century rationalists often argued that religion taught men to live in a fool's paradise, in which nature and creation were good and benevolent and men naturally humane and civilized. Such beliefs gave men no incentive to develop the necessary stoicism with which to face the difficulties which would inevitably be their lot. It is impossible to escape the feeling that they enjoyed pointing this out. C. A. Watts, for example, had ironically suggested a new Doxology:

> Praise God from whom all cyclones blow,
> Praise him when rivers overflow,
> Praise him who whirls the churches down,
> And sinks the boats, their crews to drown.[30]

The natural order seen as amoral and indifferent to man's well-being was of course the antithesis of the natural theology of an earlier generation. Paine had argued that the beauty and essential rightness of the natural creation demonstrated the existence of a rational and benevolent creator, and the earlier popularizers of science had shared his optimism if not his conclusions. G. J. Holyoake never doubted that science was revealing a benevolent and pleasant reality. But a shift of mood occurred at the end of the

---

[29] W. Archer, *William Archer as Rationalist*, Watts, London, 1925, pp. 123-4.
[30] C. A. Watts, op. cit., p. 38.

century, and a more pessimistic outlook began to prevail about the
natural order as distinct from the optimism about what man with
his new-found powers could make of it. The mood was not induced
by the self-doubt found among so many late Victorians, but was
rather the doctrine of progress interpreted in a new and stoical—
almost a Calvinist—light. Scientists were often pictured as the
ultimate stoics, facing truths before which lesser men quailed.
Many might feel shock as they realized the moral implications of
man's descent not from the angels but from the brutes; but, wrote
an author very popular with rationalists,

> . . . the only answer to these questions is that truth is truth, and fact is fact,
> and it is always better to act and to believe in conformity with truth and fact,
> than to indulge in illusions. There are many things in Nature which jar on
> our feelings and seem harsh and disagreeable, but yet are hard facts, which
> we have to recognize and make the best of . . . Progress, not happiness,
> is the law of the world; and to improve himself and others by constant
> struggles upwards is the true destiny of man.[31]

Such pessimism was not characteristic of all rationalist writings,
nor indeed of these writers in all their moods, but the undercurrent
of stoicism and grimness *was* there, and more clearly in the rationalist
than in the secular or ethical movements. In part it was joined with
a moral élitism. Scientists and rationalists were more far-seeing than
the multitude, because they had had the courage to abandon
religious illusions. At the period when this mood was at its height,
the Association produced several books interpreting Islam, Zoro-
astrianism, et cetera as predominantly stoical and therefore superior
religions.

The recognition that the progress of biological evolution had
nothing to do with human wishes or happiness had in large part
been borne in on English society by the writings of the other great
scientific advocate for Darwin, T. H. Huxley. Huxley had gained an
automatic position in the rationalist pantheon, with Bishop Wilberforce cast as a kind of poor man's Savonarola, because of his struggle
to get Darwin's ideas accepted and his insistence that they were not
reconcilable with Christian theology. He was a magnificent expositor;
his lectures to working-men and politer audiences did much to
explain scientific reasoning and findings and to make their meaning
and importance plain. His reputation as a controversialist has
obscured the subtlety of his thinking about science; he was not part

[31] S. Laing, *Modern Science and Modern Thought*, Chapman and Hall, London,
1885, pp. 281-2.

of the tradition of optimistic materialism with which he has often been identified. Indeed, his account of the limitations and potentialities of science is curiously modern; his quarrel with Spencer was to insist that ethical progress, far from being a consequence or part of biological or cosmic evolution, would largely come about through combating it. He has frequently been misrepresented subsequently on this point.[32]

Huxley saw science as essentially not a body of knowledge but a method. 'Science is, I believe, nothing but *trained and organized commonsense* . . . the man of science in fact, simply uses with scrupulous exactness, the methods which we all, habitually and at every moment, use carelessly . . .'[33] Because of the simplicity and obvious clarity of the scientific method, its sense could be intuitively grasped.

> The whole of modern thought is steeped in science; it has made its way into the works of our best poets, and even the mere man of letters, who affects to ignore and despise science, is unconsciously impregnated with her spirit, and indebted for his best products to her methods. I believe that the greatest intellectual revolution mankind has yet seen is now taking place by her agency. She is teaching the world that the ultimate court of appeal is observation and experiment, and not authority; she is teaching it to estimate the value of evidence; she is creating a firm and living faith in the existence of immutable moral and physical laws, perfect obedience to which is the highest possible aim of an intelligent being.[34]

He did not share the rationalist's adulation of the scientist: 'So far as my experience goes, men of science are neither better nor worse than the rest of the world. Occupation with the endlessly great parts of the universe does not necessarily involve greatness of character, nor does microscopic study of the infinitely little always produce humility'[35], nor did he share the contemporary fear that as the advance of science extended the sphere of matter and the reign of causation, it would gradually expel spirit and spontaneity from human thought.

Huxley was opposed to both a *laissez-faire* attitude to evolution

[32] See, for example, J. H. Buckley, *The Triumph of Time: a Study of the Victorian Concepts of Time, History, Progress and Decadence*, Harvard University Press, Cambridge, Mass, 1967, who states (p. 48) that Huxley failed to understand that progress depends on a willed evolution.
[33] T. H. Huxley, 'The Educational Value of the Natural History Sciences', *Lay Sermons, Essays and Reviews*, Macmillan, London, 1870, p. 86.
[34] T. H. Huxley, 'On the Study of Zoology', ibid., p. 130.
[35] T. H. Huxley, 'From an Episcopal Trilogy', *Science and Christian Tradition*, Macmillan, London, 1904, p. 140.

and to the naïve naturalism of many contemporary scientists. He derived both his empiricism and his separation of natural and moral law from Mill. Reality, he argued, could never be known directly but only via the human consciousness, which lay like a veil between man and the universe. 'All our knowledge is a knowledge of states of consciousness,' and this is as true of scientific knowledge as of idealist metaphysics. What distinguished both the scientist and the rational man was their capacity to remain in perpetual doubt; 'Scepticism is the highest of duties; blind faith the one unpardonable sin.'

During his lifetime Huxley became increasingly opposed to the claim that values could be derived from the facts of social change, and that reality could be directly comprehended as a unified system of laws. Oma Stanley suggests that his view of nature was at first Goethian, a loving mother, wise, purposeful and beneficient, until he read J. S. Mill's posthumously published essay on *Nature* (1874) which argued that man is either a part of nature or it is exterior to man, but that in either case it is non-moral. So that to argue that men should do something because 'nature intended it' is irrational; we cannot morally justify something on the grounds that it is part of a natural process.[36] Indeed, Huxley came increasingly to stress the harshness with which natural selection bore on the ignorant and weak, and to argue that men should use their new-found powers to reverse and check the effects of biological evolution. The key to improvement lay in widespread education, but he was well aware that this too was a selection mechanism, a weapon in 'that struggle for existence which goes on as fiercely beneath the smooth surface of modern society, as among the wild inhabitants of the woods'. Nothing in science, he declared in the Romanes Lecture for 1893, gave the idea of inevitable progress any assured support.

Huxley's popular reputation as an iconoclast and the hammer of bishops finds equally little support in his often rather sympathetic accounts of religion. He shared the contemporary dislike of Catholicism—'Our great antagonist—I speak as a man of Science—. . . the one great spiritual organization which is able to resist, and must, as a matter of life and death, resist, the progress of science and modern civilization'—but at other times he was inclined to argue that religion had always been part of, and indeed sometimes the whole of, the tradition of scholarly thought. But its incapacity to come to terms with the necessity to doubt meant that 'extinguished

[36] Oma Stanley, 'T. H. Huxley's Treatment of "Nature" ', *Journal of the History of Ideas*, Vol. 18 (1), January 1957, pp. 120–7.

theologians lie about the cradle of every science as the strangled snakes beside that of Hercules.'

'Science, the available Providence of Life . . .'

With Huxley, we begin to find the growth of uneasiness about 'moral band-wagon jumping', the basing of morality and social philosophy on biological evolution, that was to gather strength in the years immediately preceding the First World War. But at the turn of the century positivism reigned supreme, and the prevailing view of religion was that a demarcation line was being drawn between it and science which left it a very small territory indeed. What lay beyond the pale of science and reason, and whether they would ultimately grow to destroy the theological badlands or whether they would not bother to cultivate them was a matter of dispute, as was the question whether liberal Protestants could not perhaps be allowed within the pale. But rationalists generally could feel that religion and non-material explanations were on the retreat, and that the range of scientific knowledge and the benefits which flowed from it were expanding, and would do so indefinitely.

There are great dangers in generalizing about the whole of a society in this way; new pockets of dissent had already appeared in, for example, the aesthetic movement of the 1890s, or the idealism and organicism which was characteristic of both the new liberalism and part of socialism. English scientists themselves seem to have become wary very early of the attempt to generalize from biology to social life, and to have readily accepted the claim that theological explanations operated in a different sphere. Rationalists were after all men of all levels of education and sophistication; T. H. Huxley's scorn for the crudities of anti-religious propaganda may not have been very popular with them, but his writings were immensely so and his doubts must have left their mark. But in the main, the picture of the rationalist world-view that is to be gained from reading their journals and publications is as described in this chapter, and was shared by a very wide-ranging and influential élite. Increasingly, however, dark shadows began to fall on the rationalist sun.

7 THINGS FALL APART: THE RATIONALIST PRESS AFTER THE FIRST WORLD WAR

The Rationalist Press Association would have liked to issue a 6d. edition of [H. G. Wells'] *Anticipations*. However, Watts broke it gently to Wells that 'God' was mentioned several times in the book and their subscribers would not like it. 'Of course,' said Watts, 'I know you only use the word figuratively.' 'Not so figuratively as all that', said Wells.

Arnold Bennett's Journal for July, 1904.

One of the platitudes of our day is that belief in science and in progress was characteristic of our benighted Victorian and Edwardian ancestors, and that both beliefs have been abandoned; in our own times, we are sadder and wiser. Some Christian apologists have created a kind of Catch 22. We must either adhere to scientism, a wholly positivist, materialist and progressive view of human affairs, or to a mystic and pessimistic theology which reduces religion to the certainty of no earthly progress and explains most of human behaviour in terms of original sin. One of the main difficulties with this view is that frequently scientists and Christian apologists are to be found batting with the opposition. In 1893 Huxley had argued forcibly against a naturalistic ethic, and thought 'social progress means a checking of the cosmic process'; and a year later, a Scottish preacher published an immensely popular and influential explanation of the natural foundations of moral life in the 'Struggle for the Life of Others'; 'the path of progress and the path of Altruism are one. Evolution is nothing but the Involution of Love, the revelation of Infinite Spirit . . .'[1]

It is more illuminating to look at the changes in our attitudes to science and morals in terms of the structural differentiation of knowledge itself. The most conspicuous difference between the educated public at the turn of the century and ourselves is the extent to which they saw all knowledge as potentially part of the same whole or system of laws, and we see it as occurring in separate compartments. Though the popularizer may make valiant attempts to build bridges across the deep fissures which have opened up between the pursuit of knowledge and its social use, science and ethics, science and social science, and the sciences themselves, we do

[1] See Richard Hofstadter, *Social Darwinism in American Thought*, revised ed., Beacon Press, Boston, 1955, pp. 95–6; J. Kent, op. cit., p. 21.

not believe that the gulfs will ever again become firm land. Our dominant theories of knowledge and of scientific enquiry itself discount the possibility.

The falling apart of a continuous world map into separate subjects has gone together with the increasing encapsulation within universities of the creation and interpretation of new knowledge. The decline of the popularizer who interprets a large field of knowledge from a particular point of view has created problems for the Rationalist Press, as have some of the changes in the ways in which certain fields are now viewed. The following account cannot pretend to do more than touch on some of the changed attitudes to scientific knowledge that have created difficulties for the central set of assumptions of the rationalist movement. Most of these changes must also have created problems in theology.

Social Darwinism

One of the main characteristics of popular thought in the late Victorian and Edwardian period was the belief that science was an unquestionable authority. All social and political ideas which could claim an affinity with science were thereby made rational and inevitable. There was much contemporary reference to 'efficiency' both of the individual and the nation, and the set of reforms and ideologies which were part of the gospel of efficiency were justified by references to Darwinian biology. This was a biology heavily filtered through the evolutionism of Herbert Spencer, who coined its key phrase—'the survival of the fittest'.

(Darwin himself had, entirely characteristically, been uncertain of and unwilling to discuss the ethical implications of his own theories. He pointed out that the progress of civilization meant that the sick, imbecile and insane were increasingly preserved and allowed to propagate themselves. But his extreme personal sensitivity to pain and suffering and a conviction that morality must be characteristic of men and evolve as they did led him, with Huxley, to the belief that civilization involved preserving and helping the weak—if possible, by better equipping them to take part in social competition. This view did much to underlie the Charity Organization Society's distinction between the deserving and the undeserving poor; charity was best bestowed on those who could use it to help themselves.)

Social Darwinism had two aspects: internally, it focused on the struggle between individuals and was used to justify *laissez-faire;* between societies, it was used to support racist and imperialist views of the struggle between nations.[2] It was assumed that the middle classes and the Aryan races, being socially dominant, must thereby be genetically superior. Considerable protest had developed by the end of the century against both variants of these dogmas. Whilst many rationalists were sympathetic toward social Darwinism, one of the strongest arguments against it was the idealist and organic conception of the state and society which was the basis of the ethical movement. But the main source of protest came from the socialists, who protested vigorously against *laissez-faire* and many of whom were also opposed to social imperialism, either on moral grounds or because it diverted energy away from internal working-class revolution. In turn, 'Social Imperialism was designed to draw all classes together in defence of the nation and empire, and aimed to prove to the least well-to-do class that its interests were inseparable from those of the nation. It aimed at undermining the arguments of the socialists . . .'[3]

The quest for national efficiency was reflected in several ways in contemporary movements. Imperial expansion offered an outlet for trying new and efficient administrative procedures in societies where traditions need not be too much respected; much as the utilitarians had seen Benthamism put to use in India rather than England. Karl Pearson saw that wars could provide a means of natural selection between nations, and so were an essential means of progress, and his ideas were taken up by both the social imperialist and the eugenics movements. (The view that nations needed wars and competition to enable them to progress conflicted with the Spencerian view that societies could rely on internal evolution and pressure of population to bring about progress. It reflected both the growing pessimism about the rapidity and inevitability of progress, and the current uncertainty amongst anthropologists as to whether each society would proceed at its own pace along the same evolutionary track, or whether progress was spread by dissemination from the most advanced societies and so could be hurried up by imperialism and war.)

[2] Much of this section is based on L. A. Farrell, *The Origins and Growth of the English Eugenics Movement, 1865–1925*, Indiana University Ph.D. thesis, 1969.
[3] B. Semmel, *Imperialism and Social Reform: English Social Imperialist Thought, 1895–1914*, Allen & Unwin, London, 1960, p. 24; and on efficiency, see G. R. Searle, *The Quest for National Efficiency—a Study in British Politics and Political Thought, 1899–1914*, Blackwell, Oxford, 1971.

These themes were reinforced by the discovery of the poor health and physique of large numbers of recruits for the Boer War; the degeneracy of the nation was widely attributed to the low middle-class and high working-class birth-rate. The eugenics movement made rapid headway in the first two decades of the century—most Fabians and many rationalists were at least sympathetic to some of its proposals, and the 'sterilization of the unfit' became a national issue. The movement had many organizational links with the rationalists; several prominent rationalists were members of the Eugenics Society, and Darwin's son Leonard was at various times chairman both of the Society and of the Rationalist Press. The educational branch of the eugenics movement had begun as a breakaway from the Moral Education League, a part of the humanist movement set up by the ethical socieities.

One aspect of the eugenics movement which rationalists must have found appealing was that it was a sustained attempt to apply scientific methods to both political theory and social policy. It claimed to offer a scientific solution to the 'social problem', in that it explained the ill-health and maladjustment of the 'residuum' in terms of hereditary factors. The claim was reinforced by the publication in 1875 and 1912 of the American studies of the Jukes and Kallikaks families, where a poor heredity seemed to have spawned an alarming number of social undesirables. The newly emerging profession of psychiatry was much influenced by hereditarian explanations; at the turn of the century it was argued that 'hereditary tendency has more effect, is a more potential agency in the production of insanity, than all other causes put together.'[4]

An influential section of the British medical profession became alarmed by the evidence that insanity, tuberculosis and criminality were hereditary conditions; they argued that 'negative eugenics' should be used to stop the carriers reproducing themselves. This became the programme of the eugenics movement itself, who advocated that the intelligent should be encouraged to breed by selective taxation and that sick, insane and otherwise defective people in institutions should be segregated from the other sex. Very few members of the movement ever seriously advocated compulsory sterilization. It is curious, in view of the hostility of sociologists to hereditarian explanations of human behaviour, that

[4] M. H. Haller, 'Social Science and Genetics: an Historical Perspective', in D. V Glass, *Genetics*, Rockfeller University Press, New York 1968, p. 215. One of Karl Pearson's workers estimated that the force of heredity was at least five times as strong as that of the environment, Farrell, op. cit., pp. 165-6.

the Eugenics Society was formed in 1907 in response to the interest of the newly formed Sociological Society, who saw eugenics as a 'scientific sociology'. Inevitably, given the assumptions of the period, Francis Galton proposed that eugenics should become 'a new national religion'. (Religion was generally called for at points when something unpalatable had to be swallowed, or something desirable relinquished.)

Great impetus was given to the movement as a result of the research into genetics which finally separated Spencer's meliorist and Lamarckian view of the mechanisms of human progress from Darwinian evolution. It became obvious that biological evolution was a random process unrelated to the nature of social change. Man could no longer hope to create an ideal race and good society through a better environment and the growth of scientific knowledge, though the eugenic position was relatively optimistic in maintaining that once breeding came to be controlled by science, social problems would disappear. Arguments were put forward for the breeding of a natural aristocracy, and Grant Allen, a writer very popular with rationalists, thought that the emancipated woman should choose her husband—several if necessary—on the grounds of his genetic suitability.

Selective breeding had a subtler appeal to the materialist, anti-emotional sort of rationalist. 'I believe in Sir Francis Galton,' Aunt Phoebe remarked in one of H. G. Wells' novels, 'Eugenics . . . men ought to be bred like horses. No marriage or any nonsense of that kind. Just a simple scientific blending of points. Then Everything would be different.' One obvious difficulty was that the poor, backward and unfit would not benefit; why should they accept the exigencies of social progess?

At this point in the argument, in 1894 Benjamin Kidd put forward a powerful defence of Christianity. He argued that social evolution consisted precisely in the overcoming of rational self-interest, and that the motive power for this was religion. Religion was 'a form of belief, providing an ultra-rational sanction for that large class of conduct in the individual where his interests and the interests of the social organism are antagonistic, and by which the former are rendered subordinate to the latter in the general interests of the evolution which the race is undergoing.'[5] The argument that religion was the basis of morality had shifted its ground. Once supernatural sanctions had discouraged immoral behaviour; now

[5] B. Kidd, *Social Evolution*, Macmillan, 1894, p. 130.

religion had become a mechanism fostering a social emotion, something beyond the utilitarian scale of the values of science. The
argument was taken up and widely reiterated on a number of levels.
Its most powerful popular expression was Marie Corelli's best-
selling novel of the 1890s of the boy reared on rationalist dogmas
who knew everything that science could teach but could find no
reason for living; *The Mighty Atom* was only part of an active
contemporary concern that a positivist philosophy could offer no
reward commensurate with its demands. It is significant that both
the ethical movement and the labour churches were established in
the 1890s, and both were based on the view that man's natural
selfishness stood in the way of social progress and could only be
conquered by religion.

The other reasons for the decline of social Darwinism do not
seem entirely clear. Intellectually, advances in genetics made it
clear that generalizations could only really be made about breeding
populations rather than races or individuals, and that the variations
which did appear could often scarcely be looked upon as progress.
The new science of sociology began to attack the explanation of
human behaviour in hereditarian terms; Hobhouse had been led
through the influence of T. H. Green to the view that *human* progress
was less dependent on biological laws than on a self-conscious intelligence. To him, the birth of sociology marked the transition
from evolution to development, in which man could make his future
the subject of conscious moral choice and free himself from biological inevitability. Politically, members of the new socialist bodies
challenged the view that the poor were genetically inferior, and
the scientists in the 1920s and 30s who thought that there was a
scientific blueprint for social development were inclined to think that
it was not selective breeding but Soviet communism. Other explanations of human behaviour which found a large anti-social component
in all men were growing, and the very existence of a link between its
ideas and those of National Socialism did much to discredit social
Darwinism.

The changes that were brought about by advances in biology to
the general philosophy that was based upon it can be glimpsed in
The Science of Life, an immensely popular introduction to biology
first published in 1931 and frequently referred to by rationalists.
Its authors, H. G. Wells and his son and Julian Huxley, still believed that science and morality were connected and that the general
public needed to know about recent research because 'It reflects upon

the conduct of our lives throughout. It throws new light upon our moral judgements.'[6]

The authors emphasized man's descent from and biological similarity to apes, but they also stressed the difference in their mental powers which had enabled man to create an elaborate society and a high degree of self-knowledge. They defended the Darwinian view of evolution as purposeless, the selection of random variations by environmental factors, against 'life-force' or teleological theories. But through the growth of man's power to control his environment, and his growing capacity for rational as distinct from traditional or metaphysical thought, he was being enabled to break away from control by natural selection. Grave problems were posed, however, by the removal of the pressures of natural selection; over-population, and 'those untouchables [who] constitute pockets of evil germ-plasm responsible for a large amount of vice, disease, defect and pauperism.' The authors briefly flirted with the notion of 'positive breeding' but whereas Huxley was inclined to advocate it, Wells, with a firmer grasp of both political reality and what would be emotionally acceptable, overruled him.

Social progress was now seen to rest on the 'understanding and competent minority', who became part of a group mind, and this stream of 'larger, comprehensive life', representing man's intellectual achievements, enabled individuals to cast aside the crutch of belief in a personal immortality. The authors were able to assume that religion was largely the province of the ignorant and superstitious, and not likely to impede seriously the growth of knowledge and consequently of progress. When opposing a scientific to a theological view of man they were monists, but none the less inclined to insist on the value of subjective experience and the exercise of the will.

Reason Dethroned

At various times the debate on the processes of natural and social evolution impinged on the rapidly changing science of psychology, which also seemed to be leading to a view of man less congenial to the hopeful picture of the rationalist. Nineteenth-century psychologists had often assumed man's mind to be a *tabula rasa* which formed ideas out of the units of sensation caused by its contact with

[6] H. G. Wells, G. P. Wells, and J. Huxley, *The Science of Life*, Cassell, London, 1931, p. 3.

the environment, and thus education became the key to indefinite human improvement. Phrenology had led to the localization of specific mental functions in specific parts of the brain[7] and had been very popular with sceptics, for whilst they had no doubt that there was a faculty of reason which grew with evolution, there seemed to be no physiological entity to correspond to the soul or the will.[8]

Most nineteenth-century rationalists do not seem to have found intolerable the picture of man as a finite mechanism, part of a universe ruled by iron laws; as Plekhanov observed, those who believe most firmly in the iron laws of the cosmos appear to have little difficulty in regarding themselves as free agents. One of their reactions was the 'grimness' described earlier, and another characteristic one was the emphasis that it was man's *reason* which enabled him to comprehend the world. The adulation of human reason so characteristic of humanists carried with it the subtle implication that by understanding natural laws, man could in fact manipulate them; or that the exceptional man could. Bagehot's *Physics and Politics, or Thoughts on the Application of the Principles of 'Natural Selection' and 'Inheritance' to Political Society* was an immensely popular defence of social determinism, and like some social Darwinists he attacked democracy on the grounds that it was only the exceptional man who could triumph over his immediate circumstances and enable the race to progress. The English versions of this doctrine were inclined to cast the scientist or the statesman in the role of the superman. But developments in twentieth-century psychology undermined the reign of reason from within.

Darwin had shown that man was biologically part of the animal kingdom. The 1900s saw the development of instinct theory, or the explanation of much of human and animal behaviour in terms of autonomous, ineradicable and usually unpleasant instinctual traits which both drastically limited the possibility of human progress and devalued reason as a factor influencing behaviour. In America one reason for the rapid acceptance of versions of both behaviourism and Freud after the First World War was that unlike instinct theory, both allowed some role for social reform.[9]

The belief in the importance of the faculty of reason for social progress was also attacked from the opposite direction by William

[7] R. M. Young, *Mind, Brain and Adaptation in the Nineteenth Century*, Oxford University Press, London, 1969.
[8] J. Y. Simpson, *Landmarks in the Struggle between Science and Religion*, Hodder and Stoughton, London, 1925.
[9] M. H. Haller, op. cit.

James, who at the turn of the century did much to demolish Spencer's associationalist psychology. He showed how his unitary evolutionary sequences denied man any free will, and devalued his moral decisions to mere rationalizations of the inevitable. More importantly for rationalists, James dismissed the mechanist view of man which limited his legitimate mental activities to reason and cognition. It is clear from our experience of ourselves, said James, that a large part of our mental activity is taken up with our emotions, wishes, sentiments and intuitions. Our minds exist prior to and independently of our experience of the world, and because they do, they impose a purpose and a shape on our doings. Indeed, the concepts of science are thin and shallow compared with the rich and living reality of subjective experience. The *Varieties of Religious Experience* argues that it is possible to be either religious or irreligious in a more or less rationalist way, but that the essence and importance of religion lies in man's emotional response to his existence. The religious response may be organically based, but this does not explain it away; 'Scientific theories are just as much organically determined as religious emotions are; and if we only knew the facts intimately enough, we should doubtless see "the liver" determining the dicta of the sturdy atheist as decisively as it does those of the Methodist under conviction anxious about his soul.'[10]

To James, the religious response is something that helps us to adjust more easily to the fact of our dependence on an indifferent natural order. During the twentieth century, because nature is no longer seen as conscious or benevolent man's position as part of nature becomes more difficult to accept. Culture is seen, by both Malinowski and Freud for example, as something which both disguises and reduces our consciousness of ourselves as merely part of a cosmos which is indifferent to our existence.

> Our solar system, with its harmonies, is now seen as but one passing case of a certain sort of moving equilibrium in the heavens, realized by a local accident in an appalling wilderness of worlds where no life can exist . . . The Darwinian notion of chance production, and subsequent destruction, speedy or deferred, applies to the largest as well as to the smallest facts. It is impossible, in the present temper of the scientific imagination, to find in the driftings of the cosmic atoms, whether they work on the universal or on the particular scale, anything but a kind of aimless weather, doing and undoing, achieving no proper history, and leaving no result. Nature has no one distinguishable ultimate tendency with which it is possible to feel a sympathy.[11]

[10] W. James, *The Varieties of Religious Experience: a Study in Human Nature*, Longmans, Green & Co., London, 1902, p. 14.
[11] ibid., pp. 491-2.

An even more influential theory of personality to cast doubt on the strength and autonomy of reason was that of Freud. As his doctrines were popularly interpreted, much intellectual activity seemed to be a sham. Chapman Cohen, president of the secular movement and a thorough-going materialist, welcomed psychoanalysis because he thought that Freud had extended determinism to the psyche, but most rationalists did not share his enthusiasm. Psychoanalysis was neither a proper science nor were its conclusions favourable to rationalism, 'the pseudo-science which would dethrone reason and make us all the slaves of the unconscious'. Edward Clodd, Chairman of the Rationalist Press from 1906–13 and author of many of its popularized accounts of science and anthropology, found the Oedipus Complex '. . . a theory which is unproved and malicious. It is hardly worth while to dwell upon its repellent character . . .', and many rationalists objected to the 'muck-raking' by which not only religion but many of the achievements of civilization were attributed to re-directed sexuality. Rationalists were obviously not alone in their protests; their reaction must have been typical of British society. The peculiar and enhanced difficulty for the rationalist lay in his inability to retreat to a more traditional and pleasing view of the situation, committed as he was to basing his views on recent knowledge, and integrating such knowledge into a picture of human life and ethics.

In the context of the slow and painful absorption of the developments in the psychologists' view of man into the rationalist tradition, Graham Wallas, president of the Association in the late 1920s and a popular lecturer to ethical societies, reflected some of the rationalist's dilemma. His life illustrated many of the themes of the cultural *milieu* of the rationalist. He was the son of an evangelical clergyman and lost his faith at Oxford under the influence of Darwin and W. K. Clifford. He was dismissed from his post as a schoolteacher because of his irreligion, and became a worker at Toynbee Hall and a lecturer on moral issues for the Fabian Society. As the utilitarians had done, he saw social, moral and political problems as psychological at root; why did men not act democratically naturally, and was it possible to devise a political system to put their better impulses into action? At first he looked to education in morals and civics for the bridge between the psychological nature of man and a desirable socialist society, but then tried to create a revised psychological basis for stable democracy. He rejected 'free reason' as the basis of democratic politics because it had been discredited by science, but he also rejected the 'intuitionist' psychology of Kidd and contemporary European thinkers, and adopted the attempted synthesis of William James. He was impressed by the danger of instinctual and habitual patterns of behaviour being carried on into new situations; the large scale and impersonality of industrial society had created such psychological disruption that he feared that an adaptive attitude to human psychology, such as that of eugenics, would be necessary in order to achieve social efficiency and satisfaction. Wallas never resolved the conflict between his convictions that most of human nature was biologically given, but that none the less behaviour could be radically changed and the transition to collectivism was in any case inevitable.[12]

Significantly enough, Wallas was very much the 'Man of Letters', opposed to the growth of intellectual specialization or a 'value-free' social science. His insistence on trying to comprehend the 'whole man', and to retain morality and ideas as important agents in human affairs in a period when increasing stress was being laid on social conditioning and economic constraints, obviously struck many contemporaries outside the rationalist movement as old-fashioned idealism. His general and synoptic approach to the social sciences was equally unpopular with Fabian social reformers. 'His wide and conversational speculations about men in society do not impress us', wrote Beatrice Webb. The rationalist movement was increasingly separated from the far more demarcated boundaries and abstracted empiricism of the culture of English academic life.

The Savage Mind

At the time when the rationalist movement was formed, anthropology was an important part of its general view of the progress of mankind. The early accounts by Spencer and Tylor of the development of society were strongly evolutionary and cast the decline of religious superstition for a central role in the drama of human progress.[13] As White, one of the major creators of the myth of science saw it, anthropology showed that man had gradually evolved upward, and

[12] This account of Wallas is taken from M. J. Wiener, *Between Two Worlds—the Political Thought of Graham Wallas*, Clarendon Press, Oxford, 1971.
[13] For a detailed study of the influence of evolutionary ideas on Victorian anthropology, see J. S. Burrow, *Evolution and Society: a Study in Victorian Social Theory*, Cambridge University Press, London, 1966.

so refuted the theological doctrine of the Fall. A review of Tylor in *Watt's Literary Guide* concluded that 'As theology, or the science of God, wanes, anthropology, or the science of man, waxes.' The early anthropologists hoped to discern the laws of cultural development; '. . . our thoughts, wills and actions accord with laws as definite as those which govern the motion of waves, the combination of acids and bases, and the growth of plants and animals,' wrote Tylor.[14] As the rationalists did, they saw religion as beliefs—in the supernatural, in ghosts, in spiritual beings—and so as something which could be replaced by other and more rational beliefs. *The Golden Bough*, immensely widely read and influential in the popular imagination long after Frazer's methods and conclusions had been abandoned by the profession, enshrined an evolutionary theory in which magic, science and religion always existed, but magic and religion dwindled as science increased its influence in human affairs, and the more ritual and supernatural aspects of religion were more and more only to be found among the ignorant.

To the first generation of anthropologists, the salient difference between the accounts of African societies which were their main material and modern life was the large amount of social and intellectual resources savages devoted to magical practices and beliefs. Every aspect of their lives seemed impoverished and bleak thereby; to even the most liberal, they were merely pitiable. The Association published several anthropological works which described the *burden* that religion laid on man, and which drew analogies between very primitive activities such as cannibalism and their survival in a more refined and symbolic form as communion suppers, et cetera. 'In a very pregnant conclusion, Dr. Tylor broadly hints to our modern theologians that one office of ethnography is to reveal how much "time-honoured superstition" lies hid under the "garb of modern knowledge".'

This sort of comparison was considered, and not only by rationalists, to constitute a devastating attack on religion; Robertson-Smith was dismissed from his post at the Free Church College at Aberdeen. In a summary of 'The Debt of Freethought to Anthropology' in the Rationalist Press Association's Annual for 1913, it was thought that facts collected about the religions of lower cultures were the major challenge to scriptural authority because they revealed the universality of myths of the fall of man, the flood, the killing of a god and

[14] E. B. Tylor, *Primitive Culture: Researches into the Development of Mythology, Philosophy, Religion, Language, Art and Custom*, Murray, London, 1871, p. 2.

his resurrection. (The argument then went on to an unusually liberal conclusion; the efforts of missionary activities in primitive societies were disastrous precisely because in simple societies where secular life had no autonomy and abstract morality was weak, the indigenous religion was a necessary binding force.)

The influence of Robertson-Smith, Spencer, Tylor and Frazer also spread to the interpretation of classical religion. The Enlightenment had seen classical antiquity as the period of dawn of rationality and knowledge together with a lessening of superstition which was not to occur again until the end of the Dark Ages. Deists and *philosophes* characteristically underemphasized and intellectualized the role of religion in Greek and Roman civilization.[15] Jane Harrison was the first to apply the new anthropological ideas to classical Greek religion, and to insist that the literature and philosophy of the period, admirable though they were, sprang from religion but also did much to check and hold at bay those 'elements of licence and monstrosity' which were a part of the religious impulse.

Her later reading of Bergson and Durkheim only strengthened her insistence that religion, along with philosophy and art, arose from the ritual needs and practices of Hellenic civilization rather than from its intellectually much more acceptable mythology, and Gilbert Murray largely followed her in seeing recent anthropological findings as pointing to the inescapably irrational nature of all religion. Gilbert Murray became a leading official of the Rationalist Press Association; Jane Harrison, along with others of her circle, was an enthusiastic member.[16] The Association did much to popularize their new views on classical religion, but all these writers, expecially Frazer, were remarkably circumspect in their polemical attacks on Christianity or readiness to apply the new anthropological knowledge specifically to Christianity. This role was left to the popularizer; and his marginal place in the English intellectual establishment was both cause and consequence of this.

The most popular with the members of the many anthropological works published by the Rationalist Press seems to have been Grant Allen's account of *The Evolution of the Idea of God*. As Allen's biographer in the D.N.B. commented, he had 'framed an evolutionary system of his own, based on the work of Herbert Spencer.'

---

[15] P. Gay, *The Enlightment: an Interpretation: the Rise of Modern Paganism*, Knopf, New York 1967.
[16] M. Despland, 'Seven Decades of Writing on Greek Religion', *Religion: a Journal of Religion and Religions*, Vol. 4(2), pp. 118–50.

Allen made a living as a scientific popularizer, but had come to popular fame with *The Woman who Did*, i.e. abandoned marriage and satisfied her sexual needs as she wished so as to prevent the radical degeneration which was following on personal frustration and genetic mismating. *The Evolution of the Idea of God* was described 'from its earliest and crudest beginnings in the savage mind of primitive man to that highly evolved and abstract form which it finally assumes in contemporary philosophical and theological thinking.' It claimed to be concerned with the psychological origins of beliefs and not their truth, but a presentation of Christianity as largely built on borrowings from older religions, which suggested that gospel accounts of Jesus might well be fictitious and the crucifixion a description of the ritual murder of a temporary king, could hardly have been acceptable to the orthodox Christians of an ethnocentric and imperialist age. The Bishop of London was reputed to have called it 'that most dangerous of books . . .', which must have endeared it to rationalists. Allen suggested that religion served different functions for different people. The essential function for the uneducated was religious custom or practice, which had separate origins from and no necessary connections with the abstract and ethical theological elements of religion. This was a line frequently taken by both Christian and rationalist apologists searching for some sort of evolutionary *rapprochement*.

After the evolutionary school of Spencer and Tylor had been abandoned, the emphases of anthropology became rather less favourable to the world view of the Association. Stress was now laid on the argument that religion fulfilled a *function* in society, and Malinowski, by insisting that the function must ultimately be related to a biological need, made religion seem altogether less likely to wither away.

Anthropology was affected, as all social thought was, by the sense of crisis and decay of stable tradition that was so strong in Europe at the turn of the century. The problem of consciousness, according to Stewart Hughes, lay at the core of the general revolt against positivism; 'it was the period when the subjective attitude of the observer of society first thrust itself forward in peremptory fashion . . .'[17] The effects of this change in viewpoint have constituted most of the intellectual history of the social sciences in the twentieth century, and their slow retreat from positivism. If the process has been slower

[17] H. S. Hughes, *Consciousness and Society: the Reorientation of European Social Thought 1890–1930*, MacGibbon and Kee, London, 1959, p. 15.

in Britain than elsewhere, it is because much of the activity of anthropologists and sociologists has been concerned with the administration of alien peoples and with social problems; the moral worth of such activity was until recently easy to assume, and so a detached pose was more plausible.[18] But the process has also been slow because of the influence of the rationalist tradition itself on English intellectual life. The pessimism about man's natural rationality or even common sense, the complete relativism and subjectivism of many European thinkers, did not seem to be important or influential arguments to most rationalists and perhaps to most English social thinkers until the 1950s.

This is not to argue that the social sciences are now indifferent to the status of religious beliefs. The current assumption is that conventional religion is no longer a necessary part of the world view of the educated members of an advanced society, though there is confusion over whether some social and psychological needs are thereby left unfulfilled, are replaced by science or by something else which is a functional alternative to religion.[19] The definition of religion itself has changed; the early anthropological definitions, like those of the rationalists, were *intellectualist*—religion was belief. It then became something which fulfilled certain functions, mainly because of the binding force of collective ritual behaviour, and Durkheim produced a radically different view as to its social force, antipathetic equally to liberal individualism and to theologians. As Evans-Pritchard put it, 'Religion is what religion *does*'. This changed emphasis has not been explicitly commented on by writers for the Association, but it does constitute a difficulty for the original rationalist view that religion is a set of erroneous beliefs.

The recent debate amongst anthropologists and the philosophers concerning the autonomy and the universality of reason, and whether religious statements which appear to flout common-sense views of reality can be considered to be rational in any sense, has raised several questions which are fundamental to the philosophy of rationalism. Is reason something which can be defined in terms of universal criteria, or can it only be assessed in context? Can religious statements be understood by the non-believer, and what status do 'interior' and 'exterior' understandings of religion have? Is a rational and factual understanding of the affairs of life enough, or will we

[18] P. S. Abrams, *The Origins of British Sociology: 1834–1914*, University of Chicago Press, Chicago, 1968.
[19] See my *Sociologists and Religion*, Collier-Macmillan, London, 1973, for a more elaborate development of this argument.

inevitably resort to some kind of metaphysic to sustain us under suffering and uncertainty? It is both sensible and courageous for the Rationalist Press to devote much space to these issues in its journals in recent years.

The New Physics

The sciences most extensively popularized and discussed by rationalists during the early twentieth century were biology and anthropology; during the 1920s, popular interest switched to physics and astronomy. The works published by the Association in these fields were less propagandist in that they did not (and indeed could not) stress the destructive effects that the new knowledge would have on religious faith. There were several reasons for this.

The discoveries that were being made in physics, chemistry and astronomy were so abstract and non-intuitive as to require a considerable effort merely to grasp them, and analogies with social and moral life were consequently hard to draw. Scientific laws were not seen as universal causal forces, but as probabilistic and partial. J. A. Hobson attacked some of those who reported these new discoveries for having extended

> into the field of inorganic science a wild doctrine of irrationalism. Hitherto the idea of rigid determinism, though regarded as unnecessary for scientific specialists, was generally accepted as the basic principle of natural phenomena. Effects followed causes and were commensurate with them. If you knew the causes you could infallibly predict the effects. Are we to scrap this determinism alike in the world of matter and the world of mind, substituting what?[20]

He believed that if things appeared to be indeterminate, this might be due to imperfect knowledge rather than the structure of matter, and defended determinism on positivist principles for having improved the grounds of moral judgements. Vice was ugly, not sinful, goodness moral beauty, not a virtue, and this non-judgemental basis of viewing human behaviour had produced more enlightened attitudes to punishment, et cetera. The scientific doctrine of indeterminacy would have a harmful moral effect.[21]

Another reason for the antagonism of many rationalists to the new knowledge was that most of the outstanding publicists of

[20] J. A. Hobson defending the Positivist and positivist view of science, Comte memorial lecture for 1933, 'Rationalism and Humanism'.
[21] ibid.

science of the period—A. N. Whitehead, Sir Arthur Eddington, Clark Maxwell, Sir James Jeans—either were or became if not precisely Christians at least quasi-religious, and claimed, much to the indignation of the Association, that the new physics supported, or at least did not contradict, Christianity. Two attacks were increasingly made on the rationalist ideology of science.

The first was the claim that science supported religion. The universe was redrawn as decreasingly determinate, ruled by probability rather than 'iron laws', and thus it came to be hinted that mysterious forces moved behind the surface of things. The natural order was seen as wonderfully complex, but also mysterious and unknowable. The materialist and mechanistic view of the world of many scientists was replaced by a neo-idealism. '. . . The universe can be best pictured, although still very imperfectly and inadequately, as consisting of pure thought, the thought of what, for want of a wider word, we must describe as a mathematical thinker.'[22] Only abstract mathematics, Jeans thought, could express or describe ultimate reality, and the more intuitive mechanical explanations of nature were being abandoned. Matter would be reinterpreted as a manifestation of mind, and consequently man, the only thinking animal, was reinstated in a position of uniqueness and power from his more lowly place in the biologists' scheme of things. Several accounts of the history of science were produced by Christian apologists which emphasized that because science was no longer materialist it was no longer antipathetic to religion.[23]

That a number of eminent contemporary scientists were Christians disturbed the simple identity that the rationalist movement had been able to assume between scientific thought and agnosticism or atheism. A disillusion with scientists became evident; 'You cannot suppose', argued Chapman Cohen in a debate with Joad in 1928 on 'Materialism, Has it been Exploded', 'after knocking down God Almighty, that I am going to jib at Professor Eddington.' And he was joined by Susan Stebbing with a trenchant critique of the mystical tendencies in the work of scientific writers on physics.[24] Jeans and Eddington, she felt, 'approached their task through an emotional fog . . .'; to the rationalist, it was poison gas. There had been a

[22] J. Jeans, *The Mysterious Universe*, Penguin Books, Harmondsworth, 1937, pp. 169–70.
[23] See for examples J. Y. Simpson, op. cit., p. 222; L. P. Jacks, *The Revolt against Mechanism* (Hibbert Lectures for 1933), Allen and Unwin, London, 1934; I. G. Barbour, *Issues in Science and Religion*, S.C.M. Press, London, 1966.
[24] S. Stebbing, *Philosophy and the Physicists*, Methuen, London, 1937.

revival of interest in spiritualism during the First World War which had claimed several prominent scientists as members and which led the *Literary Guide* to denounce science as 'morally bankrupt'. H. G. Wells, a man fervently admired by many rationalists, disappointed and saddened them with the increasing number of his works which were set in a quasi-religious vein, and Joad complained that the Association put strong pressure on him to conform to an orthodox materialist viewpoint.[25] Scientists were occasionally proving a disappointment to the Association, and some members argued that it should return to attacking religion directly rather than relying on scholarly work to do it indirectly—'we relied too much upon professors.'

Joseph McCabe, an ex-Franciscan who had been a lecturer for the Rationalist Press, published with them a refutation of the 'literary hoax' of Jeans, Eddington, *et al.*, i.e. the claim that nineteenth-century materialism had been exploded by the new physics. He defended Darwinian biology at length, and belittled Einstein's theories as only applying to physics. He rejected any view that scientific ideas might be subject to perpetual change; theories '. . . may become as free from possible doubt as the facts themselves . . .'[26]

In 1953 the Association published a more sophisticated defence of deriving moral values from science in the post-relativity era.[27] The author distinguished between truth and reality. Philosophically the theory of reality had been used to emphasize the subjective and relative nature of human perceptions; individuals were locked each into his own series of values and world views, all of which were equally valid. He argued that in practice the sense of the reality of things is a vital function of the mind, and that this requires us to postulate an absolute universal standard of morality, to which we relate our behaviour. '. . . the mind can, and must, and does, postulate the actual existence of any conception which is necessary for the consistency of its experience, and on which depends its stability in an unknown world.' Truth was consistency; abstract ideas could consequently be treated as real if they were consistent

---

[25] See the review of *God, the Invisible King* in *Literary Guide*, June 1917, p. 81, and 'What Wells meant to my Generation', *Rationalist Annual*, 1947, p. 70. Joad claimed in 'On being no longer a Rationalist' (*Rationalist Annual*, 1946, pp. 65–75) that the Association was as intellectually bigoted as the Christian opposition, but it must be said that the Association continued to publish his attacks on them.

[26] J. McCabe, *The Riddle of the Universe Today*, Watts, London, 1934.

[27] E. C. Barter, *Relativity and Reality, a Reinterpretation of Anomalies appearing in the theories of Relativity*, Watts, London, 1953.

with material ideas of reality. Reasoning itself was a product of the imagination, and therefore ultimately unreal. 'Reasoning itself can be real and yet have no connection with reality.' The concepts of relativity were justified, finally, by experimental observations; i.e., mathematical constructs were judged by our world of experience, and this consequently must be our ultimate criterion of reality.

Fellow-travelling

The second attack that was made on the rationalist ideology of science during the 1920s and 30s was that science *was* internally connected to a social and moral philosophy, that of communism.[28] During the 1920s, the scientific community seemed on the whole to have become less interested in politics, perhaps because government support was rapidly increasing. During the 1930s, the general admiration for the social progress and scientific achievements of the Soviet Union combined with the obvious disutilities of the high unemployment and other social costs of the capitalist system led many British scientists to a concern with the 'social relations of science', i.e. the uses to which science was put and the extent to which societies could be guided by science and by scientists.

The movement produced two general results, first an interest in scientific humanism which was linked with the Rationalist Press and promoted by men such as Julian Huxley and H. G. Wells who had worked for the Association, and later in the 1930s the growth of popular Marxism and the rapid success of the Left Book Club (very similar to the Rationalist Press in structure but far more successful— it had acquired twelve thousand members after a month and grew to nearly sixty thousand by 1939) which swept many scientists into communism. Few of them joined the party, but those who were interested in the relations between science and social life rejected the liberal individualism of the rationalist's view of scientific knowledge.

The radicalization of science in the 1930s was most marked in physics and biochemistry where great advances were being made. The 'social relations of science' movement laid great stress on the application of science to human affairs, and the power that scientists had to improve them. Many scientists were inclined to be critical of conventional politics and to look for an intelligent scientific control

---

[28] N. Wood, *Communism and British Intellectuals*, Gollancz, London, 1959, and see A. Marwick, *The Deluge*, Penguin Books, Harmondsworth, 1967.

of social and economic life. Science, which was after all the pursuit of truth in the spirit of objective, rational and open-minded enquiry, was contrasted with corrupt and uncertain politicians who neither knew nor cared about the expanding horizons of knowledge. (The theme of the scientist-king is a common one among scientists, appearing especially vividly in their occasional excursions into fiction. Fred Hoyle's account of how astronomers take over from the squabbling and time-serving politicians to save humanity from *The Black Cloud* is a classic of the genre.)

In 1931, a group of members tried to persuade the Rationalist Press to abandon attacks on religion and commit itself to 'scientific humanism', the effort to make science effective in human affairs. They wanted to abandon the liberal individualism of the Association because 'the higher moral possibilities of mankind cannot be realized without the scientific control of the political and moral mechanism of the world.' One of them pointed out that the younger members of the Association were supporters of socialism and scientific humanism, but that the directors were still anti-supernaturalist and politically individualist. But, as J. B. S. Haldane argued, it was impossible to try to base social policy on science when science and scientists were not unified—'Unfortunately, there is no agreement among rationalists as to how science should best be applied to human life'—and many other scientists reiterated that moral issues could not be settled by reference to science. Most of members' letters which were published thought that scientific humanism was a 'soft-headed' and indefinite platform which would lead to 'sentimental chaos', and agreed with the directors that the aims of the Association should still be to carry on 'propaganda to the end of opening the eyes of other people who still adhere to religion'. They were also not prepared to support socialism in order to bring about rational planning, but essentially saw science as a tool to demolish superstition.

The 'social relations of science' movement was welcome to the Association in that it represented an influential body of men who believed that scientific ideas could and should be extended to social and moral life, as against the view that a stable frontier had been established between science and religion which confined science to the quantitative and the phenomenal. Whilst rationalists were eager to exclude religion from the realm of science, they wanted to extend the control of science over the disputed territories of social and moral life. The general decline in the popularity of materialist and evolutionary explanations of human life left it open to the influence of 'non-scientific' ideas such as vitalism. The 'social relations' movement itself capitalized on the work of rationalists in trying to extend scientific thinking to social and moral life, and seems to have represented a shift of interest in the British scientific community from the intellectual to the social implications of science.

During the 1930s the sales and the number of subscribers to the Association began to fall, perhaps because of an increased interest among the middle-class 'advanced' public in political ideas with which it was unsympathetic. During the 1930s, for example, the proportion of W.E.A. classes that were held on political and economic topics rose from five per cent to sixty-five. As other means of mass communication developed, it became evident that despite the relative social acceptance of atheism in the twentieth century, the battle to reach the popular audience would have to be renewed with the B.B.C. The Association found that under Reith, no discussion of rationalism or even Unitarianism was permitted, and that prominent rationalist intellectuals who were frequent broadcasters, for example on the Brains Trust, were not allowed to discuss their irreligion. The protests of the Association redoubled with the arrival of television, and after repeated attempts to bring pressure to bear on the Corporation via sympathetic M.P.s and eminent rationalists, limited concessions were made in 1947 to the extent of some experimental programmes of religious discussion. No progress was made until the Margaret Knight lectures of 1955, when a few mild protests against religious teaching in schools led to popular outcry and a ban on all such broadcasts. The publicity gained for humanism by the issue showed the extent to which opinions were changing, and by the mid-sixties the Corporation felt that public opinion had changed sufficiently to allow the occasional eminent humanist to state his position.

But although the Association had effectively lobbied for the right to use the new mass media, their very growth put its position as a publisher in jeopardy. During the Second World War, the general rise in demand for books of all kinds led to record sales. After the war, the financial position of the Association rapidly worsened. The demand for books, especially on theological issues, had greatly decreased by 1948, and production and printing costs were rising so steeply that it was becoming very difficult for small publishers to stay in business.

'The new Philosophy puts all in Doubt . . .'

On an intellectual level, general attitudes to science were not as uniformly enthusiastic as they had been. Hiroshima had provided a sharp proof of the lack of connection between scientific and moral progress. Many eminent scientists had become distressed at the extent to which the public accorded them unquestioning trust. '. . . public men in England now display a touching but alarming faith in the power of science to solve any national problem however serious,' said the President of the British Association in 1948.[29] There was a general retreat from the view that scientific knowledge could be applied directly to social and political life without being mediated by political or moral decision. The first signs of change were the attacks by Polanyi and others on the restrictions on scientific freedom in Soviet Russia. By extension, they pointed out, the social control of science anywhere was likely to have anti-liberal implications for both science and society.

These changes were connected with the general shift in the view of progress itself. At the beginning of the century, a belief in progress was seen as part of a peculiarly modern outlook linked with a belief in man's goodness and self-sufficiency and the power of science to banish suffering and evil; by the post-war period it had become the 'bastard offspring of a Christian world outlook'.[30] One of the first signs of change had been the claim that the belief in progress was merely *The Heavenly City of the Eighteenth Century Philosophers;* that it could only have sprung from a Christian soil, and had bloomed forth into various totalitarian movements for total social transformation. By this period, the contemporary tendency to assess ideas in terms of their connections with fascist and communist regimes was well under way, and proposals with any kind of positivist or social engineering flavour were suspect.

Many of the older members of the Rationalist Press were puzzled and dismayed by the growing discrepancies between contemporary thought and the traditional aims and assumptions of rationalism. During the 1930s and 40s, most of the letters about this subject to the *Literary Guide* urged the Association to concentrate on the

[29] H. Tizard, *The Passing World: Science and Social Progress*, Bureau of Current Affairs, London, 1948, p. 5.
[30] W. W. Wagar, 'Modern Views of the Origins of the Idea of Progress', *Journal of the History of Ideas*, Vol. 28(1), 1967, pp. 55–70.

surer path of attacking religion. But as F. C. C. Watts reported to the 1944 Annual General Meeting, the growing general indifference to religion made it difficult to recruit members on this basis, and he proposed to publish more popular books on ethics and science of a less directly polemical nature. Many members agreed with him and thought that rationalists should take up and combat other forms of irrational thought, and discuss the issues raised by the new social sciences and continental philosophy.

In 1947, some of the younger members of the Association together with a group of university students started *The Free Mind*, 'An Organ of Student Rationalism', in an attempt to recruit undergraduates. In addition to the usual articles on scientific, social-scientific and literary topics and news of the rationalist movement, the *Free Mind* challenged many of the shibboleths of an older generation of rationalists. It was argued that, far from science slowly triumphing until it could explain all reality as a coherent and rule-governed whole, uncertainty was unavoidable. Rationalists were criticized for believing in science in the same blind and unquestioning manner as the faithful believed in the Scriptures. 'The credulity of Rationalists is astonishing; they raise football cheers at any technological invention, however stupid, dangerous or anti-human, and they are ready to embrace any and every panacea, chemical, medical or psychological, provided someone who calls himself a scientist vouchsafes it.'[31]

These criticisms were based on the general contemporary acceptance of the distinction between scientific knowledge and value-judgements. The corollary for the Association was that whatever the discoveries of science such knowledge could have no impact on a religious understanding, which did not attempt to give a rational account of the world. It was this position which, aided by the triumph of pragmatism and linguistic philosophy, became general in the twentieth century, although many leading philosophers such as Bertrand Russell and A. J. Ayer argued forcibly against it. (Both were prominent supporters of the Association.) The trend in new theological work toward notions of commitment, leaps of faith, and the tolerance of ambiguity was part of the process.[32] This position placed traditional rationalist assumptions in jeopardy; as two directors pointed out when it was proposed to publish a history of modern thought, 'whilst there was excellent material for our purpose in the

---

[31] Letter from Conan Nicholas, *Free Mind*, October 1947, p. 24.
[32] See W. W. Bartley, *The Retreat to Commitment*, Chatto & Windus, London, 1964.

book, the suggestion that subjects like ethics lie to some extent outside the range of scientific treatment rather "sells the pass".'[33]

The group associated with *The Free Mind* argued that rationalism
could not provide a guide to life merely by supporting science and
attacking the churches; it would have to abandon scientific materialism and create its own code of ethics. The rationalist accounts of
religion, it was suggested, with their vivid accounts of Christian
hypocrisies and tortures, mainly served to arouse sadistic feelings.
Perhaps the unkindest cut of all was J. A. C. Brown's 'The Psycho-
Pathology of Rationalism', in which on the basis of his long experience in the movement he suggested the variety of unconscious
motives which underlay the beliefs of many members. The essentially religious who felt uneasily impelled to joke about God; those
terrified by emotion who defended themselves against uncertainty
and feeling by the use of reason; the closed-minded and hard-
headed materialist, opposed to psychology, psychoanalysis, tele-
pathy or anything which introduced uncertainty into a safe closed
universe. Genuine rationalism was possible, but the Association's
ignorance of social science had blinded them to the fallibility of the
mind and the inter-penetration of reason and desire; they should
seek for knowledge about themselves, and attack political and other
forms of irrationality rather than the moribund churches.[34]

Even in the humanist movement, so open to all expression of
dissension and criticism, such trenchant attacks were hard to support.
And the *Free Mind* was losing money and did not reflect the Association's general policy; several directors felt that its purpose should
have been to combat the influence of the S.C.M. In 1949 the editors
of the journal and the president of the Association resigned since
the board did not support their views, and the growth of humanist
support in the universities after the war was increasingly exploited
by the ethical movement.

The incident illustrated some of the inevitable difficulties that
result when an organization with a definite general mythology and
programme for social change is open to the implications of changing
knowledge; the intelligentsia who relayed and interpreted the new
insights were not committed either to the ideology or the practical
ends of the organization, and so had no inhibitions about launching
attacks which would have prevented the practical ends of recruiting
members and defending traditional interests. During the 1950s and

---

[33] Minutes of the R.P.A. for 9 May 1946, p. 21.
[34] *Free Mind*, Autumn 1948, pp. 3 *et seq.*

60s, a more flexible and sophisticated intellectual basis was created for defending rationalist objectives, but this in turn ran the risk of losing any distinctively rationalist nature.

It took account as far as was possible of new themes in both philosophy and the philosophy of science. Both stressed strongly the non-aggregative, non-synthetic nature of knowledge, and the 'obsolescence of the conception of science as the pursuit of truth.'[35] The Association seems to have mainly reported research in the two fields of greatest contemporary popular interest, medicine and the social sciences. It is characteristic of such research that whilst its claim to universal truth is uncertain, its human utility and social importance are usually obvious. It is also often the case that in the attempts to use such research, a religious body can be seen to be resisting, and the Association together with the other humanist bodies has found a constructive social role in initiating 'controversies on such practical questions as education, family planning, marriage, divorce, crime and punishment, and individual freedom.' Since many of its members are professional people, often teachers, doctors and paramedical workers, these issues have a direct bearing on their working lives. The group who assumed control of the Association in the 1950s introduced articles into the journal on the application of the social sciences and history to contemporary life, and it was hoped that by relegating 'destructive Rationalism' to a supplement the journal would attract those who wanted to be kept up to date with trends and controversies in the 'world of serious thought', and who would welcome informed discussion of 'questions affecting the freedom of the mind'.

The issue of scientific progress and the freedom of the mind was given impetus by the limitations which have been imposed on scientific freedom by the regimes of Nazi Germany and Soviet Russia, and a number of scholars who fled from Germany produced a series of influential works on philosophy, political theory, pre-judice and science, all of which stressed the crucial importance of possessive individualism for scientific advance. Current philosophies of science which lay stress on the importance of the 'open society' as a pre-condition for the recognition and incorporation of scientific discovery into a healthy scientific tradition have found much favour among writers for the Association. In recent years, the Association has printed many articles on one of the practical aspects of this

[35] J. R. Ravetz, *Scientific Knowledge and its Social Problems*, Clarendon Press, Oxford, 1971, p. 20.

controversy, the dubious use of psychiatry to regulate those aspects of the mind which might be thought to be not so much unhealthy as unconventional.

In a retrospect published by the Association of scientific progress in the first half of the twentieth century, A. E. Heath summarized the opinions of his contributors. Science had been impeded not by religion, but what an earlier generation of rationalists had thought was due to religion, the inherent difficulty of accepting that theories must be continually revised. We are now 'more sceptical of the lasting applicability of any particular ordering scheme.' The attempted synthesis of all scientific knowledge had been abandoned; each science had its own conceptual structure, and general ordering concepts such as holism, vitalism and behaviourism were now best treated as contextual methodological devices rather than as creeds.[36]

The major justification of religion in popular argument in Britain until the 1930s or so was that it was the necessary support of morality. The growth of openly admitted agnosticism and atheism among the eminent and the decline of organized religion among the moral classes made this argument implausible. It was succeeded by another defence of religious experience as the source of wonder, joy and emotional warmth in life. Science and scientists were and are personified as cold, materialist and the supporters of a brutally mechanistic society. A number of prominent agnostic intellectuals of the post-war period who returned to religion have given the search for warmth and meaning as their reason for doing so, and the Mass Observation report of the confused state of religious opinion in Britain immediately after the war found that rationalists were increasingly coming to doubt whether reason itself was enough, and if rational arguments were not being used to legitimate violence in human affairs.[37]

The current variant of this view is the claim that science and scientists are relatively innocent, that they explore only the thin crust of blind rationality stretched over the deeper, more complex and harsher nature of reality. Rationalists have frequently found themselves dismissed as the last supporters of the Enlightenment in a wiser world; foolishly, optimistically believing in reason, unable to comprehend or plumb the evils of existence.

In return, the Association has argued that rationalism *can* provide

[36] A. E. Heath, ed., *Scientific Thought in the Twentieth Century—an Authoritative Account of Fifty Years Progress in Science*, Watts, London, 1951.
[37] Mass Observation, *Puzzled People*, Gollancz, London, 1948, p. 41.

a sense of worship, joy and so on, and Julian Huxley's *Religion Without Revelation*, a book very popular with the Association's members, is much quoted in this context.[38] The 'positive' ethic of the Association in the post-war period has drawn very heavily on his account of evolutionary humanism. Huxley reasserted the incompatibility between scientific explanations and belief in the existence of God, but this did not mean that there was no real religion; 'religion of the highest and fullest character can coexist with a complete absence of belief in revelation . . . and . . . a personal God.' Religion was a natural phenomenon which came from the emotions common to all men, feelings of sacredness, reverence and mystery. But religion was wedded to certainties rather than the doubting and questioning which enabled such immense gains in other areas of life, and so it had changed too slowly to be of use in human affairs. Its erection of false certainties had prevented mankind from shouldering the burden of responsibility for its own actions and taking charge of the potentialities it had. It was primarily the growth of psychology, Huxley considered, which had shown us that the experience of the supernatural was located in men's minds, and anthropology which had located the origins of contemporary religion in very primitive conceptions of reality. Whilst man needed satisfaction for spiritual wants which would always take him beyond science, this need involve neither supernatural elements nor an ecclesiastical form. The new creed would be internal. Huxley added a statement of his own creed; 'I believe, first and foremost, that life is not merely worth living, but intensely precious; and that the supreme object of life is to live . . .'

Whilst Huxley thought that man's view of the world could never become fully scientific because science could never come to terms with our emotional needs, his account of science like that of many scientific popularizers is suffused with a kind of lyrical *élan*. It seems to come partly from the contemplation of the immense past procession of scientific advance and the dizzying spectacle of the complex chain of being of which man is a part, and partly from the transposition of the release which our knowledge has given us in the past to the hope which it can give us for the future. It is interesting that surveys of the religious opinions of American scientists find that an explicit rejection of supernatural religion is much the commonest among biologists, who can feel such a mystical sense of the

---

[38] A shortened version was published in the Thinker's Library series in 1940.

possibilities of evolution and of our place in nature.[39] The difficulty with this sense of *élan*, as Ronald Hepburn has pointed out, is that it is fragile.[40] We may feel exalted by the immensity of the heavens, the complexity of a fly's eye, et cetera, or we may equally well feel alienated and bored. Perhaps the greatest obstacle that the Rationalist Press now faces is the contemporary mood of ennui, the feeling that scientific knowledge has largely lost its favourable metaphysical connotations, that it can give us very little of what we really want, that the universe that it reveals to us is indifferent to our inner selves.

This feeling is perhaps the emotional residue of the falling apart of the intellectual universe of knowledge itself. The increasingly specialized and non-intuitive nature of scientific knowledge, the caution which we feel about openly deriving values from facts, has produced an ethos in which the synthesis of knowledge, the attempt to create an explicit personal philosophy which is based on formal knowledge, has come to seem old-fashioned. The latest accounts of the nature of scientific knowledge itself throw doubt on the notion of its unity or forward movement just as the history of science reveals not only the most unscientific origins of sixteenth- and seventeenth-century science among men who were the last of the *magi* before they were the first of the rationalists, but also the origins of scientific theories among the obsessions of other parts of life.

The difficulties that a philosophy which based itself upon science had to face on the intellectual level were reflected in the practical difficulties that the Association faced as an organization. By the mid-1950s, its membership had fallen to under three thousand, and this lent fuel to the increasing demand for a move away from scientific rationalism and the attack on the churches to a greater concern with the social sciences and current social problems. This inevitably brought the Association nearer to the position of the Ethical Union, which was also searching for new directions in a period of falling membership, and various liaison bodies began to be formed to prevent a duplication of efforts on the part of both movements. In 1962, the two bodies decided to form the British Humanist Association for a trial period of five years, during which time they would try to recruit both members and local groups to Humanism, the more attractive and contemporary version of their

[39] E. L. Long, *The Religious Beliefs of American Scientists*, Westminster Press, Philadelphia, 1964.
[40] R. Hepburn, 'A Critique of Humanist Theology', *Objections to Humanism*, Constable, London, 1963, edited by H. J. Blackham.

traditional beliefs, which was to offer both a personal ethic and concrete campaigns for social advance, mainly in the field of personal freedom and sexual morality. The members of the two older organizations were encouraged to transfer their membership to the new body, but the members of the Association were comparatively reluctant to do so; by 1964, only five hundred had transferred out of five thousand members. The new British Humanist Association was recruiting rapidly; publicity was bringing in about two hundred enquiries a week. The Rationalist Press was under pressure from both sides; from those of the new humanist group who accused it of dragging its feet over union, and the older rationalists who disliked what they saw as the Association's departure from its proper aims, the attack on supernaturalism and the encouragement of rational and scientific thinking. But the structure of the Association made the board comparatively invulnerable to the pressures of members.

The British Humanist Association immediately moved more actively into political life than the two older societies had done; a system of regular lobbying and letter-writing to M.P.s was organized, and so were an Agnostics Adoption Bureau and various committees on marriage law reform, health, youth, and the problems of the humanist teacher. Outside publicity increased as a result and members pressed for more political action, though the officials warned that by doing so the Association's charitable status was being jeopardized. (Registration as a charity, which enables an organization to avoid income tax, prohibits it from taking part in any political activity. Religious organizations are exempt from this prohibition, a source of bitterness to many humanists.) In 1965, the Ethical Union was struck off the list of charities, and consequently lost an annual tax rebate of about two thousand pounds. The Rationalist Press, which had been unhappy about directly involving its members in political activities with which they might not agree, and fearing its own loss of charitable status, withdrew from the British Humanist Association whose own loss of such status was inevitable.

Whilst lending such temporary financial assistance to the new Association as was thought possible, the directors of the Rationalist Press decided that the legal separation of the two bodies 'could become a permanent solution to many of the problems that had existed in the past.' They felt that the British Humanist Association's aims were in an uneasy relationship to their own, which were wider and deeper than particular political and social reforms. 'The forces of irrationality and superstition are not contained within national boundaries and they are not temporary. When laws are reformed, the need for more reason and less wishful thinking will still be there. There will always be an important role for a body which is concerned with the war rather than with particular battles.'[41] They felt that many of their overseas members wanted their publications but did not want to become part of an English social movement; aiming as they did to increase the influence of a general climate of opinion, books and magazines seemed likely to have a more universal influence than the specific social reforms derived from their contents.

Ideas and Things

Ideas are not only given significance by current problems and concerns but are also shaped and distorted by them, as the interaction of the Rationalist Press and the wider intellectual history of our society showed. The 'social problem' and its eugenic solution of the turn of the century illustrates both processes. The Association saw scientific knowledge in the way in which it is often seen, as uniquely rational, intrinsically interesting and good, and as having a displacement effect on irrational and supernatural modes of thought. The various eddies and cross-currents which created complexities and contradictions in this general outlook struck rationalists with unequal force and speed. The 'new physics' impinged very rapidly, concerned as it was both with their traditional subject-matter, the popularization of science, and with their customary heroes, the eminent popularizing scientists, here drawing unwelcome quasi-mystical deductions from their scientific work. The far more fundamental and far-reaching changes in our views of man, society, knowledge and religion which are implied by the revolutions in psychology, sociology and anthropology—the rise of *homo sociologus*, socially relative and existentially created, of a social world of shifting created meanings, the invasion of medicine by psychology— have had a much slower impact, as they have on all our imaginations.

Philip Converse's illuminating study of the relationship between the political opinions of the educationally sophisticated and highly involved and those of supporters at lower levels of information and interest showed that with declining levels of formal education, world views become increasingly split up and inconsistent. Education and involvement are in part sources of a pressure to make our

[41] Annual Report of the R.P.A. for 1964/5.

thoughts consistent.[42] Without them, the opinions of particular people and feelings about their views become more important to us than the general arguments themselves. Whilst many rationalists have been profoundly influenced by the personal world views of figures such as H. G. Wells, the Huxleys or Bernard Shaw, the very nature of rationalism makes them *more* likely to strive for a self-conscious and connected world view than the most sophisticated creators of the elements of contemporary knowledge that they borrow. They are, in a sense, more intellectual than the contemporary intellectual.

'To reduce life to exact rule and method,' said David Hume, 'is commonly a painful, oft a fruitless occupation.' The rationalist is unusual because he makes so many connections between ideas. His efforts to comprehend the world by reason and by science make him conspicuous in a society which dines from a kind of intellectual *smörgåsbord* in which complete metaphysical systems, like twelve-course banquets, are otiose. But as Hume knew, the attempt itself can be the attraction. 'Even to reason so carefully concerning it [human life], and to fix with accuracy its just idea, would be overvaluing it, were it not that, to some tempers, this occupation is one of the most amusing in which life could possibly be employed.'

[42] P. E. Converse, 'Belief-Systems in Mass Politics', in D. E. Apter, ed., *Ideology and Discontent*, Free Press, Glencoe, 1964.

8 THE RATIONALISTS

> . . . that growing body of people who, for whatever reason, tend to agnos-
> ticism but desire to be convinced that agnosticism is respectable; they are
> eager for anti-dogmatic books written by men of mark. They couldn't
> endure to be classed with Bradlaugh, but they rank themselves confidently
> with Darwin and Huxley. Arguments matter little or nothing to them.
> They take their Rationalism as they do a fashion in dress, anxious only that
> it shall be 'good form'.
>
> George Gissing, *Born in Exile*

The members of the Rationalist Press Association were not based
on local groups, but were subscribers from all over Britain and outside it. Many of them were also members of the secular or ethical
movements, but from the very limited evidence that can be gathered
about them, they did represent a different facet of humanism and
had the attitudes which are often conventionally associated with the
hard-headed atheist materialist of fiction.

The membership grew steadily from the formation of the Association in 1899 to over four thousand in the mid-1930s; it then fell
slightly, rose again during the forties when books were scarce and
in great demand, dropped to 2,700 by 1956 but began to rise again
until they had reached over five thousand in 1964. The fluctuations
of growth are dissimilar to those of the other movements, and hint
at a separate source and pattern of membership. As in the other
humanist groups, membership was often short-lived; the Association thought that many sought a temporary membership for the
sake of cheap publications. Fluctuations of membership could be
severe; in 1946, a thousand members did not renew their subscrip-
tions, and of these nearly half had only joined in the previous year.
In 1961, the results of a questionnaire revealed that over half of those
who replied had joined the Association in the previous five years.
Members were gained through advertising; the liberal quality papers
such as the *Observer* and *New Statesman* proved the most fruitful.
But the majority of members reported that they had been persuaded
to join by a friend: despite the relative anonymity and impersonality
of the Association's contacts with its members, it is more than a mass
movement.

The Association always had very few women members; Campbell
found that fewer than one in five members were women in 1963,
though this discounts those women whose husbands were subscribers on behalf of them both. As in the other humanist movements,

many of the leaders and some members were the sons of the clergy; from a very small sample, it seems that they had, on the whole, been Anglicans, Baptists or Presbyterians, and the majority of the active campaigns of the Association were directed at the established church.

The Association resembled the secular movement not only in having a low proportion of women members but in having a middle-aged membership; this was in part because the two movements overlapped. In 1963, many more secularists also belonged to the Association than belonged to any other humanist organization. In 1961, the majority of members were over forty, having joined many years previously, and in 1963 nearly a third of the members were over sixty and the largest group in their forties.[1] At this point, and probably at others, the difference in age was related to a difference in opinions; the members reported themselves as far more likely, if they were under twenty-five, to call themselves 'agnostic' and not 'atheist', and to consider that the Association spent far too much time in attacking religion. The attempted and finally successful alternations of the Association's policy and publicity in the fifties and sixties, exemplified by the appearance of the *Free Mind*, were considered to be in part the revolt of younger members against a gerontocracy.

We can guess that some of the differences of opinion between age-groups reflected their different experiences. The older a rationalist was, the more likely he would be to remember a period when the formal and informal social control exerted by the churches had been a major factor in, for example, the day-to-day running of schools, hospitals and the mass media. The younger he was, the longer, on the whole, his formal educational experience would have been, and the higher reaches of the educational system are largely secular. The post-war generation of young adults would have experienced political oppression as more important than religious, and rationalism not as in need of defence against theology, but as having to take account of developments in philosophy, political theory and psychology.

The members of the Association seem to have been predominantly professional and clerical workers, and as in the positivist movement, there were numbers of teachers, doctors, engineers and others who might have been expected to find scientism congenial. Campbell's survey of 1963 found that almost all members were either white-collar, administrative, or above all, technical and professional

[1] C. B. Campbell, op. cit., pp. 249–51.

workers.[2] The largest group, as for all the other middle-class humanist bodies, were school-teachers—who formed almost a fifth of the
Association's members. Doctors, university teachers, and scientists
were also over-represented. To explain this, Campbell develops the
general theme of a correspondence between the world view of the
professions—especially the personal service professions—and of
humanism. But it begs fewer questions to say that the Association
recruits members overwhelmingly from the middle class because of
the values which it espouses, and from certain occupations which
feel a tension between traditional behaviour, legitimated by religion,
and a reinterpretation of their role for which they are seeking a
general metaphysical support.

The rationalist and ethical movements correspond very well to
Parkin's depiction of middle-class radicalism; that is, they are
interested in moral rather than economic reform, and their motives
are part of a general view of life which is made self-consciously
explicit because it is not that of the rest of their class. That is,
they are not part of the pattern of acquiescence in religious teaching
and sporadic church attendance which is true of many middle-class
people. These movements lay emphasis on developing a philosophy
of life which is part of the general culture of liberalism rather than
an impetus to revolutionary activity, and requires considerable
interest in and familiarity with abstract ideas. The Association offers
little in the way of concrete purpose or group identity to its members,
but it offers information which is interesting in itself, and which is
discussed as part of a general philosophy of life.

Teachers and doctors are alike in that in various aspects of their
work—school assembly, Scripture lessons, abortion, sex education
the treatment of pain and death, et cetera—the norms of the professional who lacks religious belief come into conflict with other
values. That is, the autonomy, freedom of opinion and judgement
by one's peers which are the core of the professional ethic conflict
with the demands of the part of the authority structure which
enshrines ideas such as a Christian education or the sanctity of
human life, which are ultimately justified by reference to religion.
The liberal professional needs an alternative metaphysic; and in
areas in medicine and science where new moral dilemmas appear,
the humanist movement can provide a general background metaphysic to discussion of a liberal humanitarian kind. It can also
operate as a pressure group in these areas; with success, for example,

2 ibid, pp. 258–62.

over the reform of the abortion laws, and with less success in the frequently reported cases of teachers being denied headships if they will not take religious assembly.

Many who are not members of the rationalist or humanist movements have such values; many of these values are enshrined in the process of higher education itself, which predisposes its recipients to more liberal political views and an explicit rejection of religious belief. Rationalists commonly remarked, as they joined the Association, that they had been rationalists all their lives without knowing it; but this is the Association's dilemma. What precisely do they gain by joining the Association?

One answer was that they furthered the spread and influence of rationalist ideas; but when the Association has acted as a pressure group, it has steered from the Scylla of political activity. In the beginning the majority of rationalists were liberals, and, like the other humanist bodies, were affected by the centripetal pull of socialism. But a far larger proportion of members agreed with a non-political policy and were less radical than in the ethical or secular movements, and partly because of this and partly because of the Association's centralized and undemocratic structure, the founders were able to adhere to the view that rationalism was not a political doctrine, and that they should not work for any objective 'about which members might differ'. Much of their agitation has been either for secular education or for the repeal of the blasphemy laws and freedom of opinion. It was claimed that rationalism constituted a distinctive approach to life which was independent of politics; often with the positivist implication that if it were adopted, many political issues would be decided automatically. But when is an issue political?

The Association consulted its members in 1960 as to whether they considered that nuclear disarmament was a political doctrine or something which was entailed by rationalist principles. A survey of membership showed that over half the members who replied described themselves as 'left-wing', a third as 'middle-of-the-road', and only 11 per cent as 'right-wing', most of whom were elderly. There was a 'high correlation' between describing oneself as left-wing and as atheist, or being middle-of-the-road and agnostic. The right-wing members complained that the Association was 'soft on Communism', and should attack it on the same basis as it attacked religion; the left wanted a more positive opposition to war. But the majority were opposed to the Association's adopting any specific social policy on the Bomb or anything else, but would have liked to see more pressure for the secular upbringing of children and against racialism, and a distinctively humanist concept of sex and marriage.[3]

'Rationalists are a body of people', reported a committee in 1954, 'who have broken with the authoritative approach, but there is no Rationalist dogma and there cannot be an official Rationalist viewpoint.'[4] Like the secularist, the rationalist was primarily defined by his opposition to religion. In practice, as letters from members showed, the Association was pressed to take a stand on many issues and did so, losing some members as a result. Yet without commitment to some concrete issues, merely to assert the virtue of intellectual freedom and rationality would be too general and nebulous. It is interesting that at different periods, the same issues may be generally defined as 'political' or not. During the thirties, communism was less 'political' than it has now become.

Part of the rationalist's relative detachment from politics was due to the rather pragmatic and instrumental attitude which the directors believed that many members had toward the Association and to rationalism in general. Members lacked much communal involvement, and were likely to leave the Association rather than to try to influence it. The directors were conscious that many did not want to be involved in any kind of direct action, and a symposium in 1959 on religious education in schools revealed that no parents withdrew their children, for fear they might suffer social pressure. The rationalists sought intellectual reinforcement from the Association rather than a social identity.

Conversion to Rationalism

Members conveyed little about themselves to the Association, so few accounts of the process of conversion exist, and those which do are often those of eminent rationalists rather than the ordinary member. Some of the themes found in the experiences of secularists are repeated: being the child of a clergyman, or having been destined for the church; having read the Bible and the radical critiques of Paine and Blatchford. (Some rationalists were also secularists.) But in many more cases than for the secularist, the rationalist had been influenced by reading about science, not by reading about

---

[3] R.P.A. Minutes, 8 December 1960, p. 129; *Humanist*, February 1961, p. 54.
[4] R.P.A. Minutes, 19 May 1954, p. 126.

scientific findings, but by reading the accounts of science by popularizers which drew out the theme of the destruction of theology by science, or the evolution of mankind away from superstition—the kind of books, in fact, published by the Association.

The main evidence is collected in twenty accounts of 'Why I became a Rationalist', printed in 1931, and fifty of 'Books which Made me a Rationalist,' published between 1940 and 1941.[5] Even the earlier accounts lay most emphasis on what was read, but several do mention the disillusionment produced by the First World War—which was very extensively justified in religious terms, whereas the second was not. One man found the war had destroyed his faith in science as well, and of course there were some who found their faith in the trenches. Perhaps the most significant point is that by the time of the Second World War, it was not customary to expect that one's general beliefs would be either so structured or so closely allied to concrete experience as to be vulnerable to it.

The same works are repeatedly referred to in both sets of accounts. Many of them, such as Paley's *Evidences*, Chambers' *Vestiges of Creation*, Colenso on the Pentateuch, *The Golden Bough*, had in fact been written with the aim in part of reconciling religion to science; but the very framework of the debate, in which religion had become something which had to be altered and refined to accommodate it to science, was a secularizing one. Numerically, by far the most influential works were those of Haeckel, especially *The Riddle of the Universe*, and of T. H. Huxley, and there are also frequent references to a group of books—Winwood Reade's *Martyrdom of Man*, Laing's *Modern Science and Modern Thought*, Phelps' *The Churches and Modern Thought*, Draper's *History of the Conflict between Religion and Science*, White's *History of the Warfare between Science and Theology*, and the *Literary Guide* itself—which are all in essence part of the mythology of science. That is, they are accounts by popularizers of the advances of science (often rather out-of-date ones) which set it in a positivist, evolutionary and progressive context, laying stress on the extent to which both intellectual advance and social and moral progress were intimately bound up with the destruction of supernaturalism. Most of them also apply this framework to religion, and whilst they remain strongly opposed to Catholicism, some are prepared to argue for a refined, moralized form of Protestantism which will underpin men's moral and spiritual life but keep well out of the way of intellectual and social progress.

5 Both in the *Literary Guide*.

Some rationalists considered that they had been converted by reading more directly anti-religious works, not only Paine and Blatchford but also Ingersoll and McCabe. And finally there are occasional references to works from a more literary and humanist tradition—*Queen Mab*, Montaigne, *Omar Khayyam*, *Candida*, and Marcus Aurelius—where we can only guess at the perceptions that they were filtered through to emerge as arguments for rationalism.

9 THE ORIGINS OF THE ETHICAL MOVEMENT

In the discussion, there was the oddest mixture of things that were personal and petty with an idealist devotion that was fine beyond dispute. In nearly every speech she heard was the same implication of great and necessary changes in the world—changes to be won by effort and sacrifice indeed, but surely to be won. And afterwards she saw a very much larger and more enthusiastic gathering, a meeting of the advanced section of the woman movement in Caxton Hall, where the same note of vast changes and progress sounded; and she went to a soirée of the Dress Reform Association and visited a Food Reform Exhibition, where imminent change was made even more alarmingly visible . . .

She became more and more alive, not so much to a system of ideas as to a big diffused impulse towards change, to a great discontent with and criticism of life as it is lived, to a clamorous confusion of ideas for reconstruction—reconstruction of the methods of business, of economic development, of the rules of property, of the status of children, of the clothing and feeding and teaching of everyone . . .

H. G. Wells, *Ann Veronica*

The ethical movement in Britain was officially founded in 1895, had a certain vogue and success until the First World War, and then lay dormant until shortly before its renaissance as the British Humanist Association in the 1960s. The origins of the movement were due to the coming together of three separate strains of 'advanced' thought which continued to co-exist within the movement in an ultimately uneasy relationship. These strains were the idealist philosophy of the followers of T. H. Green who were trying to create a new moral view of society by teaching philosophy and civic duty; a political utopianism associated with the rise of socialism in the 1880s that called for a religious or 'purer' expression of political beliefs, a middle-class Labour Church; and a theory which was common to both the American ethical movement and the Broad Church, that there was a vital need for a national church, for a ritual expression of the newer morality. The conflict between the different kinds of organization wanted by the three factions—a philosophical discussion group combined with charitable activity, a semi-political meeting, and a religious service—was fiercer and more prolonged in the ethical movement than in the other humanist movements. The religious-substitute group had more weight, especially whilst it was led by Stanton Coit who dominated the movement until the inter-war period.

Philosophically, the ethical movement was based on a very different tradition from the intellectual, individualist mode of secularism and rationalism. Where they stressed freedom and rights, it stressed community and duty; where they laid emphasis on intellectual progress, the ethicist looked to moral redemption of the whole of man and society. Whereas they wanted to destroy religious *belief*, the ethicist was interested in the religious *experience* of worship and ritual, which he wanted to refine and replace by a religion which would worship the good and the right. The rationalist saw intellectual advance as the key to progress; the ethicist thought that 'moral endeavour is indispensable to both personal and social progress.' In combating Marxist economic materialism, the rationalist insisted on the independence both of the human mind from its social situation and of scientific ideas from economic necessity. The ethicist thought that the pursuit of the moral life was not only the supreme personal good but also the only means by which reform could be effected.

In many respects the ethical movement resembled the positivists, and when both movements were in decline most positivists joined the ethical movement. Both of them, with some doubts and dissensions, saw ritual activity as an essential part of their work; both were concerned with strengthening the organic and moral aspects of society; and both were closely involved with various aspects of the labour movement. But whereas the general influence of positivism lay in the interest and enthusiasm which many late Victorians felt for the philosophy of Comte and in the ability and social influence of some of his English disciples, the influence of the ethical movement was much less distinctive. It owed affinities to both American transcendentalism and German Idealism as they blended into the rethinking about the state and society at the end of the nineteenth century. The history of the positivist movement is far better known; that of the ethical movement is more uncertain, since its importance lies in the influence of a way of thinking about social and political life which is now very alien to us, and consequently easy to dismiss. Yet both movements offer a fascinating glimpse of the relations between socialism and the religious impulse; in some ways they were more impractical and conservative than the mass parliamentary party which was to emerge as the main focus of socialist activity in Britain, but in other ways they were far more revolutionary in that they attempted what English left-wing politics has so conspicuously lacked, a consistent vision of a radically different kind of society, to

reach which would entail fundamental change guided by philosophical principles.

The positivist movement was the earlier; its founders began to
try to recruit support in 1870, nearly twenty years before the setting
up of the ethical societies, and since both the ideas of its founder and
its own vicissitudes are fairly well known, they can be briefly
recapitulated.[1]

The Religion of Humanity

The philosophy of Auguste Comte, as interpreted by his earliest
English disciple Richard Congreve was as the name 'positivism'
implies, a total world view which extended over all human knowledge
and would ultimately contain both science and politics, as well as
becoming the basis of a new religion and a new society. The fascina-
tion of positivism as a system of thought for many mid-Victorians
was that, like Spencer's philosophy, it opened up an enormous
evolving panorama of human progress and scientific discovery, in
which everything was related to everything else. All fields of thought
and all societies evolved through three stages; all thought, and all
political judgements, were consequently relative to their social
context. To the positivist, the empiricist and pragmatic flavour of
English political and intellectual life made the contemporary lack of
social progress not surprising; how could effective political action
proceed without a basis in a clear set of ideas? As a positivist commented, the English outlook on science and evolutionism was
intellectually confused; some agreed with Herbert Spencer's views
on the planets but not on social affairs, others agreed with Darwin on
biology but not on society. 'The awkwardness of this situation is so
apparent, it is so very unsynthetic . . .'[2] The appeal for intellectual
clarity and the grasp of social relativism must have constituted part
of the link between the positivist leaders and the Marxists.

[1] For accounts of various aspects of positivism, see J. E. McGee, *A Crusade for Humanity*, Watts, London, 1931, a history of the movement itself; W. E. Simon, *European
Positivism in the Nineteenth Century*, Cornell University Press, New York, 1963, an
account of its intellectual influence, or lack of it; R. Harrison, *Before the Socialists:
studies in Labour and Politics 1861–81*, Routledge, London, 1964, devotes chapter 6 to
its relations to socialism, and S. Eisen has written several papers on the main figures
in the movement, for example 'Frederic Harrison and the Religion of Humanity',
South Atlantic Quarterly, Vol. 66 (4), 1967, pp. 574–90. Most of the quotations are from
speeches reported in the *Positivist Review*.

[2] R. G. Hember, reading a paper on 'Ethics and the Social Problem' to a joint meeting
of ethical and positivist societies, *Positivist Review*, No. 120, December 1902, p. 244.

Positivism offered to its adherents the sense of all human knowledge coming within their grasp, the vision of the progress of science
to the point where a science of society would become possible. As
with Spencer, those who were primarily interested in science found
the system finally stifling; 'long ago in Chapel Street, I used to feel
the atmosphere of a real dislike of scientific research, a disdain for
it . . .', said Patrick Geddes.[3] But whereas Spencer, true to his
nonconformist origins, had described the increasing separation of
religion from social, intellectual and political life, the converts that
Comte made were expected to do far more than merely assent to
his philosophical doctrines. They had, after a long period of training
and preparation, to take upon themselves the moral leadership of
the positivist communities, and ultimately of society. In Comte's
thought, each successive stage of knowledge encompassed all
succeeding stages, and at the time that he wrote, he saw that the
transition of positive, or scientific thought was taking place from
biology to sociology, the science which by comprehending all the
sciences became their queen. Out of scientific knowledge of society
a positive philosophy of life would evolve, which since it would
settle all conflicts, would be the salvation of mankind. The philosopher alone would rule society, not as a king but as a priest whose
religion was the service of humanity.

After the death of Clothilde de Vaux, the religious aspects of
positivism grew in importance. Comte proposed an elaborate
calendar in which week by week the benefactors of mankind would
be commemorated and the progress of human knowledge traced,
presided over by a mother and child, the symbol of the love of the
positivist for humanity. Comte looked forward to an elaborate
hierarchic arrangement of society in which women and workmen
formed dependent classes, powerless and yet adored for their moral
qualities. The positivists accepted that social inequalities were
inevitable but thought it was vital to improve the lot of the poor;
they saw the key as the moral and spiritual authority of the man who
lived in harmony with the organic unity of the future society.

How would society be moralized? Not as the social democrats
assumed—'we positivists deprecate Revolution'—and not by the
liberal methods of parliamentary democracy—'*election* is not a
natural basis for the creation of a true moral and spiritual authority'.
Both the English and the French positivist movement were divided

---

[3] 'A Current Critique of the Positivist School', *Positivist Review*, No. 343, July 1921
p. 146.

over whether positivism should exert moral influence by being embodied in a religious form—Social Catholicism—or whether they should hold meetings to instruct men in positivist knowledge, comment on history and take part in public affairs from an informed viewpoint which would itself be a mode of conviction. Sometimes those who espoused the religion of humanity termed their opponents 'incomplete' and themselves 'complete' positivists. The intellectual influence of positivism in English life—which was at times considerable—came about largely not through the activities of the movement but through the illuminating commentaries on history and public affairs of some of the positivist leaders, especially Frederic Harrison.

Comte's first English disciple, Richard Congreve, was a history fellow at Wadham College who became a positivist in 1854. His attention had been attracted to Comte's writings by J. S. Mill and he was predisposed to accept them by the fact that his faith had recently been shaken, and he wished to regain his religious belief. He had at one time intended to be ordained. He met Comte in 1849, and his interest promptly shifted from the intellectual to the devotional plane. Comte nominated Congreve as the 'Spontaneous leader' of the British positivists. Congreve moved to London, contacted promising recruits, in 1867 founded the London Positivist Society, and three years later opened a room in Chapel Street, which became the headquarters of the ritualist wing of English positivism. While Congreve had been at Wadham, he had directly or indirectly influenced three students, E. S. Beesly, J. H. Bridges and Frederick Harrison, who became positivists. Beesly and Bridges had both been intensely and passionately interested in religion; they were the sons of evangelical clergymen. Harrison was from a high church family but had gradually retreated from orthodoxy as his political opinions became more radical. 'A church must teach, bind, regulate, . .' he thought, but although he accepted the 'hierarchical sacerdotal machinery' of the religion of humanity, he felt no enthusiasm for it.

The French positivist movement had already split into two camps, a religious wing led (reluctantly and inefficiently) by Laffitte, who hoped that the movement would take over the role of the Catholic church, and a philosophical wing which had broken with Laffitte because of the authoritarian and closed aspects of Comtian thought. In 1877-8 a complex schism occurred in the English and French movements, in which Beesley, Harrison and Bridges became loosely aligned with Laffitte despite his reluctant theocracy, and Congreve, who had tried to take over international leadership of the movement, set up a separate group which hoped ultimately to take over the position of the Church of England.

The idea of taking over the Church of England was a lure to all of those who were both theologically radical and socialist in late nineteenth-century England. Just as the Broad Church movement insisted that neither dogma nor an intense personal conviction of revealed truth was as important to religion as the existence of the Anglican church, its centre as the focus of community, as the basis in which those of many different opinions could meet, so the socialists hoped that such an institution could take over and moralize the whole of society. Harrison may have felt uneasy about the sacerdotalism and ritualism of Congreve, but he and the other positivist leaders were intensely interested in the social role of the Church of England. In part they saw it as the conservatives saw it, as something which subdued the brawling individualism of the radical or rationalist to a consciousness of his place (a subordinate one) inside a community, and with Matthew Arnold, a positivist could regret 'the dignity and strength of conscious subordination and veneration toward the vast spiritual unseen, which has given place to a noisy feebleness and an impertinence of small, literal rationality.'[4] In part, they wanted to unify the nation under a moral leadership. Social progress could only come about when all parts of the community stood in a right relationship to one another and acknowledged their duties toward one another. And, in part, they wanted to unify the heart and the head; the sympathy and generosity characteristic of women and workmen which were a necessary part of a good society must be acknowledged and yet led by the scientific intellect.

The positivists, who courageously and consistently supported the rights of workmen to form trade unions and of the Irish and colonial peoples to govern their own societies by their own lights, were equally consistently opposed to negative freedom, to the striving for equal rights by groups—women, workmen—who were inherently unequal. 'The cry for equality', said Harrison, had become perverted '. . . to be a movement for the wider dissemination of physical, social and moral poison.'[5]

Originally the English positivists had jointly hoped to carry out

[4] Letter to Congreve from Henry Carson, 17 July 1884, Congreve Papers, British Museum.
[5] 'Our Social Programme', in *Positivist Review*, January 1894, p. 7.

what they interpreted as the practical aspects of Comte's philosophy;
to gather a body of adherents and establish a church of humanity,
to form schools to teach the new religion to children, and to attempt
to settle social conflicts. Congreve saw his goal as religious; his
adherents must accept the religion of humanity or nothing, and
this included submission to Comte's doctrines and to Congreve
himself as high priest of the movement. Congreve's insistence that
positivism *was* a religion and must be regarded as such was the only
way of presenting the doctrine that attracted firm adherents. Many of
their letters to Congreve stressed that their authors' interest in Comte
had arisen out of their distress and rootlessness at being no longer
able to believe in conventional Christianity; 'the need for some new
system to take the place of the old faith'. In many cases these men
were old Owenites; Congreve found them a most receptive audience.

Malcolm Quin, an ex-secularist, a strong adherent of Congreve
and a natural ritualist, described vividly the attractions of Comtism
as answering both his religious hunger and an intellectual longing
for a system.

> I was not satisfied either to see life—man in the universe—in unrelated
> sections . . . Comte's appeal to me may be easily explained. He presented
> himself to me as a master of synthesis, and of a synthesis which was an ordered
> unity of imagination, worship, doctrine, morals and life. In this he stood
> alone. He was then, and he is now, the one thinker of the modern world
> professing to offer men a religion—a religion of love, poetry and service—
> founded on science.[6]

Congreve established a chapel in Chapel Street in 1870, decorated with busts and portraits, and a tablet with the positivist sacred
formulae. Here an evening school was run, but without much success, and a service and rites of passage were created of an elaborate
and pseudo-Catholic kind. Most of those who became positivists in
the early period seem to have been high Anglicans whose loss of
faith had left them with a craving for ritual. (But feelings about kinds
of ritual are stronger and deeper than the ideas they embody;
Bridges, son of an evangelical clergyman, hated all attempts to
draw up elaborate fixed forms of liturgy or prayer, and thought that
prayer should be extempore.)

Harrison, Beesley and Bridges thought that before a church was
started knowledge of positivism should be generally spread, otherwise the movement would become yet another small sect and vulnerable to the mockery of the scientific and political élite whose ideas

[6] M. Quin, op. cit., p. 41.

they should be influencing. 'Its true business is to modify opinion, to found ideas, to infuse a moral tone into politics, to teach the Capitalist justice, to inspire labour with its true dignity, to make a human religion the source of every phase of daily life.'[7] They wanted meetings to consist of educating men in the application of positivist principles to the social and political problems of the day, and so largely confined their activities to giving talks and teaching in the positivist school. They became active in the trade union movement, since with their belief in co-operation and community as the basis of social reform they were attracted to the 'organic' aspect of union activity, and they tried, unsuccessfully, to urge the British labour movement into Comtian internationalism. Beesley became chairman of the first International, and worked hard to convince radicals of the 'historical destiny' of the proletariat. He was as convinced as the most revolutionary that unless the wealthy used their power for the public good, 'they will be exposed at frequently recurring intervals to revolutionary violence.' The attempts to reverse inequalities of wealth by democratic means could have no permanent success: 'We believe that private property is an indelible institution . . .' The working-man would overthrow the capitalist and the banker, but his victory would be moral.

The positivists in their search for *Gemeinschaft*, looked not only to a restored Catholic church but to the medieval vision so powerful among many socialists in the late nineteenth century, the return to a community purged of the anomie and individualism which gripped both manufacturer and radical. Harrison's funeral discourse on a 'normal, typical, natural workman,' a positivist carpenter, laid stress on the fact that he might have 'thrust himself into the rank of petty masters who are seeking to race into fortune. But Darkin was always proud to be a workman; he held fast to be on brotherly terms with his fellow-workmen; he was not eager to gain money! He was not anxious to be ever changing the conditions or the place of his work.'[8] To F. J. Gould, positivism helped toward an all-round view of the labour problem and ultimately the religion of humanity would govern all relations in the community. But George Jacob Holyoake, heir to an older tradition of liberal and individualist radicalism and self-help, was not convinced by the thought of the moralization of employers. 'Positivism', he said, 'is the natural religion of Capitalists.'[9]

[7] F. Harrison, *Positivist Review*, No. 242, February 1913.
[8] *Positivist Review*, Supplement for January 1897, pp. 22–3.
[9] Quoted by Stanton Coit in *Ethical World*, 19 March 1909, p. 33.

After the split in 1878 between Congreve and his Wadham disciples, Congreve, left at Chapel Street, renamed his group the Church of Humanity, and began to adopt the rituals of the Anglican church service. He became more and more 'religious' in his outlook, though his congregation restrained his greatest excesses. Several provincial positivist branches followed his lead. Quin established a Church of Humanity with elaborate neo-Catholic ritual at Newcastle on Tyne in 1887, and further small groups in the Leicester and Newcastle areas. A provincial centre founded at Birmingham in 1882 immediately split into two factions, one religious and one concerned with political and social instruction.

The Liverpool positivists who founded a church under Congreve's direction in 1880 and tried to create a form of worship found a difficulty which was to become familiar to the ethical movement, in reconciling the longing for the emotional warmth which their members recollected from religious services with their paradoxical distaste for remembrances of Christianity. Quin, who was interested in and sensitive to the nuances which made rituals seem pleasing and appropriate or inhumanly cold or queasily reminiscent of religious experiences best forgotten, had written to the head of the Liverpool church about the hymns in use there, and he reported that those they used had slowly emerged as right.

> We lay under a peculiar disadvantage in choosing hymns at the first. All the warm poetical ones—those having much colour and human feeling and sympathy—were decidedly theological in language, and to this personally I had a strong objection in principle. Then, hymns free from this, and tolerably humanly pious in thought, we found to be of the cold Unitarian tinge, and very unmoving.[10]

Not the least of the attractions of the unemancipated woman to the positivist was that she was susceptible to religious emotion. The 'complete' positivists hoped that she would win men from 'mere cleverness', and were not surprised that women formed a majority of their small congregations. One who was trying to win support from amongst the community of secularists at Leicester, found that their wives 'complained bitterly of secularism wanting to tear down the past', so he arranged a trip for them around a nearby church to explain its symbolism, and wrote approvingly to Congreve after a visit to Chapel Street that his 'Sunday morning was quite like being at Church without being Anglican . . .' The

[10] M. Quin, op. cit. p. 119.

tone of condescension was often all too apparent in those who presented 'Positivism to simple people'.

The Congrevian positivists were not in sympathy with the secular
movement for many reasons, and were in competition with it for
the conversion of the working class. Their collectivist vision of a
future planned society, free of conflicts and ruled over by a scientific
priesthood, was alien to the much more egalitarian and individualist
tradition of secularism. Secularists believed that all workmen should
learn about science as a means both of defeating superstition and
of emancipating themselves; the positivists were dismayed at the
effect Huxley was having on the working class and scientific education. His popularization of science struck them as brutally materialist
and lacking the spiritual grandeur of Comte's conception of it. And
those unequipped, as women and working-men were, to understand
the mysteries of science should not be encouraged to read and reflect
on it. 'No sign of Huxley there . . .' reported a positivist who
had lectured at Leicester secular society with relief. They found
'the usual snapping criticism' of their secularist audiences hard to
tolerate.

The positivist leaders who seceded from Congreve formed the
London Positivist Committee and began to meet in Newton Hall.
Their main purpose was to influence scholarly opinion by means of
the *Positivist Review*, to give popular expositions of positivist
doctrines, and to educate poor young men and women in the Comtian system. This was no mean feat, covering as it did most existing
scientific and historical fields, but the positivists considered that the
defect of most political activity was that it was not based on a
'common sociology or set of principles', and that the various attempts which were being made to teach science and a scientific ethic
suffered from being merely a presentation of scientific fact and not a
synthesis. 'The spirit of empirical detail is making them (contemporary men of science) . . . dull and brutal.' They criticized
the rationalists both for oversimplifying human progress by assum-
ing it to be unilinear and dependent merely on the accumulation of
knowledge, and for treating man 'as a being of pure intellect alone, or
at least as if the other parts of his nature were only the dogs that
kept his intellect down.'

In some ways their view of science, as of religion, was startlingly
sophisticated compared to that of their contemporaries; witness
Bridges, meeting with Geddes, Hobhouse, Benjamin Kidd and
others in 1903 to set up a Sociology Society, and arguing that a

science consisted not in the search for more facts but in the establishing of laws, which should be tested by their predictive power.[11] In the heyday of social Darwinism, the positivists deprecated the way in which men, who were formed by their societies and influenced by their environment from the first, were judging social life as if it were continuous with natural life and justifying imperialist and eugenicist atrocities with false biological analogies. (Far from extending biology to society, they extended society to biology and became Lamarckians.) And it is odd to find a completely contemporary structural/functional assessment of the roots and functions of religion —for example, that the Welsh revivals of the early 1900s were a vehicle of cultural protest against the breaking up of old bonds by industrialism[12]—appearing at a time long before such a sophisticated voice was heard among academic social scientists.

Unlike the other humanist bodies, it was an integral part of positivist philosophy that its leaders should establish a definitive interpretation of contemporary events; to do otherwise would be to leave their members without guidance in public life and 'render their claim to moral leadership almost a farce.' The Reverend Maurice Davies, who visited the Positivist Sunday School in 1874 and found it mainly full of trade unionists being taught politics by Harrison, left a vivid picture of the '*savants* and strong-minded ladies' sitting at the front together with George Odger, the famous working-class radical surrounded by a court of his Southwark supporters, while the working-men and one working-woman sat at the back.[13] Despite the initial objections to ritualism, after it became clear that the meetings at Newton Hall were indeed those of a small sect there was a gradual appearance of religious elements in meetings; music and a rudimentary liturgy expressing the unity of social sentiment were instituted. The leaders were, however, very touchy on the subject of religious equivalents, and avoided the use of terms such as 'festival' or 'prayer'. Harrison complained that *The Service of Man*, 'an admirable non-theological collection' of hymns was being confused with a service book; but it is difficult to see quite what else he could have expected.

The committed positivists in Britian never numbered more than about one or two hundred at any time. By 1898 nine groups had been

[11] J. H. Bridges, *Positivist Review*, No. 129, September 1903, pp. 206-9.
[12] S. H. Swinny, loc. cit., No. 147, March 1905, pp. 61-4.
[13] Rev. C. M. Davies, *Heterodox London*, Tinsley Brothers, London, 1874, Vol. 2, pp. 246-7.

formed, but most of them were very small, and the movement declined rapidly from that point on. The members were divided between a wealthy professional group, composed of doctors, lawyers, teachers and manufacturers, and a smaller group of working-men, many of whom were relatively independent and wealthy craftsmen. Unlike any of the other humanist groups, some members were part of the traditional upper class; perhaps attracted by the Anglo-Catholic flavour and strong emphasis on leadership. Many had been the sons of clergymen or come from religious families, and, unusually among humanist groups, there were many marriages among them which reinforced their cohesiveness. Like the Labour Churches, the positivists hoped to find a way of establishing fundamental social change without the divisions and violence which seemed inevitable, and with the establishment of parliamentary socialism their decline was accelerated and they merged into the ethical movement. Their anti-imperialism, particularly their support of Home Rule for Ireland and of the rights of the natives, had made them unpopular with most working-men and ultimately led to their break with the trade union movement.

The Philosophers and the Debating Societies

As has often been remarked, the extraordinary self-confidence and vitality of many Victorians had its converse in an equally characteristic anxiety and doubt. Their fears were many: revolution, cultural anarchy, rampant sexuality and a kind of decay and falling apart of a society in which traditional bonds were daily being eroded and overthrown. The appeal of such a detailed and elaborate system as positivism for some and the hostility which it evoked in others were symptoms of the doubt. One of its central aspects was the fear that the intellectually inevitable decay of traditional religion would lead to a corresponding decay in morality, especially amongst the poor who had both less reason to favour the *status quo* and were less able to appreciate the more complex philosophical defences of the virtuous life. Two ways of inculcating the necessary conceptions of morality and duty were generally considered: education and a new religion.

These themes tended to be joined together in different constellations and filled with a different philosophical content, but much of that content came, having suffered various sea-changes, from

Germany. The Broad Church tradition, for instance, attacked the atomistic and mechanistic thought of the utilitarians which had given rise to the individualist piecemeal programme of reform of the English radical, and opposed to it the vision of an ordered hierarchical society held together by 'natural' relationships and a set of common values. In such a society, the church would become a source of social power and the state would be moralized; all intellectual life would be drawn into their auspices and the disintegration of contemporary life would be checked. For some, especially if they had aesthetic interests, the natural analogy was an idealized classical antiquity or medieval England; but for others, the ideal was exemplified by Germany, where state guidance of its cultural renaissance had led to national greatness. A part of its greatness, with which Prince Albert had been particularly concerned, was the belief in the virtues of scientific education and the national direction of science.[14]

Another solution to the problem of the inculcation of duty without the aid of hell-fire was an anglicized version of the categorical imperative; the pursuit of morality for its own sake, and the judgement of religious truth solely in terms of its moral validity. The influence of Idealist philosophy became strong from the 1870s on at some universities, particularly Oxford and Glasgow, where T. H. Green and Caird used their expositions of German philosophy to preach that the utilitarian conception of man was an inadequate basis for political life. Green, a patently virtuous and morally inspiring figure, cast the evangelical tradition of moral earnestness, the call to duty and self-sacrifice, into a new key. After a period of painful struggle he had ceased to be a Christian, but thought some form of religion was essential not only to morality but to the holding together of life in an organic whole. Green laid great stress on how much was demanded of the citizens of a democracy; he inspired his students with the connection between philosophy and civic duty. One of the tasks of his ethical philosophy was to re-define religion as morality and to re-establish its beliefs in a way that could attract and hold reasonable men. To the idealists, an act was only good if the motives for carrying it out were good; and those motives were themselves part of the true general will or social conscience of all classes of the community, upon which all social progress depended.[15]

[14] G. R. Searle, op. cit., p. 31.
[15] M. Richter, *The Politics of Conscience—T. H. Green and his Age*, Weidenfeld & Nicolson, London, 1964, gives an excellent exposition of both Green's views and their social influence, on which this section is largely based.

One of the aspects of Idealism which is baffling to the empiricist and the expositor alike is its very emphasis on wholeness, the feeling that things become more 'real' and important as they become more spread out, broad and comprehensive, that the good of the individual only has any meaning in so far as it is related to the common good of all the society. In the literature of the ethical societies, there is much reference to 'unity', 'developing spirit', 'the good will', 'supreme ends' of various kinds, the shared values which underlie political activity, the unfolding and transforming nature of progress in which all things will be new and yet more fully part of the whole. Politically, Green both feared the encroachments of the state and yet hoped to moralize it; he was reluctantly forced by the grave social and economic problems of his time to advocate some measure of socialism as their only cure. The young men whom he influenced came on the whole to London, and put his influence to work in various ways; in the settlement movement, in the reshaping of the work of the state with which the Fabians were concerned, in the Charity Organization Society and in the ethical movement.

The London Ethical Society was formed in 1886 with the active support of many Idealists, among them Bernard Bosanquet, Muirhead, Bonar and Mackenzie, and attracted the interest of Henry Sidgwick, R. B. Haldane, Sir John Seeley and Leslie Stephen. Many of them seem to have had in mind some of the previous famous debating societies where questions of morality had been discussed, in particular the Metaphysical Society which had met during the 1870s for representatives of the whole spectrum of belief and non-belief to discuss the conflict between religion and science. In retrospect, the continual astonishment which its members seem to have felt at the tolerance that they all displayed and the large amount of common moral ground between them scarcely seems so surprising. Indeed one of the reasons for the decline of the society was because its members rapidly reached agreement on many issues, a difficulty with which later ethical societies were to become familiar.

The appeal of the debating group at every level of society owed much to the clubbable disposition of the English male; but the description by Henry Sidgwick of the influence of the Apostles upon him—'this spirit . . . absorbed and dominated me . . . it came to seem to me that no part of my life at Cambridge was so real to me as the Saturday evenings on which the apostolic debates were held; and the tie of attachment to the society is much the strongest corporate bond which I have known in life . . .' leads one to suspect that more was involved.[16] Perhaps part of it was that among these groups of friends, gratifyingly conscious of themselves as an élite, the earnest discussions that they held as to how the new society would be came to seem a foretaste of that society itself, in which all differences could be tackled with reason and the good will. And this in turn exacerbated the tendency of all these reformers to see the differences between men in terms of their beliefs and not of their material interests.

Contemporaries assure us that in the late 1880s and 90s, the most talked-about book was *Robert Elsmere*, Mrs Humphry Ward's account of the spiritual progress of a young man from a rationalist squire who undermines the theological basis of his faith to an Oxford philosopher, clearly Green, who inspires him to take up the fight for ethics in the East End slums, where he founds a new church which bases its creed on reason. 'The problem of the world at this moment is, *how to find a religion*? Some great conception which shall be once more capable, as the old were capable, of wielding societies, and keeping men's brutish elements in check.'[17] By temperament and habit, most of the early members of the London Ethical Society were looking for a lecturing and debating society rather than a religious movement, but this was the question around which much of their discussion centred. Could any plausible system of ethics be devised in the absence of any supernatural sanction that was not simple-mindedly and selfishly utilitarian, and how could men be induced to live by it?

The initial impetus for the founding of an ethical society at all was provided by Stanton Coit, an official of the American Ethical Society who spent six months at Toynbee Hall in 1886. Many of those who were concerned at the godless state of the poor were connected with Toynbee Hall and the university settlement movement, and Coit urged them to form an ethical society on the lines of the ethical culture movement which would provide them with leadership and guidance for their practical activities, and itself become the basis of a new community. Bonar and Muirhead sent a statement to likely sympathizers, explaining that the bond between members of such a society was the belief 'that the moral and religious life of Man is capable of a rational justification and explanation, apart from Authority and Tradition. They believe that there is at

[16] Quoted in A. W. Brown, *The Metaphysical Society: Victorian Minds in Crisis, 1868–1880*, Columbia University Press, New York, 1947.
[17] Mrs H. Ward, *Robert Elsmere*, Smith & Elder, London, 1888, pp. 446–7.

present great need for the teaching of a reasoned-out doctrine on this subject, especially where old sanctions and principles have lost their hold.'[18] The members of the London Ethical Society were not especially anxious to sever themselves from Christianity, because they saw it as gradually evolving into their own non-theocratic ethics. They united on the basis that ethics were supreme and independent both of material experience and of any reality beyond experience. But why was this so important, and how could it be made widely understood?

It was agreed that a major function of an ethical society was to teach ethics; and the philosophers associated with the society acted as speakers for Toynbee Hall and the other ethical societies as well as holding discussions among themselves. Leslie Stephen, at one time president of the Union of Ethical Societies, saw them as the meeting-place 'between the expert and specialist on the one side, and on the other, the men who have to apply ideas to the complex concretes of political and social activity.' Swan Sonnenschein, who was a member of the London Ethical Society, published many volumes (mostly at a financial loss) in the Ethical Library series by which he hoped to acquaint English philosophers with the work of Hegel, Bergson and other continental thinkers.[19] But 'teaching' was an ambiguous concept. Stanton Coit, whose ideas will be described in a later chapter, saw the influence of an ethical society as essentially religious; morally uplifting, uniting and hortatory. Most of the philosophers who belonged to the London Ethical Society rejected this 'semi-ecclesiastic' conception, but whilst some wanted to discuss and clarify moral ideas with no explicit didactic or social purpose, others were less concerned to analyse the content and relative merits of possible moralities than to inspire men with the importance of moral idealism and inculcate moral principles by moral education. Children and the working class were thought to be most in need of it, and consequently the society worked closely with Toynbee Hall, and opened a guild for poor London children.

Amidst so much moral leadership the London Ethical Society, hardly surprisingly, never developed much corporate unity; its leading members were all public figures who 'edified a thoughtful class of people with highgrade though somewhat academic lectures'

---

[18] G. Spiller, *The Ethical Movement in Great Britain*, Farleigh Press, London, 1934, pp. 1–2.
[19] F. A. Mumby, *From Swan Sonnenschein to George Allen & Unwin Limited*, Allen and Unwin, London, 1955, p. 36.

but were not prepared to act jointly with them. Bosanquet objected to any departure from an individualist conception of both social welfare and education. He disliked the 'moral suasion' of the group interested in community life—'Teach moral philosophy but do not mix up your teaching with your preaching'—and he also spent much time advocating the social gospel of the Charity Organization Society, which consisted of teaching people to help themselves and to assist the working classes to their own kind of moral perfection. He and some of the other Idealists finally withdrew and founded the London School of Ethics and Social Philosophy because they feared that the ethical movement was drifting toward the religion of humanity. Their experience of lecturing through the society and the university extension movement had shown them that there was an adequate demand, mainly among school teachers, for evening lectures on philosophy and ethics. The school closed in 1900, and together with the training programme of the Charity Organization Society was merged into the London School of Economics, in 1912.[20] The society was also handicapped by its lack of contact with socialism. It advocated some mild degree of social and political reform; 'the improvement of the present situation of many is an indispensable condition of the moral welfare of all', but in the main it saw its task as lying above and beyond politics, except in so far as it should 'encourage scientific efforts which aim at examining the conflicting theories of individualism and socialism, with a view of their being harmonized in some profounder view of life . . .'[21]

Several other of the early ethical societies were of this discussion-group type; that at Cambridge, also dominated by moral philosophers who wanted to discuss neither religion, politics, metaphysics in general nor actual ethical systems, but to explore the area of general agreement in moral behaviour; that at Halifax, which was founded to provide an ethical version of the works of 'the great single-tax prophet of San Francisco', Henry George; that at Rochester, founded by a variety of ministers to discuss ethics; and the Hampstead Ethical Society. None of these societies, apart from the last, outlived the nineteenth century, for their discussions were prone to

[20] F. J. Gould, 'The English Ethical Societies', *Reformer*, 15 October 1897, p. 225; J. R. Muirhead, *Bernard Bosanquet and his Friends*, Allen & Unwin, London, 1935, pp. 48, 91; B. Bosanquet, 'The Communication of Moral Ideas as the Function of an Ethical Society', *Ethics and Religion*, Sonnenschein, London, 1900, p. 209; E. Schell, 'Bernard Bosanquet's Theory of Moral Education', *Paedagogia Historia*, Vol. 6(1) 1966, pp. 185–205.
[21] Manifesto of the Delegates at the First Congress of the International Ethical Union, 1896, p. 2.

turn to questions of politics or to concrete social issues which revealed the divisions in what should be the ethical common bond. The feeling that Idealism should appeal to the heart, to offer sympathy and fellowship, was not consistent either with purely intellectual discussion or with dwelling on what *was* the ethicists' common identity, their rejection of Christianity. Their academic nature precluded their taking on some active tasks, such as teaching children or working in the socialist movement, which bound other societies together more effectively.

The debating society which did survive, that at Hampstead, did so because it adopted a religious form of service to encourage mutual sympathy, and because its classes, socials and educational visits helped to bind the members together. The society remained outside Coit's Union of ethical societies because its leader felt that whilst Coit was prepared to identify the ethical movement with socialism, no political party held a monopoly of morals; and the discussions among its members were on themes common among middle-class advanced liberals who were not prepared to accept the collectivism of socialism. They were concerned with the role and moral state of the working class, the breakdown of nineteenth-century liberalism and the Idealist solution in the moralized state, and the writings of Henry George—'the capitalist's last ditch', Marx had observed sardonically. The long life and cohesion of the Hampstead society were also thought to be due to its predominantly Jewish membership; the habit of close association in a minority group survived the new forms that it had taken.[22]

Liberal Judaism

The contemporary crisis in Christian theology and the concern of many middle-class liberals with 'the social problem' also had their effect on Judaism. In both America and Germany in the 1890s there were Jewish movements toward a more modernist theology and a social concern, and the ethical movement in America provided as the Unitarians did a congregation where both Christians and Jews who wanted to retain some religious adherence could meet. In England in the 1890s the leaders of the orthodox Jewish community were becoming alarmed at the number of highly educated young people who were influenced by the 'advanced' religious and political ideas

[22] Minutes of Hampstead Ethical Institute, 1900–1, and M. H. Judge, *The Ethical Movement in England*, published privately, London, 1902.

of the wider society, and 'Instead of attending to the rites of Judaism, like their forefathers, it is said that they prefer to hear *ethical discourses* outside the synagogues, and in consequence, are drifting into unbelief.'[23]

In 1899, the disquiet which was leading many Jews to join ethical societies and the new socialist bodies was focused inside orthodoxy by an article on 'The Spiritual Possibilities of Judaism today' by Lily Montagu, the daughter of a prominent member of Anglo-Jewry. A number of eminent Jews including C. G. Montefiore, yet another Balliol student who had come under the influence of T. H. Green, banded together with proposals to refine and reform orthodoxy which met with approval from many of the leaders of the Jewish community. In 1901, an association was formed to establish meetings and services on Sabbath afternoons, 'supplementary to the services provided by existing synagogues, which by their form and content might appeal to those who were unable to attend the ordinary services or to find spiritual satisfaction in them.' In these services, men and women sat together, prayers were recited in English as well as in Hebrew, some prayers were modified and instrumental music appeared.

The rationale of the changes was not only to break down the ritual barriers between Judaism and Christianity and to recast Judaism in a more universal form so that the rituals of their religion would no longer bar Jews from complete social acceptance, but also to modify Talmudic doctrine in the way towards which contemporary liberal Christians were moving. That is the aim was to substitute natural for revealed religion, so that the Messianic idea was reinterpreted as the belief in human progress, to lay stress on the natural evolution of theology which science would establish in Judaism just as it had in the physical world, and to move away from 'superstitious' ritual and substitute a more direct ethical element in synagogue meetings.

Through the additional meetings a distinct philosophy of Liberal Judaism began to emerge, and it became evident that the gulf between it and orthodoxy would probably result in the founding of new congregations. The approval of the orthodox had been given because they hoped that the new association would check the rate of recession, but now they feared that the changes themselves might lead to the assimilation of young Jews into gentile life. The rigid

[23] Quoted from *Daily Chronicle* of 31 October 1899 in *Ethical World*, 11 November 1899, p. 711.

doctrinal orthodoxy of the most recent wave of immigrants from Russia which had supported them under the most severe persecution was favourably contrasted with the doctrinal plasticity and liberalism of the new Union. In 1900, the Union established its own synagogue in a converted chapel, and became an independent religious movement. Women were formally equal from the beginning, special attention was paid to youth organizations, and in the attempt to overcome the lifeless religiosity of much of orthodoxy the movement borrowed those rituals of Protestantism which emphasized the personal choice of faith—a confirmation service, for instance. By 1931, the synagogue had become the largest synagogue in Britian, and by the 1950s there were fifteen liberal or progressive synagogues with about ten thousand members.[24]

It is interesting that although Liberal Judaism originated in the same intellectual unrest, the desire to abandon old rituals for a religion which would express an ethical and scientific spirit which had led to the ethical movement and other liberal religious groups, they declined as church-going declined or were deflected into politics, whereas Liberal Judaism flourished. Its success and strength are perhaps because it answers the need of a minority group who wish to preserve a culture and a community identity which is ultimately a religious one, but who, as educated, successful and largely assimilated members of British society do not wish to retain the practice and beliefs of orthodoxy, which both separate them from secular life and are incongruous in a culture which emphasizes that religion requires a deliberate intellectual and ethical assent. As with the liberal synagogues in America, the switch of emphasis from the *mitzvot* to the synagogue meeting and the changes in service form have made the *shape* of Judaism something which can co-exist more easily with the dominant religious mode, and so enables religious activity to be more securely separated from secular life and religious divisions to become less acute in that life.

'The Sentimental Socialist'

During the last decade of the nineteenth century, the main branches of the labour movement in England were established; the Social

[24] Rabbi Israel I. Mattuck, *Liberal Judaism*, Union of Liberal and Progressive Synagogues, London, 1947; *Strengthen our Hands*, undated pamphlet issued by the Union of Liberal Progressive Synagogues; Lily H. Montagu, *The Jewish Religious Union and its Beginnings*, n.p., n.d.

Democratic Federation, the Fabian Society, the Labour Churches
and Independent Labour Party all date from this period, as do a
host of minor and forgotten groups—the Fellowship of the New
Life, the Brotherhood Churches, the Socialist Sunday Schools,
various anarchist, Tolstoyian and Christian Socialist groups, and
the Theistic Church. The ethical movement had intellectual and
organizational connections with many of them; eventually it
absorbed the Labour Churches and the Theistic Church. In writing
about these movements, it is easy to dismiss them. They were
ultimately ineffectual, and there were plenty of contemporaries who
regarded them as mere irritating distractions from the real issues.
Many of those who were closely involved with them at the time—
Tom Mann, for instance, or Ramsay MacDonald, or Bernard Shaw
—clearly lived to regret it, and in their memoirs attempted to dismiss the movements along with their enthusiasm for them. With the
wisdom of hindsight, we look back on the 1890s and 1900s and
see the shapes of the rising parliamentary Labour party, with
its intellectually respectable Marxist left-wing and Fabian right,
and we neglect all those excitements and coalitions which at the
time seemed as likely as Labour was to replace the Liberal
party.

There were two underlying reasons why so many radicals did not
expect to see a successful parliamentary socialist party. Many feared
that a political division between Labour and Conservative could
only exaggerate a class war and the growing tendency to reject the
liberal individualism on which parliamentary democracy was based
for the neo-Hegelian mysticism of the strong state which was to be
found among both left and right.[25] And the initial hostility of the
churches to socialism and the influence of Marxist materialism on
many socialists meant that many left-wingers interpreted socialism
as either the religious successor to a dying Christianity, or as a new
kind of politics which had a progressive form of morality of its own,
detached from the parliamentary system. The early phases of
socialism as of all mass movements were marked by a sense of
euphoria, a hope for an entirely new society where moral principles
would determine all social relationships, and political factions
would be replaced by a common ethic. It was with such a hope that
many contemporary socialists supported experiments in religious
socialism.

[25] B. Porter, *Critics of Empire—British Radical Attitudes to Colonialism in Africa,
1895–1914,* Macmillan, London, 1968, p. 156.

But the exigencies of defining what work the socialist movement is to do mean that vague and inchoate faith must be replaced by a set of concrete proposals, and the process of bargaining and assessment of strengths which is necessary to achieve ends through the existing political system mean that the initial utopian emotions must adapt to changing circumstances. During this process, a good deal of antagonism between idealists and realists is inevitable. Belfort Bax, an early protagonist of the 'realistic' wing, attacked the 'sentimental' socialist's desire to be all-inclusive in his aims; 'how can a society whose aims are so high condescend to such matters of detail as *meaning*? How can a man as catholic as the "Brother of the Higher Life", or a member of the "Communion of Noble Aspirations", or of the "New Atlantic Society" be so narrow as to exclude anyone?'[26] He was part of a long tradition of savage dismissals of idealism and broader social objectives inside the labour movement. These critics underestimated the nature of the change that the 'sentimental socialist' envisaged; movements advocating widespread moral change do not need to define their objectives carefully, since it is the change of heart that is all-important; with goodwill, everything can be achieved. Their view of change is that of the evangelical.

As the labour movement in Britain began to define concrete proposals for action and procedure, the various bodies of which it was composed began to split, though with a considerably overlapping membership, to form a spectrum of groups which varied from semi-religious bodies to purely political pressure groups, and which catered for different social classes. Some were anxious to achieve a *rapprochement* with conventional religion to harness its social influence and spiritual powers. Others focused on dimensions of socialism which were later to lose any direct connection with it, such as the anti-cruelty concern of the vegetarians and the Humanitarian League, which extensively overlapped with both the Fabians and the ethicists. Initially there was a constant interchange and overlapping of membership between rapidly proliferating bodies which were more ideologically nebulous and all-embracing than they later became. The Fabians and Social Democratic Federation, for example, were at first recruited very largely from the same people, and much the same group were

[26] E. B. Bax, *The Religion of Socialism*, Sonnenschein, London, n.d., p. 100.

also active anarchists; connections which all three groups were later anxious to deny.[27]

Another socialist rivulet which was soon to go underground was the communitarian, Tolstoyian interest in the setting up of utopias and promoting the simple life. The Fellowship of the New Life, founded in 1883 by a wandering mystic 'for the purpose of common living, as far as possible, on a communistic basis, realizing among ourselves the higher life', seems in retrospect unlikely to have sired the Fabians, but in fact the year after it was founded, the more pragmatic element split off to form the Fabian movement and those more interested in religion than community moved into the ethical movement. Many, including Ramsay MacDonald, continued to support the Fellowship, the Fabians and the ethical movement; the English organizer of the Fellowship played an influential part in founding both the Fabians and the London Ethical Society, and then went to America and became a leader of the St Louis Ethical Society. A member who was both an ethicist and a Fabian thought that they 'were so intertwined with respect to both personnel and theory as to be hardly separable', and Stanton Coit, the leader of the ethical movement, was an enthusiastic Fabian who saw himself as extending the 'permeation' technique to taking over the national church for social democracy.

The intellectual picture presented by the various branches of the ethical and socialist movements at the turn of the century was very confused, in part because the whole map of social and political life was gradually being redrawn. The traditional radical dislike of the State and its apparatus—'Old Corruption'—which had been supported by both the radical manufacturers' interest in hastening the breakup of a traditional system dominated by the aristocracy, and the intellectual defence of individualism by both natural scientists and political thinkers as the basis of social progress, was being assailed from all sides. The dominant metaphor of natural selection had led many socialists to the assumption that social progress was slow but inevitable, that whilst the administrative changes involved would be complex, gradually the 'advanced' morals of socialism would percolate the whole community and there would be very little opposition. Other countries might need revolutions; English socialism had evolution on its side.

[27] A. M. McBriar, *Fabian Socialism and English Politics 1884–1914*, Cambridge University Press, London, 1962; E. J. Hobsbawm, 'The Fabians Reconsidered', in *Labouring Men—Studies in the History of Labour*, Weidenfeld & Nicolson, London, 1964, pp. 261–4.

Comtian positivism and neo-Hegelianism saw a strong and moralized state as both end and agent of social reform. The biological analogies so beloved of the period took yet another twist with Kropotkin's demonstration that Darwinism really showed that natural species survived by mutual aid. Marxist, positivist and Idealist alike pointed to the importance of the whole, the extent to which each man's existence only had meaning as part of society. All collectivist solutions to social problems came to be loosely referred to as socialist.[28]

The ethical movement, which considered it wrong to compartmentalize individual and social morality, was divided on whether the basis for social progress lay in the improvement of individual moral character, or in economic and political change. Many ethicists supported the liberal individualism of Mill, Huxley or Spencer, and thought that general well-being could only rest on personal liberty. The Idealist philosophers of the London Ethical Society and the New Liberal group thought that a social revolution was essential, but that it would be a moral one; whereas Stanton Coit and the ethical societies which followed him thought that only socialism could give practical effect to the gospel of ethics, and hoped that the Independent Labour Party in turn would introduce 'ethical elements' into its programme. Coit defended the policy of the journal of the movement, the *Ethical World*, against the criticisms of his bias in favour of socialism and the masses.

> Such critics regard ethics as a scholastic study of abstract ideas of right, duty, responsibility, the moral ideal, honesty, temperance and justice. And when we have published articles about Trade Unions, or Old Age Pensions, or Co-operation, or an Eight hour day, they have taken offence, and detected something like dishonesty. We have seemed to them now and then, from under our cloak of ethics, to protrude the cloven hoof of Socialism, politics, revolution . . .[29]

Though many ethicists and some ethical societies, including the South Place Society, did not support Coit, it was his identification of the ethical movement with socialism which gave it much of its following, and while socialism existed in an inchoate state, ethicism flourished with it.

[28] A. M. McBriar, op. cit.; E. J. Hobsbawm, 'The Fabians Reconsidered', op. cit., pp. 261–4.
[29] J. A. Hobson, *Confessions of an Economic Heretic*, Allen & Unwin, London, 1938, p. 55; Coit's editorial, *Ethical World*, 6 January 1900.

A Secular Religion

The third source of membership for the ethical movement was the tradition of the secular religion, the religion of morality, which would embody moral principles and set them in a familiar ritual pattern of worship from which all supernatural references had been removed. Several attempts have been made to explain this phenomenon, which has often been confused with a slightly different one in which essentially political or economic grievances have been expressed in religious form. Yet the intentions of the leaders of these secular religions have been clear; they have been trying to provide a support for morality in order to create an alternative to revolution, to bring about major change without class conflict.

At the turn of the century, it was common to feel that although Christianity was failing because it was intellectually untenable and identified with the *status quo*, if it collapsed political reform would become more difficult because the impetus for men to act unselfishly would have gone. Middle-class radicals found themselves in a dilemma. Men were rational and free agents, whose actions were only effective and valuable in so far as they were not compelled; yet the existing inequalities of society negated the freedom of both those whose poverty was so great that they could only live brutishly, and those who were not poor but were forced to use repression to maintain their positions, and, not being islands, were impaired by the incompleteness of the whole. On the whole, the middle-class radicals were antipathetic to the Marxist solution—'*continental* socialism' was often enough to condemn it—which excluded them as individuals as not being members of the proletariat, and seemed careless of both the costs of class warfare and its uncertain outcome.

In such a dilemma, it can be seen why they pinned such faith on the apparently improbable solution of a secular religion, which by changing men's hearts, by dispelling selfishness and bringing about a moral reformation would alone be able to 'redistribute wealth and control the sources of wealth so as to satisfy the demands of each individual. But this consciousness of the working class, in order to become dynamic, must be a moral consciousness; in other words, it must be animated not by facts, but by a standard of what must be.' In fact, without the emphasis on the ethical element, revolution would be useless, for 'only a sense of justice—only an emphasis of the moral factor—has ever produced, or will ever produce, an economic revolution in favour of a dispossessed class.'[30] The ethicist stressed as thoroughly as any revolutionary that the labour movement, by concentrating on collective bargaining and specific political issues was courting catastrophe; unless it mobilized the people as a whole rather than fomenting factions between them, civil war would break out. Should the masses concentrate on moral and physical growth and organization, then 'employers would accept invitations to conferences as courtiers to the councils of kings.' (Overcome, presumably, by the moral superiority of the workers; it is hardly surprising that 'continental' socialists condemned the ethical movement as 'the last resort of middle-class timidity'.)

Quite how many ethicists saw a secular religion as the only hope of averting revolution and how many were merely looking for personal solace is uncertain. Felix Adler, the American founder of the movement, saw membership of an ethical society as a safeguard against the complete abandonment of moral duty by those who had lost the religion which had been bound up with it for so long. Other members saw its religious worth in a simpler light.

> I feel impelled . . . to testify . . . to the meaning and worth of the ethical fellowship to me. For the last four years I have been a member of one of the Ethical Societies, and I can speak of the help and strength which it gives me in my daily duties to attend our Sunday meetings. Not only the addresses, but the instrumental music and singing, inspire me for the work of the coming week, and rest me after that of the past. It is an unspeakable comfort to meet there others who are trying to surmount the difficulties of life in the ethical spirit.[31]

Secular religions have been accounted for in two ways; as the recourse of pre-political people, who have not yet correctly identified the means of bringing social change about, and as the attempt to create a general system of values inside which socialism can flourish. But neither the ethical, positivist nor Labour Church movements can be easily explained in these ways. Their members were not pre-political; many of them were actively engaged in politics. What they seem to have had in common was the attempt to supersede politics, or to end all differences of opinion beneath an underlying moral unity. Men's hearts could be changed; and so all conflicts of interest could be overcome. However weak such a solution now appears, not only did it seem more plausible at a time when, in the recent past, evangelical fervour had indeed dramatically changed

[30] H. J. Bridges et al., *The Ethical Movement*, Union of Ethical Societies, London, 1911.
[31] Letter from F.N.B., *Ethical World*, 9 April 1898, p. 238.

men's behaviour, but before it could be seen that a socialist political party could be accommodated within the existing political system, the religious solution seemed the only alternative to the revolutionary one in bringing about fundamental social change. The idealism, in both senses, of this solution was perhaps the reason for the peak of influence of British Idealist philosophy at the turn of the century, and its rapid disappearance thereafter. Its major weakness as a political theory had been to assume that self-realization and rational moral conduct were the same, and that fundamental non-ideational conflicts of interest did not really exist.[32]

[32] A J. Milne, 'Utilitarian Social Philosophy', *Archives Européennes de Sociologie*, Vol. 8 (2), 1967, pp. 319-31.

10 ETHICAL WORSHIP—THE USES OF RITUAL

As Socialists we had, so to speak, withdrawn, divorced ourselves from the society in which we lived. We were making our own society; and since the society we had rejected had its religions and churches, so we deemed it necessary to have a religion and church likewise. But of course we had not religion at all in any true sense. We had noble aspirations and much indignation, but these are different things.

Walter Allen, *All in a Lifetime*

To both outsiders and present-day humanists, the most ludicrous and incomprehensible aspect of the religions of socialism—the ethical, positivist and Labour Church movements—has been their ritual activity, their attempts to embody their ideas and convey them by other than purely intellectual means. Such activities are commonly dismissed either as the vestiges of religion or as the products of an unusual psychological need, a sort of hunger for the trappings of religion combined with a distaste for its content. To a more sympathetic view, the men who tried to create a ritual were conscious of the need to convey something which cannot be done by means of information and arguments; they were, more or less deliberately, setting out to create artificially sets of shared sentiments and *mores* which, they believed, were vitally necessary in order to allow of true social unity and advance. The need to create that which can only grow, which we know we need but do not know how to get, was a problem with which the great sociologists of the period were vitally concerned. With the loss of public religion, custom and traditional community, social commentators increasingly talked about 'demoralization', the 'loss of nerve'; had they read Marx or Durkheim, they might have been talking about alienation or anomie.

Although we have come to realize the importance of ritual for social life it is a difficult topic to examine, since by definition, its meaning and its effects are most importantly concerned with that which cannot be put into words. It is extremely rare for rituals to be deliberately created and reflected upon; the very process almost denies its end. New rituals more commonly come about unconsciously; apparently utilitarian, rationally justifiable activities, such as meeting to protest about government policy or going to a football match, suddenly are noticed to have acquired a wealth of symbolism and meaning which expresses the feelings of the participants about their place in the world and which (often) metaphorically reverses the relationships by which they feel themselves made impotent. The important rituals which in most societies surround the stages of the life-cycle have in our society become truncated and often denied. Some might argue, following Malinowski, that the anxiety and uncertainty which surround the physiological processes of birth and death have either become redundant or surrendered to the control of the medical profession and that the impetus for secular ritual is consequently less; or, alternatively, that where the bonds of the traditional community, the reminders of common identity, have been eroded by more complex and functional relationships between those who relate to each other primarily in terms of specialized roles, rituals—which by their nature transform us totally—have come to seem out of place. Others have argued that our neglect and truncation of ritual is something which has been produced by social change and the kind of intellectual tradition which the Rationalist Press has so closely reflected, and that our need for ritual is still there and unsatisfied.

The religions of socialism tried to create rituals; for a period, and for some people more than a period, they were successful, but in the end they came to seem inappropriate and unconvincing and were abandoned. Why this should have been so is not clear, any more than why the secular religions created after the French revolution were so unsuccessful. Durkheim laid great stress on religion as essentially a shared experience, an institution which was socially necessary in order to make any set of beliefs and social bonds comprehensible and binding. He advocated that in order to prevent social dislocation and corruption, all social collectivities such as national groups, trade unions or enterprises, should adopt their own ritual and symbolism; what he does not seem to have considered were the conditions under which such bonds would become natural rather than embarrassingly artificial.

Many rituals are borrowed; the Christian missionaries who toiled among the heathen were frequently horrified to discover that the meaning of their religion had been poured from its ritual bottle and replaced with less familiar contents; that symbols such as crosses had acquired a magical power to heal or confer potency, or that the gift of Pentecost had become a literal glossolalia. But this has happened throughout the history of religions and of contact between cultures. Nadel's attempt to examine systematically on what basis Islamic rituals were borrowed and incorporated into a indigenous

African religion concluded that no reason could be discovered; the rituals which were borrowed did not seem to have been selected on the basis of either their impressiveness or their familiarity, nor because they dealt with matters which were of concern to the people who borrowed them.[1]

The creator of ethical ritual, Stanton Coit, was familiar with the works of Jane Harrison, Durkheim and Levi-Bruhl on ritual and justified his activities by reference to anthropological arguments, but his church services also had a key place in a wider political programme. Before setting up his own church, he had been a minister at South Place, but his ideas on both politics and religion and even more his unspoken assumptions about ritual clashed with those of its committee. South Place represents a community with a genuine religious tradition and feel, a *congregation*, which moved from religion as an intellectual matter long before it abandoned religion as a tradition. Coit created a ritual which became fully convincing only for a short period.

South Place—the end of the Enlightenment

To take up the story of South Place again in the 1850s: after W. J. Fox's withdrawal to radical politics, a succession of unsatisfactory ministers were appointed to the remains of the liberal unitarian congregation to 'develop the religious sentiments in conformity with the ascertained laws of natural and religious truth'. Many of these ministers had been Anglican clergymen, and whilst their theological opinions might have become liberal to the point of disappearance, their views on the sacerdotal role of the clergy and its position *vis-à-vis* the congregation had not.

The Reverend Barnett, for example, who was appointed in 1857, had tried to make the form of the services more church-like by introducing a choir, a new hymn-book and chanted psalms, and the objections voiced by many of the congregation were not to ritual as such, but to the particular flavour of mysticism and emotion, the sense of congregational unity, that Barnett was trying to introduce. The disagreements between Barnett and the committee deserve to be recorded, not only because they illuminate much about the complex connections between theological ideas and ritual forms, but because of the wordy splendours of the battle.

[1] S. F. Nadel, *Nupe Religion*, Routledge & Kegan Paul, London, 1954.

The advanced unitarians who made up the South Place congregation may have largely lost any supernatural beliefs, but they had retained a view that what a religion should do was appeal to the moral sense and satisfy the intellect; they complained that Barnett talked about nothing but 'records of the past as contained in the Bible', and had departed from natural religion—'from our pulpit the rocks and the heavens no longer sing their grand hymn of devotion and praise.' Barnett in turn had found his congregation distressingly intellectually presumptuous:

> I am told that I make a great deal too much of the Saviour for your taste. It is urged against me that I preach all about Christ, and never about Socrates; that I glorify Paul, and say nothing about Pythagoras; that I bore you with the Bible, and never read in our worship from other books; that I delight in the Psalms of David, and ignore the Confessions of Rousseau; that I revel in Isaiah and neglect Plato; that I sometimes take a lesson from Solomon, while you have a preference for Poor Richard.[2]

Barnett had tried to create a mood of religious reverence in his congregation by several means. His last sermon had preached the necessity of a liturgy, of a sense of beauty and mystery which could only be created by an emphasis on form and order in worship, which he had hoped would give 'a tone of Christian simplicity, solemnity, spirituality and earnestness'. He found the self-confident independence with which the unitarian confronted revealed truth antipathetic; 'I minister to faith, and hope, and charity, not to doubt, disputation and egoistical enlightenments. I am reverential and devout—you like criticism and rhetoric . . . I seek, however humbly, and however feebly, to reconcile your sinning and sorrowing souls to the Lord God Almighty; you are intent, instead, on a career of iconoclastic adventures and exploits.' The deficient sense of sin among the South Place congregation also meant that they did not see any saving grace in the minister or in the church itself. Barnett protested that by his exclusion from the committee, he was cut off from the congregation as a living unity; 'you regard me, not as the living minister of a living church, but the hired lecturer of a sort of secular theological association or institute. You have, for the most part, seemed to expect nothing from me but a discourse once a week . . .' The committee retorted that in their terms he was unsuccessful; many members had left the chapel, and Barnett was

---

[2] Quotations in the dispute between Barnett and the Committee are taken from the *South Place Pulpit* for May and June 1863, and M. Conway, *Centenary of the South Place Society*, Williams and Norgate, London, 1903, p. 100.

not a stimulating enough lecturer to draw large congregations. Barnett had wanted the members of the chapel to be a congregation, to have more personal contact with each other and to undertake 'educational, charitable and spiritual works'. As London grew and Finsbury had become less of a professional residential area, the congregation had grown more scattered and the close links which had held members together were replaced by a more purely intellectual appeal which drew strangers from all over London, and this in turn depended very largely on the intellectual calibre of the minister and his social contacts.

Barnett had equally wanted the congregation to feel the solemn mystery of religion, the power of the act of worship, by acknowledging this in their demeanour whilst in the chapel. 'How many times have I, with gentleness and respectfulness, but with solemn earnestness, reproved the apparent irreverence of your habits in the house and hours of our worship!' What he meant was perhaps what had struck the attention of another Anglican clergyman, visiting the chapel ten years later, who found that he could readily distinguish between strangers and regular attenders, 'since some of the habitués have a custom of walking to their very pews with their hats on, and talking quite loudly whilst sitting there, as though to enter a standing protest against any notion of consecration attending to their chapel.' The deliberate denial by some of the 'feel' of religious ritual was something which struck me when I attended South Place nearly a hundred years later. One suspects a kind of iconoclasm by committee. 'As soon as the last words of the benediction were over, the congregation resolved itself unromantically into a meeting, and a gentleman stood up on a pew seat, and discussed how best to change the chapel pulpit into a platform.'[3]

The consequence of the 'egoistical enlightenments' of his congregation had been that South Place was no longer regarded, Barnett thought, as a religious institution. He pointed out that members were conscious of its dubious reputation: 'when you would put any of my published discourses into circulation, you feel it to be necessary to tear off the title-page; because you know that, with "South Place" on the cover, no-one will read them.' Barnett's response to all this had been, with that mixture of humble solemnity and high-handedness so characteristic of evangelicals, to try to sell the chapel to the Baptists and start a church elsewhere. Whereupon

[3] Rev. C. M. Davies, *Unorthodox London: or, Phases of Religious life in the Metropolis*, Tinsley Brothers, London, 1873, pp. 13, 19.

he was sharply reminded by the committee that not only did this not lie in his powers, but he was both alien to the traditions of the chapel and intellectually not even a Christian. They reaffirmed their belief in the purpose of the chapel as being for the worship of the 'One true God alone', and 'that it recognizes a law of progression, both in the material and the moral world, and it welcomes every addition to the knowledge already gained, whether applicable to the one or the other.'

Barnett resigned, and was followed by a succession of 'advanced' ministers from less receptive congregations of whom there was an apparently endless supply for ethical and secular platforms, but matters did not improve until the appointment of Moncure Conway in 1864.

Transcendentalism and Radicalism

Moncure Conway was the son of a Virginian landowner who had abandoned the Methodist ministry when confronted with the optimistic faith and innocence of a Quaker community. He had entered the Harvard Divinity School to train as a unitarian minister, but the intellectual deism of eighteenth-century New England theologians had been swamped by the rising tide of transcendentalism. Conway immersed himself in Longfellow, Hawthorne, Holmes and above all Emerson, and from them he took a blend of an optimistic faith in the emotions and in science rather than in dogma, and a defence of radicalism in politics whereby momentous changes would be brought about for the better by the dimly perceived workings of evolution, so brilliantly anticipated by Emerson.

Conway's outspoken abolitionism made him a controversial minister and in 1863, having lost several pulpits, he went on a speaking tour of England to gather support for the abolitionist cause. South Place was one of the pulpits from which he spoke, though the chapel was shortly due to be closed. His second sermon there was 'attended by some old radicals who had rarely appeared in the Chapel since Fox's time', and Conway was persuaded to accept the charge of the congregation.

Conway's *forte* lay in a sensitivity to the nuances of beliefs and the way in which they should be reflected in the forms of service. For a rational religion, a delicate matching of belief and its expression is essential if the meeting is to retain any religious sense, and yet not offend any anti-clerical susceptibilities. Conway proposed changes in the form of the service; refusing to wear Fox's gown, converting the pews into seats, and tactfully approaching the committee over 'the composition of the prayer'.

> With the views now generally entertained at South Place as to the attributes of the Deity—as an All Wise and All Loving Father who could not change one iota of His wise and perfect laws for all the prayers of the Universe—it became very difficult indeed to shape a prayer, especially a public one, in such a manner as would be reconcilable with these beliefs in every particular . . . Instead of the prayer he proposed to substitute a devotional reading, either of his own composition or of some eminent writer—and he felt quite certain that the service would gain rather than lose in warmth, earnestness and devotion by the change he proposed.[4]

The committee, appeased equally by Conway's defences of radical political philosophy and his success as a preacher, gladly consented, and Conway's moral ascendancy over the congregation was such that although he abandoned the forms and symbolism of sacerdotalism he did, none the less, create far more congregational loyalty and unity than Barnett had been able to do.

In Troeltsch's terms, Barnett had been trying to create a church so that the institution itself, its role in society, its forms of worship and the sacerdotal role of its leader were the source of legitimacy and power, but he had been affronting the sensibilities of a group who were a denomination or sect, who were resigned to being an élite minority and who saw legitimacy as resting in a powerful and effective leader, although with an unusual source of charisma, a facility for powerful and learned arguments.

Conway was an effective leader; Count D'Alviella, who was observing and comparing attempts to modernize religion in 1885 thought that Conway had such strong personal attraction, especially in his clear and moving voice, that without him the chapel would have collapsed. And his power was only added to by the fact that his theology, although it filled the right sort of *space* for the congregation, i.e. supported advanced radical views, evolution and science, was intelligible to no one but himself. His sermons attempted to create a mood, to inspire rather than to argue. Those who met him remembered his tolerance, breadth of thought and warm heart, but remembered little of what he had actually said. He had moved, he thought with characteristic poetic vagueness, 'from dynamic theism to the theism evolved from pantheism by the poets'.

[4] Minutes of the South Place Chapel for February 1869.

Evolution was a key factor in Conway's thinking, but it was the moral and spiritual evolution of Emerson and Hegel in which mankind would progress ever upward to ever more perfect states which would comprehend all preceding stages. Faith in progress Conway thought, was fundamentally a belief in God. But God was many other things as well; Conway considered it an 'axiomatic truth' that an 'instinct compels us to render homage to the superior principle, generally embodied in the idea of God', and the conception of God also got turned into the ideal of humanity so that Jesus became the ultimate religious reformer, the representative man, who embodied 'all that is most elevated and comprehensive in the New Testament'; which as Alviella sardonically commented, meant 'everything that is conformable to the views held at South Place Chapel.' Like the transcendentalists of New England, Conway was opposed to dogma not only because the letter killeth and could not catch the spirit of religion, but because God was identical with the whole progress of humanity whose course was unforeseen, and even this sort of nebulous identity should not be pressed too far, 'for fear of identifying it with a dogmatic formula which may be found on the morrow in antagonism with some recent verification of science.'[5]

Conway was made even more acceptable to the South Place congregation by his position in radical intellectual circles—he wrote a successful life of Paine—and by his interest in contemporary developments in science and anthropology. Whereas the rationalist took from anthropology a stress on the evolution away from the *burden* of religion, Conway found in it a basis for comparative religion and the evolution of a synthesis of all morality and theology, and his sermons on these subjects attracted large attendances. He tried to attract a wide range of controversialists on these topics, and to mingle symbols of all the religious and inspiring leaders on the walls of South Place to emphasize their essential unity. Orthodox Christians found it outrageous; Dr Spurgeon complained that 'a people who are something more or worse than Unitarian' were congregating in a chapel 'adorned with tablets bearing the names of Moses, Voltaire, Jesus, Paine, Zoroaster, etc. The blasphemous association of our Lord and Thomas Paine and Voltaire creates an indescribable feeling in a Christian mind . . .', but the members of the congregation were satisfied. After Conway's first year, the

[5] Count Goblet D'Alviella, *The Contemporary Evolution of Religious Thought in England, America, and India*, Williams & Norgate, London, 1885; M. D. Conway, *Autobiography*, Cassell, London, 1904.

committee reported that they could scarcely have hoped for 'a more earnest, interesting, instructive and eloquent series of services', whose combination of 'deep philosophy' and 'stimulus to upright and useful conduct' revived the 'best memories of the Finsbury pulpit'.

The congregation of South Place was gradually losing the respectable city and manufacturing Unitarian families and gaining a more sporadic and intellectual clientele, including many of the most famous scientific, literary and 'advanced' figures of the day. Conway's 'periodical soirées for music and conversation, with picnics into the country and water parties on the Thames' were brilliant affairs. South Place retained enough of a congregational tradition to have 'a large number of ladies, some of them dressed in an elegant style'. In 1964, some members who had been brought up at South Place could recall how inspiring and sociable Conway's meetings had been, and that many families in the congregation still clung half-heartedly to their old religions. It was the easier for them to do so as Conway became more opposed to dogma or to definition of any kind. Worship was a matter of neither reason nor faith but of feeling, which must be detached from any formula; 'the religious sentiment may and must be separated from everything of the nature of dogma, belief or hypothesis.'

South Place had evolved a satisfactory pattern of ritual and theology, but its sympathetic tolerance for the most notorious radicals of the day finally began to show signs of strain in the 1880s, the decade in which economic distress among the poor became acute and a growing number of both working- and middle-class reformers were turning to collectivist solutions of various kinds. In 1886, 'Some conversation took place on the question of letting the chapel to the Communists', read an entry in the minutes, but true to their liberal traditions, they did let it with a caution 'as to dirt and smoking'. General opinion in the 1880s in London distinguished increasingly sharply between the respectable poor who were worthy of charity and help and the 'residuum', those who through chronic unemployment and poor housing had become permanently degenerate and a threat to the skilled working-classes and civilized society alike.[6] South Place, in common with many

[6] Stedman Jones, (*Outcast London*, Clarendon Press, Oxford, 1971) who considers that the middle-class view was that poverty was degeneracy until the 1880s, when there was a sudden attempt to demarcate off the 'respectable' employed poor from the 'residuum'. I have found ample evidence from earlier periods to suggest that amongst the poor at least, the concept of 'respectability' has a long and vigorous history.

other institutions of the period, began evening classes in scientific
and political knowledge for the respectable working-classes.

After Conway's resignation in 1884, a series of guest speakers
were invited, among them Leslie Stephen, Graham Wallas, Karl
Pearson, Edward Carpenter, J. M. Robertson, Frederick Harrison
and J. Allanson Picton, to speak to the congregation. South Place
rationalized the arrangement—'Truth is naturally many-sided'—
but members began to fall away, and the committee were happy to
accept Conway's recommendation of Stanton Coit, a young worker
from the American ethical movement. It is with Coit's very different
ideas on ritual and the political and social role of an ethical movement
that the remainder of this chapter is concerned.

'The most secular man of our year, but also the most spiritual'

Thus had his contemporaries summed Coit up in the Amherst year
book. He was to become the dominant figure in the English ethical
movement from his appointment as lecturer to the West London
Ethical Society in 1894 until his gradual retirement from about 1930,
when his ideas had lost much of their credibility within the movement. His leadership was based on his energetic, autocratic but
inspiring character, the wealth and generosity of both himself and
his wife, his excellence as a speaker, but also on his clear and consistent views on the functions of an ethical movement. In a movement which originated in such inchoate, complex and contradictory
viewpoints, none of which gave the actual meetings of members
much of a role, his detailed and positive conception of what the
movement as a movement could achieve gave it a coherence that its
members both needed and resented.

Coit had been born in Ohio in 1857; his mother was a spiritualist,
and Coit himself had telepathic gifts. His lack of experience of
orthodox religious communities was to make it difficult for him to
understand the anti-clericalism of many ethicists and their unease
with religious symbolism. At fifteen, he had been smitten by Emerson's insistence that the only important question was that of the
moral conduct of life: 'How shall I live?' Coit went to Amherst,
where 'my conversation must have fairly reeked of Emerson',
and in particular centred on his plea that 'Pure Ethics is not
now formulated and concreted into a *cultus*, a fraternity with

assemblings and holy days, with song and book, with brick and stone. Why have not those who believe in it and love it left all for this?"[7]

Once, when Coit was talking to a friend about his views on ethical mysticism and the moral life, he was told that his views were those of a young New York rabbi, Felix Adler, who had taken most of his congregation with him when he left his synagogue and founded the Ethical Culture Society. Coit became a full-time worker for the society, and ran moral instruction classes for its children; but Adler's views on the training of a priest in the ethical movement were stringent. He should be highly educated philosophically, but his influence was to be exerted through the minds and the hearts of his hearers to reach their wills. 'The platform of an Ethical Society is itself an Altar, the address must be the fire that burns thereon.'[8] Accordingly in 1886 Coit went to Berlin to study Kant, the philosophical basis of Adler's views, and on his way back spent three months at Toynbee Hall, where he acquired an interest in the idea of neighbourhood guilds which was to develop later into a theory of how socialism would come about.

Although Coit always regarded himself as essentially in sympathy with the American ethical culture movement, his views on many matters began to differ from those of Adler. Coit was a socialist, and socialism was an integral part of the united moral community that he hoped the ethical movement would build. But Adler was a 'pronounced and aggressive' anti-socialist, and an anti-feminist; Coit concluded ruefully, 'it is evident that there are two types of ethics. . .' (a reflection so damaging to his general philosophy that he did not pursue it). And Coit would have based his ethical church on a 'continuity with the Christian tradition', which he knew that Adler would inevitably have opposed. When Adler recommended Coit to Conway as his successor at South Place, it must have seemed a solution to the inevitable clash between the two men.

Coit was determined to make South Place a part of the ethical movement; he wanted the activities of the society to shift from intellectual discussions to ethical inspiration, and for the members to start guilds for their own children and the children of the poor. Philanthropic ventures and ethical classes proliferated; Coit

[7] S. Coit, *My Ventures on the Highway of Truth*, ms. kindly loaned to me by Lady Fleming. Emerson had, after all, once been a unitarian minister.
[8] F. Adler, 'Some Characteristics of the American Ethical Movement', in *Fiftieth Anniversary of the Ethical Movement*, Appleton, New York, 1926, pp. 6–7.

altered the order of services and wanted the congregation as well as the choir to sing hymns. He tried to have matters arranged more reverently; the congregation was requested not to dissent during meetings from the views of the lecturer, and to refrain from standing outside the doors of the chapel if they disliked the practice of hymn-singing. (This form of protest continued until hymns were discontinued in 1963.) But the committee were becoming more resistant to his demands for change, and yet again they refused to allow the minister to attend committee meetings, a resistance stiffened by the fact that many old members had begun to leave, complaining that their aesthetic sense of worship as appropriately marked by a decent plainness and simplicity was offended by the elaborate rituals that Coit was introducing, and that they thought the important thing should be the lecture, not the liturgy of the service and the congregation's charitable activities. Coit resigned in 1891, taking with him the 'young and ardent', and South Place wooed Conway back from America to resume his position as minister until 1897. Coit spoke to the various ethical societies and Labour Churches, and tried to persuade them to join his ethical movement. He gradually took over the London Ethical Society, and it was there that his personal philosophy took a concrete form in the Ethical Church.

Ethical Democracy

Coit's philosophy was based on the view that moral values had a real existence, independent of the material world, and that once the individual had had his attention drawn to them, his spiritual judgement would force him to acknowledge their authority and to attempt to realize the good life. Morality was universal and synoptic; Christianity was merely an episode in the attempts of philosophers and moralists to convey their view of the moral life to men. Religion was necessary for social cohesion, but its essence lay not in supernatural beings but in *devotion to the good*. Goodness was self-evident, a quality of character and conduct which was readily recognizable, and to do good was true religion. 'Nothing could be clearer and more definite than this doctrine . . .' When men came to realize this, they would attain inward peace, and by this personal redemption social change would become possible; 'the Ethical movement must animate single hearts before it can rise to the majesty of a social force.' To those perplexed about their religious belief, and how social change would be possible without a shared bond which would lift men above narrow self-interest, this message came as a revelation. A woman remembered how she had heard Coit lecture for the first time at South Place and

> Scales seemed to fall from her eyes, and she perceived what religion meant. 'Morality is religion', the lecturer affirmed; and as she carried the sentence home with her, it seemed to give expansion to her whole being. The old narrow Rationalism was widened by sympathy, and she saw how, in spite of theological doctrines, others might be ethical.[9]

Unlike the idealist philosophers, Coit did not see the recognition of the compelling power of absolute moral values as an individual intellectual act. His view was far more sociological; at some points remarkably Durkheimian. The good in man, Coit thought, came from his contact with society; men were drawn together by the recognition that without the binding force of ideals and moral values they could not exist. In order to act upon them they needed the help of others, and it was this striving after a common moral purpose that had drawn mankind together in religion. Religion was nothing if it was not social; the religious impulse could not exist without a church. 'The high value I place', Coit said, 'upon the spiritual discipline of ecclesiastical organization arises from my recognition of the perfectly patent connection of cause and effect existing between fellowship in the moral life and moral enthusiasm.' He criticized James' *Varieties of Religious Experience* in much the same way as Durkheim had attacked Bergson's view of religion, because James discussed spiritual experiences as if they could exist independently of a religious community.[10]

As Coit pointed out, his views were an extension of the Broad Church tradition of Coleridge, the Arnolds, and, above all, John Seeley. In their writings, the theme appears of a national church which, liberal and comprehensive in doctrine and rooted in the past traditions of the British nation, will absorb the narrow bigotries of Nonconformity and foreign sophistries of Catholicism and become at once the spiritual image of the state and its guide and support. In such a church, the conflict between science and revealed religion would be transcended, because the essential message of Christianity was that of all religions—to do good. Christians are those who accept

[9] S. Coit, 'The Ethical Movement Defined', in *Religious Systems of the World*, Sonnenschein, London, 1890, pp. 538–42; *Ethical World*, 10 December 1898, p. 785 and 3 December 1898, p. 777.
[10] S. Coit, *National Idealism and a State Church*, Williams and Norgate, London, 1907. Most of the subsequent discussion of Coit's ideas is based on this work.

the moral example which Christ set for them. He was a kind of ideal good citizen, a man who proposed a universal social morality on which society could be based. In the organic unity which such a church would give to society, conflict between social classes would be at an end, the best traditions of the society would be preserved against both the ravages of industrialism and the individualism of the utilitarians and Herbert Spencer, and the poor would take their rightful place in the life of the nation. The absence of religion, 'secularity', would merely result in the dominion of machinery and philistines; a secure state could only rest on an ethical basis, and it was the duty of the clergy to teach such a national morality to their charges.[11]

Coit extended and developed these ideas in *National Idealism and a State Church* (1907), an amalgam of idealist philosophy, Emersonian ethics, and an extension of current anthropological work on the role of religion in society; 'organic' is a favourite term. It attacked the effects of individualism in religion, politics and economic life. Men needed the help of their fellows to become good citizens in any sphere, and the religious impetus which would enable them to acknowledge their common bond was inseparable from the ritual of a church. Socialists should accordingly support the national church, since it alone created the general will needed for social change. Men were moulded by the religious and moral life of their nation. 'The real organic unit of religious life, of which any man is a member, is always the nation to which he belongs, in so far as the nation stands for social and personal ideals and principles.' The ethical movement itself was an extension of the Broad Church to two classes excluded by the Christian churches, but vitally important to the life of the nation—Jews and agnostics, who rejected Christian beliefs, and the working classes, whom both state and national church had excluded and betrayed. Only the force of religious nationalism would be able to reunite the churches and classes in England and get the working classes to attend church again. The rituals and forms of the state church, the moral standards it enshrined, would be established democratically. The existing churches and sects would become parties within it, each with its own views, but accepting the democratic decision of the people.

Because Coit, like Seeley, saw the religious unit as the nation and religious teaching as based on the traditions of the society rather

[11] R. T. Shannon, 'John Robert Seeley and the Idea of a National Church', in R. Robson, *Ideas and Institutions of Victorian Britain*, Bell, London, 1967.

than the Bible, religion became a higher form of patriotism. Progressive thinkers, he believed, were wrong to despise the patriotism which was so strong a component of contemporary social imperialism, and to hope that if it were broken down socialist internationalism would result. Patriotism was not only an ineradicable sentiment, but a necessary one to break down individualism and bring about a more unified community. 'In my judgement, the identification of religion with the unifying impulse of a nation gives to religious Modernism that cohesive principle which was fatally lacking in the individualistic rationalism of the eighteenth and nineteenth centuries.'

One of the reasons for which Coit was anxious to join forces with the Anglican church, rather than to found a competing one for non-supernaturalists, was that he felt that those who had already left the churches had become too tainted with rationalist individualism to be responsive to the organic conception of ethical socialism. 'It is not the man of the world, it is not the isolated Agnostic, it is not the individualist, who knows how to appreciate the new revelation that has come in his own day.' The contemporary political socialists were *laissez-faire* individualists who could not really believe in state control, especially since their views were buttressed by the atomistic individualism of the nonconformist churches to which many of them still belonged. The Anglican, on the other hand, was already a socialist in his religion, since he believed in its union with the state and a social and organic role for the church, and should become a political socialist. But the Anglican church was marked by the class exclusiveness of the landed gentry, and its unwillingness to acknowledge the rights and sufferings of the poor had alienated them from it. Coit hoped that socialists would see that their movement was a religion, and so band themselves together to constitute a church.

> When socialists more profoundly grasp the inner secret and more widely survey the scope of the movement, they will be sure consciously to assert the religious and spiritual character of their philosophy and their mission. They will then constitute themselves a church as well as a political party. When they do, their fervour for their church will be exactly like that of the Anglican for his . . .

The Ethical Community

The decline of community was seen from the 1860s on as a major evil which was responsible for class antagonism, the appalling living conditions of the poor and their brutalization, and the difficulty of mobilizing the sense of duty of the leaders of the community to improve its lot. At this period, the Idealists and liberals generally thought that parliamentary legislation was far less significant in promoting social welfare than private philanthropy and the various forms of mutual aid which had been developed by working-men. Craft unions, co-operatives, benefit societies and mutual improvement societies were all seen as forms of community, which the state would oversee and harmonize so that society became a harmonious whole.[12] The contemporary reformer appealed to the sense of guilt of the wealthy and educated; the East End was seen as a disgraceful monument to their abandonment of the labouring classes amongst whom they no longer lived and to whom they gave only a sporadic charity.

One solution which was proposed was that the rich should return to live among the poor and resume their neglected role as leaders of the community. The settlement movement, in particular the founding of Toynbee Hall in 1883, provided an institutionalized structure for idealistic young men to spend a short period among the poor, helping and teaching them and their children. Coit, who had spent a short period at Toynbee Hall, was an enthusiast for the idea of creating a community, but in many respects he was more egalitarian and less paternalist than the English workers in the movement. He believed, for example, that 'all the people, men, women and children, in any one street, or any small number of streets . . . shall be organized in a set of clubs, which are by themselves, or in alliance with those of other neighbourhoods, to carry out, or induce others to carry out, all the reforms—domestic, industrial, educational, provident, or recreative—which the social ideal demands.'[13] The poor, he thought, had only been debased by a bad environment, from which the neighbourhood guilds would rescue and rapidly raise them to the morality and personal habits of the upper classes. He made vague references to a religion of eugenics which would cope with the problem of those who could not be raised.

Coit's belief in the natural goodness and creativity of the poor made him exceptionally liberal for his time; his advocacy of selective breeding reinforced by public opinion make him seem reactionary in ours. But we must see a thinker in the context of his own time;

---

[12] M. Richter, 'Intellectuals and Class Alienation: Oxford Idealist Diagnoses and Prescriptions', *Archives Européennes de Sociologie*, Vol. 7(1), 1966, p. 12.
[13] H. J. Blackham, *Stanton Coit, 1857–1944*, Favil Press, London, n.d., pp. 7–8.

an interest in eugenics was common among extremely liberal men in the pre-Hitler period, since it was considered a humane means of preventing the cruel consequences of social Darwinism, and had close connections with family planning, a concern of the most 'advanced'. 'Eugenics co-operates with the workings of Nature . . .' said Galton; '. . . what Nature does blindly, slowly and ruthlessly, man may do providently, swiftly and kindly'. The ethical movement in the thirties was both inclined to favour selective breeding and consistently condemnatory of Hitler.

To Coit, the main problem in implementing a socialist society was to make effective the moral force which would bind men together and make them act ethically, and his solution to this question was to use religious techniques. Christianity, he thought, had sapped men's self-confidence by teaching them that they were weak and evil and should be humble. They were naturally both good and sane, and by the means of science and social democracy, the kingdom of heaven could indeed be built upon earth. Men were not merely rational animals; and the antagonism to religion which many who had left Christianity expressed, alienated them from group bonds and tended to individualism and sterile intellectuality. Ritual and ceremonial were the most vital part of religion, for they were a language which expressed and reinforced the interior states which led to social unity and recognition of the good. Consequently, it was vital that the rituals used should be sensitively developed and aesthetically pleasing. Coit condemned very strongly the hideous tastelessness of positivist ritual; their unimaginative prayers— 'foolish and incapable utterances'—which neglected the literary talents of the day. Shaw, Chesterton and Elgar were examples of talent which should be turned to good use, and it was very important that not only the liturgy but the music, setting and priestly garments of ethical worship should be aesthetically satisfying so as to fire the imagination. The personification of abstract forces such as 'Virtue' or 'England' would make men feel an identity with them and be moved by them.

In 1906, there were forty-two ethical societies and in all of them, Coit thought, a service was conducted embodying some at least of his principles. Their propaganda instrument would be his manual of songs and ceremonies, and he hoped that eventually enough people would be attracted for the Prayer Book to be once again overhauled, and the ethical movement to become the basis for the national church.

The Ethical Church

Coit's views on the role of ritual in social change were worked out in the society that he led and controlled, the West London Ethical Society, later to become the Ethical Church. In 1891 Coit and his supporters had left South Place, and at first merged with the caucus of Idealist philosophers in the London Ethical Society. But Leslie Stephen, Bernard Bosanquet and several other members protested at the socialism, ritualism, and attempt to inspire rather than inform of Coit and his circle, who split off again to form the West London Society. In a letter to the members of the new society Coit explained the distinctive nature of his own views. The purpose of members of the society meeting together was to make them aware that they were spiritually members of one another. Part of the bond between them was the bond of Reason, which would be strengthened by the Sunday lectures on the performance of duty. But an equally important bond was that of Feeling, and here Coit condemned the type of freethinker often found in London 'whose dissipation consists in the much attending of lectures and discussions, who mean to become learned, who glory in their religious emancipation, hate forms and ceremonies, and are violently moved against all recognition of emotion . . .' It was this 'unsocial intellectuality' which had made the educated agnostic fancy that he need not attend Sunday lectures and did not need 'humble, simple, human communion in the truth'. Henceforth, his society would follow its own path; it would cultivate and satisfy the whole man.[14]

Coit took with him to West London the form of service, essentially nonconformist, in use at South Place: ethical hymns, readings from religious or ethical texts, and a long discourse. Out of it evolved what can only be called ethical High Anglicanism; the order of service in 1913, for instance, was organ voluntary, introductory sentence, a canticle, a meditation, two minutes of silence, a hymn, a lesson, an anthem, the discourse, an anthem, the invitation to fellowship, a hymn, and the dismissory sentence. Over the next ten years or so, he founded many societies, predominantly in London, and by 1907 the West London Society was well-established. Two well-attended services were held every Sunday, and there were over four hundred subscribers.

In association with the church, Coit hoped to found the manifold

[14] S. Coit, *Letter to the Members of W.L.E.S.*, n.p., 1894.

activities in the community which ethical religion was to unite. He started ethical classes for children, a local branch of the I.L.P., which he housed in a hall which he hoped would ultimately become a centre for political, trade union and ethical activity in North Kensington. To him, socialism was an integral part of the ethical life, but his vision of socialism was wider than politics. 'I am what I should make bold to call a psychological and ethical as well as a merely economic socialist. I am an all-round socialist, while others seem to me often one-sided, partial, and lacking insight into the mental dynamics of reform.'

Like many other observers, Coit had seen that whereas in private life men fairly readily acknowledge moral responsibility for one another, public life is far more anomic. His solution to the problem was to try to merge the two; he wanted to reunite in his guilds the areas of life that industrialism had separated, in order to bring moral principles more effectively to bear upon them. He wanted trades unions to be reorganized on a neighbourhood basis, so that the family would become 'a potent psychological and social factor in the Labour Movement.' At present, he felt, the movement was concentrating too much on specific issues such as collective bargaining; it needed to be organized 'under a definite yet comprehensive programme, touching all sides of life, and based on the fundamental principles of an ideal social organism.'[15]

During the early years, the discourse at West London was often given by an eminent socialist such as Ramsay MacDonald, Keir Hardie or Philip Snowden. As it had done in the Labour Churches, this limited the amount of ritual that could be developed, for such men were both unable and unwilling to assume the role of priest. Coit was active in the labour movement in the 1890s and 1900s; he was an enthusiastic Fabian, seeing himself as permeating religion as the Fabians were permeating government, and he supported the wing of the society which wanted it to identify itself with the labour movement and with spiritual as well as economic reform. The ethical societies would be the churches of socialism, 'the educational and moral centres of Democratic life.' But he found that whilst socialists were willing to hear him speak on socialism, they were not interested in the ethical movement. When he started an ethical society in the East End, those members he turned into socialists drifted into the local S.D.F. branch. Coit was never a Marxist

---

[15] S. Coit, in *Ethics*, 1 March 1902, p. 65; and in *Ethical World* for 8 and 22 January 1898.

socialist, but his views on egalitarianism were perfectly sincere. Despite the great discrepancy in social status between the select professional members of his congregation and the local active working-class socialists, he insisted that at ethical church suppers they should all sit down and eat together.

After his unsuccessful stand as a socialist candidate in 1905, Coit's interest in socialism lessened. The labour movement was rapidly losing its role as a morally redemptive movement which should transform all the relations of society, and concentrating on specific policies and forming purely political organizations. Coit's conception of an organic and idealist socialism had less currency; Idealism was discredited as an academic philosophy, the fear of revolution was less, and Coit quarrelled with the many pacifists in the I.L.P. and left the Labour party. As the West London Society became more ritualized, socialist speakers became less frequent.

The changes in the form of service were slow but consistent from 1900 on. Instrumental music, a choir, and a chanted liturgy were introduced, and hints appeared of the postivists' liturgical calendar: a Woman Sunday, a Spring Festival to include the dedication of members' children, a universal litany to be intoned once a month, and 'Ten Words of the Moral Life' to be sung by new members. (Their phrasing is strongly reminiscent of the Collects and the Ten Commandments: 'Each one of us hears the Spirit of Duty saying within him: I am the supreme judge of men and of gods; thou shalt exalt nothing above me,' for example.)

In 1909 Mrs Coit bought a Methodist Church on Queensway, and Coit's ritualistic tendencies could be given free rein. Gradually appropriate decorations were added: portraits and quotations from various advanced thinkers and reformers lined the entrance, and the interior conveyed a wealth of symbolism and imagery. Ethicists maintain that the general effect was both impressive and beautiful. The interior and pulpit were designed by Walter Crane with a dark blue carpet, a gold-starred blue ceiling, and a picture by Crane showing men passing the torch of humanity to one another down the ages. There were statues of Christ, the Gautama Buddha, Socrates, Pallas Athene and Marcus Aurelius, and a shrine to Kwan Yin to illustrate the essential unity between all good men and teachers of mankind. There were stained glass windows of Florence Nightingale, Elizabeth Fry and St Joan (including a small figure of Bernard Shaw).

The music was composed and directed by Kennedy Scott, formerly the organist to a Carmelite church and founder of the Oriana Choir. He and Coit devised an elaborate form of service in which choir and congregation responded to litanies intoned by a cantor. Coit wrote a cycle of ethical anthems, 'Saviours', to be performed to Palestrina's *Missa Brevis*, and thus 'a deep mine of devotional music of the highest order has at last been opened up for use in England in the expression of modernist ideas.' Many visitors to the ethical church were attracted by the high standard of performance of baroque music; elsewhere in England it was rarely performed at the time.

In other barely perceptible ways, the audience showed signs of becoming a congregation. A thriving social club grew up, and many testimonies were given to the moral and intellectual strength which was created by the service. Coit officiated at marriages and naming ceremonies in his doctoral gown, later to be replaced by one designed by a sub-committee. Members had begun to treat the church as sacred: the doors were to be shut and no one to be allowed in during the service, a room in the building was no longer to be used for dancing, political and controversial literature was to be excluded from the bookstall, and a popular membership supper was held once a month after the service. The medieval flavour was sharpened by the formation in 1913 of a Religious Drama Society and of an Ethical Preachers' Guild to train preachers for all the advanced churches and societies with which Coit was now in contact. There were continual requests for members to attend extra singing practices, week-night lectures, and a gamut of social events.

By 1911, the ethical church had made a considerable impression on religious life in London. It had over five hundred members and its congregations were swollen by interested observers, some of whom at least came to mock and stayed to pray. One of them, R. O. Prowse, wrote two novels about Coit and the church. The ritualistic leanings of the audience must have been increased by the fact that some were not merely former Anglicans but former clergymen. Coit commented in 1913 that hardly a month went by without him 'being approached with offers of service by men who are, or recently have been, recognized preachers in the older religious organizations. . . . It is not too much to say that . . . there are hundreds at our disposal.'[16]

Like the other humanist movements, the Ethical Church was pressed to take action over both women's rights during the period of suffragette agitation, and over nationalist sentiments during both

[16] *Ethical World*, 15 September 1913, p. 139.

the Boer and First World Wars. Coit tackled both questions in his inimitable way. Having initially quarrelled with Adler because of his hostility to divorce, his own conceptions of society as a spiritual unity and the tendency of idealists to subordinate the part to the whole led him to criticize the liberal individualist views on personal morality of Shaw, Wells and other socialists, and to demand a greater recognition of the social worth of monogamous marriage. Many of his congregation were suffragettes, and demonstrations were announced in the church at the same time as signatures were demanded for a manifesto condemning violence. Coit, turning again from political to spiritual power, proposed that a 'spiritual concentration service be held every Tuesday evening for the advancement of social justice to women . . . those attending be recommended to practise deep breathing, and that the meeting be arranged so as to begin with the statement of a theme for meditation, followed by a few moments for deep breathing, then by a further statement, in more elaborate form of the theme, then by a further longer period of silence.' Whether this proposal was taken up or not is obscure, but in accordance with Coit's belief in the potential and actual power of the Anglican church in the nation's life, a party of suffragettes from the ethical movement '. . . wearing flaming scarves, marched on Sundays to Westminster Abbey and St. Paul's to crowd the pews in silent demand for a public answer to the question previously sent to the preacher, as to the religious worth of the call for the vote.'[17]

As Coit's sympathy with the labour movement weakened and his conception of the religious role of the ethical movement grew more definite, so the nationalist element in his thinking grew stronger. Each nation had a separate religious destiny; and during the First World War, which Coit ardently supported, he added a sub-heading to the *Ethical World* 'Object: to Deepen the Devotion of British Subjects to the Moral Destiny of the Empire'. The ethical movement was composed of socialists, many of whom were pacifists and as staunchly opposed to the war; when the I.L.P. declared their opposition, Coit left the labour movement, and many ethicists who found his fervent patriotism and militarism distasteful left the church. The universal dismay and disillusionment brought about by the war made the ethicists' hopes of a united moral society in a community of nations seem less plausible, and even Coit's proposals for an All Nations Service where international unity would be signified

[17] Minutes of West London Ethical Society for 1913; *News and Notes*, October 1957, p. 2.

by a ceremonial lowering of national flags before an inscription of common moral values do not seem to have been received with much enthusiasm.

By the end of the war, the membership of the church had been halved to three hundred members, and the sense of division among members, the declining numbers, and poverty (Coit's personal fortune had largely been invested in Germany, his wife's home) had made the elaborate ritual seem less convincing. Perhaps as a result of congregational pressure, conferences began to be held on the subject of the discourse after the Sunday services, to demonstrate 'our belief in debate and testimony as a principle of religious life', and it was generally agreed that these had not, as some had feared, 'lowered the religious tone of our service nor detracted from the impressiveness of our social worship'. But there was a delicate balance between making the religious service seem credible to members and yet allowing spontaneous behaviour from another context. One woman who had frequently attended the ethical church at its ritualistic height revisited it after some time and found the form of the meeting had changed.

> Once there was applause—it grated upon me exceedingly. The whole service seemed to lose its spiritual unity and *raison d'être*. It was the only time that I felt the old rationalistic Adam rising within me, spurning the singing of hymns and the whole churchly *mise en scène* as uncalled for in connection with what suddenly appeared to me as a mere lecture.[18]

There is no inherent reason why applause and hymn-singing should not form part of a coherent meeting, but the cultural tradition of British society is to dissociate them. They are felt and perceived as incompatible because our social experience makes us feel that church services are one kind of thing, where a certain range of moods and behaviours are appropriate, and political or discussion meetings are another. The corrosive effects of the dominant values of society may make the mixture seem ridiculous. A member complained that ethical societies catered for half-hearted people who wanted to go to church on Sunday because it looked respectable:

> They assume a mock solemnity which is trying to people who have not been accustomed to church services. At one society everyone is requested to silently meditate for five minutes on the good life. This always seems to me intensely comic, and I know several members of the society who have the same feeling.[19]

[18] *Ethical World*, 1 September 1914, pp. 137–8.
[19] Letter to *Humanist*, 1 June 1918, p. 95.

The shame-faced expressions of Labour leaders, struggling to
find a countenance which expresses both respect for and detachment
from the singing of 'The Red Flag' at party conferences, are expressing exactly the same problem. In the early stages of the labour
movement when the ritual was set up, the mood was indeed that of
comradeship, unity, an emotional sense of martyrdom, kinship with
an international revolutionary tradition; the spirit died, but the
letter lives.

Despite the occasional expressions of unease at ritual, Coit
continued to implement an ever more elaborate form of service. In
1923, a scripture table was placed below the pulpit from which the
service was conducted, and in the following year an altar was set up;
a pillar of Skyros marble inscribed 'An Altar to the Ideal, the True,
the Beautiful, the Good', which was 'convenient for namings and
marriages'. Coit argued on setting up the altar 'I feel that, although we
have not known it, we belong unmistakably to that class of religious
communities which sets up altars.' But altars imply objects of
worship; Coit justified his action by referring to the contemporary
psychological theories of the role of religion of Durkheim, Levi-
Bruhl, Jane Harrison, Cornfield and many others. He thought that
'no-one could count it superstitious to believe that he *might*, or
degrading to think that he *should*, open his heart to the Ideal of
Truth, Beauty and Goodness', and were he to do so, Ideal energy
would take possession of his character and spiritual experience.[20]

Despite the increased ceremonial, the unity of the congregation
was crumbling as all the other activities in social work, teaching and
meeting for various purposes died away. Marriages and namings
were still fairly frequent, but the congregation was beginning to age
and new members were not coming forward, In 1932, Coit appealed
for a successor from among would-be Christian ministers, and
received over ninety applications from Unitarians, Wesleyans and
Anglicans for the post. About half held an orthodox ministerial
appointment, and whilst their religious beliefs may have changed
their belief in the usefulness of their role had not; they were part of
that group of ministers who have come to define their task increasingly in terms of moral or welfare activities. Finally, Harry Snell, a
labour politician and president of the Ethical Union, H. J. Blackham,
who had been attracted to Coit by his translation of Hartmann's
Ethik, and one of Coit's daughters became assistant ministers.

[20] *Ethical Message*, May 1923, pp. 7, 21.

Declining numbers and financial stringency forced Coit to cut down the musical part of the service and to limit its length to one and a half hours and the discourse to forty minutes—even so, the length of the service testifies to the dedication of the members. Gradually his devotional and aesthetic interests gave way to H. J. Blackham's interest in public issues and social problems and the discussions after the services were restarted.

The disruption of the Second World War when many members moved from London, and the proof yet again that common moral values did not seem to be enough to unite nations, made the services seem less successful and the psychological acceptance of them more fragile; 'it was right in principle to have discussions in the Church, but the difficulty of incorporating them satisfactorily in the service was recognized.' By the end of the war Coit had died, and the service had been largely stripped of ritual. Creed and hymns were omitted, candles and red robes were no longer used, partly because there was less money to pay for the music which went with them, and partly because Blackham urged the remaining attenders to accept that given the immense decline in the prestige and influence of the Christian churches, the rationale of the ethical church was impossible. He argued that moral ideals were not things which could be worshipped, only implemented; and that they should seek to provide for ordinary men a method of interpreting their experience rather than deifying it.

The remaining service was variously criticized for being too warm, too cold, but the proposal to finally abandon the Anglican service-form led to a 'deadlock of the liturgically-minded versus the rest', and complaints that the church was rapidly shedding the emotional and Idealist part of its work that Coit had considered so important. The financial difficulties of the church meant that it was let to a Christian congregation, and it was finally sold to the Catholics in 1954; it became more difficult to make the liturgy seem convincing in a small room, and it was abandoned for a period of music and recitation, followed by an address and discussion.

The meetings of the church had become more akin to those of other ethical societies, now mainly defunct, and during the 1950s it rejoined the ethical movement and changed its name once again to the West London Ethical Society. When I attended its meetings in 1964, most members could recollect but did not always regret the greater lavishness and closer camaraderie of the ethical church in its heyday, but the overall tone had become very academic, and the only relics of its ritual history were the reading before the lecture and some of the ornaments rescued from the ethical church.

Rites and Meanings

From these attempts at ritual with their various vicissitudes, some tentative generalizations can be made. Each member of a society brings to ritual occasions a pre-history in which certain things go readily together and others are jarring. For ritual to be effective, disconcerting juxtapositions must be avoided; this is just as much of a problem in orthodox denominations, as witness the tension over changes in liturgy or the attempts of ministers to introduce symbols and references to other areas of life into church services. But in ethical services, men met from different religious traditions; united by the fact that they had ceased to believe in them, they were none the less divided by their warring ghosts. At South Place, ministers might have rejected certain aspects of being a minister, but none the less if they came from an Anglican tradition as Barnett did, or a quasi-Jewish one as Coit did, they were irked by the wholly different role and expectations of a nonconformist tradition. Religious beliefs were less important than religious shapes; but the members of South Place, having evolved from an orthodox Unitarian body, were at least agreed on the shape that their religion should have, and able to resist incompatible elements extremely effectively by pointing out that they were alien to their *traditions*— not to their beliefs. A firm sense of tradition, which was in part a tradition of intellectual openness and argument, held their members together.

Coit had both a clear intellectual rationale and considerable charisma as a leader in creating a service akin to that of the Church of England; but many of his members, even his young preachers, came from more dissenting backgrounds, and whilst they did not deny the need for ritual, there were attempts on several occasions to cut down on the liturgy, the emphasis on the leader of the service, and to increase the length and importance of the discourse and the involvement of the whole congregation in singing hymns. Coit was right to see the tradition of individualism in English radical life as something which was destructive of his ideals, but what he failed to see was that those who had explicitly rejected orthodox religious beliefs were bound to have done so in terms of an ethic of personal autonomy and liberty. As Durkheim argued, the individualism which was so strong a component of the personal ethic of liberals in the late nineteenth and twentieth centuries was itself a religion, in which man was at the same time both believer and God. Each man worshipped not himself but what he held in common with all other men and what led him to respect them—their common humanity.[21]

Just as Coit did, Durkheim distinguished between the anomic, *laissez-faire* individualism of Spencer and the philosophical radicals, 'that egoistic cult of the self', and the individualism of Kant, in which the individual can find meaning and satisfaction only in that which makes him part of all other men and makes them and their rights sacred to him. 'This cult of man has for its first dogma the autonomy of reason and for its first rite freedom of thought.' Simply because a set of beliefs is widely held, argued Durkheim, it acquires a moral supremacy which gives it a religious character, and in any case, just because it is generally held, it is inescapable. He stands the argument of the religious conservative on its head; men need a religion, it is true, to bind society together and make them act unselfishly, but the religion that they now need is that of individualism, of faith in political and intellectual liberty. Any attempt to destroy this faith—here he has in mind the *anti-Dreyfusards*—will destroy the bonds of sentiment which prevent social dissolution.

Durkheim's argument can be nicely illustrated by considering the ritual activities which Coit devised partially as a result of his work. The congregation of the Ethical Church were indeed from sufficiently diverse backgrounds and of such varied ideas as only to have their humanity and a belief in theological liberty in common; by the act of common worship, they were bound more closely together in fellowship. But when Coit attempted to extend rituals to symbolize matters on which intellectually they diverged—the unity of nations, for example—he was less successful. He saw, rightly, that those most responsive to his ideas would be those already members of orthodox religious congregations, not those who had abandoned both religious belief and its ritual expression. But he assumed that they would have an extremely sophisticated view of the relationship between theological beliefs and their ritual expression—that when they had abandoned, partly for intellectual and partly for moral reasons, their belief in supernatural beings, none the less their attachment to *communitas* and to the ritual that symbolized their acceptance of common ends

[21] E. Durkheim, 'Individualism and the Intellectuals', *Political Studies*, Vol. 17(1) 1969, pp. 14–30, first appearing as a pro-Dreyfusard defence of liberalism in 1898.

would be preserved intact. But it is precisely the splitting apart of the layers of intellectual meaning, myth, symbols and ritual which constitutes the decline in their significance.[22]

Sociologists have attached little importance to ritual behaviour, partly because they mainly come from and study societies which are Protestant, dominated by scientific utilitarian modes of thinking, where men live in open social groups and most of their relationships with each other are in terms of fairly narrowly defined roles. Various ideas have been put forward by anthropologists to explain rituals which would suggest that they will not flourish under such circumstances. Many rituals are concerned with the transition of the individual between two states, or with his transference between two roles. The crossing of the boundary is dangerous; it is effected by the use of ritual which sets apart both the occasion and its participants, and which makes the crossing irreversible.[23] But in our society, the transition between childhood and adult life, between being single and being married, between being a member of one group and of another, even between being alive and being dead, no longer has this magical, irreversible, final quality. Gluckman argues that in all societies, men are united in some contexts and opposed in others, and that much ritual and ceremonial acts to cloak conflicts and to set them in a wider context of unity, whereas in modern urban societies we use empirical procedures such as law, or meet with each other in terms of specialized segregated roles.[24]

The power of religious rituals derives not only from the fact that men are collectively involved in expressing something but because the rituals are themselves or refer to a kind of supernatural power. One way of resolving the knotty conundrum as to what is religion and what magic is to consider ritual both as magically efficacious in itself or as a channel for divine power or grace, *and* as expressing a set of ideas or supplicating the attention of a deity. An effective ritual is many things to many men; a communion wafer is officially a symbol, but according to folk wisdom if a worshipper malignly carries it away in his mouth unconsumed, it may turn to flesh, or become a source of power in itself which can be used for black magic. And the potency of ritual derives in part from the power of its symbolism, in which the worlds of inner experience and public

[22] P. S. Cohen, 'Theories of Myth', *Man*, Vol. 4(3), September 1969, p. 352.
[23] This is the view of Malinowski and Van Gennep.
[24] M. Gluckman, 'Les Rites de Passage', in *Essays on the Ritual of Social Relations*, Manchester University Press, Manchester, 1962.

meaning are fused by the homology of the community and the human body.[25]

Seen in these terms, Coit's rituals were an attempt to walk on water. Their rationale was purely aesthetic and intellectual; they have a polite, anaemic, late Victorian quality. They were urged on a group of highly deracinated people, drawn from all over a large metropolis, who had broken with the political and religious traditions of their society, who were highly educated and sophisticated. Their aesthetic appreciation and moral sense might have been keen, but they were alien to the world of magical boundaries and symbolic expression.

In some respects, Coit had misunderstood Durkheim, at the same point where he often contradicted himself. Men cannot be given ideas and feelings by ritual which they do not otherwise have. Ritual can only express, reinforce and give a numinous quality to that which exists already. There *have* been successful rituals which have expressed the ideas of the humanist movement; the 'egoistical enlightenments' of the South Place congregation, the traditions which surrounded Bradlaugh's speeches and debates, the provincial radical culture which the secularists were heir to when they rode out in charabancs to picnic in the Pennines, carrying banners with pictures of Paine. The movement has its heroes and myths, an 'encapsulated history' of progress, struggle and victory. Coit, the 'positive' secularists and the labour churches were more imprisoned by a religious tradition than they knew; when they tried to create community, they turned from that which they had already to mimic a religious model which was itself losing its power.

[25] M. Douglas, *Natural Symbols—Explanations in Cosmology*, Cresset Press, London, 1970.

11 FROM ETHICISM TO HUMANISM: THE DISCOVERY OF A ROLE

> The sentimental Socialist, though not necessarily Christian, retains essentially the introspective attitude of Christian ethics. He forms societies, the members of which are supposed to pledge themselves to infinitely high aims . . . The young people of the well-to-do middle class, for whom sentimental socialism possesses attractions, think human nature susceptible of higher aims than the current ones, and meet in drawing rooms for the apparent purpose of passing resolutions to that effect.
>
> E. Belfort Bax, *The Religion of Socialism*

The outstanding feature of the history of the ethical movement has been the confusion over its role and purpose. Was it a religion, of socialism or morality, or was it secular? Should it engage in more than debate over ideas? These ambiguities were not so much solved as overridden by other concerns in the transition to humanism in the 1960s. The fundamental difficulty was over the relation between morals and society; is there a single moral code to which all members of British society do or should adhere, or are there several sorts of morality, attached to different political beliefs? In one sense, the history of the ethical movement is that of the decline of the Victorian belief that moral ideas are the basis of action and therefore that society can only be unified by shared ideals.

When the delegates from four London ethical societies met in 1895 to form a federation, their aims were:

> By purely natural and human means to assist individual and social efforts after right living.
>
> To free the current ideal of what is right from all that is merely traditional or self-contradictory, and thus to widen and perfect it. To assist in constructing a theory or science of Right, which, starting with the reality and validity of moral distinctions, shall explain their mental and social origin, and connect them in a logical system of thought.

That is, in contrast to Coit, the remainder of the ethical movement rejected any religious sanction for moral conduct or any rapprochement with the churches, and during the first few years of its life it was mainly concerned with resisting the force of Coit's personality and defining a separate mode of work. In other ways it was less decisive, but seems to have believed that ethics evolved with society and that the task of moral rethinking was to ensure that there was no time-lag in this process, so that the moral code remained both strong and in key with the problems of the times. Ethicists rejected religion as a means of doing this and looked instead to education, both to the education of adults in moral philosophy with which many of the Idealist philosophers were concerned, and to the moral education advocated by many who worked in the labour movement. The importance of education in their eyes and the belief that morals could be inculcated through formal education was doubtless connected with the fact that many members were teachers.

Educating the Moral Sense

The humanist movement has been specifically concerned with two aspects of education, secular and moral. Secular education, which has been of prior concern to the secular movement and the Rationalist Press, is the attack on religious instruction in schools; the attempt to have it either omitted, or made more syncretist, or to have more attractive alternatives provided for those children whose parents withdraw them from religious instruction. The ethical movement, together with the positivists, labour churches and part of the labour movement, has been more concerned with *moral* education.

On a wider level, both factions gave to education the prominence which was attached to it by most nineteenth- and twentieth-century radicals. Man, no longer the creature of tradition or of original sin, is instead a source of great potentialities; by means of a good education, he can be vastly improved. Reason, the key to human betterment, is its own guide to education; the truth, for Robert Owen and for many others, was *naturally* superior to error. Thus education should aim to enhance and develop that already within the child, and his most important innate capacity is his moral sense. The ethical movement believed that Christianity never had been or was no longer capable of providing children with a systematic training in ethical conduct, and that a more scientific and refined process of moral education could be devised. Many members spent much time and effort in devising and giving series of lectures in moral education, and in its early stages the movement undertook as its main aim to hold ethical classes for children and to train ethical teachers and lecturers. In 1897 it founded the Moral Instruction League, to introduce systematic moral instruction into schools.

After 1902, the league moderated its aim to that of supplementing religious instruction, was supported by many Christians and eugenicists, gained considerably wider influence and success and became increasingly separate from the ethical movement. After 1914 morality seemed less important than civics, to which the League turned its attention for the few remaining years of its life.[1]

Some ethicists were more interested in the provision of moral education for adults and children outside the schools, and worked in the Neighbourhood Guilds and settlement movement. Many ethical societies, urged on by Coit, did set up ethical Sunday schools for either their own children or the children of the poor, and these were often linked with local socialist Sunday schools. Others took a more radical line; education should itself be moralized, since its chief aim should be 'the formation of character'.

But just as the ethical movement was to find that a moral sphere was hard to clear of weeds and fence off from the rampant growths of religious and political life, moral education proved a tender plant to rear. For what should children be taught about politics? (An area of life clearly in need of being moralized.) And should they be taught that virtue was rewarded? Felix Adler saw moral education as a kind of conditioning agent; children should be taught that good always triumphed. Apart from a few gifted teachers, the tone of the lessons seems too often to have been repellently didactic. Just as the ethical societies themselves were absorbed into the I.L.P., most ethical Sunday schools were merged with the socialist ones. With the resignation in 1898 of F. J. Gould, who had been the prime mover of moral education, the interest of the ethical movement waned.

Coit's resignation as a member of the Council of Ethical Societies in 1900 was also a factor in the decline of interest in moral education. He was succeeded by Harry Snell, a member of the I.L.P. and later a Labour minister and member of the Privy Council who led the movement until just before the Second World War. It had become evident that Coit's objectives at West London and those of the rest of the ethical movement were different, and in 1914 Coit had left the Union of Ethical Societies and called on other ethical groups to throw in their lot with the church. After Coit's departure, the Union framed a simpler set of objectives for itself; it tried 'by purely

[1] B. Sacks, *The Religious Issue in the State schools of England and Wales, 1902–14*, University of New Mexico Press, Albuquerque, 1961; H. Silver, *The Concept of Popular Education*, MacGibbon and Kee, London, 1968.

human and natural means to help men love, know and do the right . . . and to affirm that moral ideas and the moral life are independent of beliefs as to the ultimate nature of things and as to a life after death.'

Behind these apparently innocuous objectives lay a powerful force in radical thought just after the turn of the century. Evolutionary theories of social change were becoming less self-confident, and all justifications for state interference in social progress became regarded as 'socialist'. The biological analogies of social processes were now less fashionable, but the ethical movement retained the 'organic' metaphors of Hegel and the evolutionists which centred on the idea of the Good Will, the *sine qua non* for the peaceful or successful transition to socialism. The unity of society was impeded not only by warring religions but by the antagonism between capital and labour. The ethical movement hoped that it could establish an area outside both religion and politics where a more open and democratic examination of contemporary national and international problems could take place. The dilemma sharpened with the coming of the Russian revolution. Socialists, it now seemed, had to choose between democracy and socialism, just as radicals had been divided over pacifism and imperialism. Many of them used the 'organic' metaphors so beloved of the Idealists to attack the ideas of social imperialism; cultures could only grow and develop in their own way.[2]

Just as the relationship between religious and social divisions had weakened the claim of Christianity to embody the moral unity of the nation, so, the ethicist feared, the growing attachment of the labour movement to particular political and economic factions was weakening its claim to represent the moral ideals of the whole British people. This was increasingly leading to the structural differentiation of political and religious life and of individual and social morality. The ethical movement feared that this would make genuine progress impossible; 'moral endeavour is indispensible to both personal and social progress'. To the ethicist, ethics was independent both of religion and of particular political programmes; the ideal of the good life was a concrete unity. But as the Union came to realize, the difficulty 'of commending Ethical Religion to the man in the street is how, with force and clarity, to relate its basic principles to the pressing problems of individual, national and international

[2] B. Potter, op. cit., pp. 156–70.

life, whilst carefully avoiding those political and social matters concerning which men and women differ.'[3]

During the first decade of the twentieth century, this seemed to be an intellectual but not a practical problem. From 1896, several new ethical societies were established each year until 1910. By 1927, seventy-four had been founded and forty-six affiliated to the Union; but their existence was often brief. They were a hetero-geneous bunch. Some were local labour churches, secular societies or positivist groups whom Coit had persuaded to affiliate to the Union. Others were old religious congregations, which had either, like South Place, evolved into agnosticism or whose ministers had led a break-away movement from their Unitarian or Presbyterian bases. Some Unitarian churches wavered for some time between ethicism and orthodoxy; the older members of the Unitarian congregation at York rescued it from ethicism by appealing to the Trust deeds.

Some Unitarians and whole congregations became so 'advanced' that they moved not only into the ethical movement but out of it again into the I.L.P. Sometimes the process was telescoped; Plumstead ethical society was forced to close down because of the counter-attraction of a local Unitarian minister who had become a leading figure in the labour movement at Woolwich; when the central Unitarian body had protested, he had broken away and filled his church by preaching the gospel of social ethics. The members of the Plumstead society who were too intensively concerned with local labour politics for the health of ethicism, were drawn into the church.

Not all the ethical societies founded on churches had once been Unitarian congregations. A Baptist preacher at Abertillery had begun special Bible classes for young men to discuss politics and liberal theology, and when his deacons scented heresy and protested the young men resigned from the church and set up an ethical society with a flourishing Sunday school, a congregation of two to three hundred on Sunday evenings, and classes on Marxist econom-ics. Another Baptist minister at Liverpool had found that his 'advanced' views attracted many 'seekers after truth and social reform', and resigned and started a very ritualist ethical church.[4] Coit was of course delighted at these proofs that the churches were

[3] H. Snell, *The Ethical Movement Explained*, Ethical Union, London, 1935; Minutes of the Executive Committee of the Ethical Union for January 1935.
[4] Minutes of Council of Union of Ethical Societies, May 1899; *Ethical World*, 15 December 1907, p. 92, 15 May 1908, pp. 37–8, 15 November 1910, p. 173.

coming over to the gospel of ethics and social democracy, and not only he but many other ethicists found that old religious congregations were persistent and successful bases for ethical societies.

By 1905, the ethical movement was prospering. Fifty societies had been formed, four-fifths of which were still in existence, and the fourteen societies which reported their members had between them 1112 members. The influence of many societies was greater than their membership, for the *average* number of attenders at Sunday meetings was often greater than, sometimes twice as great as, the number of members. For example, two societies formed at Neath and Merthyr Tydfil just after the Welsh revivals attracted an enormous following. At Neath a thousand people attended the first few meetings, with passionate singing and questioning far into the night at the Enquirers' meetings. From Merthyr there were frequent reports of wildly enthusiastic adherents. Ethical hymn-singing, which was frequently deplored in English congregations as lacking any nonconformist brio, was long and fervent; ethical hymns were altered so that they could be sung to 'Eventide' and other favourites from the Bethel. Both societies, and many English ones, had members who were mostly also members of a local labour society, and at first the dual allegiance did much to consolidate the membership. By 1912, the Ethical Union had two thousand members.

Ethicists

The nature of the members of the ethical movement is largely obscure until the series of surveys that were made with the transition to humanism in the 1950s. For the early period I have been able to find biographical details for seventy-two members, mainly appearing between the 1890s and 1950s as obituaries, and as always these concern the leading rather than the average members of the movement. But they do point to the fact that ethicists were not drawn from the same groups as either secularists or rationalists, though they were ultimately joined by many members of the positivist movement. The biographies give several clues as to the meaning and attraction that the ethical movement had to its members.

Politically, most ethicists were left-wing; only one is described as conservative and three as 'old-fashioned liberal'. The others, if they were not members of the labour movement, Fabian society or a variety of reform movements—Poor Law Reform, secular education, euthanasia, the Malthusian League, women's suffrage—were at least 'progressive'. The number of early members who were suffragettes is very high, but unlike most suffragettes, they were also socialists. Many of them were members of the ethical church, since Stanton Coit was a prominent worker for women's rights.

Occupationally, ethicists came from the professional part of the middle classes. The largest group were teachers and workers in education, and ethical lecturers were often recruited from the university teachers who were members of the movement. There were many other members of the established professions, including four doctors, and a number with private means. There are mentions of five workers and one trade union official. Local ethical societies seem to have varied in their social composition; whereas Coit's congregation was select—'silks rustle, and kid gloves glisten'—other groups from poorer areas of London or the North reported themselves as humbler and frequently complained that the tone of the movement was too academic and that the concern with philosophical topics had driven working people away.[5]

The most striking occupational group of these members are the twelve ex-ministers or priests, and the number of members who had been active Sunday school teachers in the churches, often transferring readily to the ethical Sunday schools. The previous religion of most members had been Anglican or Congregationalist; the remainder were almost all ex-Catholics, Jews, Unitarians or Presbyterians. Whilst this is to be expected in so middle-class a movement, it also explains the lessened interest in matters of doctrine and greater concern with the moral and social role of the church of the ethicist as compared with the secularist or rationalist. But as the secularist maintained, the lack of concern of the ethicist with the errors and dangers of religion was partly to be explained by the fact that the movement did not begin until the churches themselves were less concerned with scriptural authority than the moral content of religion, and it was less explicitly used as an agent of social control.

The obituaries of members are twice as often of men as of women, but men, in this as in other organizations, were more likely to become leaders. To members of the movement the high proportion of women was striking, especially in contrast to their relative rarity in secular and rationalist gatherings. The evidence that was collected just after the turn of the century is contradictory, but the most thorough survey found that in twelve London societies women were

[5] F. J. Gould, *The Reformer*, 15 October, 1897, p. 223.

only just in the minority of attenders, and the highly ritualized meetings had a large majority of women. Many meetings were also attended by a large number of children, suggesting that they were indeed the family meeting-places that Coit had hoped for.[6]

The conversion experiences of some ethicists are like those of the secularists—the themes of the inability to believe in the Bible, to accept Christian teaching as morally justifiable, the attack on the defects of ministers, all reappear. Walter Gregory, for instance, who had been brought up as a Baptist but became a Pentecostalist, found that one Sunday 'at the East London Tabernacle, Archibald Brown, who had received a letter criticizing his sermon on infant baptism, read it from the pulpit, tore it up and threw the pieces among the congregation. He then reasserted that the baby who was not baptized would not go to heaven. A primitive sense of the artificiality and wickedness of such teaching roused young Gregory . . .', and he began to spend his Sunday evenings first at a pub in Hackney frequented by secularists, and later with the East London Ethical Society.[7]

As for the secularists, for many ethicists the move from orthodox religion to ethicism was intertwined with the move to socialism; both were seen as 'scientific' doctrines attracting 'seekers after truth and social reform'. Many early ethicists were by no means hostile to the churches. Rather, they missed the habit and consolation of church-going, and might well have rejected Christianity intellectually long before they ceased to attend church, having often moved from denomination to denomination and finally even into and out of Unitarianism in the search for a tolerable theology. William Kent, for example, a government clerk, child of a Wesleyan printer from the East End, read Blatchford's attacks on Christianity as a socially reactionary force in the 1890s. Disturbed in his faith, he began to read Rationalist Press reprints, and for an anxious night was converted to agnosticism by T. H. Huxley. His religious dilemmas finally seemed to have found a solution in Campbell's new theology of around 1911, which to his Methodist friends and himself seemed to offer a new and wholly ethical role for religion. But his successful proselytizing among his Bible class created resistance among the Methodist establishment, and he moved first to an Independent church and then to an ethical society. After a brief

---

[6] R. Mudie-Smith, *The Religious Life of London*, Hodder and Stoughton, London, 1904.
[7] *Ethical World*, 15 March 1908, p. 7.

return to orthodoxy via Spiritualism he settled down in the ethical movement, and 'gradually lost the habit of feeling that he had to hear someone on Sunday'.[8]

For most ethicists, there was no sharp rejection of Christian belief and worship but merely a gradual minimal shift of beliefs, a progressive depersonalization of god to an abstract ethical principle, a move from an idealist theology to philosophical idealism. Many English people must have ceased to be orthodox Christians in just the same way. A growing humanitarianism is a common theme; Thomas Watt, for instance, became an agnostic because of the cruelty of the natural order. A god who could allow it did not deserve his allegiance, so he replaced him by a conception of an abstract deity who embodied the highest human ideals. Like other critics of religion, many ethicists abandoned Christianity because they felt it took too pessimistic and sin-laden a view of what man was and could achieve. One of the most outspoken exponents of this view was first an Anglican and then a Presbyterian minister, until he unfrocked himself in 1948. He objected strongly to sin— 'the word is a horrid one . . . it created the very thing that it was trying to destroy. Healthy-mindedness can only come about by the adoption of a positive attitude . . .' He had suggested to his Presbyterian congregation that they should abandon the word, with tumultuous results. The worst aspect of Anglicanism was 'that it requires of its devotees an incredible amount of personal debasement. Think of the amount of self-depreciation involved to any ordinary, decent person in continually having to say and believe "We acknowledge and bewail our manifold sins and wickedness . . ." ' To him, 'Man's scientific achievements give the lie to his supposed helplessness and worthlessness, and prove him a veritable demi-god!'[9]

From such scanty evidence, only tentative conclusions can be drawn about the meaning of the ethical movement to its members, but they support the view that it acted as a substitute religion more often than as an anti-religious organization.

The Impact of Socialism

The ethical movement had moved too close to the labour movement for it to remain independent of it. As socialists increasingly realized

[8] W. Kent, *The Testament of a Victorian Youth*, Heath Cranton, London, 1938.
[9] Letter in *Ethics*, 17 March 1906, p. 87; G. E. Jaeger in *News and Notes*, January 1951, pp. 2–4.

that political power and concrete social and economic reform lay within their grasp the redemptive solution of the ethical movement, 'moral change', was discarded for practical politics. Ethicists began to feel that they were not *doing* anything.

A well-known worker in the English Socialist movement implored me, a short time ago, to desert the Ethical Movement and undertake work more immediate and practical. Leave off posing as a social monk, he said, and come out and rough it once more with the workmen on some immediate, practical, and concrete issue.[10]

Members moved from the ethical to the labour movement; those who might have joined it turned to socialism instead; and even entire ethical societies transformed themselves into branches of the I.L.P. The Plumstead society which closed in 1908 because its members wanted to take a closer interest in social reform, the Cardiff society which had shut down in the previous year 'because of the labour movement', and the Merthyr society which transformed itself into an I.L.P. branch, were examples of a widespread exodus which began in about 1907 and continued into the post-war period. Moral unity became increasingly difficult as the issues of pacifism and rights for women created factions among the left wing; as with socialism, the ethical movement was damned if it did support them, and damned if it didn't. As Snell pointed out, some members left whatever was said on current affairs, but if nothing was said even more would leave. Moral and political neutrality was killing them.

In the inter-war period, the movement changed its objective from that of a mass movement, the inspiration of radical politics, to an emphasis on the fellowship that ethicism could provide. The statements of principle which emerged between the wars have the air of skirting difficult issues and concentrating on what was certain about the movement; that to its devoted members, 'it was becoming the home of the soul,' and was 'a comfort and a joy to those who lived in the light of its principles.' The feeling of fellowship in which members sustained one another in an ill-defined faith took over from the conscious striving after a secular church. The Union continually strove after a satisfactory definition of principles, but as one official observed, intellectual consensus was irrelevant to unity. '. . . The elaboration of principles—above a modest and indispensable minimum—has little practical significance. The generality of the members, as a sheer matter of fact, however deplorable it may be,

[10] H. Snell, 'Is the Ethical Movement Practical?', *Democracy*, 21 September 1901, p. 528.

do not study these principles and when questioned by their friends as to their faith can only offer homely answers.' Many members who were dismayed at the ineffectuality of the Union remained within the movement because they were convinced of the importance of what it was trying to do. Looking at the world, '. . . the lack of all positive and constructive thought upon the great questions of life is equally and appallingly evident'.[11]

During the 1930s, several attempts were made to redefine the movement's purpose. A Forum was held at South Place on the 'True Purpose of the Ethical Movement': 'the topic, it must be confessed, possesses little novelty for some of us . . .' Pleas were made for the movement to take sides in the contemporary battle between Fascism and Communism, '. . . for moral principles became sterile unless they were translated into action'. The policy of trying to represent what lay beyond politics was condemned as 'middle-class, dilettante, comfortable and detached'. It did seem to be the case that with the increased interest during the 1930s not only in practical politics but in political philosophy, the areas of common morality which the ethical movement had been able self-confidently to assume would unite all men of good will had now largely disappeared. There seemed to be less good will and reliance on moral guidance about.

During the 1930s, there were various indications in the magazine of the movement that members increasingly thought that the problem was not so much that English society lacked a common morality, as that in concrete cases men failed to relate their moral principles to their behaviour whether they possessed specific ideals or not. The hope that a common definition of duty would emerge in the meetings of the movement was replaced by the view that the purpose of the meetings was 'to make us more clearly and completely aware of what we are and what we are doing, and of what we ought to be and what we ought to be doing; of the world and its demands, and of our unity within it; of the duties and enjoyments proper to human beings; of the good life, and the society which we should help to create and of which we should be worthy.' Religious ritual, which would have had to have been based on a common creed, was no longer seen as an appropriate means. 'The method is the appeal of words to the imagination, the conscience, the reason; organized discussion of principles and problems, of ideas, views and plans;

[11] *Ethical Societies Chronicle*, October 1929, p. 1.

social action.. . . . If the meeting has been successful it should be possible to feel that in tendency it has served to make the mind clearer and the will firmer and more responsive; that it will, in effect, improve the quality of the person and of the life lived.'[12]

One consequence of secularization was that now the crucial dilemmas of the society were expressed not in metaphysical but in political terms. To prove that moral values could be maintained without a religious faith was an obsolete issue; rather, liberal and democratic values were being challenged by new totalitarian doctrines from both left and right. The letters and articles in the journals of the thirties were largely concerned with Fascism and Marxism and Stalinism.

Rethinking

By the Second World War, the individual membership of the Union had dwindled to just over a hundred, and only eight societies remained, all in London. After the war, a determined effort at rethinking the principles of the movement, largely instigated by H. J. Blackham, was begun in the hopes of attracting some younger and less middle-class members. To Blackham, the ethical movement now faced a generation totally removed from religion, and thus there was no point in trying to salvage a religious tradition. The new philosophy which emerged was presented under the name of humanism. Apart from a greater concern with social issues and being avowedly non-religious, it is difficult for the outsider to distinguish it from ethicism. Greater attempts were made to relate it to concrete thought and problems, and the fact that most members thought that it succeeded in this is perhaps more important than whether it did so more than ethicism had done.

'Humanism', like 'ethicism' presented problems of definition, often avoided by giving a rapid historical sketch of the various meanings of humanism from the Greeks onward. As some theologians indignantly protested, this was to borrow many Christian clothes. H. J. Blackham held that 'Humanism proceeds from an assumption that man is on his own and this life is all, and an assumption of responsibility for one's own life and for the life of mankind . . .' Humanism was not a secular creed but an attitude of mind. Morality

---

[12] 'How to Form an Ethical Society', pamphlet No. 4 in *The Way to a Common Faith*, Watts, London, 1945, pp. 2–3 and 4–5.

was a function of society; but man could control his actions, and so make mankind an end in itself.[13] Perhaps the frail demarcation from old ethicism is most clearly seen in the difference between a movement concerned to develop an alternative to religion to prop up a moral code, and a movement which strove to adapt morality to contemporary problems, and yet to keep it liberal and guided by reason. Moral ends were now seen as man-made and no longer absolute. These antitheses, although insisted on, were much stronger than the actual distinction between the two phases of the movement since both had laid stress on evolution and liberty of thought; the humanist movement rejected moral relativism. In short, like other social movements it encapsulated history, choosing from the history both of Western civilization and of itself that which explained its present form.

Politically, humanism became identified with liberal individualism; frequent reference was later to be made to the Popperean justification of the open society, and the journals of the forties are full of accounts which show that for humanists, as for many others, Stalin's Russia had largely destroyed the political appeal of Marxism. The Marxist wing did not give up their position within the movement easily. *The Plain View*, which from 1946 to 1961 worked out the philosophical position of humanism, carried a running dispute between the Marxist members, primarily Archibald Robertson, and the rest. Robertson claimed that almost no members of the movement were right-wing, and the only obstacle to its identification with Marxism were the old Kantian liberals. The movement should now become the scientific philosophy of labour. To an old member, this was all too reminiscent of the battles he had fought in 1907 to prevent the movement becoming 'leftist': 'The idea that the man who votes Conservative must belong to a different ethical world to the man who votes Labour is pernicious nonsense . . .'[14]

Ultimately, influenced by the declining popularity of communism and Marxist ideas in Britain during the 1940s, it was agreed that the ethical movement, whilst holding left-wing views on most issues, should not ally itself with any political party or dogma. Just as previously ethicism had been defined by showing how it differed from Christianity, now humanism came to be defined as a world view neither Christian nor Marxist. There *were* fundamental moral

[13] From a long definitional discussion in H. J. Blackham, *Humanism*, Penguin Books, Harmondsworth, 1968.
[14] Letter in *The Plain View*, July 1946, pp. 215-6.

principles which it was its duty to assert, and thus it stood at the head of all those excluded from the other two major world dogmas, Catholicism and communism.

At the 1950 annual conference of the Ethical Union, H. J. Blackham argued that the movement should declare itself humanist. However, '. . . there was more argument as to what was the position on doctrinal matters of the founders of the Movement than on the proposal that the position of non-commitment or agnosticism about the nature of the universe should be superseded by a definite affirmation of Humanism, many holding that the official outlook had always been humanist. . .'[15] A large part of the meaning of humanism to members was the belief in the importance of all men deciding their moral values and activities for themselves, and this was a theme increasingly stressed with the attack on political totalitarianism and the strenuous defence by the movement of many kinds of negative freedom: freedom from censorship, from educational indoctrination, from political control, from social and legal pressures on personal morality, the defence of church disestablishment and of participatory democracy. Humanists were even—the acid test—prepared to argue that minority religious groups should not be arbitrarily interfered with. In other ways the movement was highly interventionist, arguing for world government, population control, the control and beneficial uses of science, and more enlightened legislation on race relations and penal policy.

It can be argued that such a heterogeneous collection of objectives stems less from a specific philosophy than from the position of the movement as a disadvantaged minority which has a vested interest in freedom from censorship, et cetera, which is equally likely to be found among religious groups in Communist countries. There is much truth in this argument; as has been pointed out many times, the humanist movement is not only fortified by episodes of vigorous opposition, it is even defined by them. Much the same objections could be made against the philosophy of classical liberalism, with which humanism is intellectually closely connected. Both movements are caught between openness, freedom and so on as a general principle, and a strong sense that some beliefs and policies are more open, free, rational, and so on, than others. This was frequently a hotly debated issue in the humanist meetings that I attended. When did a justifiable dislike of Catholic influence become intolerance?

[15] *News and Notes*, May 1950, p. 15.

Should humanists keep an open mind about extra-sensory perception, or was it incompatible with a scientific or rational view of man ?
I can only record my impression that many humanists were and are
very open-minded, interested in new ideas, prepared to listen reasonably receptively to the opposition, et cetera, and regard such qualities
as what makes a good humanist. It is also true that as the opposition
to irreligion has waned and the humanists' positive views have
become more widely held, they have not noticeably slackened in their
support for negative freedom.

Without any very definite assent being given by members, the idea
that the ethical movement was humanist became accepted. Though
membership was still very small, by 1951 an optimistic sense began
to appear that the movement was standing for something definite, a
part of and a response to modern life. After numerous conferences
and study groups, precise definitions of belief at last seemed possible.
Because the movement had abandoned all pretensions to being a
religion the secular movement and Rationalist Press regarded it
with more favour, especially since the small size of all three made
them more ready to seek unity. Initiative toward this came mainly
from the Ethical Union, and new local groups often combined the
members of all three bodies.[16] The movement also began to affiliate
to various social reform bodies; it established formal ties with the
N.C.C.L., the National Peace Council, the United Nations Association and the Howard League, and the Divorce Law Reform League
and Abortion Law Reform Association were formed and largely
run by members of the ethical movement. In 1950, after repeated
overtures South Place affiliated to the Union, and the Humanist
Council, the first of a series of bodies jointly sponsored by the
Rationalist Press and the Union, was set up.

These attempts to create a new ethos were not yet reflected in a
growing membership, and there were doubts about the high intellectual level of propaganda and the loss of links with the labour movement which some members felt had at least provided a contact with
reality. In 1954, the President pointed out that the movement now
had six affiliated societies, none of which was flourishing, and two
hundred and fifty members, many of whom were elderly. There was
considerable discontent: 'Since the war there have been eight years
of theory and little else . . .' And yet, as previous generations of
ethicists had discovered, if the movement tried to advocate those
largely moral reforms which stood outside the political sphere, it

[16] *News and Notes*, June, pp. 1–2.

inexorably acquired a crankish air. As an ethicist had wearily remarked,

> Is not the Ethical Movement identified in the minds of many . . . with 'pious Pacifism', the abolition of the death penalty, anti-vivisection, and even a lurking suspicion of anti-capitalist sympathies. To these aims . . . there are some who would not scruple to add Communism, Sex Reform, and Nudism to our inventories of duties . . .

The only solution, as in the case of the secular movement, was for changes in the wider society to make the changes identified with the humanist movement seem more pressing and important. The immediate cause of the rapid growth of the movement after 1955 was the immense publicity given to humanism and to the social position of the irreligious by the radio broadcasts by Margaret Knight on morals without religion. The publicity and controversy advertised the humanist bodies more widely than they could have done themselves, and many new members appeared who had held humanist beliefs for years but had not known of any organization to relieve their isolation. The new presentation of beliefs, more advertising and more publicity began to result in growth. New groups were formed at the rate of several a year from 1955 onward, and officials quickly realized that the universities and other institutions of higher education were a promising source of active if often shortlived members and groups. In 1967 there were seventy local humanist groups, but half had been formed in the last four years.

A different kind of member was demanding a different kind of humanism. A group organizer remarked of the Orpington and Brixton groups that the members were relatively young and radical; philosophical and ethical discussions did not appeal to them, and it was only in the context of discussion about social problems that abstract moral issues acquired any meaning for them. In this connection, the Union began several practical services for its members, including a counselling service and an Agnostics Adoption Society. (Most adoption agencies require prospective parents to state that they will bring up the child in a specified religious faith.)

During the late 1950s and early 1960s, the form which humanist rethinking mainly took was concerned with issues of personal and especially sexual morality. The projected legislation on homosexuality, divorce, abortion, euthanasia, racial integration, the treatment of illegitimacy and the provision of contraceptives involved a host of moral issues in which traditional religious positions and humanism stood in sharp contrast. During the early period of the ethical movement, its leaders were mainly concerned to show that traditional moral standards could be justified without reference to a deity, and tried for both tactical and ideological reasons to dissociate the movement from the 'free love' wing of progressive opinion during the thirties. But during the 1950s opinions changed considerably and humanism was able to both profit from and contribute to the change. Its appeal to university students, who are likely to be liberal on such questions of personal morality and to be deeply concerned with them at that stage in their lives, must have been related to the predominance of this sort of issue. Older members protested that humanism seemed to be about sex and nothing else.[17]

The distaste for the compromises of politics characteristic of many humanists found especially strong support in the operations of the politics of conscience. As the ethical movement began to back moves for legislative change and to contact sympathetic M.P.s, they were often found to be voting against their convictions because of constituency pressures, largely channelled through the church lobbies. The attempts of the Union to provide pressure groups, research and eminent supporters to combat the lobbies did much to give its members a sense of a useful role, which was increased by the growing dissension within the churches. It also created much publicity for the activities of the humanist movement, which in turn attracted more members.

Growth

The growth of social movements is usually as closely recorded as their decline is shrouded; the growth of humanism is no exception. In 1954, a member summing up the state of the movement said that there were six societies—all but one in London—and two hundred and fifty members of the Union. The new members who joined were mainly over forty, so the membership as a whole was still ageing.

[17] Dilemmas arose for the movement in the conflict between the commitment to the 'new morality' and the broader one to the open mind. During the passage of the Abortion Bill through parliament in 1968, Baroness Wootton, a leading member of both the humanist and rationalist bodies, voted against a clause of the Bill and in consequence was not re-elected to the Vice-Presidency of the British Humanist Association. Many members protested at censorship being exerted in this way, but others believed that the new political role of humanism made at least minimal agreement on such issues necessary for official members.

In 1959, a survey of local groups had replies from twenty-seven 'humanist' groups and two that were still called 'ethical'; thirteen of them were university societies, and these were much the larger. An important change in membership was noticeable. 'Older humanist groups have almost twice as many women as men, while there are nearly twice as many men as women in the newer humanist groups.' Four years later, the university groups had split off and were run by a separate body, the University Humanist Federation. Of the remaining thirty-two local groups, twenty-five had been founded in the previous seven years but it was evident that the existence of many of them would be fleeting. They met comparatively seldom and took no communal action on any political or social issue. The regular attenders at all the groups numbered only six hundred, but the membership and the number of local groups was steadily growing. By this time the Ethical Union was jointly with the Rationalist Press sponsoring a new organization, the British Humanist Association. Campbell's survey of the seventeen hundred members of the B. H. A. found that its members were now predominantly male, young adults, and highly educated professionals. All three bodies had a predominance of school-teacher members—about a fifth—but the B.H.A. also had a growing proportion of university teachers, G.P.s, and physical and biological scientists; it was a marginally more professional membership than that of the two older organizations, themselves predominantly composed of professionals.[18]

The Association continued to grow; in 1967, there were seventy local groups, and forty-one further groups in universities, colleges and schools. It was widely thought that the Margaret Knight broadcasts had been the crucial factor in arousing interest in organized humanism and that they had also marked a watershed in the relations between humanists and Christians in Britain, in that the debate over the lectures was the last occasion on which it was argued by influential religious figures that those without religious belief were unequal citizens who should, because of their exclusion from a central part of national life, be kept out of public positions.

In 1965 the Ethical Union was removed from the register of charities, and this brought relations between the three movements to a crisis. Members of both the Ethical Union and the humanist body

[18] *News and Notes*, April 1954, February 1960, March, 1964; C. B. Campbell, 'Membership Composition of the B.H.A.', *Sociological Review*, November 1965; *HumanistNews*, December 1960, pp. 1-2.

had been arguing with increasing force that they should forgo their charitable status for a more active part in politics, and many felt that it was the rationalist members who were still too attached to a 'negative secularist and purely anti-Christian attitude' rather than to the broader social role and reduced interest in the churches of the new humanism. The Ethical Union was merged into the British Humanist Association, and they abandoned charitable status for a position as a pressure group for both their members and the non-Christian part of the population. The Association's members heartily endorsed the decision to concentrate on the social questions of concern to its members 'affecting the quality of human relationships and community life, which are too often ignored by central and local government because they are inconvenient and lacking in organized support.'

The Association is at present successfully pursuing this path. Increasing publicity has brought an increase in members, though they are still apparently not likely to stay for long in the movement. University humanist societies, for example, find few of their members going on to join local groups after they have gone down— perhaps three years is about the length of time needed to work out a philosophy of humanism? In 1967, the secretary and H. J. Blackham retired, to be replaced by representatives of the post-war humanist generation.

The Limits of Moral Action

Throughout its history, the ethical movement has been concerned with the nature and limits of moral action. The impact of Idealism on secular thinking was much the same as its impact on theology. It shifted the source of authority from external principles—the Scriptures, utilitarian arguments—to the inward witness of reason and the conscience. To Matthew Arnold, religion was 'morality touched by emotion', and it was this aspect of religion that the ethicist tried to retain. The philosophical limitations of this doctrine are clear, but what is less certain is when and why it lost its emotional credibility. Within the ethical movement with its strong ties with socialism, the rise of the view that socialism was not the basis of the coming society but was a set of principles which a political party should attempt to realize as much as possible in the existing one, that these were *interests*, or represented interests only, provided a dilemma for ethicists. It separated political from moral action at the cost of making the latter seem relatively peripheral and ineffectual, and it eroded that area of action on which, it had been supposed, all men of good will could agree.

A theme which is constantly sounded in the autobiographies and novels of the first two decades of this century is the attack on 'cant' and 'sham'. Cant meant both Victorian sexual morality and the conventional practice of religion, but it meant more than this; it seems to have meant the rather carefully cultivated moral garden of the high Victorian period, the anxious exclusion of those rampant and poisonous jungles of motive and feeling which men such as Ibsen, Nietzsche, Sorel and the beginnings of vorticism and surrealism were beginning to concern themselves with. The appalling slaughter of the First World War, and the attack of the anti-imperialists of the left on ethnocentrism did much to focus the attack on older modes of thought and feeling.

In a period of such iconoclasm and cynicism, the original moral charter of the ethical movement, that 'all earnest-minded people of any or no religion are convinced of the importance of honesty in our dealings with others, of purity in our lives, of kindness toward the weak, and of justice toward all', and that on this rock they could build their church, was doomed. The assumptions of the previous century of the goodness, the simplicity, the natural feeling of man in his better aspects, the desirability of curbing and disciplining the worst by an internal moral agent, the conscience, were all alike dissolved. 'Feeling' and emotion were no longer the allies of justice and reason.

Church-going declined rapidly amongst the middle classes, and the private practice of or reference to religion became even rarer. But by the 1950s the problem had changed again. Political activity had become largely justified in terms of very limited moral goals, and a younger generation sought for a means of widening political horizons beyond compromise and interest to problems such as those of world peace, world poverty, and of trying in a non-partizan way to improve the quality of peoples' lives without the odious connotations of 'charity'. The humanist movement of the late fifties and sixties appealed to this new and highly educated generation, just as did the Campaign for Nuclear Disarmament. Higher education in itself is likely to bring with it the rejection of formal religious beliefs and a general humanitarianism, and thus to provide recruits for a movement such as the humanist movement, a 'general social back-ground' in Smelser's terms, rather than a movement with an explicit practical goal.

Changes in political life may themselves erode the movement again. The traditional concern of the rationalist and humanist with issues such as population control, ecology, the husbanding of natural resources and their success in bringing them to national attention, has paradoxically led to their absorption within traditional interest politics, just as a general background to and critique of radical ideas can now be drawn from a different tradition, the anarchism and neo-Hegelianism of the New Left. The humanist movement is part of the tension within political life itself between immediate, expedient action based on technical considerations and a narrow calculation of interest, and a search for that idealism and general philosophy which alone can provide a long-term guide to political life. Shaw, Wells and Orwell, the guiding stars of the older generation of both Labour M.P.s and humanists, have as yet no successors.[19]

[19] S. J. Ingle, 'Socialism and Literature, the Contribution of Imaginative writers to the Development of the British Labour Party', *Political Studies*, June 1974, Vol. 22(2), pp. 158–68.

12 THOUGHT AND ACTION

Belief is favourable to the human mind, were it for nothing else but to
furnish it entertainment. An infidel I should think, must frequently suffer
from ennui.

James Boswell, *The Journal of a Tour to Corsica.*

All religions and social or political movements possess a set of
beliefs—an ideology—which define the movement, its aims and its
members. Not all members will share exactly the same views, and
so successful movements create mechanisms for defining their
boundaries and pronouncing on permissible ranges of variation. The
boundaries must be neither too vague nor too concrete and inflexible;
members must have a reasonably clear conception of the aims of the
movement to guide their behaviour, yet it must be flexible enough to
contain different viewpoints and adapt to differing circumstances.
It is possible, however, for a movement to form and continue without a well-defined ideology but with only a vague and general sense
of its purpose, and several recurring features of all the humanist
organizations can be more fully understood if they are looked at in
this light.

What are the likely consequences where the belief system of a
movement is very indefinite? If its purposes have never been clearly
established each decision that is taken cannot be judged against
agreed criteria nor can it be submitted to some person or body
who, it is agreed, can decide what action should be taken. The
humanist bodies have possessed neither agreed courses of action
not accepted authorities, for their members wish above all to make
up their own minds on the contents and the purposes of their beliefs.
Consequently, uncertainties and disagreements have been endemic.
They have been limited by three factors: the movements have been
decentralized, so that decisions taken by central bodies and by local
groups have had little relation to each other; the movements have
been defined by opposition to an outside group—Christianity; and
the process of argument and discussion over philosophy and aims
has become defined as something that is good in itself, and central
to humanism. These factors are interrelated. The central organizations have been unable to acquire much power because the ideology
of the movement is opposed to authority; authority is commonly
seen as illegitimate and harmful because it is compared to religious

authority; and discussion is correspondingly seen as good because it is 'rational'.

(There are few studies of organizations or movements whose goals or values are in dispute. Such a situation should be distinguished from the far more common and understood case of discrepancies between the *formal* and *informal*, or *overt* and *latent* goals of an organization. Sometimes goals become less certain because of changes within or outside the organization, but usually such uncertainty is temporary and is often concealed by the assumption that formal goals and values are unquestionable; they seem not so much to express the beliefs of members but to act as masks, protective ideologies which conceal or resolve difficulties not overtly faced.)

For the humanist movement, the problem has been to what extent specific values and activities, on which members may differ, can be legitimately derived from general and nebulous values which they all accept. The belief in argument and discussion as a method of deciding this acts in the context of meetings as a protective ideology, since it presupposes two premises which are rarely examined; that there is a single truth which is recognizable and reachable, and that it is to be reached by free discussion. The condemnation of religion can also act as a protective ideology, since it becomes both a defining characteristic of the movement and a method of uniting otherwise dissident opinions. Yet the very protection that these mechanisms afford prevents the emergence of a generally accepted consensus, either of ideas or of feeling. The definition of the aims of religious groups can emerge more easily since they can be defined as 'above' politics or specific issues, and the appropriate behaviour, reverential and non-argumentative, is itself part of the bond between the individual and the group.

The Purpose of Purposes

The ideology of a movement should define three things: the nature of the organization, its goals and methods, and who may properly join and work for it. The humanist bodies in Britain—and indeed, elsewhere in the world—have been ambiguous on all three counts. The reasons for the ambiguity are essential to an understanding of the difficulties that the humanist movement has had to face.

The most general ambiguity which all of the humanist bodies have had to face is as to whether they are secular religions, however defined, or pressure groups on behalf of the non-theological. Are they social or psychological substitutes for religion, alternatives to it, or modes of transcending and overcoming it? Are they separate from political life, a part of the political process, or its basis? The dilemma is not merely ideological, but has to be faced over and over again on the most concrete level, in the running of the meetings. It is on the concrete level, on the whole, that it has been argued out, so that the issue (say) of whether members should try to come to know one another outside meetings or not has been divorced from the question of what literature can be sold on the bookstall. Underlying specific arguments has been the previous experience of humanists of two different sorts of meeting, the religious and the political.

We intuitively assume the purposes of a religious meeting to be to unify the group and to relate it to something outside itself; to promote fellowship, common values and experiences, to be expressive rather than instrumental. Culturally, we expect that such a meeting would in the ideal-typical case be held on a Sunday morning, consist of an address not followed by applause and discussion, to be preceded and followed by readings and singing. The audience would be expected to be a congregation, i.e. to attend the entire meeting, refrain from smoking, talking or informal behaviour during it, to display some kind of moral unity and to attend other activities— Sunday schools, evening classes, rites of passage—run by the group. A tendency toward overt symbolism would culminate in a specially decorated building, a choir and a speaker, all with the hallmarks of the sacred, the set apart and forbidden. By contrast, a meeting with a more educational or political function is usually held on a week-night, consists of a lecture or debate, often on a social or political issue, followed by applause and discussion. In place of a hymn, there might be a song or recital by a member, or the ritual of the democratic election or the committee meeting itself to structure the meeting. The audience would come and go more freely, and they might smoke, talk or read papers and feel no constraint to know one another or agree with each other outside joint political, social or proselytizing activity. The leader of the group would act as chairman or organizer, and no attempt would be made to set him apart or decorate the room.

These two sorts of meeting have been conventionally connected in our society with two broadly different purposes, the religious and the social or political, and whilst the type of meeting that each holds is not in every point functionally necessary to the general purpose of the movement, none the less there are strong conventional assumptions about the form that services or discussion groups and political gatherings will take. If the *nature* of a new organization is clearly identified, then the appropriate form of the meeting can be assumed. But humanists, who are not agreed or even individually certain of the purposes of their movement cannot use them to devise an appropriate meeting, and can only feel that the demands they intuitively expect the meeting to satisfy are going unmet. And yet the criticisms which they have voiced at various points—'lack of unity'; 'too like a church'; 'no inner life'; 'wishy-washy sermonizing'; show what is at stake.

The problem has been compounded by the inflamed sensibilities of many humanists on the subject of religion. They looked back on their religious pasts with either vigorous antipathy or wistful regret; and with such varying motives and divided loyalites found it hard to achieve a satisfactory framework for the meeting. As was discussed in Chapter 10, those who attended meetings where an attempt was made to evoke group unity might suddenly find an incongruous element destroy their ability to take the plausibility of the meeting for granted; and their neighbour might equally find the whole enterprise absurd. The mixture itself created its own problems. South Place reported in 1907 that

> The Society is feeling the inconsistency apparent between the platform and the choir, when a lecture on Rationalism is introduced with solos or anthems having supernatural implications, and the members are pleading for harmony between the whole of the readings, meditations, and lecture. . . . this difficulty is constantly confronting other Ethical Societies . . .

Meetings which took the shape of religious services did succeed in concealing the potential disunity of their members, but the suppression of important differences of opinion could in the long run prove fatal. 'Where the end is to create a religious tradition, it also carries within itself the seeds of disintegration.'

Most humanist meetings have adopted the form of a political meeting or discussion group; but this has its own difficulties. Is the purpose of the meeting to attack religion? And if it is for more than this, what outlook and reforms should it espouse? Such a temptingly open group attracts its own problems:

> . . . at a discussion where any person may speak, there are invariably a number of persons with fads or obsessions which are made to appear relevant to any topic. Some of the smaller societies have certainly received their *coup*

de grace in consequence of a failure to restrain the loquacity of faddists and cranks.[1]

The ethical and secular societies which I visited during the course of my research had talks on a wide range of ethical, political and social problems, but the discussion was more uniform. A few members took up much of the discussion with passionate statements about their own preoccupations, and those who organized meetings have always had to restrain 'persons who wish to air their own views or who are habitual fault finders'. Such persons are by no means restricted to humanist groups, as a visit to almost any meeting would confirm, but whereas religious groups can control them by a service which makes audience intervention unseemly, and political groups are attached to a national context of action and have their own procedures to control interruptions, humanist groups have been more vulnerable. Humanists have feared that their very openness and tolerance attracts the garrulous and obsessive, and that the slight flavour of eccentricity has possibly repelled potential members and prevented the emergence of any accepted position. Chairmen have generally been very tolerant to the most discursive who usually do not respond to the fidgets or complaints of the irritated, and when, very rarely, speakers have been attacked for talking too much, chairman or other members have generally quashed the attack by reasserting their belief in free speech—'That's what Humanism (or Ethicism, or Secularism) is about.' But the belief that argument is fruitful is itself subjected to strain since consensus is not reached, and at many points pressure has built up inside the movements for them to stop talking and *do* something.

Some groups, for example the Society of Friends, hold meetings which are apparently far more unstructured than those of the humanists, but the strength of tradition creates order. In the case of the Friends most Quakers are made aware by their education and upbringing of the permissible range of opinion and behaviour at meeting, and by tacit agreement the Elders of the meeting tend to speak first and far more often. The preoccupation with one issue also found among them is explicable to them as 'a concern', and Elders are empowered to restrain the too-frequent expression of a concern. Speaking at a Quaker meeting is to be understood as a separate prompting by the inner light; statements related to those of previous speakers are not encouraged, and any sort of discussion is out of place.

[1] *Humanist*, 1 May 1919, p. 76.

Humanist groups have on the whole lacked such controls. Few of those active in the movement come from humanist families, and there are no collective sentiments about the purpose of meetings for them to imbibe, nor any shared understanding as to who should regulate speaking at meetings. Some secularist meetings have tried to impose order by rigid time-tabling, by dividing discussion time equally between all those who initially notify their wish to speak. But the chairmen who try to impose such order find the ethos of individuality goes against them; at the meetings which I attended, someone would eventually be sure to say 'He's as bad as the Pope', and regimentation would have to be abandoned for bonhomie. Some groups have lasted long enough to create their own traditions, the secular societies at Leicester or Failsworth, for example, or South Place, and it is significant that all three have felt able to argue that proposed changes were against their *traditions*, rather than having to rely on arguing them out from the aims of humanism.

The humanist groups have all laboured diligently to achieve clear expressions of their goals and principles, but many of these are so general and call for such fundamental changes that the resources of the movement are evidently too small to achieve them. In part, the problem has been that of converting very general objectives, such as the defence of rationality or the autonomy of ethics, or statements such as 'man must assume responsibility for himself', into more specific policies and ways and means of implementing them. Not only are the policies and philosophies of the movement consequently endlessly debated, but they are, in the broadest sense, very radical. They challenge universal commonsense assumptions, such as that religion, even if untrue, does no harm, and in that sense they stand outside the wider society. At the same time, humanism is not a total ideology for most of its members, and there are no concentrations of humanists in certain localities or social *milieux* such that shared definitions can be assumed. Humanists, unlike many sectarians, are not detached from the wider society; indeed, their beliefs lead them to take an active part in it. Thus their radicalism is constantly jeopardized by the prevailing commonsense, empiricist outlook of English society, yet they cannot achieve the insulation from taken-for-granted reality which would enable them to resist it.

The effect on the humanist bodies themselves of a congruence or lack of it between general assumptions outside and the intellectual rationale inside the movement can clearly be seen. The decline of the *philosophe* aspect of the radical tradition and the rise of the Marxist jeopardized the secularist's view of reality; the decline of philosophical Idealism had an equivalent effect on the ethicist. Even more markedly, the context of assumptions about science, religion, thought and reality in which the Rationalist Press was founded buoyed it up at first and then slowly ebbed away. This is not to claim that the intellectual structures of meaning and ends which the movement has created are in any sense untrue; merely that they can be both less defined and stronger if they are immersed in the general sea of social reality and assumptions. Once the sea has withdrawn, they stand more nakedly exposed to Matthew Arnold's chill winds from the borders of the world. Recently, the humanist movement has again created a structure which brings it into the tide of our everyday interests and concerns.

I can only mention here the obvious importance of the outside forces which have borne upon the movement and affected its fortunes. The conditions under which a large and active humanist movement can be created have changed. In the nineteenth century, success was clearly related to the existence of numerous individuals with recently lost religious faith, churches which appeared to be both influential and vulnerable, and the weakness or relative unattractiveness of movements which sought to change the structure of society.[2] These conditions ceased to obtain among the Protestant working class from about 1890; the mass socialist movements which appealed to the kind of men who became secularists were all formed in the early 1890s. In the middle class, the growing dissent among the intelligentsia had spread far enough by the 1890s for the Rationalist Press to find an adequately large market for its publications, and the middle-class retreat from church attendance had gone far enough by the first decade of this century to give the basis for a mass ethical movement. Obviously changes occurred at an uneven rate in different regions, social groups and communities. Unitarianism felt the wind of change long before Catholicism did, because of the nature of both the religion and its adherents.

As this century has proceeded, falling church attendances and the gradual secularization of public life have made anti-clericalism an increasingly peripheral issue, and the pool of those with previously strongly held religious beliefs has both dwindled and been diverted into other channels; political activity or even psychotherapy are both likely 'solutions'. The humanist movement languished for some time because of this, but by redefining its concerns and methods

[2] I am indebted to Hugh McLeod for his helpful suggestions on this point.

has been able to attract a more professional membership who are interested in questions of ethics and an informed world view from a secular stance. In this, they are rivals not only with other pressure groups but also with political parties, which have recently extended their attention to neglected areas of social and moral concern, partly as a result of the success of the British Humanist Association itself.

In the absence of strong conventional models of conduct and belief, or charismatic leaders such as Bradlaugh or Coit who could create their own area of conviction, members have been forced by lack of favourable conditions for the movement's growth to seek for a philosophy which is explicit, but too wedded to freedom to make it binding. The ebb and flow of certainty amongst humanists about their beliefs is revealed on a mundane level by the fact that almost every issue of the humanist journals in this century, until the last five years or so, has included a letter or an article asking or attempting a definition of what humanism—or secularism, rationalism or ethicism—really is.

The ideology of a movement needs to define not only its nature and purpose but who may become a member. The humanist movement has in practice been completely open about recruitment; whilst Christians were sometimes formally barred from membership they could attend meetings. Some members, particularly those nineteenth-century workmen caught up in the toils of a 'respectability' from which their opinions debarred them but the lack of which generally led to unregulated behaviour, wanted to bar all those with the failings which were a source of Christian criticism. The central bodies have resisted the demand to expel members who were not atheist or 'respectable' enough, since tolerance and acceptance is a central strand of humanism. At the same time, they have tried to avoid involving the movement in socially disliked issues; to make explicit the distinction between members who advocated neo-Malthusianism, free love, et cetera and an organization which did not. The more explosive the issue, the harder it was to dissociate the two.

The solution of the humanist movement to all these problems has been to adopt a structure in which neither local groups nor central bodies must adhere to a common point of view, so that they can accommodate themselves to the views of their members, and also to create a strong defence of conflict and disagreement as something which is healthy and valuable. Whilst this may have contributed to the rapid turnover of membership which has been characteristic of all the groups, it has also served to limit conflict and to recognize the inevitable disagreements which must arise in a movement where the members are largely united by what they do *not* believe in, and by the independence and resistance to authority which drove them to make their dissent explicit in the first place.

Such a solution to internal dissent within a group seems to be a rare one, although it is equally characteristic, as far as can be seen, of humanist groups in Holland, Australia and the United States.[3] To adopt the view that differences of opinion are healthy requires that members combine a strong intellectual and emotional belief in the virtues of argument and discussion with a high degree of tolerance toward those who differ from them. This prerequisite may help to account for the high degree of both formal and informal education among members of the movement, and the fact that the largest occupational group of humanists at present are teachers, a profession which in the last thirty years has attempted to move away from an authoritative 'telling' to a faith in free criticism and finding out for oneself.

Another factor limiting conflict over the ends of the humanist movement is that during the late nineteenth and early twentieth centuries there were many different bodies, so that whilst many humanists belonged to more than one body, they could adhere most strongly to that which most nearly represented their views. The movements can be grouped according to the predominant class composition of their membership and whether they were trying to *replace* or revivify religion or whether they were trying to *destroy* it, (*see* Figure 1 on following page).

The Process of Joining

The processes by which men and women hear about, become interested in, contact, join and finally become active members of churches, political parties and social movements remain largely obscure. Explanations of conversion tend to assume either that there

---

[3] S. Warren, *American Freethought 1860–1914*, Columbia University Press, New York, 1943; N. J. Demerath and V. Thiessen, 'On Spitting against the Wind: Organizational Precariousness and American irreligion', *American Journal of Sociology*, Vol. 71, May 1966, pp. 674–87; F. B. Smith, *Religion and Freethought in Melbourne, 1870–90*, M. A. Thesis, University of Melbourne, 1960. Accounts of Dutch movement in *News and Notes*, June 1952, p. 7. and February 1954, p. 7.

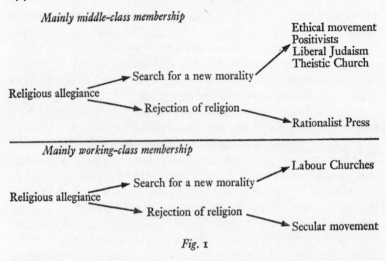

Fig. 1

is a strong misilarity between the views of an individual and the
ideology of a group, or else that the ideology is largely irrelevant;
the movement offers emotional gratification to the convert by giving
him an opportunity to satisfy various psychological drives. Such
explanations, Lofland argues, are based on the unreasonable assumption either that 'joiners' possess distinct ideas before they come into
contact with a movement, or that people who belong to groups with
peculiar beliefs must originally have been peculiar people.[4] In the
study of both religious and political movements, an implicit distinction is often made between mainstream, 'reasonable' churches
or parties whose membership can be explained either in terms of
rational calculation or traditional allegiances, and fringe, deviant,
'wild' sects whose membership is assumed to have various pathologi-
cal characteristics. Many authors implicitly invoke the prejudicial
assumption of *The True Believer*, that those who rapidly change
between very different movements—especially if one of them is the
Communist Party—or movements which have a high turnover of
membership, are *ipso facto* unrealistic, sectarian, totalitarian,
et cetera.

These views ignore the very general mental set with which the
'seeker' approaches movements, into which any number of ideologies
may conveniently slot, at least for a time. Cult members only need
to hold a few very general beliefs, such as the conviction that events
have a pattern and a purpose which can be revealed to us by forces

[4] J. Lofland, *Doomsday Cult*, Prentice-Hall, New Jersey, 1966, pp. 29–62.

outside our experience, for a wide range of movements to offer them answers. The various humanist bodies very rarely converted members to their beliefs; rather they had been made generally receptive to a humanist outlook by a variety of general social processes described in the chapters on membership, and the problem for the movement has been to persuade them that it is worth while to join an organized body to further their ideas. Humanist bodies lack the power of those sects which transform men's view of the world and themselves; they do not create new beliefs but mobilize those which are already there.

Because the aims and methods of the movement were so diffuse and general, members came to it from very different routes and with different preconceptions. People who move between small religious groups with roughly similar views have been termed 'seekers', but it is likely that there are also some who move between social, political and religious groups. Whilst most humanists have not been 'seekers', the patterns of movement which were fragmentarily glimpsed by contemporaries suggest that the various humanist bodies were points on more than one sort of pilgrimage. One such was the 'liberal religion' circuit, in which each body could act at various times to replace Unitarianism as a 'feather-bed for falling Christians'. Another was an interest in science, which can be tentatively divided into the religions of science such as positivism, spiritualism and phrenology, or more recently Scientology, and a belief in scientific knowledge and control which is more akin to the Rationalist Press, Progressive League, and eugenics movement. Humanism could also be a point on a radical or socialist circuit along with a wide spectrum of reformist groups, centred on varying sub-circuits such as humanitarianism, personal liberty of various kinds, and moral regeneration; and the last pilgrimage was that concerned with a new morality, which might lead members to groups interested in moral education or the reform of the law relating to personal morality. These pilgrimages and circuits were well-worn at some periods and not others, and over time the first has declined and the way-stations of the others have changed.

The result of these connections is a cannibalizing or osmotic tendency in which movements which are on a common circuit recruit members from each other, and large movements are likely to engulf smaller ones, since their success is attractive. The humanist movement is particularly vulnerable since, like the peace movement, it is less a movement oriented to a particular set of reforms than a general social background from which more specific movements have emerged, or by which they are supported.[5] As these movements have emerged, they have drawn members away from humanism since they may no longer consider issues such as women's rights as a part of humanism but as important movements in their own right. The nature of the osmotic process can be readily understood in the humanist movement, because members moved between groups, very often along friendship links; they were taken to meetings of new groups by friends they had made in the old one. Leaders would often use their membership in one group to advocate another, as when Mrs Besant and others proselytized for socialism in the secular societies.

The general drift of movement along the circuits is connected with the social and intellectual history of the society as a whole. Socialism drew members away from all the humanist movements in the 1890s and 1900s, and women's suffrage and communism amongst others exerted a similar briefer attraction; their force must also have been felt by many other individuals and groups as they grew to power and saliency in the wider society. It is impossible to assess accurately all the currents and eddies which brought seekers into the humanist bodies at various points and drew them out again, but Figure 2 attempts a very simplified representation of the main progressions that have been discussed for the century after 1830.

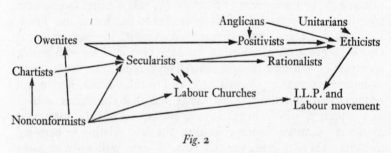

Fig. 2

In the same way, changes in religion itself produced changes in motive for those who became humanists. The obsession with the brutality and malevolence of Christian beliefs about death, hell and redemption of many late nineteenth-century liberals grew much less in the twentieth century, as eschatology changed and the general social concern with and concrete experience of death declined.

[5] For a discussion of the distinction, see N. Smelser, *The Theory of Collective Behaviour*, Routledge, London, 1962, p. 273.

Contemporary fears of chaos—of economic decay, riots and random violence—are unconnected with a formal religious framework.

Underlying circuits of movement there lay broad categories of motive for becoming a humanist; the dislike of organized religion, the search for another system of knowledge, a firmer basis for morality, or a morality of politics. The decline of support for orthodox religion, connected to the general network of radical ideas, meant that resistance to religion was commonly focused on the arbitrary and rigid nature of religious authority, of church or minister, and a corresponding emphasis that the heart was the best guide to religious life. Not many who came to feel about organized religion in this way joined the humanist movement; many more would have joined nonconformist churches or abandoned organized religion altogether. And those who did enter the humanist movement had insufficient long-term motive to stay there. Their antagonism to religion was itself jeopardized by increasing secularization and the growing assumption that religion, whether true or untrue, was not very important, and to insist on attacking it both unkind and ridiculous.

A second reason for the rejection of religion was the intellectual one; the search for another and more adequate system of knowledge, and the belief—at its strongest at the end of the nineteenth century— was that this could be a wholly scientific one. Secularism, rationalism and positivism all owed members to this general conviction, but a wide range of other systems of thought and movements such as 'scientific' socialism and spiritualism must also have benefited from it. The attractions of a complete system of knowledge, one which would explain everything and resolve all moral doubts, were very great to a generation who were witnessing the final disappearance of a sacred canopy. The popularity of many thinkers to nineteenth century audiences was partly due to their very scope, the sense that they gave that everything could be fitted into a cosmic plan. The intellectual changes which brought about the fragmentation of knowledge, the separation of facts and values and the peremptory insistence on the arbitrary and subjective nature of thought created difficulties for the humanist movement, as well as for theology and other intellectual systems. The attack on 'cant' and 'sham', the Edwardian reaction to the late Victorian love of the grand system, made rationalists out of some and total sceptics out of others.

A third reason for rejecting religion was the search for a firmer basis of morality, the fear that since the churches were failing to tackle the grave problems of contemporary life, anarchy would result unless a new source of personal idealism were to evolve. In searching for this, it was natural until a few decades ago to turn to religion, so widely assumed to be the support of morality and to lead men to acts of selflessness and generosity. Many of the searchers were also looking for the rituals, the links with community, the mythopoeic power, of remembered religion. As organized religion lost its majority support it lost the role as the centre of the community which some humanists were trying to recreate. Those who had been drawn to the idea of a liberal religion had always been subjected to a stream of abrasive comments from both humanists and outsiders.

> Seeing that the members of the Battersea Ethical Society have avowedly decided that discussion of doctrine is unseemly, that sermons should be subjects of meditation, not of controversy; and that the test of its 'services' is the extent to which Saturday's sinners find themselves comforted and strengthened on Sunday for a fresh plunge into sin on Monday, I asked why, in the name of common sense, its members do not join the Congregational Free Church, where they will find everything they want well organized in comfortable chapels, and done much better than they can do it with their present resources . . .

scoffed Bernard Shaw.[6] And as religion lost its power and familiarity, the idea of acting as a replacement for it became less attractive.

A fourth circuit which brought some men and women to humanism may be called that of the morality of politics, or religion of socialism. In the earliest periods of political movements, many members feel an immense upsurge of idealism and moral enthusiasm which lends the movement a spiritual or religious force. The movement seems on the verge of transforming the whole of life, and politics and religion become one. Some English socialists sought for a new church to express their idealism, and others thought that socialism itself was a religion. William Morris reflected in 1883 that 'Hyndman is sanguine of a speedy change happening somehow, and is inclined to intrigue and the making of a party . . . I think the aim of socialism should be the founding of a religion.' The writers who inspired men to socialism in Britain—Carpenter, Blatchford, Shaw, Morris and Wells—saw their political beliefs as part of a general humanism and for a time supported one branch or other of the movement. The nature and place of the boundaries between political and religious life, which we experience as secure and evident, is in reality shifting

---

[6] *Ethics*, 20 June 1903, p. 199.

and uncertain. The writers who have attempted to explain humanism have often foundered on the uncertainty of what seems to be obvious.

The Boundaries of Politics and Religion

The explanations of humanist and other puzzlingly hybrid movements take three general forms; the religious substitute, the pre-political manifestation, and the new religion which underlies radical change. The first explanation is used by those who have, consciously or not, a functional explanation of religion. If religion has specific social or psychological functions, is a piece in a societal jigsaw puzzle, then men and groups who lack religion but have other beliefs or allegiances are said to be using communism et cetera as a substitute. Such an explanation of humanism is common among both its critics and sociologists, but it is both static and rigid. Religion is not a *thing*, a constant component, but something the shape and boundaries of which can fluctuate and change, the meaning of which is different at different times and for different men.[7] Unless we are to equate it with something as broad as 'any general value-system', we cannot assume any fixed place for it; and just as religion changes its form and its emphases, so does humanism.

The ambiguity of the distinction between religious and political behaviour has been remarked on where what look like essentially economic or political deprivations have been expressed in a religious form, or where apparently essentially religious emotions are vented in a secular context. Explanations of this sometimes assume a kind of backwardness or irrationality of societies or men which prevents them from correctly rendering what is Caesar's to Caesar. Accounts of cargo cults and of other religions of the dispossessed assume that had the desire for restitution been seen as a political or economic demand, it would have been a more effective one. This explanation has been criticized very effectively in the context of the third world, but it is equally dubious when applied, as Hobsbawm applies it, to the explanation of millenial movements in more advanced societies.[8]

[7] For a more extended version of this argument, see my *Sociologists and Religion*, op. cit.

[8] For a sustained critique of this kind of explanation of new religions in the Third World, see B. R. Wilson, *Magic and the Millenium*, Heinemann Educational Books, London, 1973; C. B. Campbell, *Towards a Sociology of Irreligion*, Macmillan, London, 1971, gives a humanist version of the religious substitute argument; E. Hobsbawm, *Primitive Rebels*, Manchester University Press, Manchester, 1955, p. 127.

It is assumed that their members are 'principally confined to backward communities within the wider society', those not born into capitalism. This is evidently not true of the humanist bodies since they were formed at a time when all men had access to political citizenship, and many humanists were actively engaged in politics. Nor is it clear, as I shall go on to argue, that we can equate political with effective action.

There is a further general explanation of secular religions, which is that they form part of a counter-culture and help it to deny 'commonsense' assumptions about the limits of possible social change and the fixed nature of man and reality, so as to make possible a more radical political transformation. Thus Worsley: 'There is a heavy emphasis in all cults upon a new morality. The social order is to be transformed by radical political and economic changes. But the new order must also have a new morality; it cannot continue with the outworn indigenous ethics . . .'[9] The close links of all the humanist bodies with radicalism and socialism, the origin of most of them at the socialist renaissance of the 1890s and their decline as it became more securely established as a mass party and less messianic in its aims, are evidence of this. But many socialists found their rationale in nonconformity, Marxism or politics itself; why did some look for an explicit 'religion of socialism'?

Rather than postulating a psychological or functional need for religion, we could examine their reasons for wanting a secular religion. Among the reasons that they gave, a constant theme occurs; that *only* a religion can create moral change, can 'change men's hearts'. The political process of itself cannot sufficiently change society; in its operations, the compromises necessary to democratic politics will deflect radicals from the real changes that are needed. Only a religion could so morally unify society as to break down established structures of self-interest, to bring about the major changes which were needed to realize a good society and (perhaps) to avert revolution. Just as our confidence in the power of religion fluctuates, so does our confidence in the political process.

The growth of the British humanist movement from the 1960s seems due neither to a revival of belief in liberal religion nor to a sudden influx of the previously devout looking for an alternative, but rather to a growth of interest in the moral and social issues which lay, at that time, outside the sphere of conventional politics. The broadening of the range of political debate to many of the areas with

[9] P. Worsley, *The Trumpet Shall Sound*, MacGibbon and Kee, London, 1957, p. 251.

which humanism has been concerned is partly a measure of its success as a lobby, and partly of the strength of the social changes which created new, though often short-term, members for the humanist movement and changed the boundaries of the political system.

Living with Uncertainty

As a consequence of the variety of motives which have brought men to humanism, and the difficulty of establishing an agreed-upon set of beliefs or mode of operation, the movement has been beset by disagreement as well as co-operation. The nature of its membership has been such that the usual methods of definition and exclusion have not been employed nor has it retreated to a wholly pragmatic and short-term programme of action. The concern of members for the tolerance of difference, openness to new knowledge, and yet a clear and democratically established basis for operations, has kept the movement open to an extent which members sometimes feel to make it either intolerable or ineffectual.

To the old debate with the materialists, as to whether it is the ideas of a movement or its mode of organization and social base which determine its success, the humanist movement backs up its answer with its own history. Despite the relative strength of humanist beliefs in British society, the very nature of those beliefs subjects any movement trying to further them to continuing uncertainty and strain.

BIBLIOGRAPHY

I. Select list of secondary sources on the humanist movement and the intellectual and social life of Britain in the last century. (Published in London, unless otherwise stated.)

Abrams, P. S. *The Origins of British Sociology, 1834–1914*, University of Chicago Press, Chicago, 1968.

Adams, W. E. *Memoirs of a Social Atom*, 2 vols., Hutchinson, 1903.

Adler, F. *An Ethical Philosophy of Life*, Appleton, 1913.

— et al. *The Fiftieth Anniversary of the Ethical Movement, 1876–1926*, Appleton, New York, 1926.

— *Life and Destiny, or, Thoughts on the Ethical Religion*, McClure Philips, 1903.

Aldred, G. A. *No Traitor's Gait!* 2 vols., Strickland Press, Glasgow, 1955.

Allen, G. *The Evolution of the Idea of God*, Watts, 1931.

Almond, G. *The Appeals of Communism*, Princeton University Press, New Jersey, 1954.

d'Alviella, Count Goblet. *The Contemporary Evolution of Religious Thought in England, America and India*, Williams and Norgate, 1865.

Annan, N. *The Curious Strength of Positivism in English Political Thought*, Oxford University Press, 1959.

— *Leslie Stephen: his Thought and Character in Relation to his Time*, MacGibbon and Kee, 1951.

Anon. (G. W. Foote ?). *Death's Test, or, Christian Lies about Dying Infidels*, Freethought Publishing Company, 1882.

Anon. 'Popular Infidelity in the Metropolis', *The Journal of Sacred Literature and Biblical Record*, Vol. VI., January 1865.

Anon. *The Religion of a Layman*, Waddie, Edinburgh, 1907.

Anon. 'The Religious Heresies of the Working Classes', *Westminster Review*, Vol. XXI., January 1862.

Archbold, E. and Lee, H. W. *Social Democracy in Britain—Fifty Years of the Socialist Movement*, Social Democratic Federation, 1935.

Archer, W. *William Archer as Rationalist*, Watts, 1925.

Armytage, W. H. *Heavens Below: Utopian Experiments in England, 1560–1960*, Routledge, 1961.

Arnstein, W. L. *The Bradlaugh Case*, Oxford University Press, 1965.

Aveling, E. B. *A Godless Life the Happiest and Most Useful*, Freethought Publishing Company, 1882.

Ball, F. C. *Tressell of Mugsborough*, Lawrence and Wishart, 1951.

Ball, W. P. *Mrs. Besant's Socialism: an Examination and Exposure*, Progressive Publishing Company, 1886.

Banks, J. A. *Prosperity and Parenthood: a Study of Family Planning among the Victorian Middle Classes*, Routledge, 1954.

Barbour, I. G. *Issues in Science and Religion*, S. C. M. Press, 1966.

Barclay, T. *The Autobiography of a Bottle-Washer*, Backus, Leicester, 1934.

Barker, J. *Life of Joseph Barker, written by Himself*, Hodder and Stoughton, 1880.

Barter, E. G. *Relativity and Reality: a Re-interpretation of Anomalies Appearing in the Theories of Relativity*, Watts, 1953.

Bartley, W. W. *The Retreat to Commitment*, Chatto and Windus, 1964.

Bax, E. B. *The Religion of Socialism*, Sonnenschein, n.d.

— *Reminiscences and Reflections*, Allen and Unwin, 1918.

Beck, C. E., ed. *The English Catholics, 1850–1950*, Burns Oates, 1950.

Becker, C. L. *The Heavenly City of the Eighteenth-Century Philosophers*, Yale University Press, New Haven, 1932.

Becker, H. S. *The Outsiders*, Free Press, Glencoe, Ill., 1963.

Benn, A. W. *History of English Rationalism in the Nineteenth Century*, 2 vols., Longmans, 1906.

Benny, J. *Bradlaugh and Hyndman: a Review and Criticism of the Recent Debate on Socialism*, Benny, 1884.

Bernstein, E. *My Years of Exile*, Parsons, 1921.

Besant, A. *An Autobiography*, Fisher Unwin, 1893.

— *The Law of Population: its Consequences, and its Bearing upon Human Conduct and Morals*, Freethought Publishing Company, 1877.

— *Life, Death and Immortality*, Freethought Publishing Company, 1886.

— and Foote, G. W. *Is Socialism Sound? Verbatim Report of Four Nights Debate in the Hall of Science*, Progressive Publishing Company, 1887.

Bettany, F. C. *Stewart Headlam*, John Murray, 1926.

Bibby, C. *T. H. Huxley*, Watts, 1959.

Bithell, R. *The Creed of a Modern Agnostic: paper read to the London Dialectical Society*, Routledge, 1883.

Bitner, E. 'Radicalism and the Organization of Radical Movements', *American Sociological Review*, Vol. XXVIII (6), 1963.

Blackham, H. J. *Humanism*, Penguin Books, 1968.

— *The Human Tradition*, Routledge, 1953.

— ed. *Objections to Humanism*, Constable, 1963.

— ed. *Stanton Coit, 1857–1944*, Favil Press, 1948.

Blatchford, R. *God and My Neighbour*, Clarion Press, 1903.

— *My Eighty Years*, Cassell, 1931.

— *The New Religion*, Clarion Pamphlet No. 20., n.d.

Bocock, R. J. 'Ritual: Civic and Religious', *British Journal of Sociology*, Vol. XXI (3), 1970.

Booth, C. *Life and Labour in London*, Third Series, Macmillan, 1902.

Bradlaugh, C. *The Autobiography of Mr. Bradlaugh*, Austin, 1873.

— *England's Balance Sheet*, Freethought Publishing Co., 1884.

— *The Freethinker's Textbook*, 3 vols., Charles Watts, n.d.

— *Humanity's Gain from Unbelief, etc.*, Watts, 1929.

— *Some Objections to Socialism*, Freethought Publishing Co., 1884.

— *Supernatural and Rational Morality*, Freethought Publishing Co., 1886.

— *Will Socialism Benefit the English People?*, Freethought Publishing Co., 1884.

— Besant, A., and Watts, C. *The Freethinker's Textbook*, 3 vols., Charles Watts, n.d.

Bradlaugh-Bonner, C., and Bonner, A. *Hypatia Bradlaugh-Bonner, the Story of her Life*, Watts, 1942.

Bradlaugh-Bonner, H. *Charles Bradlaugh*, 2 vols., Fisher Unwin, 1894.

Brennan, T., Cooney, E. W., and Pollins, H. *Social Change in South West Wales*, Watts, 1954.

Bridges, H. J. *The Emerging Faith—Answers to Questions on Ethical Religion*, Watts, 1937.

— et al. *The Ethical Movement—its Principles and Aims*, Union of Ethical Societies, 1911.

Briggs, A., *ed. Chartist Studies*, Macmillan, 1962.

Brown, A. W. *The Metaphysical Society—Victorian Minds in Crisis, 1869–1880*, Columbia University Press, New York, 1947.

Buckley, J. H. *The Triumph of Time*, Harvard University Press, Cambridge, Mass., 1967.

Budd, S. *Sociologists and Religion*, Collier-Macmillan, 1971.

Burrow, J. W. *Evolution and Society: a Study in Victorian Social Theory*, Cambridge University Press, 1966.

Bury, J. B. *History of Freedom of Thought*, Williams and Norgate, 1913.

Bury, J. B. *The Idea of Progress*, Macmillan, 1920.

Cairns, W. D. *The Army and Religion*, Macmillan, 1919.

Campbell, C. B. 'Membership Composition of the British Humanist Association', *Sociological Review*, Vol. XXIII (3), 1965.

— *Towards a Sociology of Irreligion*, Macmillan, 1971.

Cannon, W. F. 'The Normative Role of Science in Early Victorian Thought', *Journal of the History of Ideas*, Vol. XXV, 1964.

Carpenter, E. *My Days and Dreams*, Allen and Unwin, 1916.

'A Catholic Freethinker', *Mr. Bradlaugh the Model Protestant*, Catholic, Freethinker flysheet, n.d.

Clark, E. T. *The Psychology of Religious Awakening*, Macmillan, 1929.

Clayton, J. *The Rise and Decline of Socialism in Great Britain, 1884–1924*, Faber and Gwyer, 1926.

Clifford, W. K. *The Ethics of Belief*, Watts, 1947.

— *Lectures and Essays*, Watts, 1918.

Clodd, E. *Memories*, Chapman and Hall, 1916.

Cockshut, A. O. J. *The Unbelievers*, Collins, 1964.

Cohen, C. *Almost an Autobiography—Confessions of a Freethinker*, Pioneer Press, 1940.
— *Bradlaugh and Ingersoll*, Pioneer Press, 1933.
— *Essays in Freethinking*, Pioneer Press, 1923.
— *The Other Side of Death*, Pioneer Press, 1922.
— *Socialism and the Churches*, Pioneer Press, 1919.
— and Joad, C. E. M. *Materialism, has it Been Exploded?*, Watts, 1928.
Cohen, P. 'Theories of Myth', *Man*, Vol. IV (3), 1969.
Coit, S. *Ethical Culture as a Religion for the People*, E. W. Allen, 1887.
— *Ethical Democracy—Essays in Social Dynamics*, Grant Richards, 1900.
— *National Idealism and a State Church*, Williams and Norgate, 1907.
— ed. *Social Worship, for Use in Families, Schools and Churches*, 2 vols., West London Ethical Society, 1913.
Cole, G. D. H. *British Working-class Politics, 1832–1914*, Routledge, 1941.
— *The Life of Robert Owen*, Macmillan, 1930.
— *Richard Carlile, 1790–1843*, Gollancz, 1943.
Coleman, T. *The Railway Navvies*, Hutchinson, 1965.
Collet, S. D. *George Jacob Holyoake and Modern Atheism*, Trübner, 1885.
— *Phases of Atheism*, Holyoake, 1860.
Cominos, P. T. 'Late Victorian Sexual Respectability and the Social System', *International Review of Social History*, Vol. VIII (1 and 2), 1963.
Converse, P. E. 'Belief Systems in Mass Politics', in D. E. Apter, *ed.*, *Ideology and Discontent*, Free Press, Glencoe, Ill., 1964.
Conway, M. D. *Autobiography*, 2 vols., Cassell, 1904.
— *Centenary of the South Place Society*, Williams and Norgate, 1904.
— *Life of Thomas Paine*, Putnam, New York, 1892.
— *The Voysey Case from a Heretical Standpoint*, Thomas Scott, Ramsgate, n.d.
Cooper, T. *Life of Thomas Cooper, written by himself*, Hodder and Stoughton, 1872.
Courtney, J. E. *Freethinkers in the Nineteenth Century*, Chapman and Hall, 1920.
Courtney, W. L., *ed. Do We Believe?*, Hodder and Stoughton, 1905.
Cowling, M. *Mill and Liberalism*, Cambridge University Press, 1963.
Creasey, C. H. and Eve, A. S. *Life and Work of John Tyndall*, Macmillan, 1945.
Crowther, M. A. *The Church Embattled—Religious Controversy in Mid-Victorian England*, David and Charles, Newton Abbott, 1970.
Cruse, A. *After the Victorians*, Allen and Unwin, 1938.
Dangerfield, C. *The Strange Death of Liberal England*, Constable, 1936.
Davies, C. M. *Heterodox London, or Phases of Freethought in the Metropolis*, 2 vols., Tinsley Brothers, 1874.

— *Unorthodox London*, Tinsley Brothers, first series 1873, second series 1875.

Davies, D. R. *In Search of Myself*, Bles, 1962.

Davies, E. T. *Religion in the Industrial Revolution in South Wales*, University of Wales Press, Cardiff, 1965.

Demerath, N. J. and Thiessen, V. 'On Spitting against the Wind: Organizational Precariousness and American Irreligion', *American Journal of Sociology*, Vol. LXXII, (6), 1966.

Douglas, M. *Natural Symbols—Explorations in Cosmology*, Cresset Press, 1970.

Durkheim, E. 'Individualism and the Intellectuals', translated version in *Political Studies*, Vol. XVII (1), 1969.

Eisen, S. 'Frederic Harrison and the Religion of Humanity', *Southern Atlantic Quarterly*, Vol. LXVI (4), 1967.

Ellegard, A. 'The Darwinian Theory and Nineteenth-Century Philosophies of Science', *Journal of the History of Ideas*, Vol. XVIII (3), 1957.

— *Darwin and the General Reader—the reception of Darwin's Theory of Evolution in the British Periodical Press, 1859–1872*, Göteborgs Universitets Arsskrift, Vol. LXIV (7), Göteborg, 1958.

Elliott-Binns, L. E. *The Development of English Theology in the later Nineteenth Century*, Longmans, 1952.

Ellis, H. *My Life*, Heinemann, 1940.

Engels, F. *Socialism, Utopian and Scientific*, Sonnenschein, 1892.

Ensor, R. C. K. *England, 1870–1914*, Clarendon Press, Oxford, 1936.

Eppel, E. M. and M. *Adolescents and Morality*, Routledge, 1968.

Erikson, K. T. *Wayward Puritans, a study in the Sociology of Deviance*, Wiley, New York, 1966.

Ernest, C., and Hithersay, R. B. *Sketch of the Life of Saladin*, Stewart, n.d.

Eros, J. 'The Rise of Organized Freethought in Mid-Victorian England,' *Sociological Review*, Vol. II (1), 1954.

Ethical Union *The Way to a Common Faith*, 5 parts, Watts, 1945.

— *Ethical Leaflets*, n.p., n.d.

Faulkner, H. U. *Chartism and the Churches—a study in Democracy*, Columbia University Press, New York, 1916.

Festinger, L. *et al. When Prophecy Fails: Millenial Dreams in Action*, Harper, New York, 1956.

Flaws, G. C. *Life of Saladin*, Watts, 1883.

Fleming, D. *John William Draper and the Religion of Science*, University of Pennsylvania Press, Philadelphia, 1950.

Foote, G. W., *ed. The Hall of Science Libel Case, with a Full and True Account of the 'Leeds Orgies'*, Forder, n.d.

— *Rome or Atheism—the Great Alternative*, Forder, 1892.

— *Secularism the true Philosophy of Life*, Freethought Publishing Company, 1879.
— and McClaren, A. D. *Infidel Death-Beds*, Pioneer Press, 1933.
Fox, F. *Memoir of Mrs. Eliza Fox*, Trübner, 1869.
Froude, J. A. *The Nemesis of Faith*, Chapman, 1849.
Garnett, R. *The Life of W. J. Fox, Public Teacher and Social Reformer*, Bodley Head, 1909.
Gasman, D. *The Scientific Origins of National Socialism: Social Darwinism in Ernst Haeckel and the German Monist League*, MacDonald, 1971.
Gellner, E. A. 'French Eighteenth Century Materialism', in D. J. O'Connor, *ed.*, *A Critical History of Western Philosophy*, Free Press, Glencoe, Ill., 1964.
Gillispie, C. C. *The Edge of Objectivity: an Essay in the History of Scientific Ideas*, Princeton University Press, New Jersey, 1960.
— *Genesis and Geology: a study in the relations of Scientific Thought, Natural Theology and Social Opinion in Great Britain, 1790–1850*, Harvard University Press, Cambridge, Mass., 1951.
Gilmour, J. P., *ed. Champion of Liberty: Charles Bradlaugh*, Watts, 1933.
Gluckman, M., *ed. Essays on the Ritual of Social Relations*, Manchester University Press, 1962.
Golding, H. J. *Experimentalism and Marriage*, Ethical Union, 1933.
Gorer, G. *Death, Grief and Mourning*, Cresset Press, 1965.
Gosse, E. *Father and Son*, Heinemann, 1909.
Gould, F. J. *Chats with Pioneers of Modern Thought*, Watts, 1898.
— *History of the Leicester Secular Society*, published by the Society, Leicester, 1900.
— *Hyndman, Prophet of Socialism, 1842–1921*, Allen and Unwin, 1948.
— *Labour's Unrest and Labour's Future*, Watts, 1919.
— *Life Story of a Humanist*, Watts, 1923.
— *The Pioneers of Johnson's Court: a History of the R.P.A. from 1899 onwards*, Watts, 1935.
Gouldner, A. W., *ed. Studies in Leadership*, Harper, New York, 1950.
Gowans-White, A. *The Story of the R.P.A., 1899–1949*, Watts, 1949.
Grant, A. C. 'Combe on Phrenology and Free Will: a Note on Nineteenth-Century Secularism', *Journal of the History of Ideas*, Vol. XXVI (1), 1965.
Grant, J. *The Great Metropolis*, Saunders and Otley, 1837.
Gross, J. *The Rise and Fall of the Man of Letters*, Weidenfeld, 1969.
Haeckel, E. *The Riddle of the Universe at the Close of the Nineteenth Century*, Watts, 1904.
— *The Wonders of Life: a Popular Study of Biological Philosophy*, Watts, 1904.
Haller, M. H. 'Social Science and Genetics: an Historical Perspective', in D. V. Glass, *ed.*, *Genetics*, Rockefeller University Press, New York, 1963.

Hardy, A. C. *Science and the Quest for God*, Lindsey Press, 1951.

Harrison, A. *Frederic Harrison: Thoughts and Memories*, Heinemann, 1926.

Harrison, B. *Drink and the Victorians: the Temperance Question in England 1815–1872*, Faber, 1971.

Harrison, F. *Autobiographical Memories*, 2 vols., Macmillan, 1911.

Harrison, J. F. C. *Learning and Living, 1790–1960: a study in the history of the English Adult Education Movement*, Routledge, 1961.

— *Robert Owen and the Owenites*, Routledge and Kegan Paul, 1969.

Harrison, R. *Before the Socialists—Studies in Labour and Politics, 1861–1881*, Routledge, 1964.

— 'Professor Beesly and the Working-Class Movement', in A. Briggs and J. Saville, *eds.*, *Essays in Labour History*, Macmillan, 1960.

Hawton, H. *The Feast of Unreason*, Watts, 1952.

— *The Humanist Revolution*, Pemberton, 1963.

— *The Thinker's Handbook—a Guide to Religious Controversy*, Watts, 1950.

Hearnshaw, J. F. C., *ed.* *The Social and Political Ideas of some Representative Thinkers of the Victorian Age*, Harrap, 1933.

Heath, A. E., *ed.* *Scientific Thought in the Twentieth Century—an Authoritative Account of Fifty Years Progress in Science*, Watts, 1951.

Henriques, U. *Religious Toleration in England, 1787–1833*, Routledge, 1961.

Himmelfarb, G. *Darwinism and the Darwinian Revolution*, Chatto and Windus, 1959.

Hobsbawm, E. J. *Labouring Men—Studies in the History of Labour*, Weidenfeld and Nicolson, 1964.

— *Primitive Rebels—Studies in Archaic Forms of Social Movement in the Nineteenth and Twentieth Centuries*, Manchester University Press, Manchester, 1959.

Hobson, J. A. *Confessions of an Economic Heretic*, Allen and Unwin, 1938.

Hobson, S. G. *Pilgrim to the Left*, Arnold, 1938.

Hoffer, E. *The True Believer: Thoughts on the Nature of Mass Movements*, Harper, New York, 1951.

Hofstadter, R. *Social Darwinism in American Thought*, revised edn., Beacon Press, Boston, 1955.

Holdsworth, W. S. 'The State and Religious Nonconformity: an Historical Retrospect', *Law Quarterly Review*, Vol. XXXVI (2), 1920.

Holyoake, A. *Secular Ceremonies*, Austin, 1870.

— and Watts, C. *The Secularist's Manual of Songs and Ceremonies*, Austin, 1870.

Holyoake, G. J. *Bygones Worth Remembering*, 2 vols., Unwin, 1905.

— *John Stuart Mill as some of the Working Classes knew Him*, Trübner, 1873.

— *The Last Trial for Atheism in England*, Trübner, London, 1871.

— *Life and Character of Richard Carlile*, Austin, 1849.

— *Life and Last Days of Robert Owen of New Lanark*, n.p., 1859.
— *The Limits of Atheism: Or, Why Should Sceptics be Outlaws?*, Brook, 1874.
— *The Logic of Death: or, Why should the Atheist Fear to Die?*, Watson, 1851.
— *The Logic of Life: deduced from the Principles of Freethought*, Austin, 1870.
— *Public Speaking and Debate*, Farrah, 1866.
— *Secular Responsibility*, Trübner, 1873.
— *Sixty Years of an Agitator's Life*, Unwin, London, 1893.
— and Bradlaugh, C. *Secularism, Scepticism and Atheism*, Austin, 1870.
Houghton, W. E. 'Victorian Anti-Intellectualism', *Journal of the History of Ideas*, Vol. XIII (3), June, 1952.
— *The Victorian Frame of Mind, 1830–1870*, Yale University Press, New Haven, 1957.
Howarth, O. J. R. *The British Association for the Advancement of Science*, published by the Association, 1931.
Hughes, E. C. *Consciousness and Society: the Reorientation of European Social Thought, 1890–1930*, MacGibbon and Kee, 1959.
Hughes, H. Price. *The Atheist Shoemaker—a Page in the History of the West London Mission*, Hodder and Stoughton, 1889.
— *Life of Hugh Price Hughes*, Hodder and Stoughton, 1904.
Huxley, J. *Religion Without Revelation*, Watts, 1941.
Huxley, T. H. *Critiques and Addresses*, Macmillan, 1890.
— *Lay Sermons, Essays and Reviews*, Macmillan, 1870.
— *Science and Christian Tradition*, Macmillan, 1904.
Hyndman, H. M. *Record of an Adventurous Life*, Macmillan, 1911.
Ingle, S. J. 'Socialism and literature: The Contribution of Imaginative writers to the Development of the British Labour Party', *Political Studies*, Vol. XXII (2), June 1974.
Inglis, K. S. *Churches and the Working Classes in Victorian England*, Routledge, 1963.
— 'The Labour Church Movement', *International Review of Social History*, Vol. III (3), 1958.
Irving, W. *Apes, Angels and Victorians; a joint biography of Darwin and Huxley*, Weidenfeld and Nicolson, 1955.
Jacks, L. P. *The Revolt against Mechanism*, Allen and Unwin, 1934.
Jackson, J. A. *The Irish in Britain*, Routledge, 1963.
Jackson, T. A. *Solo Trumpet*, Lawrence and Wishart, 1953.
James, W. *The Varieties of Religious Experience: a Study in Human Nature*, Longmans, 1902.
Jeans, J. H. *The Mysterious Universe*, Cambridge University Press, Cambridge, 1930.
Judge, M. H. *The Ethical Movement in England*, Kingdom Road, Hampstead, 1902.

Keans, S. *Both Worlds Barred*, Unwin, 1894.

Kegan, P. C. *Memories*, Kegan Paul, 1899.

Kent, J. *From Darwin to Blatchford: the Role of Darwinism in Christian Apologetic 1875–1910*, Dr Williams Trust, 1966.

Kent, W. *London for Heretics*, Watts, 1932.

— *The Testament of a Victorian Youth*, Heath Cranton, 1938.

Kidd, B. *Social Evolution*, Macmillan, 1894.

Knight, W., ed. *Memorials of Thomas Davidson, the Wandering Scholar*, Ginn, Boston, 1907.

Kuhn, T. S. *The Structure of Scientific Revolutions*, University of Chicago Press, Chicago, 1962.

Laing, S. *Modern Science and Modern Thought*, Chapman and Hall, 1885.

— *A Modern Zoroastrian*, Watts, 1903.

Lansbury, G. *My Life*, Constable, 1928.

Lawson-Jones, W. *A Psychological Study of Religious Conversion*, Epworth Press, 1937.

Layard, G. D. *Mrs. Lynn Linton, her Life, Letters and Opinions*, Methuen, 1901.

Leeds Secular Society. *The Converted Lecturer, or, Mr. Gordon's Repudiation of Secular Principles Examined*, Summergill, Leeds, 1862.

Liveling, S. *J. H. Bridges, a Nineteenth Century Teacher*, Kegan Paul, 1926.

Lloyd, J. T. *From Christian Pulpit to Secular Platform*, Pioneer Press, 1903.

Lofland, H. *Doomsday Cult*, Prentice-Hall, New Jersey, 1966.

Lond, T. *Secularism: What is it? Answered by a Working-Man*, Ward, 1859.

Long, E. L. *The Religious Beliefs of American Scientists*, Westminster Press, Philadelphia, 1964.

Lovejoy, A. O. *The Great Chain of Being*, Harvard University Press, Cambridge, Mass., 1951.

McBriar, A. M. *Fabian Socialism and English Politics 1884–1914*, Cambridge University Press, 1962.

McCabe, J. *A Biographical Dictionary of Modern Rationalists*, Watts, 1920.

— *Edward Clodd, a Memoir*, Lane, 1932.

— *Eighty Years a Rebel—an Autobiography*, Haldemann-Julius, Girard, Kansas, 1947.

— *From Rome to Rationalism: or, Why I left the Church*, Watts, 1896.

— *George Jacob Holyoake*, n.p., 1922.

— *Life and Letters of George Jacob Holyoake*, 2 vols., Watts, 1896.

— *The Riddle of the Universe Today*, Watts, 1934.

— *Twelve Years in a Monastery*, Watts, 1912.

McGee, J. E. *A Crusade for Humanity—the History of Organized Positivism in England*, Watts, 1931.

— *A History of the British Secular Movement*, Haldemann-Julius, Girard, Kansas, 1947.

Mackay, C. R. *Life of Charles Bradlaugh, MP.*, Gunn, 1888.

Mackenzie, J. S. *Autobiography*, Williams and Norgate, 1936.

McLachlan, *The Unitarian Movement in the Religious Life of England*, Allen and Unwin, 1934.

McLeod, H. *Class and Religion in the Late Victorian City*, Croom Helm, 1974.

Mann, T. *Tom Mann's Memoirs*, Labour Publishing Co., 1923.

Marty, M. E. *The Infidel—Freethought and American Religion*, World Publishing Co., Ohio, 1961.

Marwick, A. *The Deluge—British Society and the First World War*, Penguin Books, Harmondsworth, 1967.

Mass Observation. *Puzzled People, a study in Popular Attitudes to Religion, Ethics, Progress and Politics in a London Borough*, Gollancz, 1947.

Mattuck, I. I. *Liberal Judaism*, Union of Liberal and Progressive Synagogues, 1947.

May, R. *Death's Test on Christians and Infidels—Echoes from Seventy Death Beds*, n.p., 1882.

Milne, A. J. 'Utilitarian Social Philosophies', *Archives Européennes de Sociologie*, Vol. VIII (2), 1967.

Mineka, F. *The Dissidence of Dissent : the Monthly Repository, 1806–1838*, University of North Carolina Press, Chapel Hill, 1944.

'A Monmouthshire Farmer'. *The Path I Took and Where it Led Me*, Watts, n.d.

Montagu, L. R. *The Jewish Religious Union and its Beginnings*, n.p., 1927.

Morley, J. *Recollections*, 2 vols., Macmillan, 1917.

Mudie-Smith, R. *The Religious Life of London*, Hodder and Stoughton, 1904.

Muirhead, J. H. *Bernard Bosanquet and his Friends*, Allen and Unwin, 1935.

Mumby, F. A. *Publishing and Bookselling*, Cape, 1930.

— and Stallybrass, F. H. S. *From Swan Sonnenschein to George Allen and Unwin Limited*, Allen and Unwin, 1955.

Murphy, H. R. 'The Ethical Revolt against Christian Orthodoxy in Early Victorian England', *American History Review*, Vol. LX (4), July 1955.

Nadel, S. F. *Nupe Religion*, Routledge and Kegan Paul, 1954.

Nethercot, A. H. *The First Five Lives of Annie Besant*, Hart-Davis, 1961.

— *The Last Four Lives of Annie Besant*, Hart-Davis, 1961.

Norman, E. R. *Anti-Catholicism in Victorian England*, Allen and Unwin, 1968.

Okey, T. *A Basketful of Memories*, Dent, 1930.

Owen, R. *The Life of Robert Owen, written by Himself*, facsimile of first edition by Knight, 1971.

Pack, E. *The Parson's Doom*, Freethought Socialist League, n.d.

— *Trial and Imprisonment of J. W. Gott*, Freethought Socialist League, 1912.

Packe, M. St J. *The Life of John Stuart Mill*, Secker and Warburg, 1954.

Patterson, A. T. *Radical Leicester: a History of Leicester 1780–1850*, University College, Leicester, 1954.

Pease, E. R. *History of the Fabian Society*, Fifield, 1916.

Pelling, H. *The British Communist Party—a Historical Profile*, Black, 1958.

— *The Origins of the Labour Party, 1800–1900*, Macmillan, 1954.

Percival, P. *Failsworth Folk and Failsworth Memories*, Hargreaves, Manchester, 1901.

— *The Position of Positivism, with some remarks on the Position of Secularism*, Heywood, Manchester, 1891.

Persons, S. *Free Religion—an American Faith*, Yale University Press, New Haven, 1947.

Petersen, H. *Havelock Ellis—Philosopher of Love*, Riverside Press, Cambridge, Mass., 1928.

Porter, B. *Critics of Empire—British Radical Alternatives to Colonialism in Africa, 1895–1914*, Macmillan, 1968.

Prowse, R. O. *James Hurd*, Heinemann, 1913.

— *The Prophet's Wife*, Gollancz, 1929.

Quin, M. *Memoirs of a Positivist*, Allen and Unwin, 1924.

Ratcliffe, S. K. *The Story of South Place*, Watts, 1955.

Raven, C. E. *Natural Religion and Christian Theology* Cambridge University Press, 1953.

Ravetz, J. R. *Scientific Knowledge and its Social Problems*, Clarendon Press, Oxford, 1971.

Reade, W. *The Martyrdom of Man*, Trübner, 1877.

Redford, A. *Labour Migration in England, 1800–1850*, Manchester University Press, Manchester, 1964.

Reid, F. 'Socialist Sunday Schools in Britain 1892–1939', *International Review of Social History*, Vol. XI (1), 1966.

Reid, W. H. *The Rise and Dissolution of the Infidel Societies of the Metropolis*, Hatchard, 1800.

Richter, M. 'Intellectual and Class Alienation: Oxford Idealist diagnoses and prescriptions', *Archives Européennes de Sociologie*, Vol. VII (1), 1966.

— *The Politics of Conscience: T. H. Green and his Age*, Weidenfeld and Nicolson, 1964.

Ritchie, J. E. *The Religious Life of London*, Tinsley Brothers, 1870.

Robertson, J. M. *Charles Bradlaugh*, Watts, 1920.

— *History of Freethought in theNineteenth Century*, 2 vols., Watts, 1929.

— *Life Pilgrimage of M. D. Conway*, Watts, 1914.

— *Modern Humanists Reconsidered*, Watts, 1927.

— *Socialism and Malthusianism*, Freethought Publishing Co., 1885.

Sacks, B. *The Religious Issue in the State Schools of England and Wales*, *1902–1914*, University of New Mexico Press, Albuquerque, 1961.

Salt, H. S. *Seventy Years Among Savages*, Allen and Unwin, 1921.

Schell, E. 'Bernard Bosanquet's Theory of Moral Education', *Paedogogia Historia*, Vol. VI (1), 1966.

Searle, G. R. *The Quest for National Efficiency—a study in British Politics and Political Thought, 1899–1914*, Blackwell, Oxford, 1971.

Semmel, B. *Imperialism and Social Reform: English Social Imperialist Thought, 1895–1914*, Allen and Unwin, 1960.

Shannon, R. T. 'John Robert Seeley and the Idea of a National Church', in R. Robson, *ed.*, *Ideas and Institutions of Victorian Britain*, Bell, 1967.

Sheldon, W. L. *An Ethical Sunday School*, Sonnenschein, 1900.

Silver, H. *The Concept of Popular Education: a study of Ideas and Social Movements in the Early Nineteenth Century*, MacGibbon and Kee, 1965.

Simon, W. M. *European Positivism in the Nineteenth Century: an Essay in Intellectual History*, Cornell University Press, New York, 1963.

Simonsson, T. *Face to Face with Darwinism—a Critical Analysis of the Christian front in Swedish Discussion of the Later Nineteenth Century*, C.W.K. Gleerup, Lund, 1958.

Simpson, J. Y. *Landmarks in the Struggle Between Science and Nature*, Hodder, 1925.

Singer, C. *A Short History of Biology*, Oxford University Press, Oxford, 1931.

Skinner, Q. 'Meaning and Understanding in the History of Ideas', *History and Theory*, Vol 8 (1), 1969.

Slosson, E. E. *Major Prophets of Today*, Little, Brown, Boston, 1914.

Smelser, N. J. *The Theory of Collective Behaviour*, Routledge, London, 1962.

Smith, F. B. 'The Atheist Mission', in R. Robson, *ed.*, *Ideas and Institutions of Victorian Britain*, Bell, 1967.

Smith, W. S. *The London Heretics 1870–1914*, Constable, 1967.

Snell, H. *The Ethical Movement Explained*, Ethical Union, 1935.

— *Men, Movements and Myself*, Dent, 1936.

Society of Ethical Propagandists. *Ethics and Religion*, Sonnenschein, 1900.

Soutter, F. W. *Fights for Freedom*, Unwin, 1925.

— *Recollections of a Labour Pioneer*, Unwin, 1923.

Spiller, G. *The Ethical Movement in Great Britain*, Farleigh Press, 1934.

— (*ed*. V. Spiller). *Gustav Spiller, 1864–1940*, V. Spiller, Barking, 1940.

Stanley, O. 'T. H. Huxley's Treatment of "Nature"', *Journal of the History of Ideas*, Vol. XVIII (1), 1957.

Starbuck, H. D. *The Psychology of Religion*, Walter Scott, 1899.

Stark, R., and Glock, C. Y. *American Piety: the Nature of Religious Commitment*, University of California Press, California, 1968.

Stebbing, S. *Philosophy and the Physicists*, Methuen, 1937.

Stedman-Jones, G. *Outcast London*, Clarendon Press, Oxford, 1971.

Stephen, L. *An Agnostic's Apology*, Watts, 1931.

Thompson, A. *Here I Lie—the Memorial of an Old Journalist*, Routledge, 1937.

Thompson, E. P. *The Making of the English Working Class*, Gollancz, 1964.

Thompson, L. *Robert Blatchford: Portrait of an Englishman*, Gollancz, 1951.

Thompson, P. 'Liberals, Radicals and Labour in London, 1880–1900', *Past and Present*, Number 27, April 1964.

Tizard, H. *The Passing World: Science and Social Progress*, Bureau of Current Affairs, 1948.

Tressell, R. *The Ragged-trousered Philanthropists*, Lawrence and Wishart, 1955.

Trevelyan, J. P. *Mrs. Humphry Ward*, Constable, 1923.

Trevor, J. *My Quest for God*, 'Labour Prophet' Office, 1897.

Tribe, D. *100 Years of Freethought*, Elek, 1967.

— *President Charles Bradlaugh, M.P.*, Elek, 1971.

Tuckwell, Rev. W. *Reminiscences of a Radical Parson*, Cassell, 1906.

Turner, B. *About Myself, 1863–1930*, Toulmin, 1930.

Tylor, E. B. *Primitive Culture*, Murray, 1871.

Union of Liberal Progressive Synagogues. *Strengthen Our Hands*, n.p., n.d.

Vivian, P. *The Churches and Modern Thought*, Watts, 1907.

Wagar, W. W. 'Modern Ideas of the Origins of the Idea of Progress', *Journal of the History of Ideas*, Vol. XXVIII (i), 1967.

Walker, D. P. *The Decline of Hell*, Routledge, 1964.

Wallace, A. R. *My Life*, Chapman and Hall, 1908.

Wallas, G. *William Johnson Fox*, Watts, 1924.

Ward, Mrs H. *Robert Elsmere*, 3 vols., Smith and Elder, 1888.

Watts, C. A. *A Defence of Secular Principles*, Austin, 1871.

— *The Meaning of Rationalism*, Watts, 1905.

— *A Personal Statement to the Freethought Party*, n.p., 1902.

— *The Philosophy of Secularism*, Austin, n.d.

— *A Refutation of Mr. Bradlaugh's Inaccuracies and Misrepresentations*, n.p., 1877.

Watts, J. and 'Iconoclast', *Half-Hours with Freethinkers*, Watts, 1865.

Wearmouth, R. F. *Methodism and the Struggle of the Working Classes, 1850–1900*, Backus, Leicester, 1954.

— *Methodism and the Working-class Movements of England, 1800–1850*, Epworth Press, 1937.

Webb, B. *My Apprenticeship*, Longmans, 1926.

Webb, C. J. *A Study of Religious Thought in England from 1850*, Clarendon Press, Oxford, 1933.

Webb, R. K. *The British Working Class Reader, 1790–1848*, Allen and Unwin, 1955.

Wells, H. G. *Experiment in Autobiography*, 2 vols., Gollancz, 1934.

—, Wells, G. P. and Huxley, J. *The Science of Life*, Cassell, 1931.

Wheeler, J. M. *Biographical Dictionary of Freethinkers*, Progressive Publishing Co., 1889.

White, A. D. *A History of the Warfare of Science with Theology in Christendom*, 2 vols., Macmillan, 1896.

White, W. H. *The Autobiography of Mark Rutherford, Dissenting Minister*, Unwin, 1881.

Whitehead, A. N. *Science and the Modern World*, Cambridge University Press, Cambridge, 1927.

Whitmore, Rev. C. J. *Seeking the Lost—Incidents and Sketches of Christian Work in London*, Nisbet, 1876.

Wickham, E. R. *Church and People in an Industrial City*, Lutterworth Press, 1957.

Wickwar, W. H. *The Struggle for the Freedom of the Press, 1810–1832*, Allen and Unwin, 1928.

Wiener, M. J. *Between Two Worlds—the Political Thought of Graham Wallas*, Clarendon Press, Oxford, 1971.

Willey, B. *More Nineteenth Century Studies—a Group of Honest Doubters*, Chatto and Windus, 1956.

Williams, G. *Rowland Detrosier*, St. Anthony's Press, York, 1965.

Wilson, B. R. *Magic and the Millenium: a Sociological Study of Religious Movements of Protest among Tribal and Third-World Peoples*, Heinemann Educational Books, 1973.

Winsten, S. *Salt and his Circle*, Hutchinson, 1951.

Wood, N. *Communism and British Intellectuals*, Gollancz, 1959.

Worsley, P. *The Trumpet Shall Sound*, MacGibbon and Kee, 1957.

Yinger, J. M. 'Contraculture and Subculture', *American Sociological Review*, Vol. XXV (5), 1960.

Young, G. M. *Victorian England; Portrait of an Age*, Oxford University Press, 1960.

Young, R. M. 'The Impact of Darwin on Conventional Thought', in A. Symondson, *ed.*, *The Victorian Crisis of Faith*, S.P.C.K., 1970.

— *Mind, Brain and Adaptation in the Nineteenth Century—Cerebral Localization and its Biological Conception from Gall to Ferrier*, Clarendon Press, Oxford, 1970.

II. Unpublished Materials

(i) Theses
(ii) Manuscripts
(iii) Minute-Books and Annual Reports

(i) Theses

Billington, R. *Leicester Secular Society, 1852–1920 : a Study in Radicalism and Respectability*, Dissertation, University of Leicester, 1968.

Campbell, C. B. *Humanism and the Culture of the Professions: a Study of the Rise of the British Humanist Movement, 1946–1963*, Ph.D., University of London, 1968.

Farrall, L. A. *The Origins and Growth of the English Eugenics Movement, 1865–1925*, Ph.D., University of Indiana, 1969.

Rowell, D. G. *Death and the Future Life in the Religious Thought of Nineteenth Century England*, Ph.D., University of Cambridge, 1968.

Royle, E. *George Jacob Holyoake and the Secularist Movement in Britain, 1848–1861*, Ph.D., University of Cambridge, 1968.

Smith, F. B. *Religion and Freethought in Melbourne, 1870–1890*, M.A., University of Melbourne, 1960.

Summers, Rev. D. F. *The Labour Church and Allied Movements of the Late Nineteenth and Early Twentieth Centuries*, Ph.D., Edinburgh University, 1958.

(ii) Manuscripts (I am indebted to the holders of these manuscripts for allowing me to consult them)

Coit, Stanton. *My Ventures on the Highway of Truth* (Lady Fleming).

Cutner, H. *G. W. Foote, his Life and Times* (National Secular Society).

Gimson, S. A. *Random Recollections of the Leicester Secular Society*, Part I, 1932, Part II, 1935 (Leicester Secular Society).

Papers of and letters written to Richard Congreve in the British Museum Library.

Papers of and letters written to George Jacob Holyoake in the offices of the Co-operative Union, Manchester, and the Bishopsgate Institute Library, London.

Scrapbook of Members of Leicester Secular Society.

Card Index of Professor W. M. Simon on members of the English Positivist Movement.

Stanton Coit's book of press cuttings.

(iii) Minute-Books and Annual Reports

The Secular Movement

N.S.S. Executive Minute-Book for 1875–77.

Minute Books of the Committee Meetings of the Leicester Secular Society, 1877–1944.

National Secular Society's Almanac for 1870–86, and Secular Almanac for 1890–1904.

Rationalist Press Association

Minute Books and Minutes of A.G.M.s and Board Meetings 1905–65. Annual Reports for 1901–65.

The Ethical Movement

a. *Ethical Union*
Minutes of Congress, 1896–1946.
Minutes of A.G.M.s, 1946–64.
Minutes of Council Meetings, 1896–1904, 1912–38, 1950–58.
Minutes of Executive Committee, 1923–38, and General Purposes Committee, 1955–59.
Subscription Lists, 1940–46.

b. *Ethical Societies*

Minutes, Annual Reports and Membership lists of the Emerson Ethical Brotherhood (Forest Group), 1916–20.
Maps and miscellaneous writings of the Forest Group.
Minute Books of the West London Ethical Society or Ethical Church, 1901–44.
West London Ethical Society's Annual Reports, 1892–1928.
Study Circle on Comparative Religions, 1912–13.
Secular Education League, 1907–11.
Hampstead Ethical Society, Minutes for 1900–26 and records of lectures.
Minutes of Sheffield Ethical Society, 1903–17, 1921–34.
Minutes of South London Ethical Society, 1917–38.
Minutes of Parliament Court Chapel, later South Place, 1807–20, 1836–41, 1853–1963, and Annual Reports 1807–20, 1836–1965.
Minutes of Women's Group of the Ethical Movement, 1920–6, 1934–44.

III. Magazines and Periodicals

The Secular Movement

The Oracle of Reason, 1842–3, ed. G. J. Holyoake,
The Cause of the People, 1848, ed. W. J. Linton and G. J. Holyoake.
The Reasoner, 1846–61, ed. G. J. Holyoake. From 1847 it appeared with a supplement, the *Utilitarian Record*. It was restarted as *The Counsellor*, 1863–4, and Holyoake attempted to revive the *Reasoner* in 1871–2.
The Commonwealth, 1849, ed. G. J. Holyoake.

The Investigator, 1854–59, ed. Robert Cooper, then 'Anthony Collins', then 'Iconoclast' (Bradlaugh).

The National Reformer, 1860–90 ed. mainly by Bradlaugh, then until 1893 by J. M. Robertson, when it passed out of the secular movement.

The Propagandist, 1862, ed. W. Maccall.

The Secular Chronicle, Birmingham, 1872–9, ed. G. H. Reddalls, then Mrs H. Law, then G. Standring.

The Secular Review, 1876–7 ed. by G. J. Holyoake, then by Watts. In 1876 Foote and Holyoake founded the *Secularist*, which Holyoake also retired from. Watts and Foote then combined the *Secular Review and Secularist*, subsequently the *Secular Review;* Foote was replaced by W. S. Ross in 1878.

The Freethinker, 1881 to present, edited first by G. W. Foote.

The Present Day, 1883–6, ed. G. J. Holyoake.

The Agnostic Annual, ed. Charles Watts 1884 until it passed into the rationalist movement.

The Truthseeker, Bradford, 1898–1915, ed. P. Gott, called *The Secularist* for part of 1902.

The Pioneer, 1903–4, ed. G. W. Foote.

Secular Work, 1896–7, edited anonymously. Anti-Foote and pro-socialist and Bradlaugh.

Freethought News, Bradford, 1947–52, ed. F. J. Corina.

Rationalist Press Association

Agnostic Annual, 1884 to present, renamed *Agnostic Annual and Ethical Review* in 1901, then *Rationalist Press Association Annual and Ethical Review* in 1908, then *Rationalist Annual* from 1926 on.

Watts' Literary Guide, 1885 ed. C.A. Watts, renamed *Literary Guide* in 1894, in 1956 renamed *The Humanist* and became the journal of the British Humanist Association.

The Free Mind, 'An Organ of Student Rationalism', 1946–9.

The Rationalist Review, 1954–6, distributed to members with the *Literary Guide*.

Ethical Movement

South Place Magazine, 1895, renamed *The Monthly Record* from 1920 on.

The Ethical World, 1898–1916, ed. S. Coit. Renamed *Democracy* and then *Ethics* in 1901, *Ethical Review* in 1906, then *Ethical World* in 1907.

The Ethical Church Monthly, 1937–45.

The Ethical Review, 1901. Journal of Hampstead Ethical Institute.

The Ethical Movement, 1916–23, renamed *Humanist* in 1917.

The Ethical Societies Chronicle, 1923–39, ed. R. Dimsdale Stocker.
The Plain View, 1944–61, ed. H. J. Blackham.
News and Notes, ed. M. L. Burnet, 1941, renamed *Humanist News* in 1964.

The Positivist Review, 1893–1923, renamed *Humanity—the Positivist Review*, in 1923.

Index